The Politics of
International
Economic Relations

The Politics of International Economic Relations

JOAN EDELMAN SPERO
Professor of Political Science, Columbia University

LONDON
GEORGE ALLEN & UNWIN
Boston   Sydney

To Michael, Jason, and Benjamin

First published in 1977

ISBN 0 04 382018 2 Hardback
     0 04 382019 0 Paperback

Acknowledgments

Table on Estimated Oil Producer State Revenues and Their Use in 1974 used by permission of *World Financial Markets*, January 21, 1976, published by Morgan Guaranty Trust Company.

Table on Energy Consumption, Oil Consumption, and Oil Imports: United States, Western Europe, and Japan, 1962 and 1972. Reprinted by permission of *Daedalus*, Journal of the American Academy of Arts and Sciences, Boston, Massachusetts. Fall 1975, *The Oil Crisis: In Perspective*.

Cover design: Mies Hora

Manufactured in the United States of America

Preface

This book is the outgrowth of several years of teaching international political economy to both undergraduate and graduate students at Columbia University. It reflects my attempt to confront the dearth of both theoretical and empirical analyses of the politics of international economic relations and to bring international political economy back to the study of international politics.

My work has benefitted greatly from my continuing dialogue with my students and from the suggestions and criticisms of political scientists and economists, academicians and practitioners of international political economics. I am grateful to Samuel Edelman, Robert Hormats, J. C. Hurewitz, Robert A. Isaak, Wilfrid L. Kohl, Stephen D. Krasner, Ned Lebow, Edward L. Morse, Zygmunt Nagorski, Jr., Donald J. Puchala, and Elliot Zupnick, all of whom offered valued advice on the manuscript. I am especially thankful to Catherine B. Gwin who served as research assistant, colleague, and valued critic.

The student staff of the Institute on Western Europe of Columbia University maintained their good cheer while helping me chase down footnotes and locate materials. Janet Rigney, Virginia Etheridge, Janis Kreslins, and Helena Stalson of the Council on Foreign Relations were undaunted by my numerous requests for assistance. Toby Weiss assisted patiently in the preparation of the bibliography and Miriam Levy did the lion's share of the typing. Working with Barry Rossinoff, Glenn Cowley, and Martha Goldstein of St. Martin's Press has been a delight.

For its generous support throughout this entire project, I wish to thank the Institute on Western Europe of Columbia University.

Above all, I am grateful to my husband Michael who provided a unique combination of support and exhortation to finish which enabled me to complete the study.

Contents

The Politics of
International
Economic Relations

Introduction: The Link Between Economics and Politics

The interaction of politics and economics is an old theme in the study of international relations. From seventeenth-century mercantilists to twentieth-century Marxists, students of relations among states have dealt with the problems of international political economy. Yet in the twentieth century the study of international political economy has been neglected. Politics and economics have been divorced from each other and isolated in the analysis and theory, if not in the reality, of international relations.

One reason for this divorce is to be found in the theoretical heritage of modern Western academe. The heritage which has shaped much of the modern study of politics and economics—and which is responsible for bringing about the artificial separation of economics and politics—is liberalism. Liberal theorists rejected the age-old concept of a unified political and economic order and replaced it with two separate orders.

First, argued the liberals, an economic system exists based on the production, distribution, and consumption of goods and services; these economic processes operate under natural laws. Furthermore, they maintained, a harmony exists in these laws and in the economic system; such natural harmony operates best and to the benefit of all when political authority interferes least with its automatic operation. Economic activity was seen by them to be the preserve of private enterprise, not of government.

Second, they argued that the political system consists of power, influence, and public decision making. Politics, they asserted, unlike economics, does not obey natural laws or harmony. Politics is unavoidable and government is necessary for essential services—defense, law, and order. But, for them, government and politics should not interfere with the natural economic order. Indeed, in an international system, their only hope for peace and harmony is for politics to be isolated from economics, for the natural and harmonious processes of free trade to operate among nations bringing not only prosperity, but peace, to all.[1]

Such theoretical separation has led to, and has been reinforced by, the specializations of modern academe. Since the nineteenth century, economics and political science have developed as separate disciplines, focusing on separate processes, and each to a great extent ignores the common ground where the two overlap and interrelate. Consequently, international political economy has been fragmented into international politics and international economics. Economists have, for the most part, ignored the role of political factors in international economic process and policy,[2] while students of international politics have ignored economic issues in relations among states.[3]

Two political and economic developments following World War II have reinforced this formal division of analysis. In the early postwar years, significant agreement was reached by the major world powers on postwar international economic relations. In the West, the Bretton Woods system of international economic management established the rules for commercial and financial relations among the major industrial states. In the East, Soviet hegemony in Eastern Europe provided the foundation for a separate and stable international economic system. Finally, during the first postwar decade, the greater part of the Third World remained politically and economically subordinate. Linked with the developed countries of the West in formal and informal imperial relations, these states had little choice but to acquiesce to the international economic system established for them. As a result of the establishment of agreed structures and rules of international economic interaction, conflict over economic issues was minimized and the significance of the economic aspect of international relations seemed to recede. While certain developments such as the European Economic Community and the problem of the British pound surfaced from time to time, international economic interaction was relegated to the level of "low" politics.[4]

Another postwar development which caused international economic relations to recede was the emergence of the Cold War. The major problems of international relations which preoccupied decision makers and observers alike were security issues: the Soviet Union's domination of Eastern Europe and the development of Soviet nuclear capability; the

division of Germany; the forging of the North Atlantic Treaty Organization (NATO) and American nuclear strategy; the Korean conflict, Vietnam, and the problems of limited war. Thus analysis of international
relations focused on what seemed to be the subjects of "high" politics, on
security and security-related issues. Systems analysis, decision-making
theory, strategy and game theory, simulation, conflict resolution—all
were based on the primacy of security issues.

The mid-1970s reality of international relations is now undermining
the separation of economics from the study of international politics. The
givens of the postwar decades which shaped the study of international
politics—economic consensus and security conflict—are collapsing. Security issues seem to have reached a plateau. East-West *détente* has replaced
the Cold War. The United States and the Soviet Union have demonstrated a willingness and an ability to reach major agreement on security
issues. West Germany's Eastern policy or *Ostpolitik* seems to have
alleviated an important source of instability in Eastern Europe. Finally,
the long war in Vietnam is at an end, and the developed countries are at
peace.

At the same time, the broad agreement on economic rules established after World War II has collapsed under the weight of powerful
new forces. In the West, the Bretton Woods system of international
economic management has broken down. The renewed economic vigor of
Western Europe and of Japan, the strain on the United States' balance of
payments, the oil crisis, and inflation have led to the disintegration of the
postwar international monetary system. The growth of the European
Economic Community as an economic power, the dynamics of Japanese
trade, and the recession of the 1970s threaten established commercial
relations. The development of new international patterns of production
pose a multifaceted threat to the traditional economic and political order.
In the East, the Soviet Union and the Communist states of Eastern
Europe have found their closed system too restrictive for economic
development and are turning to the West for trade and technology. In the
South, the newly independent Third World countries with new economic
problems and new economic demands have entered the world arena. The
major political concerns of these countries are economic: development,
aid, trade, foreign investment, and ultimate independence. Their demand
is for no less than a restructuring of the international relations between
the haves and have nots. Therefore, as the postwar economic consensus
disintegrates and as security issues recede, economic issues are reemerging
as the focus of international relations.

Thus, if theory and analysis are to maintain touch with reality, it
will be necessary to bridge the gap between economics and politics, to
explore the interface between economics and politics in the international

system. This study will examine one aspect of that interface: the way in which international politics shape international economics.

THE POLITICAL DYNAMICS OF INTERNATIONAL POLITICS

Those students of international politics who have examined the interaction between economics and politics have most always examined the way in which economic reality has shaped politics.[5] There is, for example, a body of thought that maintains that economic resources determine strategic and diplomatic power. Analysts have pointed out the ways in which a country's gross national product, the quantity and quality of its resources, and its international trade and financial position determine its military strength. The literature demonstrates that the impact of economics on politics is quite important. The early industrialization of Great Britain in the nineteenth century, for example, was a significant resource base for British political power and an important factor in shaping Great Britain's domination of that century's international economic and political structure. Similarly, the economic power of the United States was important in creating America's military and political dominance in the twentieth century.

Just as economic factors shape political outcomes, so political factors shape economic outcomes. Students of international politics, however, invariably overlook the political determinants of international economic relations. While not denying the important influence of economics upon politics, this book will be concerned with that other side of the coin which has been frequently ignored: the political dynamics of international economics.

There are three ways in which political factors shape economic outcomes. *First, the political system shapes the economic system*, as the structure and operation of the international economic system is, to a great extent, determined by the structure and operation of the international political system. *Second, political concerns often shape economic policy*, as important economic policies are frequently dictated by overriding political interests. *Third, international economic relations, in and of themselves, are political relations*, as international economic interaction, like international political interaction, is a process by which state and nonstate actors manage, or fail to manage, their conflicts and by which they cooperate, or fail to cooperate, to achieve common goals. Let us now look in more detail at these three political dimensions of international economics.

THE POLITICAL SYSTEM AND THE ECONOMIC SYSTEM

The structure and operation of the international economic system is to a great extent determined by the structure and operation of the international political system. Production, distribution, and consumption have throughout modern history been shaped by diplomatic and strategic factors.

During the mercantilistic period between the fifteenth and eighteenth centuries, two principal political characteristics shaped economic interaction. First was the development of powerful nation states from the ruins of medieval universalism and local particularism—the emergence of new centralized political units—England, France, Spain, Sweden, Prussia, Russia—whose policy goal was the consolidation of power, both internally, vis-à-vis local power structures, and externally, vis-à-vis other states. Second, in the mercantile political system, was the competition among these many, nearly equal, states. Because power was distributed fairly equally, relatively minor changes could be very important in the overall power position of a state. But despite the significant competition for power, there were important limits to competition. There was a common political culture, including a consensus on royal legitimacy. There were also limits to state capability. State administration was weak, armies were small and mercenary, and, therefore, military and diplomatic objectives were limited.

The impact of the political structure on the economic structure of mercantilism was profound. The economic realm became the main arena for political conflict. The pursuit of state power was carried out through the pursuit of national economic power and wealth; the process of competition, limited by political reality, was translated into economic competition. All international economic transactions were regulated for the purpose of state power.

Because mercantilists believed that wealth and power were intimately associated with the possession of so-called precious metals, governments organized their international trading structures for the purpose of maintaining a favorable balance of trade to accumulate these metals. There were controls on exchange markets and the international movement of precious metals, along with regulation of individual and general commercial transactions through tariffs, quotas, and prohibitions of some transactions. States gave subsidies to export and import substitution industries and sometimes engaged in production or trade.

Mercantilist states also acquired colonies for the purpose of favorable trade balances and for the political goal of self-sufficiency. Colonies existed to accommodate the mercantile interests of the metropole, and strict state regulation of the colonial economy existed to serve these ends. It was the reaction to such mercantilist policies—the regulation of production, of exports and imports, and the control of shipping—which led the American colonies to rebel against England.

Thus in the mercantile period, it was the nature of the emerging state and the nature of the state system which in large part shaped economic interaction—and when that political structure changed, when Great Britain rose to political dominance, the economic system also underwent a dramatic change.[6]

In the nineteenth century, the political system was characterized by the balance of power on the continent and by Great Britain's power overseas. On the continent, Russia and France were constrained by the territorial realignments of the Congress of Vienna, and the four major continental powers were controlled through their own rivalries. This enabled Great Britain to play a balancing and mediating role. With its geographic position off the European continent and its predominance on the seas, Great Britain was able to control Europe's access to the rest of the world by denying overseas colonies to continental states. This naval power combined with the decline of the continental powers meant that the greater part of the non-European world was independent or under British rule.

Because of this political system of a balance of power on the continent and British power overseas, Great Britain achieved a head start in economic development and was able to establish an international economic system that centered on Britain. The basis of the system was free trade.

The political roots of free trade may be traced back to the Napoleonic period when the French emperor imposed the continental system: an economic embargo on Great Britain. The Napoleonic embargo encouraged a transformation of the British economy from trade with the continent to trade overseas. After the defeat of France and the end of the embargo, Britain continued on the established path. With the repeal of the Corn laws, the navigation laws, and the gradual removal of tariffs, however, Britain developed an exchange system of domestic manufactures for overseas raw materials. Treaties with and among other European states expanded the system to the continent, and trading dominance was reinforced by British investment overseas. Vast amounts of capital flowed out of Great Britain in the nineteenth century to the United States, Canada, Latin America, and the nontropical areas of the empire. And the City of London emerged as the world's financial center.

Thus in the nineteenth century, military and political dominance enabled Britain to adopt and internationalize a liberal economic system.

But, once again, when the political system began to change at the end of the nineteenth century, when British power waned, the liberal economic system also began to decline, and a new imperialist system emerged.[7]

The roots of nineteenth-century imperialism are complex and elusive. But two political factors were crucial to its development. The first was the decline of British dominance that stemmed from the rise of rival political, military, and economic powers, in particular, the United States and Germany. And, second, the disruptive influence of these new powers was reinforced by the emergence of modern nationalism. The increasingly powerful rival states, and Britain as well, were motivated by the unruly forces of national identity, national pride, and the quest for national self-fulfillment and power. More nearly equal power relations and the new nationalism led to a highly competitive international system, one increasingly less constrained by Great Britain's balancing and overseas domination, which had stabilized the earlier nineteenth-century system.

These crucial political changes permitted the operation of other important forces: the political pressures of a newly powerful capitalist class, along with the military; the escapades of various adventurers (explorers and fortune hunters); important technological and communications developments, which facilitated control of overseas territories; and the action and reaction dynamic of imperial competition. International political conflict increased, but often it was acted out not in Europe—at least not until 1914—rather, it occurred in Asia and Africa. In the space of a few decades much of Asia and virtually all of Africa were divided up by Western Europe and the United States.

This new imperialism was the basis for a new international economic system. European political domination led to economic domination and exploitation. As in the days of mercantilism, colonies were integrated into an international economic system which was designed to serve the economic interests of the metropole. The political victors controlled investment and trade, regulated currency and production, and manipulated labor, thus establishing structures of economic dependency in their colonies which would endure far longer than their actual political authority.[8]

The imperialist system and the residual domination of the United Kingdom in the West finally collapsed under the strain of World Wars I and II. In the post–World War II period, a new political and economic system based on the hostile confrontation of two superpowers emerged. Politically, the new system was bipolar. In the West, there was a hierarchy, with the United States as the dominant political and military power over a weakened Europe and Japan; in the Third World, nations in great part remained politically subordinate to the old imperial powers; in the East, the Soviet Union was the overwhelmingly dominant political and military power. And, finally, East and West confronted each other in the Cold War.

This international political system shaped the postwar international economic system. For political reasons, the East and West were isolated into two separate economic systems. In the East the Soviet Union imposed a Communist international economic system based on the concept of a socialist commonwealth and, for political reasons, sought to make the other members of the socialist commonwealth economically dependent on the Soviet Union and economically isolated from the West. In the West U.S. military and political dominance was matched by U.S. economic dominance. America's liberal vision shaped the economic order in the West. The principles of the international economic system were again as in the period of British hegemony: free trade and free capital movements. Within such a system American trade, American investment, and the American dollar predominated. Thus, politics have shaped economics in the postwar era. And in the 1970s, as before, it is to a great extent the changing political scene which caused the breakdown of the postwar economic system. The decline of American power and increasing pluralism in the West, a superpower détente, and a new political consensus in the underdeveloped countries are now leading to a new international economic system.

POLITICAL CONCERNS AND
ECONOMIC POLICY

In addition to shaping economic systems, political factors also influence economic policies. Throughout history, as we have seen, national policy has shaped international economics. In the mercantile period governments regulated economic activity and acquired colonies. In the nineteenth century the British repealed the corn laws and the navigation acts and turned to free trade. At the end of that century, public policy turned to the annexation of territory in Asia and Africa. In the years since World War II, American foreign policy has focused on a multilateral, free trading system.

These national policies were, in turn, determined by internal political processes. Economic policy is the outcome of a political bargaining process in which different groups representing different interests conflict over different preferred policy outcomes. Group conflict occurs, for example, between groups favoring low tariff barriers and those advocating protection, between advocates of foreign economic assistance and its opponents, between those favoring energy independence and those advocating reliance on foreign sources of energy. The outcome of political conflict is determined by power. The different strength of competing groups shapes the outcomes of foreign economic policy. Thus mercantilism may be viewed as the outcome of a political conflict between particularist local powers and the rising power of the central government; free trade was the product of a conflict between the landed class, which advocated protection, and the rising bourgeois class, which supported free trade; imperialism reflected the political power of the ascendent military and capitalist classes; U.S. liberalism was determined by the support it enjoyed among powerful business and labor groups.

Very often, what shapes the political bargaining process are overriding strategic and diplomatic interests. Economic policy is frequently either shaped by political concerns or becomes an explicit tool of national strategic and diplomatic policy. Trade policy is frequently consciously linked with political goals. Embargo has been an economic tool of political warfare throughout history. France applied an embargo to weaken Great Britain during the Napoleonic wars; the League of Nations called for an embargo of Italy after the invasion of Ethiopia in an effort to end that aggression in 1935; the United States since 1949 has embargoed trade with communist countries in an effort to weaken military capability; the recent Arab oil embargo of the United States and the Netherlands was an effort to alter their pro-Israeli foreign policy.[9]

Trade policy has also been used for defensive military purposes. Alexander Hamilton argued that the fledgling United States should develop a domestic manufacturing system through trade protection to avoid dependence on foreign sources of supply which could be cut off in time of political conflict or war.[10] A similar policy recently advocated calls for the United States to develop its domestic energy resources to avoid the consequences, both economic and political, of dependence on foreign sources of supply.

Foreign aid is another familiar economic tool used for strategic and diplomatic ends. The Marshall Plan, under which the United States gave $17 billion in outright grants to Western European countries to rebuild their economies after World War II, was designed to make Western Europe impervious to aggression by the Soviet Union. Foreign economic assistance to underdeveloped countries has been used to win friends for the West or the East during the Cold War. Foreign aid has also been used by former colonial powers to retain political influence in those newly independent former colonies.

INTERNATIONAL ECONOMICS AS INTERNATIONAL POLITICS

Finally, international economic relations, in and of themselves, constitute political relations. International politics may be defined as the "patterns of political interaction between and among states."[11] And, as with all politics, international politics involves goal-seeking behavior and a process of deciding who gets what, when and how.[12] Thus international relations are political when they involve the interaction of different groups in goal-seeking pursuits.[13]

Interaction among groups in the international system ranges from conflict to cooperation. At one extreme pure conflict occurs as when the interests of groups involved are diametrically opposed: if one group realized its goal, the other cannot achieve its objective. For example, in a conflict over territory one state will gain the territory and one will lose it. At the other extreme cooperation exists. In such a situation groups share a common interest and all benefit from the furtherance of their shared interest. For example, allies have a common interest in ensuring their common defense, or colonies have a common interest in achieving independence, or trading partners have a common interest in maintaining beneficial trading relations.

Most international interaction involves elements of both conflict and cooperation, since, even in situations of extreme conflict, there is often an element of cooperation. For example, despite the severity of the confrontation between the United States and the Soviet Union over placing missiles in Cuba in 1962 or over the Middle East war of 1973, both superpowers' interest in preventing the escalation of these conflicts into nuclear war and holocaust led to cooperation as resolution. Conversely, in situations involving high levels of cooperation, there is often an element of conflict, and even when groups share interests, there is usually conflict over specific interests and specific solutions. For example, all states may want to establish and maintain a stable international monetary system, but certain of these states have a preference for a particular type of monetary system, such as, a fixed exchange rate or a floating exchange rate regime, which satisfies their more specific national interests. Thus within a framework of common goals, states conflict over the best means to achieve their common end.

In domestic politics, goal-seeking behavior is regulated by government which has the authority to make decisions for a society and the power to enforce those decisions. The peculiar characteristic which distinguishes international politics from internal politics is the absence of government. In the international system no legitimate body has the authority to manage conflict or achieve common goals by making and enforcing decisions for the system; instead, decision-making authority is dispersed among many governmental, intergovernmental, and nongovernmental groups.

Because of the absence of government, the central problems of international politics are the adjustment or management of conflict and the achievement of cooperation. The means by which state and nonstate actors manage, or fail to manage, their conflicts and the ways in which they cooperate, or fail to cooperate, to achieve common goals is the central subject of international politics. Over the centuries actors have deliberately or inadvertently developed rules, institutions, and procedures to manage international conflict and cooperation. These forms of managing international order have varied over time, over space, and over issues. They range from balances of power to alliances to international organizations, from hegemony to colonialism to international law. When there are effective rules, institutions, and procedures, conflict takes place within agreed limits, and cooperation is facilitated. When there are no effective rules, institutions, and procedures, conflict may be unregulated and cooperation impossible to achieve. In such a situation international conflict may escalate into war.

The subject of international economic relations may also be viewed as the management of conflict and cooperation in the absence of government. As with all international political interaction, economic interaction ranges from pure conflict to pure cooperation. Some economic relations involve high levels of conflict. Wealth is an important goal of groups in international politics, and the pursuit of wealth in the presence of scarce resources leads to conflict—over access to markets, over control of raw materials, over the control of the means of production. Such conflict often is linked to conflicts over power and sovereignty. The confrontation of producers and consumers over the price of oil, for example, is a challenge by producers to the power of both the developed countries and the oil companies. The outcry in Canada, Europe, and the Third World against multinational corporations is, in part, a reaction to an infringement of sovereignty. Much of international economic interaction, however, has a high level of cooperation. Many states share the goals of a stable monetary system, expanding trade relations, and rising production, though they differ over the means of achieving these ends. Some favor fixed exchange rates, whereas others prefer a float. Some advocate tariff reductions on textiles, whereas others forcefully oppose them. Some favor growth through free trade, whereas others feel free trade inhibits growth. Some feel multinational corporations are a vital new road to economic growth, whereas others feel they perpetuate underdevelopment.

As with all international politics, states have deliberately or inadvertently established rules, institutions, and procedures to manage international conflict and cooperation. International economic management varies with time, place, and issue area. Mercantilism, free trade, and imperialism have been different historical forms of trade management. The gold standard and the dollar system have at different times regulated international monetary relations. Sometimes, such as during the nineteenth-century gold standard or the twentieth-century dollar system, management is effective. At other times, such as during the Depression of the 1930s or the monetary crisis of 1971–1973, management breaks down.

In some relations, such as those among the developed market economies, there are complex and effective management rules, institutions, and procedures. In other relations, such as those between developed and less developed countries, rules, institutions, and procedures either are not developed or are the subject of great conflict. Finally, in some areas, such as international trade, complex rules have been formally established, international organizations created, and informal procedures developed. In other areas, such as international production, international management relies on more rudimentary forms of control.

This book is a study of the way in which groups have managed or have failed to manage international economic relations since World War II. It is an examination of the system established after the war, its collapse, and the possibilities for developing new forms of management. The emphasis is on management by states or governments, for two reasons. First, according to this study, it appears that, since World War II, states have increasingly intervened to manage the international economy and that they are quite likely to increase that intervention in the years ahead. Second, this review concludes that states should intervene in the market to improve its functioning and to enhance its ability to meet the goals of the members of the system.

THREE SYSTEMS

To understand the nature of international economic conflict, cooperation, and their management, this study will examine management in three subsystems of the larger international economic system: the Western system of interdependence, the North–South system of dependence, and the East–West system of independence. This delineation of the international economy into three subsystems, especially that of separating the Western from the North–South systems, is artificial, since interactions and problems overlap all systems in the real world. Nevertheless, political processes and political problems are different in the three subsystems. Individual examinations will allow us to focus on those different processes and problems and, it is hoped, will enhance our ability to understand them.

The Western system includes the developed market economies of North America, Western Europe, and Japan.[14] These states are wealthy, highly developed, and capitalistic. They have their major international economic interactions with each other and are involved with each other in a dense system of mutual economic interaction. This dense system of mutual interaction is the major management problem of the Western system. Since World War II there has been a vast increase in economic interaction among developed market economies. Increased interaction in the financial and monetary field has developed through the common international use of the American dollar, the internationalization of banking, the monetary consequences of multinational corporations, and the creation of the Eurocurrency and Eurobond markets. There has also been a vast increase in international trade due to economic growth, trade liberalization, a decrease in transportation costs, and the broader horizons of businessmen. The major expansion in world trade in the postwar period has been generated by developed market economies. Another form of expanding interaction is the internationalization of production with the increased flow of direct investment and the reorganization of production and marketing on an international scale.[15]

These and other forms of increased interaction have led to a significant degree of interdependence—that is, actors or events in one part of the system have the ability to influence actors or events in another part of the system.[16] Thus individual countries' economic policies and events are increasingly sensitive to the economic policies and events of other members of the system. The monetary, trade, and investment policy in one country in the Western system now has a direct impact on the monetary, trade, and investment policy in other countries in the system. Thus, at a time when governments are seeking increased control of their economies, these governments are discovering that the national economy is increasingly open to external influence. Some Western countries are more sensitive or more vulnerable than other countries. The United States, in particular, has been able to control the impact of interdependence better than some nations, partly because the international aspect of the American economy is smaller than that of other members of the system and partly because of America's economic power.[17]

While contributing to economic prosperity, interdependence has also created a critical political problem. Quite simply, interdependence seems to have grown faster than the means of its management, and there is a real question—in the wake of interdependence—as to whether or not there are adequate means to manage international economic relations. From the perspective of the individual state, interdependence interferes with national policy and with a nation's ability to control its economy. Greater interaction increases the number of disturbances with which national decision makers must cope, for now, disturbances arise not only from within the economy but also from without. Interdependence also creates forces which interfere with traditional measures of national economic policy. This weakening of policy measures is especially important in an era of the welfare state when national governments are increasingly desirous of controlling their national economies. Thus interdependence weakens national management.

At the same time, international management is inadequate. Present structures and present leadership are incapable of controlling interdependence. Thus the Western international economic system seems to be at a crossroads. As one analyst put it,

> the advanced, market-economy countries are reaching the point where they face a basic choice: either to move forward to new far-reaching forms of collective management of problems they can no longer handle separately or to put the brakes on their growing interdependence and, by more or less arbitrary measures, to bring problems once more within the span of national control. [18]

In part two we will examine the problem of interdependence and the possibility of the management of interdependence.

The second subsystem of international economic interaction is the North–South system of relations among the developed market economies and the Third World, the less developed economies of Africa, Asia, and Latin America. Unlike the Western system, which is composed of relatively similar and equal actors, the North–South system is one of disparity and inequality between North and South in gross national product per capita. In 1972, the developed market economies had an average gross national product of $3,670 per capita, whereas the underdeveloped countries had an average gross national product of $280 per capita. [19] There is inequality also in annual per capita growth in North and South. In the 1950–1960 period, the developed market economies grew at an average rate of 2.8 percent a year, whereas the underdeveloped countries grew at an annual rate of 2.4 percent; in the 1960–1970 period, the developed market economies grew at an average rate of 3.9 percent per year, whereas the underdeveloped countries grew at an average annual rate of 2.6 percent. [20] In other words, the gap between North and South, between rich and poor, is widening.

The major problem of this unequal system is dependence. Whereas interdependence involves a high level of mutual economic interaction and mutual sensitivity, dependence denotes highly unequal economic interaction and highly unequal sensitivity. Dependence exists when a Southern country has a high level of economic interaction with a Northern country, when that interaction is of great importance to the national economy, and when, therefore, the Southern country is influenced by actors or events in the Northern state. The Northern country, on the other hand, does not have a high level or qualitatively important economic interaction with the Southern state and is not influenced by actors or events in the Southern country. Interdependence is a relatively symmetrical relationship; dependence is an asymmetrical relationship.

Dependence usually takes one or more forms. There may be trade dependence. Most Southern countries earn a large percentage of their gross national products from trade with the North. Most of the Third

World countries have a small internal market and thus depend on the larger Northern markets for the sale of their product. Thus a dependent country is highly sensitive to factors in the North—both market and political—which shape Northern demand and thus influence their trade. Furthermore, a large percentage of Southern countries' exports are often concentrated in a single or a small number of primary products, which reinforces sensitivity to foreign demand by making the country highly vulnerable to fluctuations in demand for the principal product. Finally, a large percentage of Southern countries' trade is often directed to a particular Northern market, which again accentuates the sellers' sensitivity and vulnerability to demand conditions of that single market. Trade dependence, then, is characterized by the Southern economy's significant dependence on trade with the North and the high levels of sensitivity to factors in the North which influence that trade.[21]

A second form of dependence is in the area of investment. A large percentage of the domestic stock of investment in Third World countries is often owned by Northern investors. Northern foreign investment tends to control the most important sectors of production: raw material production, export industries, the dynamic sectors of the economy, new investment.

A third form of dependence is monetary dependence. In some cases—the best example being the franc zone—the currency of the dependent Southern country is directly linked to the currency of the dominant Northern country, which thereby manages or significantly influences both the external and the internal monetary policy of the country. Monetary dependence also occurs when an underdeveloped country in a chronic balance-of-payments difficulty becomes dependent on external balance-of-payments assistance through the International Monetary Fund, which then reserves the right to shape and to influence domestic and foreign monetary policy.

Aid also creates dependence. Foreign economic assistance to the South is often concentrated on one Northern source, allowing manipulation, management, and decision making from outside. Furthermore, aid may reinforce Northern trade and investment dominance.

Usually, these economic dependencies—trade, investment, money, aid—are reinforced by other types of relationships with the North: cultural ties, alliances and treaties, more informal political ties, and military links ranging from military aid to military intervention.

In political terms the dependent Southern country is subject to management by the dominant country or countries of the North. The most obvious example of exclusion from management of the underdeveloped countries has been in the major economic institutions of the North—the International Monetary Fund, the International Bank for Reconstruction and Development, and the General Agreement on Tariffs and Trade—institutions that were created by the developed countries and reflect their dominant power. In the broader sense, economic decisions of developed Northern countries have an effect on the economic development of dependent countries. Agricultural, trade, and monetary policies made by the North directly affect the South. Thus the underdeveloped countries feel that the system is illegitimate because they do not have access to decision making, because they are excluded from the management role.

Furthermore this political structure means that management decisions made by the North reflect the interests, desires, and goals of the North, not those of the South. And this adds another dimension to dependency—the feeling among the underdeveloped countries that not only do they not share in the management of the system, they do not share in the resources and the benefits of the system, and that the system exists to perpetuate the South's dependent status. The impact of dependence is seen as the perpetuation of dependency and underdevelopment.

Thus the political interest of the underdeveloped countries is (1) to share in the management of the system and (2) thereby to benefit to a greater extent from the system. Their goal is to change the system of dependence. In part three we will examine the problem of dependence and the attempts of Third World countries to manage dependence.

The final international economic subsystem to be examined is that between the East and the West. The East–West relationship is one of independence, wherein partners in the system have few interactions and little impact on each other. Such has been the case in relations between the developed market economies of the West and the planned economies of the Communist states of Eastern Europe and the Soviet Union. The Cold War led each side to isolate its system from the other. Led by the United States, the West established a set of legal and administrative barriers to trade with the East, whereas the East followed a policy of economic and political isolation within a socialist commonwealth. Reinforcing the political choice of independence was the divergence of the two economic systems. Thus political choice and the divergent economic systems led to the economic independence of East and West. Socialist states and developed market states developed their own, separate economic institutions. The socialist states, for example, did not participate in the International Monetary Fund, the General Agreement on Tariffs and Trade, and the International Bank for Reconstruction and Development. East–West trade was small. And there were no capital or investment flows.

Had the system remained independent, there would have been little interest in examining the East West system of management. But, in recent years the political and economic bases for independence and isolation have changed. Détente and new economic problems in the East have led to efforts to increase East–West economic interaction. Laws are changing, policies are being modified, and economic interaction—trade, joint ventures, even Eastern membership in Western institutions—is increasing. The problem to be examined in part four is this attempt to move away from independence toward greater international economic interaction.

NOTES

1. For readings on the classical liberal school, see Adam Smith, *An Inquiry into the Nature and Causes of the Wealth of Nations*, Edwin Cannan, ed. (New York: Modern Library, 1937); James Mill, *Elements of Political Economy*, 3rd rev. ed. (London: Henry G. Bohn, 1844); John Stuart Mill, *Principles of Political Economy*, 7th ed. of 1871, J. W. Ashley, ed. (London: Longmans, Green & Co., 1909). For twentieth-century liberals, see Norman Angell, *The Great Illusion 1933* (New York: Putnam 1933); Cordell Hull *Memoirs*, 2 vols. (New York: Macmillan, 1963). For a critique of the political implications of liberal theory, see Edward Hallett Carr, *The Twenty Years' Crisis, 1919–1939: An Introduction to the Study of International Relations*, 2nd ed., (New York: St. Martin's, 1962); Kenneth N. Waltz, *Man, The State, and War: A Theoretical Analysis* (New York: Columbia Univ. Press, 1954, 1959).

2. There are, of course, important exceptions: See, for example, Richard Cooper, *The Economics of Interdependence* (New York: McGraw-Hill, 1968); François Perroux, *L'Economie du XXe Siècle*, (Paris: Presses Universitaires de France, 1961); Paul A. Baran and Paul M. Sweezy, *Monopoly Capital: An Essay on the American Economic and Social Order* (New York: Modern Reader, 1966). The last citation represents one school which is a major exception to the general isolation of economics and politics, the Marxists.

3. Again, there are exceptions: See, for example, David P. Calleo and Benjamin M. Rowland, *America and the World Political Economy* (Bloomington, Ind.: Indiana Univ. Press, 1973); Klaus Knorr, *Power and Wealth: The Political Economy of International Power* (New York: Basic Books, 1973); Edward L. Morse, *Foreign Policy and Interdependence in Gaullist France* (Princeton, N. J.: Princeton Univ. Press, 1973). Other studies in international political economy have been made by "practitioners" and a few scholars with a joint economics and political science background: See, for example, Harold Malmgren, *International Economic Peacekeeping in Phase II* (New York: Quadrangle Books, 1972); Susan Strange, *Sterling and British Policy, A Political Study of an International Currency in Decline* (New York: Oxford Univ. Press, 1971).

4. High politics are those issues of primary importance to top decision makers, whereas low politics are those issues of lesser importance relegated to lesser levels of authority. See, for example, Stanley Hoffmann, "Obstinate or Obsolete? The Fate of the Nation-State and the Case of Western Europe," *Daedalus*, 95 (Summer 1966), 862–915.

5. See, for example, Knorr, *Power and Wealth: The Political Economy of International Power*.

6. For a classic study of mercantilism, see Eli F. Heckscher, *Mercantilism*, 2 vols., transl. by Mendel Shapiro (London: George Allen & Unwin, 1936), especially Vol. 1, pp. 19–30. See also Jacob Viner, "Power versus Plenty as Objectives of Foreign Policy in the Seventeenth and Eighteenth Centuries," *World Politics*, 1 (October 1948), 1–29.

7. See Robert Gilpin, "The Politics of Transnational Economic Relations," in Robert O. Keohane and Joseph S. Nye, Jr., eds., *Transnational Relations and World Politics* (Cambridge, Mass.: Harvard Univ. Press, 1972), pp. 55–56; Alexander K. Cairncross, *Home and Foreign Investment, 1870–1913: Studies in Capital Accumulation* (Cambridge: Cambridge Univ. Press, 1953); Albert H. Imlah, *Economic Elements in the Pax*

Britannica: Studies in British Foreign Trade in the Nineteenth Century (Cambridge, Mass.: Harvard Univ. Press, 1958).

8. The literature on nineteenth-century imperialism is vast. For political interpretations, see, for example, Carlton J. H. Hayes, *A Generation of Materialism, 1871–1900* (New York: Harper & Row, 1941); William Langer, *The Diplomacy of Imperialism* (New York: Knopf, 1935); Parker T. Moon, *Imperialism and World Politics* (New York: Macmillan, 1926); Joseph A. Schumpeter, *Imperialism and Social Classes* (Oxford: Basil Blackwell, 1951). For economic interpretations, see John A. Hobson, *Imperialism: A Study* (Ann Arbor, Mich.: Univ. of Michigan Press, 1965): V. I. Lenin, *Imperialism: The Highest Stage of Capitalism* (New York: International Publishers, 1969). For overall analysis of different theories, see George Lichtheim, *Imperialism* (New York: Praeger, 1971); E. M. Winslow, *The Pattern of Imperialism* (New York: Columbia Univ. Press, 1948).

9. See, for example, Yuan-Li Wu, *Economic Warfare* (Englewood Cliffs, N.J.: Prentice-Hall, 1952); Albert O. Hirschman, *National Power and the Structure of Foreign Trade* (Berkeley, Calif.: Univ. of California Press, 1945).

10. Alexander Hamilton, "Report on the Subject of Manufactures," in Arthur Harrison Cole, ed., *Industrial and Commercial Correspondence of Alexander Hamilton Anticipating his Report on Manufactures* (New York: A. M. Kelley, 1968), pp. 247–320.

11. Donald J. Puchala, *International Politics Today* (New York: Dodd, Mead, 1971), p. 1.

12. Harold D. Lasswell, *Politics: Who Gets What, When, How* (Cleveland, Ohio: World Publishing Co., 1958).

13. Puchala, *International Politics Today*, pp. 3–4.

14. One might also add Australia, New Zealand, and South Africa.

15. Richard N. Cooper, *The Economics of Interdependence* (New York: McGraw-Hill, 1968).

16. Oran Young, "Interdependencies in World Politics," *International Journal* 24 (Autumn 1969), 726.

17. Cooper, *The Economics of Interdependence*; Robert O. Keohane and Joseph S. Nye, "World Politics and the International Economic System" in C. Fred Bergsten (ed.), *The Future of the International Economic Order: An Agenda for Research* (Boston: Heath, 1973), pp. 121–126; Kenneth Waltz, "The Myth of National Interdependence," in Charles P. Kindleberger, ed., *The International Corporation* (Cambridge, Mass.: M.I.T. Press, 1970), pp. 205–223.

18. Miriam Camps, *The Management of Interdependence: A Preliminary View* (New York: Council on Foreign Relations, 1974), p. 43.

19. International Bank for Reconstruction and Development, *World Bank Atlas* (Washington, D.C.: International Bank for Reconstruction and Development, 1974), p. 8.

20. United Nations Conference on Trade and Development, *Handbook of International Trade and Development Statistics, Supplement 1973* (New York: United Nations, 1974), p. 91.

21. See Benjamin J. Cohen, *The Question of Imperialism: The Political Economy of Dominance and Dependence* (New York: Basic Books, 1973), pp. 155–160.

Part One

An Overview

1

The Management of International Economic Relations Since World War II

During and after World War II, governments developed and enforced a set of rules, institutions, and procedures to regulate important aspects of international economic interaction. For nearly two decades, this order, known as the Bretton Woods system, was effective in controlling conflict and in achieving the common goals of the states which had created it. The political bases for the Bretton Woods system are to be found in the coincidence of three conditions: the concentration of power in a small number of states, the existence of a cluster of important interests shared by those states, and the presence of a dominant power willing and able to assume a leadership role.[1]

The Bretton Woods system was dominated by the developed countries of North America and Western Europe. The concentration of both political and economic power in these states enabled them to make and impose decisions for the entire system. They faced no challenge from the Communist states of Eastern Europe and Asia, including the Soviet Union. These states, isolated from the rest of the international economy by the nature of their centrally planned economies and by deliberate policies of isolation, interacted with each other in a separate international economic system. Moreover, they were not challenged by the less developed countries. Unlike the Communist countries, the less developed countries were closely integrated into the world economy. They traded mostly with the developed states, their most advanced industry was, in many cases, owned by European or American corporations, and they shared the same international monetary system. Because of their political and economic weakness, however, these states had no voice in management. Finally, the developed states faced no challenge from Japan. Weakened by the war, and lacking the level of development and the political power of North America and Western Europe, Japan remained subordinate and outside the management group for much of the Bretton Woods era. The concentration of power facilitated management by confining the number of actors whose agreement was necessary to establish rules, institutions, and procedures and to carry out management within the agreed system.

Management was further facilitated by a high level of agreement among the powerful on the goals and means of international economic management. The foundation of that agreement was a shared belief in capitalism and liberalism. The developed countries differed somewhat in the type of capitalism they preferred for their national economies. France, for example, preferred greater planning and state intervention, whereas the United States favored relatively limited state intervention. Nevertheless, all relied primarily on market mechanisms and on private ownership. For the international economy they all favored a liberal system, one which relied primarily on a free market with the minimum of barriers to the flow of private trade and capital. The experience of the 1930s, when proliferation of exchange controls and trade barriers led to economic disaster, was fresh in the minds of public officials. While they disagreed on the specific implementation of this liberal system, all agreed that an open system would maximize economic welfare.

Some also felt that a liberal international economic system would enhance the possibilities of peace. The belief in liberalism had a security dimension, the belief that a liberal international economic system would lead not only to economic prosperity and economic harmony but also to international peace.[2] One of those who saw such a security link was Cordell Hull, the U.S. secretary of state from 1933 to 1944. Hull argued that

> unhampered trade dovetailed with peace; high tariffs, trade barriers, and unfair economic competition, with war . . . if we could get a freer flow of trade—freer in the sense of fewer discriminations and obstructions—so that one country would not be deadly jealous of another and the living standards of all countries might rise, thereby eliminating the economic dissatisfaction that breeds war, we might have a reasonable chance of lasting peace.[3]

The developed countries also agreed that the liberal international economic system required governmental intervention. In the postwar era public management of the economy has become a primary activity of government in the developed states.[4] Employment, stability, and growth have become important subjects of public policy. The role of government in the national economy has been associated with the assumption by the state of the responsibility for assuring the economic well-being of its citizens. The welfare state grew out of the Great Depression, which created a popular demand for governmental intervention in the economy, and out of the theoretical contributions of the Keynesian school of economics, which demonstrated the need for governmental intervention to maintain adequate levels of employment. In many developed states, such as Great Britain, the welfare state went beyond intervention at the macrolevel and assumed responsibility for and intervened at the sectoral or microlevel. Thus governments also became the guardians of key domestic economic sectors.

At the international level, governmental intervention also evolved from the experience of the 1930s. The priority of national goals, independent national action in the interwar period, and the failure to perceive that those national goals could not be realized without some form of international collaboration resulted in economic and political disaster. The failure to control beggar-thy-neighbor policies such as high tariffs and competitive devaluations contributed to economic breakdown, domestic political instability, and international war. The lesson learned was that, as Harry D. White, a major architect of the Bretton Woods system, put it:

> the absence of a high degree of economic collaboration among the leading nations will . . . inevitably result in economic warfare that will be but the prelude and instigator of military warfare on an even vaster scale.[5]

To ensure economic stability and political peace, states agreed to cooperate to regulate the international economic system.

The common interest in economic cooperation was enhanced by the outbreak of the Cold War at the end of the 1940s. From that time, cooperation became necessary to face the common enemy. The economic weakness of the West, it was felt, would make it vulnerable to internal Communist threats and to external pressure from the Soviet Union. Economic cooperation became necessary not only to rebuild Western economies and to ensure their continuing vitality, but also to provide for their political and military security. In addition, the perceived Communist military threat and the common interest in defending the West against that threat led the developed countries to subordinate economic conflict to common security interests. There was a greater willingness to compromise and to share economic burdens because of the common security problem.

The developed market economies also agreed on the nature of international economic management, which was to be designed to create and maintain a liberal system. It would require the establishment of an effective international monetary system and the reduction of barriers to trade and capital flows. With these barriers removed and a stable monetary system in place, states would have a favorable environment for ensuring national stability and growth. The state, not the international system, bore the main responsibility for national stability and growth. Thus members of the system shared a very limited conception of international economic management: regulation of the liberal system through the removal of barriers to trade and capital flows and the creation of a stable monetary system.

Finally, international management relied on the dominant power to lead the system. That leader was, of course, the United States. As the world's foremost economic and political power, the United States was clearly in a position to assume the responsibility of leadership. The American economy, undamaged by war and with its large market, its great productive capability, its financial facilities, and its strong currency, was the dominant world economy. Economic strength was paralleled by military power. The ability to support a large military force plus the possession of an atomic weapon made the United States the world's strongest military power and the leader of the Western alliance. The European states, with their economies in disarray due to the war, their production and markets divided by national boundaries, and their armies dismantled or weakened by the war, were not in a position to assume the leadership role.

The United States was not only able, it was also willing, to assume the leadership role. American policy makers had learned an important lesson from the interwar period. The failure of American leadership and the country's withdrawal into isolationism after World War I were viewed as major factors in the collapse of the economic system and of the peace. American policy makers believed that after World War II the United States could no longer isolate itself. As the strongest power in the postwar world, the United States would have to assume primary responsibility for establishing political and economic order. With the outbreak of the Cold War, another dimension was added to the need for American leadership. Without American leadership economic weakness in Europe and Japan would lead to Communist political victories. Thus the strength of the American economy, the lessons of the interwar period, and Cold War security incentives made American leadership necessary and palatable economically and politically at home.

Furthermore, the Europeans and Japanese—economically exhausted by the war—accepted this leadership. They needed American assistance to rebuild their domestic production and to finance their international trade; indeed, they needed it to survive. The political implications of American leadership were viewed as positive. It was felt that American economic assistance would alleviate domestic economic and political problems and encourage international stability. What the Europeans feared was not American domination but American isolation. The history of America's late entry into World Wars I and II was fresh in their minds. Thus they actively sought American leadership.

Willing and able, throughout the Bretton Woods period the United States mobilized the other developed countries for management and in some cases managed the system alone. The United States acted as the world's central banker; it provided the major initiatives in international trade negotiations; and it dominated international production.

The coincidence of three favorable political conditions—the concentration of power, the cluster of shared interests, and the leadership of the United States—provided the political capability equal to the tasks of managing the international economy. It enabled the Europeans and Japan to recover from the devastation of the war, established a stable monetary system and a more open trade and financial system that led to a period of unparalleled economic growth.

By the 1970s, however, the Bretton Woods system was in shambles and the management of the international economy was gravely threatened. Important changes in each of the three political bases of the Bretton Woods system undermined political management. Power was challenged; leadership weakened; the consensus on a liberal, limited system dissolved.

Although the developed countries remained the dominant political and economic powers, states outside the group have challenged their right to manage the system, the major challenge having come from the less developed countries. During the Bretton Woods period, countries of the Third World became increasingly dissatisfied with the system which shaped their economies but excluded them from management and from what they felt was an equitable share of the wealth. This dissatisfaction combined with political independence led to the end of the era of their willing acquiescence. The less developed countries have sought to increase their power to gain access to the management and thus to the rewards of the international economic system. The developed countries, for the most part, have tried to deny them that access.

A different and also less important challenge to the dominant power of the developed countries has come from the Communist countries. During Bretton Woods these countries were isolated from most international economic interaction and management. But in the 1960s and 1970s the Soviet Union and the countries of Eastern Europe sought greater participation in the international economy. That participation could prove disruptive to the international economy, as was demonstrated by the Russian grain purchase of 1972. Because of their power to disrupt and because of the different nature of their economies, the integration of Communist countries into the system will require new rules, structures, and procedures.

In addition to external challenges to the power and authority of the developed countries, power has shifted internally. In the 1960s Europe experienced a period of great economic growth and dynamism in international trade. Six and then nine European countries united to form the European Economic Community, an economic bloc rivaling the U.S. economy and a potential political force. Japan's economic development was even more spectacular. In the 1960s Japan became a major world economic power and joined the developed country condominium. At the same time the United States, still the world's dominant economy, faced important problems. On the international side a weakened dollar and a declining balance of trade undermined American international economic power.

This shift of power toward greater pluralism was matched by a shift in attitudes regarding American leadership. Increasingly, Europe and Japan were dissatisfied with the prerogatives which leadership gave the United States and the way in which the United States exercised these prerogatives. The clearest example of this dissatisfaction was growing European and Japanese criticism of the dollar system and American balance-of-payments deficits. The United States for its part was increasingly dissatisfied with the costs of leadership. While the Europeans and Japanese criticized American deficits, the United States criticized the refusal of these countries to allow the United States to devalue the dollar. As domestic economic problems emerged in the late 1960s, U.S. leaders began to feel that the costs of economic leadership outweighed the benefits.

The relaxation of security tensions reinforced the changing attitudes toward American leadership. During Bretton Woods the Soviet threat united the West behind American leadership and encouraged economic cooperation. Détente and the lessening of the perceived security threat undermined the security argument for Western economic cooperation and for American leadership. Europe and Japan were no longer willing to accept American dominance for security reasons, and the United States was no longer willing to bear the economic costs of leadership for reasons of security.

The weakening American leadership undermined the system based on that leadership. While U.S. dominance was increasingly unsatisfactory for America as well as for Europe and Japan, no new leader emerged to fulfill that role. Europe, although economically united in a common market, lacked the political unity necessary to lead the system. West Germany and Japan, the two strongest economic powers after the United States, were unable to manage the system by themselves and, in any case, were kept from leadership by the memories of World War II. Unless and until there developed some new form of multilateral management or a new system of leadership, the future of international economic management would be in doubt.

Finally, by the 1970s the agreement on a liberal and limited system, which was the basis of Bretton Woods, had collapsed. States no longer agreed on the ends and the means of management. The most vociferous dissenters from the liberal vision of international management were the less developed countries. In their view the open monetary, trade, and financial system perpetuated their underdevelopment and their subordination to the developed countries. They sought to revise the rules, institutions, and procedures of the system to make possible their development and their economic independence. More than that, they sought to make that development a primary goal and responsibility of the system. Thus they also dissented from the consensus on limited international economic management. International management, in their view, should be positive, activist, and more interventionist.

For many in the developed countries as well, liberalism was no longer an adequate goal of management. The challenge to liberalism in the developed countries grew out of its very success. The reduction of barriers to trade and capital made possible a vast expansion in international economic interaction among the developed market economies: increased international capital flows, the growth of international trade, and the development of international systems of production. As a result, national economies became increasingly interdependent, increasingly sensitive to economic policy and events outside the national economy. Because of the influence of external events, states found it increasingly difficult to manage their national economies.

Interdependence led to two reactions and two different challenges to liberalism. One reaction was to erect new barriers to limit economic interaction and, with it, interdependence. An open international system, in the view of many, no longer maximized economic welfare and most certainly undermined national sovereignty and autonomy. Another reaction was to go beyond liberalism, beyond the idea of a limited management to new forms of international economic cooperation which would manage interdependence. An open system, according to this viewpoint, maximized welfare but required, in turn, new forms of international management which would assume responsibilities and prerogatives formerly assumed by the state.

The final challenge to liberalism is from the Communist countries. Their centrally planned, state trading systems are antithetical to free markets. If they are to be integrated into the world economy, new forms of management will be required to regulate East–West trade, investment, and financial flows.

External challenges to the power of the developed countries, the internal weakening of leadership, and the collapse of the liberal consensus undermined political management. Without an effective system of control, the international economy entered a period of chaos and crisis: the monetary system collapsed, states began to put up new barriers to trade, a handful of oil producers forced the powerful developed countries to submit to their demands, the Third World called for a new international economic order and threatened to wreak havoc on the world economy if they did not get that order. In the absence of management, economic conflicts escalated to the highest political levels and became contests of political power.

The major political problem facing the international economy and a crucial problem of all international relations is whether it is possible to develop new forms of political management and whether those forms will be able to deal with three key problems of our time: the control of interdependence, the achievement of equity and the end of Third World dependence, and the reintegration of the Communist world into the international economy.

NOTES

1. On the idea of the need for a leader, see Charles P. Kindleberger, *The World in Depression, 1929–1939* (Berkeley, Calif.: Univ. of California Press, 1973).
2. Kenneth Waltz, *Man, the State and War* (New York: Columbia Univ. Press, 1969).
3. Richard N. Gardner, *Sterling-Dollar Diplomacy: The Origins and Prospects of Our International Economic Order*, Exp. ed. (New York: McGraw-Hill, 1969), p. 9.
4. Andrew Shonfield, *Modern Capitalism: The Changing Balance of Public and Private Power* (London: Oxford Univ. Press, 1969).
5. Gardner, *Sterling-Dollar Diplomacy: The Origins and Prospects of Our International Economic Order*, p. 8.

Part Two

The Western System

2

International
Monetary
Management

In July 1944, as Allied forces were moving across France, representatives of forty-four nations met on a beautiful estate in Bretton Woods, New Hampshire to create a new international monetary order. Foremost in the minds of these officials was the collapse of the international monetary system in the 1930s. Economic nationalism—competitive exchange rate devaluations, formation of competing monetary blocs, and the absence of international cooperation—in those years had contributed greatly to economic breakdown, domestic political instability, and international war. The goal of those present at Bretton Woods was to establish an international economic system which would prevent another economic and political collapse and another military conflict. It was the international consensus that previous monetary systems which had relied primarily on market forces had proved inadequate.[1] Henceforth governments acting together would have to assume the responsibility of managing the international monetary system. As early as 1936 in the Anglo-French-U.S. Tripartite Agreement, the major states began to cooperate to stabilize their currencies. During World War II monetary cooperation was expanded through various agreements and through a vast amount of monetary planning for the peace. Now, at Bretton Woods, officials were prepared to establish a publicly managed international monetary order.

The way to Bretton Woods had been paved by the United States, as the interwar period had led American policy makers to conclude that one of the chief causes of the economic and political disaster had been the failure of American leadership. During World War II, U.S. leaders decided that America would have to assume primary responsibility for establishing a postwar economic order. That order would be designed to prevent economic nationalism by fostering free trade and a high level of international interaction. A liberal economic system, ensured by international cooperation, would provide the foundation for a lasting peace. Thus in two years of bilateral negotiation, the United States and the United Kingdom, the world's leading economic and political powers, drew up a plan for a new system of international monetary management. In the end the plan reflected to a great extent the American vision of the postwar monetary order.[2]

The Anglo-American plan, approved at Bretton Woods, became the first publicly managed international monetary order. For a quarter of a century international monetary relations were stable, providing a basis for growing international trade, economic growth, and political harmony among the developed market economies.

On another summer day, twenty-seven years later, the president of the United States appeared on television to announce to the United States and the world the end of Bretton Woods. On August 15, 1971, President Richard M. Nixon—without consulting with and barely forewarning the other parties to the Bretton Woods Agreements—declared that the United States would no longer abide by the rules and procedures at the heart of the international monetary order. Since that day monetary officials and heads of state have grappled unsuccessfully with the problem of reestablishing order and stability in international monetary affairs. Whether they will succeed remains an open question. If they do not succeed, economic prosperity, political stability, and, if the 1930s are a guide, even international peace may be threatened.

In this chapter we examine monetary management during Bretton Woods, the reasons for its collapse, and the possibilities for devising new means of monetary management.

THE ORIGINAL BRETTON WOODS

In actuality, Bretton Woods never functioned as the United States and the others who signed the agreement had planned. The new order was intended to be a system of limited management by international organization. Two public international organizations, the International Monetary Fund (IMF) and the International Bank for Reconstruction and Development (IBRD, known as the World Bank) were, for the first time in history, to perform central bank functions for the international system.

The rules of Bretton Woods, set forth in the articles of agreement, provided for a system of fixed exchange rates. Public officials, fresh from what they perceived as a disastrous experience with floating rates in the

1930s, concluded that a fixed exchange rate was the most stable and the most conducive to trade. Thus, all countries agreed to establish the parity of their currencies in terms of gold and to maintain exchange rates within 1 percent, plus or minus, of parity. The rules further sought to encourage an open system by committing members to the convertibility of their respective currencies into other currencies and to free trade.[3]

The IMF was to be the keeper of the rules and the main instrument of public international management. Under the system of weighted voting, the United States was able to exert a preponderant influence in that body. IMF approval was necessary for any change in exchange rates. It advised countries on policies affecting the monetary system. Most importantly, it could advance credits to countries with balance-of-payments deficits. The IMF was provided with a fund, composed of contributions of member countries in gold and in their own currencies. The original quotas planned were to total $8.8 billion. In the event of a deficit in the current account, countries would be able to borrow up to eighteen months, and in some cases, up to five years from this fund.

Despite these innovations in public control, the original Bretton Woods placed primary emphasis on national and market solutions to monetary problems. It was expected that national monetary reserves, supplemented when necessary by IMF credits, would finance any temporary balance-of-payments disequilibria. No provision was made for international creation of reserves. New gold production and the holdings of national currencies were assumed sufficient. In the event of a structural disequilibrium, it was expected that there would be national solutions—a change in the value of the currency or an improvement by other means of a country's competitive position. Few means were given the IMF, however, to encourage such national solutions.

It had been recognized in 1944 that the new system could come into being only after a return to normalcy following the disruption of World War II. It was expected that after a brief transition period—expected to be no more than five years—the international economy would recover and the system would enter into operation. To facilitate postwar recovery, the planners at Bretton Woods created another institution, the International Bank for Reconstruction and Development we noted earlier. The IBRD, or World Bank, had an authorized capitalization of $10 billion and was expected to make loans of its own funds to underwrite private loans and to issue securities to raise new funds to make possible a speedy postwar recovery.[4]

From 1945 to 1947 the United States actively pressed for implementation of the Bretton Woods institutions in the expectation that the new structure would effectively manage the international monetary system. The United States participated in the IMF and the IBRD, providing resources to these institutions and pressing other countries to do likewise. To facilitate postwar recovery and to allow for the implementation of the Bretton Woods agreements, the United States gave financial assistance: $3 billion in relief funds and, more importantly, a large, $3¾ billion, loan to Great Britain, which was expected to enable that country to complete reconstruction and to return the pound to convertibility.

By 1947, however, the United States recognized that the Bretton Woods system was not working and, in fact, that the Western system seemed on the verge of collapse. World War II, it was becoming clear, had destroyed the European economic system, which had been based largely on international trade. The sources of Europe's foreign earnings had been wiped out. Its productive capacity had been destroyed or disrupted; its overseas earnings had turned into debts; its shipping was decimated. Western Europe was faced with vast import needs, not only for reconstruction but for mere survival. The problem was reflected in large balance-of-payments deficits. In 1946 the total European balance-of-payments deficit with the rest of the world amounted to $5.8 billion[5]; by 1947 it had risen to $7.6 billion.[6] European monetary reserves were depleted. By 1948 Western Europe had only $6.7 billion of reserves to pay for these huge deficits,[7] whereas the United States was running huge balance of trade surpluses: $6.7 billion in 1946 and $10.1 billion in 1947. American reserves were immense and growing fast: to $25.8 billion in 1948 and to over $26 billion in 1949 (see Table 2-1).

The Bretton Woods institutions were unable to cope with the problem. The modest credit facilities of the IMF were clearly insufficient to deal with Europe's huge deficits. The problem was further aggravated by a reaffirmation by the Board of Governors of the provision in the Articles of Agreement that the IMF could make loans only for current account deficits and not for capital and reconstruction purposes. Only the United States contribution of $570 million was actually available for IBRD lending. In addition, because the only available market for IBRD bonds was the conservative Wall Street banking market, the World Bank was forced to adopt a conservative lending policy, granting loans only when repayment was assured. By 1947 the IMF and the IBRD themselves were admitting that they could not deal with the system's economic problems.[8]

The economic crisis of 1947 was directly linked with crucial political problems. The governments of Italy and France, faced with pressures from powerful labor unions, were highly unstable. Britain, as a result of its economic difficulties, was withdrawing from India and Palestine and abandoning political and security commitments to Greece and Turkey.

More importantly, it seemed that the Soviet Union was willing and able to take advantage of the West's economic plight and resultant political instability to further its aims of territorial expansion in Europe.

The Soviet Union had forcibly established Communist governments in the countries it occupied at the end of the war: Hungary, Rumania, Poland, and Bulgaria. It had pressured Iran and Turkey for territorial concessions. Communist guerrillas were making significant headway in Greece. Large Communist parties in the governments of Italy and France seemed to be seeking to take advantage of labor unrest. And the Soviet Union was refusing to cooperate with the Allies on a postwar settlement for Germany. It seemed that the Soviet leaders were waiting for the economic collapse of Western Europe, which they expected would be to their political advantage.[9]

It was in 1947, and because of these circumstances, that a new system of international monetary management was born. In that year the United States stepped in to fill the economic gap left by Bretton Woods. During the next two years there would develop a new international monetary system—the dollar standard—based on unilateral American management.

UNILATERAL AMERICAN MANAGEMENT

From 1947 to 1960 the United States was both able and willing to manage the international monetary system. The strength of the American economy, the lessons of the interwar period, and security incentives made American leadership acceptable economically and politically at home. And, out of necessity, the Europeans and the Japanese accepted this American management. Economically exhausted by the war, they needed American assistance to rebuild their domestic production, finance their international trade, and provide a setting for political stability. Thus after 1947 the United States began to manage the international monetary system. It did so by performing two functions necessary for a monetary system: provision of liquidity and adjustment.

Just as any national economy needs an accepted money, so the international economy requires an accepted vehicle for investment, trade, and payments. Unlike national economies, however, the international economy lacks a central government which can issue currency and manage its use. In the past this problem has been solved through the use of gold and through the use of national currencies. In the nineteenth and twentieth centuries gold played a key role in international monetary transactions. Gold was used to back currencies; the international value of currency was determined by its fixed relationship to gold; gold was used to settle international accounts. Supplementing the use of gold in this period was the British pound. Based on the dominant British economy, the pound became a reserve, transaction, and intervention currency.

By 1947 it was clear that gold and the pound could no longer serve as the world's money. Gold production was insufficient to meet the demands of growing international trade and investment. And, because of the weakness of the British economy, the pound was hardly up to the task of serving as the primary world currency. The only currency strong enough to be used to meet the rising demands for international liquidity was the dollar. The strength of the American economy, the fixed relationship of the dollar to gold ($35 an ounce), and the commitment of the American government to convert dollars into gold at that price made the dollar as good as gold. In fact, the dollar was better than gold: it earned interest; it was more flexible than gold; it was needed to buy crucial imports for survival and reconstruction.

But the strength of the dollar and the economic need for it were not sufficient to create the dollar system. Natural economic processes were creating a huge dollar shortage. The United States was running huge balance-of-trade surpluses, and U.S. reserves were immense and growing. It was necessary to reverse this flow. Dollars had to leave the United States and become available for international use. In other words, the United States would have to reverse the natural economic processes and run a balance-of-payments deficit. And that is just what happened.

From 1947 until 1958 the United States deliberately encouraged an outflow of dollars, and, from 1950 on, the United States ran a balance-of-payments deficit which provided liquidity for the international economy. Dollars flowed out through various American aid programs: the Truman plan for aid to Greece and Turkey, aid to various underdeveloped countries, and, most important, the Marshall Plan, the European Recovery Program. From 1948 to 1952 the United States gave sixteen Western European countries $17 billion in outright grants.

Another source of dollar liquidity for the international monetary system grew out of the American commitment to meet Soviet threats with Western political and military force. Such a policy required significant military expenditures. Vast sums were needed for troops, equipment, and, as in the case of Korea, for war. The only country capable of paying for such expenditures was the United States. The United States did not carry out significant foreign military expenditures with the express purpose of providing dollars for the international monetary system. However, it was willing to bear the cost and suffer the balance-of-payments consequences of such expenditures because it recognized that its allies were in no position to share the burden and because, with the vast international payments imbalances, the monetary consequences were viewed as beneficial. Thus the dollar became the world's currency and the United States became the world's central banker, issuing dollars for the international monetary system.

In addition to providing liquidity, the United States assumed the international management of imbalances in the system. The United States took several steps which facilitated adjustment in the short term. It dealt with its own huge balance-of-trade surplus and the European and Japanese deficits by foreign aid and military expenditures. In addition the United States abandoned the Bretton Woods goal of convertibility and encouraged European and Japanese trade protectionism and discrimination against the dollar. For example, the United States absorbed large volumes of Japanese exports while accepting Japanese restrictions against American exports. It supported the European Payments Union, an intra-European clearing system which discriminated against the dollar. And it promoted European and Japanese exports to the United States. Finally, the United States used the leverage of Marshall Plan aid to encourage devaluation of many European currencies in 1949 and to promote national programs of monetary stabilization.

To encourage long-term adjustment, the United States promoted European and Japanese trade competitiveness. Policies for economic controls on the defeated Axis countries were scrapped. Aid to Europe and Japan was designed to rebuild productive and export capacity. In the long run it was expected that such European and Japanese recovery would benefit the United States by widening markets for American exports.

The system worked well. Europe and Japan recovered and then expanded. The American economy prospered in spite of or partly because of the dollar outflow which led to the purchase of American goods and services. Yet by 1960 the American-managed system was in trouble.

MULTILATERAL MANAGEMENT UNDER U.S. LEADERSHIP

The economic foundation of American management of the international monetary system was confidence in the American dollar, confidence based on the strength of the American economy, the vast American gold reserves, and the commitment to convert dollars into gold. But, ironically, the system also relied on a process which eventually undermined the very confidence on which the structure was built. That process was the constant outflow of dollars from the United States. The system relied on an American deficit and on foreign holding of dollars to provide sufficient liquidity for international transactions. If, however, the deficit continued and if outstanding dollar holdings abroad became too large in relation to gold reserves, confidence in the dollar—and thus the entire system—would be jeopardized.

By 1958 the United States no longer sought a payments deficit. The European and Japanese recoveries were nearly complete. Balances of payments were improving and official reserves were growing steadily. By the end of 1959 European and Japanese reserves equaled those of the

United States. American gold holdings, however, had fallen from $24.4 billion at the end of 1948 to $19.5 billion at the end of 1959. More importantly, dollars held abroad had risen from $7.3 billion in 1948 to $19.4 billion at the end of 1959. The excess of American gold holdings over foreign dollar holdings had fallen from $18.1 billion to $0.5 billion. In 1960, for the first time, foreign dollar holdings exceeded U.S. gold reserves.[10] The United States discovered that its deficit was out of control. Private long-term capital outflow, caused to a great extent by direct investment abroad, and foreign military and aid expenditures were resulting in a rising balance-of-payments deficit. By 1960 that deficit had risen to $3.7 billion (see Table 2–1).

The weakness of the dollar was aggravated further by the weakness of the pound. The British currency had retained a minor role as an international currency primarily in the Middle East and Commonwealth countries. By the end of the 1950s, it was under severe pressure in international exchange markets. The United States could not handle the increasing problems of sterling alone. Vast sums were needed beyond the capability of the United States to support the pound in times of crisis. Furthermore, a run on the pound tended to spill over into a run on the dollar. The problem of the dollar was also accentuated by the return to convertibility of European currencies at the end of 1958. Convertibility made possible large speculative international capital flows which could be directed against the pound or the dollar.

In November 1960 the United States experienced the first run on the dollar. International speculators began to convert dollars into gold on the London market. Then in 1961 there was a run on the pound. As a result of these crises, there emerged a feeling that the system of American management was inadequate. The dollar system, to be sure, had not collapsed. There was still a common perception of a need for cooperation to support the system. The United States was still able to play a strong leadership role. The dollar and its basis, the American economy, remained healthy. But the United States could no longer manage the system alone. Henceforth, the United States would be forced to join in collective management, to seek the cooperation of other members of the system, to make concessions.

At the end of the 1950s, the IMF, largely inactive in the period of U.S. unilateral management, began to play a more important role. When the Suez crisis of 1956–1957 led to pressure on the pound and the franc and to United States refusal of support, Britain and France turned to the IMF for assistance. When their currencies became convertible in 1958, the Europeans began to turn to the IMF for funds to finance temporary balance-of-payments disequilibria. Increases in the fund's quotas at this time facilitated the more active role.

The major functions of monetary management, however, were performed by a multilateral elite from the major states. One important new form of multilateral management was central bank cooperation.

Since 1930 European bankers had met together regularly at the Bank for International Settlements (BIS) in Basle, Switzerland, but the United States had never become a member and had never participated in their frequent meetings.[11] After the dollar crisis of 1960, however, the U.S. central bank, the Federal Reserve, joined the monthly meetings. The highest officials of the Federal Reserve Bank of New York, which manages the international transactions for the U.S. Federal Reserve, the highest officials of the board of governors, and, very often, the chairman of the U.S. Federal Reserve participated in an active way in the monthly meetings of central bankers.

U.S. participation enabled the Basle group to control important aspects of the international monetary system. The bankers performed the function of ad hoc crisis management. In 1961 they supported the pound; in 1964 the lira and the pound; in 1967 the pound. The group also regulated the price of gold. In 1961 the bankers agreed to centralize gold dealings through a "gold pool," buying gold when it fell below $35 an ounce and selling when it rose above that limit. Until 1968 this pool controlled gold speculation. The bankers also cooperated in exchange markets and began to play an important role in the burgeoning Eurodollar market, investing and intervening in that market and accumulating information about it. Finally the bankers regularly exchanged information about national policies affecting the international monetary system.

A second management system developed at this time was the Group of Ten, composed of finance ministers and, in a subsidiary group, their deputies. Because IMF facilities were insufficient to handle the pound crisis of 1961, an ad hoc arrangement by central bankers was devised to save the British currency. It was recognized, however, that such ad hoc schemes were insufficient to deal with large speculative crises against the pound or the dollar because of the substantial funds required.

The United States proposed that any additional available funds be given automatically to the IMF to manage such currency crises. These supplemental funds would be controlled by the IMF in which the United States and the United Kingdom, through their weighted votes, controlled decisions.

The Europeans were willing to contribute additional funds, but they insisted that these funds be under their control. And so a group of ten industrial countries—Belgium, France, Germany, Italy, the Netherlands, Sweden, Canada, Japan, the United Kingdom, and the United States— met in Paris in December 1961 and created the General Arrangements to Borrow, a fund outside IMF jurisdiction and under the control of the

Table 2-1 U.S. Balance of Payments, 1946–1975

[Millions of dollars; quarterly data seasonally adjusted, except as noted]

Year or quarter	Merchandise [1][2]			Military transactions			Net investment income		Net travel and transportation expenditures	Other services, net [3]	Balance on goods and services [1][4]	Remittances, pensions, and other unilateral transfers [1]	Balance on current account
	Exports	Imports	Net balance	Direct expenditures	Sales	Net balance	Private [3]	U.S. Government					
1946	11,764	−5,067	6,697	−493	(10)	−493	554	6	733	310	7,807	−2,922	4,885
1947	16,097	−5,973	10,124	−455	(10)	−455	807	50	946	145	11,617	−2,625	8,992
1948	13,265	−7,557	5,708	−799	(10)	−799	975	85	374	175	6,518	−4,525	1,993
1949	12,213	−6,874	5,339	−621	(10)	−621	989	73	230	208	6,218	−5,638	580
1950	10,203	−9,081	1,122	−576	(10)	−576	1,146	78	−120	242	1,892	−4,017	−2,125
1951	14,243	−11,176	3,067	−1,270	(10)	−1,270	1,317	151	298	254	3,817	−3,515	302
1952	13,449	−10,838	2,611	−2,054	(10)	−2,054	1,267	140	83	309	2,356	−2,531	−175
1953	12,412	−10,975	1,437	−2,615	192	−2,423	1,283	166	−238	307	532	−2,481	−1,949
1954	12,929	−10,353	2,576	−2,642	182	−2,460	1,594	213	−269	305	1,959	−2,280	−321
1955	14,424	−11,527	2,897	−2,901	200	−2,701	1,775	180	−297	299	2,153	−2,498	−345
1956	17,556	−12,803	4,753	−2,949	161	−2,788	2,054	40	−361	447	4,145	−2,423	1,722
1957	19,562	−13,291	6,271	−3,216	375	−2,841	2,174	4	−189	482	5,901	−2,345	3,556
1958	16,414	−12,952	3,462	−3,435	300	−3,135	2,008	168	−633	486	2,356	−2,361	−5
1959	16,458	−15,310	1,148	−3,107	302	−2,805	2,147	68	−821	573	310	−2,448	−2,138
1960	19,650	−14,758	4,892	−3,087	335	−2,753	2,270	17	−964	612	4,073	−2,300	1,774
1961	20,108	−14,537	5,571	−2,998	402	−2,596	2,832	105	−978	628	5,563	−2,514	3,048
1962	20,781	−16,260	4,521	−3,105	656	−2,448	3,177	134	−1,155	845	5,074	−2,628	2,446
1963	22,272	−17,048	5,224	−2,961	657	−2,304	3,227	98	−1,312	996	5,930	−2,742	3,188
1964	25,501	−18,700	6,801	−2,880	747	−2,133	3,926	9	−1,149	1,078	8,533	−2,769	5,764
1965	26,461	−21,510	4,951	−2,952	830	−2,122	4,143	26	−1,284	1,426	7,140	−2,841	4,299
1966	29,310	−25,493	3,817	−3,764	829	−2,935	3,543	55	−1,332	1,404	4,552	−2,917	1,635
1967	30,666	−26,866	3,800	−4,378	1,152	−3,226	3,865	41	−1,751	1,652	4,380	−3,107	1,273
1968	33,626	−32,991	635	−4,535	1,392	−3,143	3,941	63	−1,548	1,671	1,620	−2,933	1,313
1969	36,414	−35,807	607	−4,856	1,528	−3,328	3,471	156	−1,763	1,878	1,020	−2,976	−1,956
1970	[12] 42,469	[12] −39,866	[12] 2,603	−4,855	1,501	−3,355	3,631	−112	−2,023	2,220	2,966	−3,248	−281
1971	43,311	−45,579	−2,268	−4,819	1,926	−2,893	5,659	−956	−2,315	2,537	−237	−3,642	−3,879
1972	49,388	−55,797	−6,409	−4,784	1,163	−3,621	6,208	−1,888	−3,024	2,803	−5,930	−3,779	−9,710
1973	71,379	−70,424	955	−4,658	2,342	−2,317	8,188	−3,009	−2,862	3,222	4,177	−3,841	335
1974	98,309	−103,586	−5,277	−5,103	2,944	−2,158	13,351	−3,229	−2,692	3,830	3,825	[13] −7,182	[13] −3,357
1973:													
I	15,423	−16,334	−911	−1,174	347	−827	1,953	−629	−714	767	−361	−755	−1,116
II	16,958	−17,189	−231	[14] −1,236	455	−781	1,967	−759	−779	749	166	−1,015	−849
III	18,451	−17,737	714	−1,072	531	−541	1,964	−801	−667	884	1,553	−900	653
IV	20,547	−19,164	1,383	−1,177	1,009	−168	2,304	−820	−702	823	2,820	−1,173	1,647
1974:													
I	22,464	−22,587	−123	−1,166	663	−503	4,014	−769	−513	886	2,992	[13] −2,966	[13] 26
II	24,218	−25,677	−1,459	−1,324	678	−646	2,745	−781	−717	936	78	−1,865	−1,787
III	25,034	−27,349	−2,315	−1,279	766	−513	3,161	−807	−721	960	−235	−1,265	−1,500
IV	26,593	−27,973	−1,380	−1,335	837	−498	3,431	−872	−741	1,049	989	−1,088	−99
1975:													
I	27,188	−25,358	1,830	−1,303	954	−349	2,165	−989	−572	1,093	3,178	−1,175	2,003
II	25,692	−22,314	3,378	−1,209	804	−405	2,235	−843	−393	1,043	5,015	−1,183	3,832
III P	26,716	−24,690	2,026	−1,113	1,241	128	2,572	−794	−480	1,095	4,547	−1,047	3,500

[1] Excludes military grants.

[2] Adjusted from Census data for differences in timing and coverage.

[3] Fees and royalties from U.S. direct investments abroad or from foreign direct investments in the United States are excluded from net investment income and included in other services, net.

[4] In concept, equal to net exports of goods and services in the national income and product accounts, although the two series may differ because of revisions, special handling of certain items, etc.

[5] Excludes liabilities to foreign official reserve agencies.

[6] Private foreigners exclude the International Monetary Fund (IMF), but include other international and regional organizations.

[7] Includes liabilities to foreign official agencies reported by U.S. Government and U.S. banks and U.S. liabilities to the IMF arising from reversible gold sales to, and gold deposits with, the United States.

[8] Official reserve assets include gold, special drawing rights, convertible currencies, and the U.S. gold tranche position in the IMF. Minus sign indicates increase.

(Footnotes continued on following page.)

SOURCE: *Economic Report of the President* (Washington, D.C.: U.S. Government Printing Office, 1976), pp. 274–275.

[Millions of dollars; quarterly data seasonally adjusted, except as noted]

Year or quarter	Long-term capital flows, net — U.S. Government [5]	Long-term capital flows, net — Private [6]	Balance on current account and long-term capital	Nonliquid short-term private capital flows, net [6]	Allocations of special drawing rights (SDR)	Errors and omissions, net	Net liquidity balance **	Liquid private capital flows, net [6]	Official reserve transactions balance **	Changes in liabilities to foreign official agencies, net [7]	Changes in U.S. official reserve assets, net [8]	U.S. official reserve assets, net (unadjusted, end of period) [9]
1946				−253		155					−623	20,706
1947				−236		861					−3,315	24,021
1948				−131		1,115					−1,736	25,758
1949				158		717					−266	26,024
1950				75		−124					1,758	24,265
1951				−227		354					−33	24,299
1952				−41		497					−415	24,714
1953				183		220					1,256	23,458
1954				−556		60					480	22,978
1955				−328		371					182	22,797
1956				−479		390					−869	23,666
1957				−174		1,012					−1,165	24,832
1958				−145		361					2,292	22,540
1959				−89		260					1,035	21,504
1960	−885	−2,100	−1,211	[11]−1,405		−1,060	[11]−3,677	[11]273	−3,403	1,258	2,145	19,359
1961	−885	−2,182	−20	[11]−1,200		−1,032	[11]−2,252	[11]904	−1,348	742	606	18,753
1962	−882	−2,606	−1,043	[11]−657		−1,165	[11]−2,864	[11]214	−2,650	1,117	1,533	17,220
1963	−1,151	−3,376	−1,339	[11]−968		−406	[11]−2,713	[11]779	−1,934	1,557	377	16,843
1964	−1,352	−4,511	−100	−1,643		−954	−2,696	1,162	−1,534	1,363	171	16,672
1965	−1,539	−4,577	−1,817	−154		−506	−2,478	1,188	−1,290	67	1,222	15,450
1966	−1,478	−2,778	−2,621	−104		575	−2,151	2,370	219	−787	568	14,882
1967	−2,337	−2,909	−3,973	−522		−189	−4,683	1,265	−3,418	3,366	52	14,830
1968	−2,164	1,190	−2,287	231		446	−1,611	3,252	1,641	−761	−880	15,710
1969	−1,949	−44	−3,949	−640		−1,492	−6,081	8,820	2,739	−1,552	−1,187	16,964
1970	−2,045	−1,434	−3,760	−482	867	−476	−3,851	−5,988	−9,839	7,362	2,477	14,487
1971	−2,376	−4,383	−10,637	−2,347	717	−9,698	−21,965	−7,788	−29,753	27,405	2,348	12,167
1972	−1,334	−69	−11,113	−1,542	710	−1,884	−13,829	3,475	−10,354	10,322	32	13,151
1973	−1,490	177	−977	−4,238		−2,436	−7,651	2,343	−5,308	5,099	209	14,378
1974	[13]1,119	−8,463	−10,702	−12,936		4,698	−18,940	10,543	−8,397	9,831	−1,434	15,883
1973:												
I	−334	57	−1,393	−1,543		−3,875	−6,811	−3,818	−10,629	10,409	220	12,931
II	54	−290	−1,085	−1,497		863	−1,719	2,270	551	−568	17	12,914
III	−442	1,706	1,917	59		−150	1,826	492	2,318	−2,305	−13	12,927
IV	−769	−1,297	−419	−1,257		726	−950	3,399	2,449	−2,434	−15	14,378
1974:												
I	[13]1,411	264	1,701	−3,908		1,014	−1,193	1,745	552	−342	−210	14,588
II	484	−999	−2,302	−5,265		1,313	−6,254	2,054	−4,200	4,558	−358	14,946
III	83	−2,157	−3,574	−1,458		1,135	−3,897	4,014	117	886	−1,003	15,893
IV	−860	−5,570	−6,529	−2,305		1,236	−7,598	2,730	−4,868	4,731	137	15,883
1975:												
I	−474	−2,199	−670	1,929		2,067	3,326	−6,587	−3,261	3,586	−325	16,256
II	−354	−2,431	1,047	−970		843	920	−2,634	−1,714	1,743	−29	16,242
III p	−563	−1,357	1,580	−1,335		−37	208	4,711	4,919	−4,577	−342	16,291
IV p											89	16,226

[9] Includes increases (in millions) as follows: for 1969, $67 resulting from revaluation of the German mark in October 1969; for 1971, $28 in dollar value of foreign currencies revalued to reflect market exchange rates as of December 31, 1971; for 1972, $1,016 resulting from change in par value of the dollar on May 8, 1972; and for 1973, $1,436 resulting from change in par value of the dollar on October 18, 1973.

Beginning July 1974, valuation of SDR and reserve position in the IMF based on a weighted average of exchange rates for the currencies of 16 member countries. On a pre-July 1974 basis, reserve assets for December 31, 1974 are $15,812 million and for December 31, 1975, $16,366 million.

[10] Not available separately.

[11] Coverage of liquid banking claims for 1960–63 and of liquid nonbanking claims for 1960–62 is limited to foreign currency deposits only; other liquid items are not available separately and are included with nonliquid claims.

[12] Data beginning 1970 not strictly comparable with earlier data.

[13] Includes extraordinary U.S. Government transactions with India.

[14] Includes return import into the United States, at a depreciated value of $22 million, of aircraft originally reported in 1970 III sales as a long-term lease to Australia.

**These balances have been used to measure exchange market pressures on the dollar. Under current floating exchange rate conditions, these pressures are inadequately reflected in the balances.

members of the newly formed Group of Ten.[12] The members committed themselves to lend up to $6 billion to the IMF in cases where the Group of Ten collectively determined that such credit was necessary.

The Group of Ten soon assumed other important roles in monetary management. It became a forum for discussion and exchange of information as well as a vehicle for proposals for and negotiation of monetary reform. The group also served a crisis management function. In the midst of the 1968 dollar crisis, it negotiated the two-tier gold system. This agreement created two markets for gold sales: a private market in which the price of gold could fluctuate freely and a public market where the group agreed to sell each other gold at $35 an ounce. The agreement stopped the crisis and eased the pressure on the American gold supply.

A third form of multilateral management emerged in Working Party Three of the Organization for Economic Cooperation and Development (OECD). In this OECD forum, finance ministers and their deputies discussed economic policies, exchanged information, and studied the operation and reform of the monetary adjustment process.

In addition to these multilateral elite networks, there was a series of bilateral arrangements between the United States and other members of the Group of Ten which supported the multilateral management system: swap arrangements, standby credit lines to be used by central bankers for crisis management, special American bonds which countries agreed to hold in lieu of converting dollars into gold, and German agreements to purchase American military equipment and to continue to hold large amounts of American dollars to offset the cost of American troops stationed in Germany.

Finally, there were unilateral efforts by the United States to shore up the system by improving the American balance of payments. These measures were, in large part, a response to the increasing concern and pressure of other members of the system for a reestablishment of confidence in the weakening dollar. In 1963 Congress and the Kennedy administration instituted an interest equalization tax on foreign securities designed to make borrowing in the United States less desirable and thus to reduce capital outflows. The Johnson administration established capital restraints on American foreign investment. This program was a direct response to the announcement by French President Charles de Gaulle in 1965 that he would convert current surpluses of dollars into gold and would reduce France's dollar holdings. Other programs such as the tying of foreign aid, a decrease in duty-free tourist allotments, and programs to encourage American exports were instituted. It is important to note that these actions were all special measures designed to correct the balance-of-payments situation. American monetary and fiscal policy generally remained unconstrained by balance-of-payments disequilibria, and the United States maintained an expansionary economic policy despite growing balance-of-payments difficulties.[13]

The various multilateral management mechanisms consisting of networks of monetary elites improved the functioning of the adjustment process by preventing and containing currency crises. They also achieved a major reform of international liquidity. Bretton Woods had established no means for the international regulation of liquidity, whereas the dollar system relied on the United States to act as the world's central banker. Now, individual nations took an important step toward international control of world reserves.

In the early 1960s inadequate liquidity was seen as a crucial problem. Once the United States solved its balance-of-payments problems—and it was felt that the United States would solve them[14]— there would be a liquidity shortage and a need to provide alternate forms of international money. The problem of the future, it was believed, would not be too many but too few dollars. The British in 1962 were the first to propose creating a new international reserve asset. But it was not until 1965, when the United States adopted the policy of creating such an asset, that reform negotiations began seriously.

From 1965 to 1968 there were multilateral negotiations among the Group of Ten countries under U.S. leadership to devise new international means of creating reserves. After five years of tortuous and precarious negotiation, agreement was reached to create Special Drawing Rights (SDRs), artificial international reserve units created by joint agreement by the IMF. Importantly, the new form of international liquidity would be managed not by the United States alone but by the Group of Ten jointly, for the Europeans were given a veto power on the creation of new SDRs.[15] SDRs could be used to settle accounts among central banks.

It was decided that 10 billion dollars of the new "paper gold" would be created between 1970 and 1972. This sum was small compared with total world reserves at that time, close to 100 billion dollars in 1970. It became even smaller when countries decided to stop SDR creation after the distribution of under $6 billion because there was no need for more liquidity.[16] Nevertheless, for the first time in history the international monetary system had an internationally created and managed asset.

The SDR agreement was the height of multilateral cooperation. It demonstrated the ability of the management system, not only to contain crises and to create jerry-built structures to support the system, but also the ability of the managers to move toward systemic reform. Yet it was just at this point that the system began to crack. In eighteen months between 1967 and 1968, three major currency crises signaled the end of effective monetary management: the crisis and the devaluation of the pound in November 1967, the dollar crisis of March 1968, and the crisis of the French franc and the German deutsche mark in November 1968.

FORCES OF CHANGE

In the 1960s and the 1970s there occurred important structural changes which eventually led to the breakdown of management. One change was the development of a high level of monetary interdependence. The stage was set for monetary interdependence by the return to convertibility of the Western European currencies at the end of 1958[17] and of the Japanese yen in 1964. Convertibility facilitated the vast expansion of international financial transactions which created monetary interdependence.

The new interdependence was created, first, by the internationalization of banking. In the 1960s the number of multinational banks expanded rapidly. In 1965 only thirteen American banks had branches abroad; by the end of 1974 there were 125 U.S. banks with foreign branches. The assets of foreign branches of U.S. banks rose from about $9.1 billion in 1965 to over $125 billion in 1974.[18] Concomitantly, there was an expansion of foreign banks in the United States. The number of foreign branches and agencies in New York City rose from forty-nine in 1965 to ninety-two in 1974. Total assets of these branches and agencies in the same period rose from $4.8 billion to $29 billion. By the end of 1974 foreign banks operating in the United States had total assets of $56 billion.[19]

Another aspect of the internationalization of banking has been the emergence of international banking consortia. Since 1964 various banks have formed international syndicates, and by 1971 over three-fourths of the world's largest banks had become shareholders in such syndicates.[20] Multinational banks can and do make huge international transfers of capital not only for investment purposes but also for hedging and speculating against exchange rate changes.[21]

Monetary interdependence was also a result of the internationalization of production. Large multinational corporations now control vast liquid assets. It has been estimated that approximately 200 American multinational firms control about $25 billion in cash or cash-equivalent assets. They also control perhaps another $100 billion of inventory and accounts receivable which can be used as collateral to raise funds. It has been argued that similar liquid assets are controlled by non-American international business. The financial officers of these large corporations are able to move these vast sums from country to country, taking advantage of interest rate spreads or expected exchange rate adjustments. In the 1960s and 1970s, as crises multiplied, the financial officers of these corporations developed the experience and skill at such transfers. For many multinationals the movements of such capital has become a part of good management.[22]

A final source of monetary interdependence is the market for Eurocurrencies. Eurodollars are dollars in the form of bank deposits held and traded abroad, primarily in Europe. Branches of American banks or foreign banks outside the United States accept dollar deposits and lend those deposits in the form of dollars. Other Eurocurrencies are primarily German deutsche marks and Swiss francs held abroad. The Eurodollar and Eurocurrency markets originated in the late 1950s and grew to huge proportions in the 1960s and 1970s.[23] The market has flourished largely because it is controlled neither by state regulation nor by constraints of domestic money markets. Thus it has been able to establish highly competitive interest rate levels which have attracted vast sums.

The exact size of the Eurocurrency market is uncertain. Estimates by the Bank for International Settlements show its fantastic growth in the 1960s and 1970s to over $200 billion in 1974 (see Figure 2-1). The Eurocurrency market, thus, is a large uncontrolled international capital market. Because it consists largely of short-term funds, it is highly mobile and highly volatile.

These new forms of monetary interdependence made possible huge international capital flows. During the Bretton Woods era countries were

Figure 2-1   The Growth of Eurodollar and Eurocurrency Markets, 1967–1973

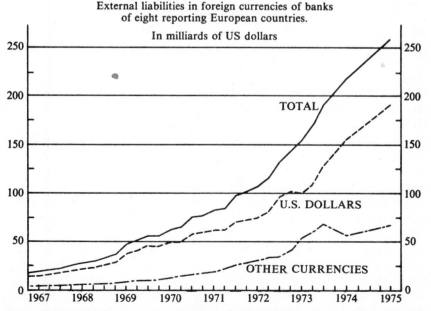

External liabilities in foreign currencies of banks of eight reporting European countries.

In milliards of US dollars

Source: Bank for International Settlements, *Forty-Fourth Annual Report* (Basle: Bank for International Settlements, 1974), p. 158.

reluctant to alter exchange rates formally even in cases of structural disequilibria. Because such changes had a direct impact on certain domestic economic groups, they came to be seen as political risks for leaders. Officials usually sought to avoid changes unless and until market forces overwhelmed them and forced a significant alteration. As a result official exchange rates often became unrealistic in market terms. This provided a virtually risk-free temptation for speculators. They could move from a weak to a strong currency hoping to reap profits when a revaluation occurred. If, however, monetary authorities managed to avoid revaluation, they could return to other currencies with no loss.[24]

The combination of risk-free speculation with the availability of huge sums was highly destabilizing. The movement of billions of dollars or pounds or deutsche marks or francs from country to country in a few days or even a few hours during a currency crisis became common. Countries, committed to maintain the fixed value of their currency within a plus or minus 1 percent, and unwilling to take the political risks of altering exchange rates, were forced to intervene to stabilize values in the face of huge pressures from enormous monetary movements. It was expected that there would be national solutions—a change in the value of the currency or an improvement in other ways of a country's competitive position.

Monetary interdependence also increasingly interfered with national economic management. The desire for economic control has been a major characteristic of postwar government, and a major tool for that control has been monetary management. Interdependence, however, undermines national monetary tools. Interest rates, for example, have become a less effective means of managing the national economic system. Low interest rates, used to stimulate an economy, might simply lead to an outflow of capital to countries with higher interest rates. In April and May 1971, a lowering of interest rates in the United States led to an outflow of capital. Conversely, high interest rates used to manage inflation may be undermined by capital inflows attracted precisely by those higher interest rates. Such was the case in Germany in 1969 and 1971. The need to defend fixed exchange rates in an interdependent system also interfered with domestic monetary management. When Germany found it necessary to absorb large amounts of dollars to maintain the value of the deutsche mark in 1969 and 1971, its domestic attempts to deflate the economy and to control inflation were seriously challenged.

For a long time the United States was the one country which was not interdependent in this sense. Huge capital flows had less effect on the vast American economy than on the smaller European and Japanese economies. The United States was further insulated by its sophisticated domestic monetary management. Finally, as long as other countries would absorb dollar outflows, the United States did not have to take domestic measures to balance international accounts. American national economic policy was not influenced by the international position of the dollar or by monetary interdependence. Thus in the 1960s the United States was able to rely on special balance-of-payment measures and avoid restrictive monetary or fiscal policy. However, during the late 1960s and early 1970s, influential American leaders began to perceive that the U.S. economy was being constrained by the international monetary system.

The clearest negative effect of the monetary system was on American trade. By the late 1960s the dollar was overvalued partly due to inflation induced by expenditures on the Vietnam war, and partly because other countries had altered their exchange rates to account for inflation while the value of the dollar had not been altered. This overvalued dollar led to declining exports and increasing imports (see Table 2–1), which had an adverse impact on domestic employment at a time when the economy was sluggish and employment was what was then thought severe, about 6 percent.

The simple solution for any country aside from the United States in this position would have been to devalue the currency and to reestablish a competitive trade position. And, although after 1968 the United States wanted to change the relationship of the dollar to other currencies, it could not because other members of the system that were holding vast sums of dollars and were enjoying trade surpluses refused to allow a realignment of currencies and threatened to devalue their own currencies should the United States unilaterally devalue. The United States, it should be noted, was not without fault on this issue. In fact, what the United States wanted was not a devaluation of the dollar but the revaluation of other currencies, which would have improved American trade competitiveness without raising the domestic political problem of devaluation.

U.S. policy makers also perceived a negative effect of the monetary system on investment. An outflow of dollars for investment purposes was encouraged by an overvalued dollar. This led to pressure at home from labor unions that were starting to talk about the export of American jobs. Yet another area in which the United States became constrained was in fiscal policy. Such policies had never been subject to external considerations. Now there emerged a major conflict. The Europeans and the Japanese demanded a deflationary American policy, arguing that the dollar outflow and the expansion of the American economy was causing inflation abroad. This call for restraint was in direct conflict with President Nixon's political desires for reelection in 1972—and his desire to reinflate the American economy in 1970 to provide a better setting for that election. Thus interdependence finally touched even the United States.

A second structural change which undermined monetary management was increased pluralism. The United States was no longer the dominant economic power it had been for almost two decades. By the mid-1960s Europe and Japan had become international economic powers in their own right. With total reserves exceeding those of the United States, with higher levels of growth and trade, and with per capita income approaching that of the United States, Europe and Japan were narrowing the gap between themselves and the United States.

The shift toward a more pluralist distribution of economic power led to a renewed sense of political power and to increasing dissatisfaction with American dominance of the international monetary system and, in particular, with the privileged role of the dollar as the international currency. The Europeans and Japanese resented the prerogatives that the monetary system provided for the United States. As the world's central banker the United States, through its deficit, determined the level of international liquidity. In an increasingly interdependent international economy, American policy and the American deficit thus influenced economic conditions in Europe and Japan. In addition, as long as other countries were willing to hold dollars, the United States could carry out unlimited foreign expenditures for political purposes—military activities and foreign aid—without the threat of balance-of-payments constraints. And American business could invest abroad at cheap exchange rates without payments constraints. Such prerogatives of American dominance had been acceptable to a war-weary Europe and Japan. They became increasingly unacceptable to a recovered and revitalized Europe and Japan.

Dissatisfaction with the political implications of the dollar system was increased by détente between the United States and the Soviet Union. The Soviet threat had been an important force in cementing the Western monetary system. The need for the American political and security umbrella helped make American economic domination palatable for Europe and Japan. The decline in the security threat loosened the cement and allowed submerged economic tensions to surface.

Reinforcing the relative decline in American power and the dissatisfaction of Europe and Japan with the system was the continuing decline of the dollar. Despite large and persistent deficits, it had seemed possible until 1965 that the dollar drain might be reduced or eliminated and that confidence in the system could be preserved. In 1963 an important study which shaped official thinking in the United States and abroad predicted a return to payments equilibrium by 1968.[25] But the Vietnam conflict and the refusal of the Johnson administration to pay for it and for its Great Society programs through taxation resulted in an increased dollar outflow to pay for the military expenses and in rampant inflation, which led to deterioration in the American balance of trade position (see Table 2-1). By the end of the 1960s large payments deficits seemed chronic.

The new pluralism made monetary management more difficult. One example of the problem was the long and difficult negotiation over the SDR reform. Negotiations lasted five years, almost failed several times, and, in fact, took so long that, by the time agreement was achieved, the problem of liquidity shortage which it had been intended to solve had been transformed into liquidity excess.

In conclusion, monetary interdependence had grown faster than international management. New problems created by interdependence, including huge international capital flows, placed stresses on the fixed exchange rate system and interfered with national economic management. In the face of these problems, there was decreased cooperation, an absence of leadership, and, finally, a breakdown in management.

PARALYSIS OF MANAGEMENT

From 1968 to 1971 there was a paralysis of international monetary management. Central banks were unable to control the large currency flows in the system and were unable to contain the sterling crisis of 1967 and the franc–deutsche mark crisis of 1968. Even the expansion of the bilateral swaps and the creation of new multilateral swaps were insufficient to control these vast short-term capital flows.

Cooperation in the Group of Ten also deteriorated. To be sure, there was some cooperation. Members, with the exception of France, continued to hold dollars. They also carried out two SDR allocations. But they were unable to move on further monetary reform, even though after 1968 there was a general recognition of the need for reform. There was increasing national intransigence. The Europeans and the Japanese complained about the American deficit, but they would assume no responsibility for their growing surpluses. The Germans and Japanese were intransigent regarding revaluation. France reduced its dollar holdings to a minimum, and called for a return to the gold standard. The French also refused to join the SDR reform until the last minute, and in 1968 De Gaulle refused to devalue the franc in the face of widespread speculation.

Most important was the American withdrawal from cooperation and leadership. The United States, as has been noted, had begun to experience the domestic pinch of interdependence and a dollar-based international monetary system. Furthermore, the U.S. administration sought to preserve the pivotal role of the dollar by a revaluation of other currencies against the dollar which its partners adamantly refused. The resultant dissatisfaction was to lead to U.S. abnegation of monetary leadership and monetary cooperation and to a policy of "benign neglect." There was benign neglect from 1968 on, first, in managing the existing system. The United States let others defend the existing exchange rate system; it permitted a huge foreign dollar buildup; it was passive in the currency crises of 1969 and 1971. The United States also followed its domestic policies regardless of international consequences and disregarded the inflationary consequences of the huge dollar outflow in other parts of the system. In 1970, for political reasons, President Nixon reinflated the economy, and as a result primarily of resultant capital outflows the balance-of-payments deficit soared. In the summer and spring of 1971, there was a run on the dollar, and for the first time in the twentieth century the United States went into balance-of-trade deficit.

There was benign neglect also in monetary reform. The United States no longer sought to mobilize the system for reform as it had done in the 1960s. Part of the reason was that the United States was no longer able to lead the system. Any U.S. initiatives for reform were quickly rejected by the Europeans and the Japanese. Another reason was that the United States really did not want any major reform; it wanted to keep the dollar at the center of the system and to maintain a system of fixed rates. All it really wanted was a realignment of exchange rates to improve the trade competitiveness of the United States.

By late summer 1971 benign neglect was no longer a sustainable policy. There was a decline in the American gold stock to $10 billion versus outstanding foreign dollar holdings estimated at about $80 billion, a worsening in the balance of trade, rampant inflation, and widespread unemployment. There were also political problems due to the economic situation, pressure to do something not only from the Democrats but from the Republicans who had an eye to the 1972 elections.

On August 15, 1971, President Nixon—without consulting the other members of the international monetary system and, indeed, without consulting his own State Department—announced his New Economic Policy: henceforth, the dollar would no longer be convertible into gold, and the United States would impose a 10 percent surcharge on dutiable imports.[26] August 15, 1971 marked the end of the Bretton Woods period. The history of the international monetary system since that date has been one of the attempts to reimpose an order on the system.

THE SMITHSONIAN AGREEMENT: CRISIS CONTROL WITHOUT REFORM

The shock of August 15 was followed by efforts under U.S. leadership to develop a new system of international monetary management. Throughout the fall of 1971, there was a series of multilateral and bilateral negotiations of the Group of Ten seeking to develop a new multilateral monetary system. The major outcome of that process of international negotiation—the first new attempt at international monetary management—was the agreement reached at the Smithsonian Institution in Washington in December 1971.

The negotiations and the Smithsonian Agreement achieved some successes. Above all, they preserved a minimum level of international monetary cooperation, following a series of significant disagreements that persisted throughout the fall of 1971 over the price of gold, over dollar devaluation as opposed to revaluation of other currencies, over cross rates among currencies other than the dollar. The United States, feeling able to alter the rules and to improve its position, took a forceful leadership role in seeking an agreement, using the import surcharge and dollar inconvertibility as weapons to force European and Japanese compromises. American negotiating tactics resembled more the rough style of Texas than the gentlemanly exchange of Basle. However, the United States also made important concessions. American negotiators finally agreed to devalue the dollar, even though they had argued that they would accept only a revaluation of other currencies. And the United States agreed to a relatively smaller devaluation—about 10 percent—than it had originally sought.

Despite the 10 percent U.S. import surcharge, the Europeans and the Japanese did not impose countervailing duties. There was no drift into protectionism. And the solution that emerged was truly a compromise.

There was also some reform of the system. The price of gold was changed; that is, the dollar was devalued in relation to gold. There was a realignment of other exchange rates. And, finally, there was a provision for some increased flexibility in exchange rates. Currencies after Smithsonian would float within a plus or minus 2¼ percent of parity, twice the range of the Bretton Woods agreement. Smithsonian also provided breathing space for reform: it was a temporary agreement which, it was hoped, would give the participants time to negotiate a long-term monetary reform.

When he announced the agreement at Smithsonian, President Nixon called it, "the greatest monetary agreement in the history of the world." His optimism was exaggerated, for in the end Smithsonian did more to demonstrate the problems rather than the possibilities of multilateral monetary management.

Smithsonian was the lowest common denominator of multilateralism. It was a form of crisis control, not a reform of the system. The increase in flexibility was insignificant in the face of huge capital flows. The realignment of exchange rates did not constitute a basic change in the system. Smithsonian did prevent deterioration in the system—a further hardening of trade restrictions, of capital controls, of multiple exchange rates—but it did not solve the fundamental problems of managing interdependence. It did not solve the problem of adjustment in a fixed exchange rate system with differing national policies and the possibility of huge international capital flows. Moreover, it did not resolve the role of the dollar, which remained inconvertible. Smithsonian offered no alternate form of international liquidity.

The monetary negotiations leading to Smithsonian also demonstrated the extent of political conflict regarding the international monetary system. Throughout the fall, the Europeans were unable to agree on a common policy, the French and the West Germans taking different positions. Only the weapon of the U.S. import surcharge and a last minute compromise by Nixon and French President Georges Pompidou enabled even the limited system of Smithsonian to be established.

"The greatest monetary agreement in the history of the world" lasted a little over a year. Soon, massive currency flows led to new pressures on the Smithsonian rates. National currency controls to hold back the pressure on the new rates proliferated. In June 1972 Great Britain and Ireland floated their currencies. A new currency crisis developed in January and February 1973. Even a second 10 percent devaluation of the American dollar at that time could no longer save a fixed exchange rate system. By March 1973 all major world currencies had withdrawn support from fixed exchange rates and were floating. Management was left to the market and in a minor way to central bankers that intervened in exchange markets on a somewhat cooperative basis to prevent extreme fluctuations.

THE COMMITTEE OF TWENTY: THE ELUSIVENESS OF REFORM

At the time, this new system was seen as temporary, providing a sufficient interval for the nations involved to reach a new political compromise on monetary reform. In 1972 a Committee on Reform of the International Monetary System and Related Issues, the Committee of Twenty, had been established within the IMF to develop a major reform of the international monetary system. The committee was composed of the members of the Group of Ten plus representatives of developing countries. The committee was charged with developing new means of managing the quantity of the world's reserves, establishing a commonly accepted currency or currencies in which members of the system had confidence, and developing new adjustment mechanisms. It was hoped that these tasks could be accomplished and that management could be reestablished by the end of 1973.

The committee agreed on general principles for reform. Regarding liquidity, there was to be an increase in the use of SDRs as the world's currency and a diminished role for other currencies, including the dollar, and for gold. Principles for adjustment were set forth: exchange rates were to be more flexible, with the possibility of floating rates in particular situations; inconvertible balances (i.e., of the dollar) were to be returned to convertibility; the adjustment process was to be more symmetrical; cooperation was to be developed to deal with disequilibrating capital flows.[27]

However, agreement on general principles and agreement on the details of monetary reform proved to be two very different things. Indeed, the statement of principles seemed to be deliberately ambiguous to cover fundamental differences. There was great conflict over the specific application of the generally agreed principles, over the nature of controls on surplus and deficit countries, over the conditions for floating, over the role of gold and the dollar, and over conditions for dollar convertibility. Each country or group of countries advocated solutions most favorable to it; there was little compromise.[28]

While the committee debated, the international monetary system went out of control. The system of fixed exchange rates collapsed and the float emerged. Double-digit inflation erupted. Inflation in the United States resulted largely from economic mismanagement. In the late 1960s the vast dollar outflow created by inflation led to an overvalued dollar, and the policy of benign neglect transformed U.S. inflation into global inflation. The boom of the 1970s created commodity shortages which reinforced the inflationary processes already in train. This new phenomenon disrupted the committee's plans for monetary reform. Reform had concentrated on the provision of adequate liquidity for the system; suddenly, the problem became the contraction of excess liquidity. The committee stressed stable but adjustable exchange rates, but different national rates of inflation made stability impossible. Inflation also increased national desires for more flexible or even floating exchange rates, to provide a degree of isolation from external inflation. By exacerbating the problem of international management in an interdependent world, global inflation further demonstrated that in an interdependent system management depends on the coordination of economic policies heretofore considered strictly national prerogatives.[29]

Finally, while the committee debated, a handful of oil exporters engineered a dramatic rise in the price of petroleum. The highlights of the oil crisis are well known.[30] On October 6, 1973, war erupted in the Middle East; on October 16 the Arab oil-producing states declared an embargo on oil going to the United States and to the Netherlands and instituted general production reductions; on that same day, October 16, the oil-producing states made the first in a series of major price increases. Within a year the price of oil quadrupled—from about $2.50 per barrel of Persian Gulf oil in early 1973 to $11.65 per barrel of gulf oil in 1974. As a result huge sums—an estimated $70 billion in 1974 alone—were transferred from oil-consuming countries, primarily from the developed market economies, to the oil-producing states.[31]

The impact of this price change on monetary management was profound. It created a major new problem of recycling. Under the ideal free trade model, the surplus earnings of the oil-producing states would be channeled back to oil-consuming countries in the form of the import of goods and services. However, the transfer of resources to the oil-producing states has simply been too vast to be absorbed by them without causing intolerable inflation. Despite vast development needs and huge arms expenditures, these states as a whole simply cannot, in the near future, absorb enough imports to make up for the loss to the consuming countries. In 1974 the surplus of the oil-producing states was over $50 billion.[32] Estimates of the size of unabsorbed earnings in coming years suggest that they will be huge. One study estimates that the surplus will amount to $400–$450 billion by 1980[33]; a more conservative study estimates that the peak accumulation will occur in 1978 and will amount to approximately $250 billion, after which surpluses will gradually decline.[34]

This huge surplus created a major problem. Most oil-consuming countries have been unable to reduce oil consumption sufficiently to eliminate their deficits or to increase exports sufficiently to cover the gap. They must borrow to pay for their deficits. The only sources for such borrowing are countries with surpluses from oil earnings. Thus the international monetary system must provide mechanisms for transferring earnings from oil-surplus to oil-deficit countries. This is the recycling problem.

The mechanisms used for recycling in 1974 suggest some of the possibilities of control and some of the problems (see Table 2–2). The surpluses of 1974 and 1975 were recycled primarily through private banks which accepted deposits of oil-exporting countries and loaned these funds to oil-importing countries. In addition, oil funds were recycled through government bills and through direct loans and investment by oil-producing states. Finally, some recycling was effected through various international institutions such as the IMF and the World Bank, which borrowed from the oil producers and made loans to oil consumers. Thus, in the first year, the private system was the primary monetary manager.

After 1974 the ability of the private market to manage recycling was severely limited. Private banks were increasingly hesitant to assume the responsibility of financing vast deficits of countries considered questionable credit risks. Unfortunately, the needy—including not only the underdeveloped nations of the world but Italy and Great Britain as well—were no longer good credit risks. In addition, a continuing role of private banks in recycling would have required their increasing their ratio of deposits and credits to capital. Most banks felt that that limit had already been reached and that they could no longer accept vast oil country deposits. In 1975 bank recycling slowed significantly, and another area of

Table 2-2   The OPEC Surplus and Its Disposition
(billions of U.S. dollars)

	1974	1975
Financial surplus	$52.0	$29.5
Investments in the United States	11.0	5.5
Bank deposits	4.0	—
Treasury bills	5.4	0.8
Bonds and direct loans	1.2	3.3
Equities	0.4	1.4
Investments in the United Kingdom	7.2	0.2
Bank deposits (in £)	1.7	0.2
Treasury bills (in £)	2.7	0.4
Government bonds (in £)	0.9	(0.9)
Equities and property (in £)	0.7	0.3
Direct loans (foreign currency)	1.2	0.2
Eurocurrency bank deposits	22.7	7.0
International organizations	4.0	2.9
IMF oil facility	1.9	2.7
World Bank and other regional development institutions	2.1	0.2
Grants and loans to developing countries	2.5	4.0
Direct loans to developed countries other than U.S. and U.K.	4.5	2.0
Other net capital flows[a]	0.1	7.9

[a]Includes investments in Eurobonds, other portfolio investments, direct investments, and local currency bank deposits in countries other than the United States and the United Kingdom as well as debt repayments.

Morgan Guaranty Trust Company of New York, *World Financial Markets*, March 1976, p. 10.

private management—the international bond market—began to be used, but this market cannot fill the gap between private capabilities and total need either. The market alone simply cannot manage recycling.

Another way to manage recycling is to let the oil-producing states do it themselves. Oil producers have made major commitments to both developed and developing countries for loans and have begun to make direct investments in consuming states. Oil country management, however, poses several problems. Oil states make loans to and invest in countries of their choice. For example, the vast majority of loans and grants to developing countries have gone to the Arab and Moslem nations. Thus oil producer management will not necessarily assure financial transfers to those needing such assistance. Furthermore, politically motivated loans raise questions; not only questions about efficiency but also about political influence. Direct investment also raises the specter of political and economic influence. There is an increasing fear in consuming countries that important sectors of industry and banking will be purchased by oil producers, reducing national control of these crucial sectors. Finally, the sums involved are simply too vast for the oil producers to manage themselves. Thus, while oil producer management will be important, it is neither a total nor a satisfactory solution.

The float, inflation, and the monetary consequences of the oil crisis overwhelmed the Committee of Twenty. On January 17–18, 1974, the committee, meeting in Rome, concluded that, because of the turmoil in the international economy, it would be impossible to develop and implement a comprehensive plan for monetary reform.[35] The Committee of Twenty was replaced by an interim committee to deal with more short-term problems.

TOWARD JAMAICA: MANAGEMENT IN THE INTERIM

The first task of interim management was to control problems arising from the rise in oil prices. International recycling schemes have been devised. In 1974, there were small stopgap programs: a German loan of $2 billion to Italy, a European Economic Community (EEC) facility of $3 billion, and a $3 billion IMF facility for oil-induced deficits. For a long time, however, states were unable to go beyond these crisis control mechanisms to agree on a more significant recycling program. The EEC pushed for an $8–12 billion facility within the IMF to finance overall payments deficits. The United States proposed a $25 billion financial net, outside the IMF and controlled by the Group of Ten. There was a deadlock for several months between these two proposals, until finally, in January 1975, there was a compromise. A facility of $6 billion was set up within the IMF and a general agreement—still to be implemented—was reached to establish a $25 billion net with the OECD. Thus there seems to be an awareness of common interest in establishing recycling facilities among the Group of Ten and an ability to organize for that interest.

However, there has been less interest in, and action on, other monetary management problems created by the rise in the price of petroleum. One such problem is debt repayment, the long-term transfer of resources from oil consumers to oil producers. Once adequate facilities are created for recycling, managers must turn to this larger long-term problem which involves, essentially, an income redistribution from oil-consuming to oil-producing states. Private mechanisms and management by oil producers will play a part in debt repayment. Bank intermediation and direct investment and loans by oil producers are two mechanisms for such transfers. But, again, international management will be necessary. Several possibilities have been put forward: the joint development of alternate energy sources to reduce the size of oil surpluses, various debt-structuring proposals, and proposals for international funds or trusts to channel long-term investment by oil producers. A key to debt repayment will be the maintenance of vital economies in the developed world.[36]

Another significant oil-related problem yet to be dealt with is the shift in monetary power. The most obvious power shift has been from oil consumers to oil producers. The control of vast oil earnings means that several countries outside the traditional management, Group of Ten-developed, market economies have the power to influence and to disrupt the system. New mechanisms must be developed to integrate the new monetary powers into the system.

The new oil rich seem to have been integrated in the sense that they seem to recognize that they have an enormous stake in the system. And they have followed responsible investment policies: there have been no rapid movements of capital, the time spans of these investments are gradually becoming longer and, thus, more stable, and these investments have been rather widely distributed. Although oil producers are tacitly cooperating with the system, more formal management mechanisms must be developed to integrate the new monetary powers into the network of elite management. Oil producers may become more active participants in the IMF by increasing their quotas and thus their voting power. Under a recent revision of IMF quotas, for example, the share and vote for members of the Organization of Petroleum Exporting Countries (OPEC) will double from 5 percent to 10. These nations may play a management role in new mechanisms developed for recycling or may participate in some way in the Group of Ten or other informal elite networks.

Finally, the oil crisis has led to a shift in power within the Group of Ten. Almost overnight most of Western Europe and Japan went from payment surpluses to severe payment deficits: Italy was virtually bankrupt; the United Kingdom and France were not far behind· the United States, West Germany, and Switzerland fared better—the United States partly because it is less dependent than others on foreign oil, Germany because it started with a strong balance-of-payments position, and all three nations because they received large deposits of surplus oil monies.[37]

The management consequences of the shift within the Group of Ten are unclear. It may facilitate management by reestablishing American dominance, making Europe and Japan once again dependent on the United States. It may force Germany to assume a greater leadership role or, it may simply increase the paralysis of management by creating a gulf between most of Europe and Japan on the one hand and the United States and perhaps West Germany on the other, with Europe and Japan influenced by their vulnerability to and their fear of an oil embargo and the United States and Germany influenced by their relative self-confidence and their lesser degree of vulnerability. Thus the oil criris has further jolted the pluralist management structure.

By 1975, when the immediate problems arising from the oil crisis had been brought under some control, there was an attempt to tackle exchange rate and reserve problems. The float remained technically illegal under the IMF articles of agreement. Although central bankers continued to consult regarding exchange rate intervention, there were no regularized means for managing different national exchange rate interventions. There was no change in the status of gold or the dollar and no increase in the use of SDRs. Thus, there was no international means of regulating the level of international liquidity and controlling world inflation.

Merely getting to the negotiating table proved a difficult task. The Europeans and Japanese, dissatisfied with the wide and arbitrary fluctuations of currencies under the float and fearing a permanent threat to their exports because of the weakening of the dollar, were eager to resume negotiations. The United States, satisfied with its increased exports due to the lower value of the dollar and fearing pressure for a return to fixed rates, resisted any proposals for change. For the first time in the postwar era, France and the EEC assumed the leadership role. Under strong pressure from the French in July 1975, the EEC agreed to urge the United States and Japan to return to the bargaining table. This pressure, combined with skillful West German diplomacy, eventually brought the United States to participate in multilateral negotiations in the fall of 1975 and winter of 1976.

At the IMF meeting of September 1975, at the meeting at Rambouillet, France in November 1975, and at the IMF meeting in Jamaica in January 1976, the five monetary powers took some steps in the direction of exchange rate management and the modification of international reserve assets.[38] They legalized the float, but they also made it possible for countries who wished to maintain fixed exchange rates, such as certain members of the EEC, to do so. At the insistence of France, provisions and means were made for returning to a generalized fixed exchange rate system at some future time. It was the general consensus, however, that the float is here to stay. For that reason, states sought to bring the float under control by creating a formal system of consultation to manage exchange rates. Finance ministers and their deputies have been required to meet frequently to discuss policy; central bankers must consult daily about exchange rate conditions and intervention activities; certain guidelines for intervention have been established. Intervention will counter disorderly or erratic exchange movements but will refrain from countering changes which reflect fundamental economic or financial conditions, such as different interest or inflation rates. Exchange rate intervention to gain unfair competitive advantage was specifically prohibited.

The guidelines, however, are slim and ambiguous. It remains to be defined just what exactly constitutes an erratic movement as opposed to a fundamental trend and just when exactly intervention is an unfair course of action. At the insistence of the United States, no specific numerical guidelines have been defined.

Thus agreement on exchange rate management will depend on consensus among monetary officials. While these officials have developed procedures for and experience in close consultation since 1960, cooperation in the 1960s relied on strong American leadership, whereas in the 1970s American leadership has been less effective and, in any case, is pressing for greater reliance on market forces and less managed intervention. Managing a float under these conditions will require not only more frequent consultation but also a high level of willingness of all parties to cooperate and compromise.

Another problem of joint management of exchange rate intervention is the absence of sanctions to discourage disruptive behavior. Under the reform agreements, the IMF is given authority to monitor exchange rate policies of members and to make binding recommendations. Failure to adhere to these recommendations might allow the IMF to deny loans and thus serve as a sanction. As yet no guidelines and no experience in IMF sanctions have been developed. And, even if they are established, the denial of IMF credit may not deter states—especially the powerful—from taking disruptive action. In sum, the agreements reached in the January 1976 meeting in Jamaica provide mechanisms for cooperation but in no way assure international control of the float.

In 1975 the powers also reached some agreement on reserve assets. A step toward the demonetization of gold was made in the IMF by the elimination of an official price of gold, the proposed disposal of one-third of the fund's supply of gold, and the removal of the fund's obligation to make and receive payments in gold. The Group of Ten agreed not to take action to peg the price of gold and not to increase collective gold holdings by buying gold.

It is not clear if these measures will result in the end of the role of gold as an international reserve asset. These steps could lead gold to be regarded as a commodity like any other precious metal whose price fluctuations would thus make it inappropriate for use as a reserve asset. However, many countries including France are not reconciled to the demonetization of gold. For countries with a history of monetary instability, gold remains a stable asset. For those opposed to U.S. dominance, gold remains an alternative to the dollar. While the IMF changes regarding gold are permanent, the Group of Ten agreement is subject to renegotiation after two years.

There has been no agreement on the dollar. The United States continues to reject any change in the role of the dollar, and other countries have not pressed for a change. Proposals for reducing the role of the dollar by making it possible or necessary to exchange dollars for SDRs or other reserve assets remain in abeyance.

The future of the SDR is also in doubt. Unless and until the SDR or some other internationally controlled asset becomes the primary source of world liquidity, there can be no international management of liquidity. Several steps have been taken to improve the SDR's position as a reserve asset: the interest rate has been increased, SDRs are now valued according to a "market basket" of currencies to make them more stable, and countries have greater freedom to deal in SDRs. Because of its stability, the SDR is increasingly being used as an international unit of account. Yet its use as a reserve asset remains limited. Because no agreement has been reached on the dollar, the dollar remains as the major reserve asset. Because of excess world liquidity no new SDRs have been or are about to be created, and with the present float the need for new reserves will probably not increase significantly. Thus the recent agreements leave not only the nature of reserve assets but also their quantity outside the realm of international management.

It also remains to be seen whether states will muster the political will and skill to establish a new monetary order and to manage the system within new rules, institutions, and procedures. The agenda of reform is long and complex. The political process of reform is fraught with difficulties. Gone are those simpler days when the United States, along with the United Kingdom, could draw up a constitution for a world monetary order. In a world in which monetary power is more widely dispersed, reform will depend not on the preferences of a dominant power but on the negotiation of several key powers. Primary among them is the United States. Monetary power is now more widely dispersed, but it is not equally dispersed. The United States remains the most powerful of the Group of Ten. Unless and until the United States assumes an active role, reform will be impossible.

The experience of the Committee of Twenty suggests that in a multilateral system agreement will be piecemeal and long in coming. It may depend as much on trial and error and on the development of common law as on formal negotiations. Such a process is not necessarily bad. Constitutions often do not work as planned. Bretton Woods, for example, never operated as the United States intended. But, in the Bretton Woods period, there was a dominant power to step in and establish new rules for regulating conflict. Today, although the United States is necessary, it is not sufficiently dominant to fulfill its earlier role. The danger in this present multilateral system is that with incomplete reform crises may go unregulated, cumulate, and wreak havoc.

Reform will also be complicated by interdependence. In an interdependent world, international monetary management will inevitably confront national sovereignty. The management of interdependence, if it is to occur, will require new forms of international authority which assume responsibilities once thought the prerogative of national government. Control of exchange rate flows and international control of liquidity, for example, will interfere with national fiscal and monetary policy and ruffle national feathers.

It is possible—though by no means certain—that states will eventually reestablish control. The consensus among the powerful on the need for cooperation and joint management persists in word if not always in deed. Leaders of the developed states have time and again stressed the theme of interdependence and the need to cooperate to maintain economic prosperity and political stability. The behavior of the new oil powers suggests that they share this view. Important mechanisms for consultation and policy coordination still operate. What will be done with this framework remains to be seen.

NOTES

1. For earlier systems of management, see Robert Triffin, *The Evolution of the International Monetary System: Historical Reappraisal and Future Perspectives* (Princeton, N.J.: International Finance Section, Department of Economics, Princeton University, 1964); Stephen V. O. Clarke, *Central Bank Co-operation, 1924–1931* (New York: Federal Reserve Bank of New York, 1967).

2. Richard N. Gardner, *Sterling-Dollar Diplomacy: The Origins and Prospects of Our International Economic Order*, exp. ed. (New York: McGraw-Hill, 1969), Chaps. 1 and 2.

3. Ibid., Chaps. 3–5, 7; J. Keith Horsefield, ed., *The International Monetary Fund, 1945–1965: Twenty Years of International Monetary Cooperation*, Vol. 1 (Washington, D.C.: International Monetary Fund, 1969), pp. 10–118.

4. Edward S. Mason and Robert E. Asher, *The World Bank Since Bretton Woods* (Washington, D.C.: The Brookings Institution, 1973), pp. 11–36.

5. United Nations Economic Commission for Europe, *A Survey of the Economic Situation and Prospects of Europe* (Geneva: United Nations, 1948), p. 54.

6. United Nations Economic Commission for Europe, *Economic Survey of Europe in 1948* (Geneva: United Nations, 1949), p. 112.

7. International Monetary Fund, *International Financial Statistics, Supplement 1972* (Washington, D.C.: International Monetary Fund, 1972), p. iv.

8. Mason and Asher, *The World Bank Since Bretton Woods*, pp. 105–107, 124–135.

9. See, for example, Dean G. Acheson, *Present at the Creation: My Years in the State Department* (New York: Norton, 1969); Ellen Clayton Garwood, *Will Clayton: A Short Biography* (Austin, Tex.: Univ. of Texas Press, 1958); George F. Kennan, *Memoirs, 1925–1950* (Boston: Little, Brown, 1967). Joseph Jones, *The Fifteen Weeks* (New York: Viking, 1955).

10. Ibid., pp. 2–3. For an early warning about the vulnerability of the dollar and the dollar-based system, see Robert Triffin, *Gold and the Dollar Crisis: The Future of Convertibility* (New Haven, Conn.: Yale Univ. Press, 1960).

11. The Bank for International Settlements was a consortium of European central banks originally established in 1930 to implement a plan for rescheduling German reparations.

12. Switzerland joined in 1964 to make the Group of Ten in fact a group of eleven.

13. G. L. Bach, *Making Monetary and Fiscal Policy* (Washington, D.C.: The Brookings Institution, 1971), pp. 111–150.

14. See Walter S. Salant et al., *The United States Balance of Payments in 1968* (Washington, D.C.: The Brookings Institution, 1963).

15. Stephen D. Cohen, *International Monetary Reform, 1964–1969* (New York: Praeger, 1970); Fritz Machlup, *Remaking the International Monetary System: The Rio Agreement and Beyond* (Baltimore, Md.: Johns Hopkins Press, 1968). For a discussion of the political barriers to reform, see Henry G. Aubrey, *Behind the Veil of International Money* (Princeton, N.J.: International Finance Section, Department of Economics, Princeton University, 1969).

16. International Monetary Fund, *Annual Report 1972* (Washington, D.C.: IMF, International Monetary Fund, 1972) p. 28.

17. This was convertibility for nonresidents. Full convertibility came in 1961.

18. Richard A. Debs, "International Banking." An address before the tenth annual convention of the Banking Law Institute, New York City, May 8, 1975, p. 3.

19. Ibid.

20. Michael von Clemm, "The Rise of Consortium Banking," *Harvard Business Review* (May–June 1971), 125–142.

21. See, for example, conclusions of U.S. Department of the Treasury, *The New York Times*, August 15, 1973, pp. 47 ff.

22. Sidney M. Robbins and Robert B. Stobaugh, *Money in the Multinational Enterprise: A Study in Financial Policy* (New York: Basic Books, 1973); Lawrence B. Krause, "The International Economic System and the Multinational Corporation," *The Annals*, 403 (September, 1972), 93–103.

23. There are many theories regarding the origins of the Eurodollar market. Some have traced it to the placing of dollars by Soviet Union and Eastern European central banks in London and Paris instead of in the United States for political reasons. Another impetus for the market came in 1957 during a crisis and run on the pound, when the British government prohibited British banks from using sterling to finance trade between third countries. To maintain their markets, the British began to make offerings in dollars. Yet another factor has been the availability of dollars, encouraged by Federal Reserve Board Regulation Q (no longer in operation), which set ceilings on interest rates that American banks could offer on loans. Because banks abroad were not controlled by Regulation Q, they could offer higher rates and thus attract dollars. See, for example, Paul Einzig, *The Euro-Dollar System: Practice and Theory of International Interest Rates*, 4th ed., (New York: St. Martin's, 1970); Geoffrey Bell *The Eurodollar Market and the International Financial System* (New York: Wiley, 1973).

24. See James E. Meade, "The Case for Variable Exchange Rates," *The Three Banks Review* 27 (September 1955) 3–27; Elizabeth Stabler, "The Dollar Devaluations of 1971 and 1973," in *Commission on the Organization of the Government for the Conduct of Foreign Policy, Appendix*, Vol. III, (Washington, D.C.: U.S. Government Printing Office, 1976), pp. 119–159.

25. Salant et al., *The United States Balance of Payments in 1968*.

26. On the crisis, see Susan Strange, "The Dollar Crisis 1971," *International Affairs*, 48 (April 1972), 191–215. For a congressional analysis, see the important Reuss report to the U.S. Congress, *Action Now to Strengthen the U.S. Dollar*, Report of the Subcommittee on International Exchange and Payments of the Joint Economic Committee, 92nd Congress, 1st Sess (Washington, D.C.: U.S. Government Printing Office, 1971).

27. Committee on Reform of the International Monetary System and Related Issues (Committee of Twenty), *International Monetary Reform: Documents of the Committee of Twenty* (Washington, D.C.: International Monetary Fund, 1974), p. 8. For an excellent discussion of the problems of monetary reform, see Benjamin J. Cohen, *Major Issues of World Monetary Reform*, prepared for the Commission on Critical Choices for Americans, August 1974. One additional aspect of monetary reform not discussed here is the question of increasing the flow of resources to the developing countries through monetary reform. See Y. S. Park, *The Link Between Special Drawing Rights and Development Finance* (Princeton, N.J.: International Finance Section, Department of Economics, Princeton University, 1973).

28. See *International Monetary Reform: Documents of the Committee of Twenty.*

29. See Cohen, *Major Issues of World Monetary Reform.*

30. See Chapter 9 of this text.

31. International Monetary Fund, *Annual Report 1975* (Washington, D.C.: International Monetary Fund, 1975), p. 12.

32. Ibid.

33. Khodadad Farmanfarmaian, Armin Gutowski, Saburo Okita, Robert V. Roosa, and Carrol L. Wilson, "How Can the World Afford OPEC Oil?," *Foreign Affairs,* 53 (January 1975), 203.

34. Morgan Guaranty, *World Financial Markets,* March 1976, pp. 6-8.

35. *International Monetary Reform,* pp. 216-219.

36. For example, see Farmanfarmaian et al., "How Can the World Afford OPEC Oil?," pp. 201-222; Hollis B. Chenery, "Restructuring the World Economy," *Foreign Affairs,* 53 (January 1975), 242-263.

37. International Monetary Fund, *Annual Report 1975,* pp. 12-15.

38. International Monetary Fund, *Proposed Second Amendment to the Articles of Agreement of the International Monetary Fund: A Report by the Executive Directors of the Board of Governors* (Washington, D.C.: International Monetary Fund, March 1976). For an analysis of the agreements, see Edward M. Bernstein et al., *Reflections on Jamaica* (Princeton, N.J.: International Finance Section, Department of Economics, Princeton University, 1976).

3

International Trade and Domestic Politics

The international monetary policy of various nations has been left largely to their respective central bankers, finance ministers, and a handful of cognescenti who can fathom the intricacies of exchange rate management, Special Drawing Rights (SDRs), and Eurodollar markets. Trade policy, however, is the stuff of domestic politics. Tariffs, quotas, and nontariff barriers are familiar issues for a broad range of economic groups, from wheat farmers to cotton textile producers, from Volkswagen dealers to computer manufacturers, from the AFL–CIO (American Federation of Labor–Congress of Industrial Organizations) to the National Association of Manufacturers to the American Farm Bureau. The intricacies of trade policy are not only well known, they are also the subject of frequent and often highly charged domestic political conflict, for the simple reason that trade policy often determines prosperity or depression, profits or bankruptcy, survival or death for many industries.

In America, the U.S. Constitution has accentuated political conflict over trade policy by giving Congress the power to levy tariffs and to regulate foreign commerce. Conflict within Congress and between Congress and the Executive is a central characteristic of American trade policy. Because Congressmen are responsible to their constituents, and therefore responsive to their economic concerns, there is often pressure within Congress for a trade policy which reflects and protects those special interests. Furthermore, the demands of a relatively small number of interest groups directed at Congress may snowball into national trade policy. For example, the Smoot-Hawley tariff of 1930, the most protectionist law of the century, was enacted when an attempt to help depressed agricultural groups led to protectionist moves by other groups.[1]

Unlike Congress which tends to link trade policy with particular domestic interests, the United States Executive may have a different perspective and different priorities and often links trade policy with larger foreign policy and foreign economic goals. Thus, for example, since the 1930s American presidents have advocated free trade as the preferred economic policy for broad economic and strategic reasons. In their effort to carry out a policy of reducing tariffs, however, presidents have been constrained by Congress. Most importantly, the president needs Congressional approval for any trade agreement, yet the very process of approval raises the threat of interest-group opposition. Presidents have tried to overcome this legislative constraint by asking Congress to delegate authority to the president to conclude trade agreements without subsequent congressional approval. Since 1934 Congress has regularly delegated such power for specifically limited periods of time and with specific constraints.

Domestic politicization has been an important constraint on international management. It is not possible in trade as it is in the monetary system for a relatively small elite to manage relations. Trade management must take into account a large number of actors and interests. It is also not possible, as it is in the monetary system, for one nation to manage international trade. Leadership is possible; unilateral management is not. In this chapter we examine the evolution of trade management in the face of domestic political constraints.[2]

The same factors which led to the creation of a managed international monetary system after World War II also led to the attempt to subject trade for the first time to systematic international control. National protectionism and the disintegration of world trade in the 1930s created a common interest in an open trading order and a realization that states would have to cooperate to achieve and maintain that order. Public officials recognized that the beggar-thy-neighbor policies of the 1930s had resulted in both economic and political losses for everyone. The retreat into protectionism in the interwar period led not only to economic disaster but also to international war. In the postwar era mechanisms for guarding against such economic nationalism, for reducing and regulating restrictions on trade, would have to be created.

The most extreme expression of the belief in free trade was to be found in the United States in the person of Secretary of State Cordell Hull, who believed in the liberal theory that free trade would lead to economic prosperity and international peace.[3] His argument for a more open system was translated into U.S. State Department policy and thereby into American foreign policy. As expressed in a State Department memorandum,

> A great expansion in the volume of international trade after the war will be essential to the attainment of full and effective employment in the United States and elsewhere, to the preservation of private enterprise, and to the success of an international security system to prevent future wars.[4]

A second force for international trade management growing out of the interwar period was the American willingness to lead the system. Just as in monetary relations, the United States learned from the Depression that the system needed a leader and that the United States would be the major candidate for that role. As the State Department put it,

> The only nation capable of taking the initiative in promoting a worldwide movement toward the relaxation of trade barriers is the United States. Because of its relatively great economic strength, its favorable balance of payments position, and the importance of its market to the well-being of the rest of the world, the influence of the United States on world commercial policies far surpasses that of any other nation. While the cooperation of the United Kingdom will be essential to the success of any broad program to reduce trade barriers, the prospective post-war position of the United Kingdom is such that its cooperation can be attained only if it is assured that strong leadership will be furnished by the United States.[5]

As early as 1934 the United States began to press for the implementation of a system of free trade.

Despite the perception of a common interest in management and in an open system and despite the willingness of the United States to lead the system, the control of trade in the postwar period would be constantly limited by domestic politics. Domestic political conflict would make it difficult to translate the generally perceived common goals into an international order for trade.

THE HAVANA CHARTER

The conflict between domestic politics and international management began with the Havana Charter, the first attempt to build an order for international trade. The charter was an essential part of the plan to create a new, internationally managed economic system in the postwar era and, like the rest of that plan, was a product of strong American leadership. American efforts to create an open system dated from the Reciprocal Trade Agreements Act of 1934, a product of Cordell Hull's liberal vision.

Under that act the United States concluded numerous agreements reducing certain of the high tariffs of the early 1930s. During World War II the United States used its international position as a political and security leader to obtain commitments to a postwar international commercial order based on the freeing of international trade. In 1945, the United States presented a plan for a multilateral commercial convention which would regulate and reduce restrictions on international trade. The convention offered rules for all aspects of international trade—tariffs, preferences, quantitative restrictions, subsidies, state trading, international commodity agreements—and provided for an International Trade Organization (ITO), the equivalent of the IMF (International Monetary Fund) in the area of trade, to oversee the system. In 1946 the United States called for an international conference to discuss this American proposal and to implement a new trading order.[6]

Agreement on a new international order for trade, however, was more difficult to achieve than agreement on a monetary order. The process of negotiation was very different from that of Bretton Woods, where the United States and the United Kingdom were able to dominate decision making and where there was little disagreement on the features of a desired system. The United States clearly played a leadership role in the negotiation process, but, because each participant faced important domestic political constraints, the United States was unable to impose its plan on others. Britain, for example, insisted on provisions for its Imperial Preference System; other Europeans insisted on safeguards for balance-of-payments problems; the underdeveloped countries demanded provisions for economic development. The result was a long, delayed international negotiation. Discussion began in 1943; final negotiations did not take place until 1947. In the end, all, more or less, got their way. The Havana Charter was a complex compromise, an agreement which embodied in some way the wishes of everyone, but which in the end satisfied no one.[7]

Hobbled as it was by domestic political constraints, the charter might have become operational—had it not been for domestic politics in the United States. Although the United States under the Roosevelt and Truman administrations had been a strong advocate of a new trading order and had led the international system through the complex negotiating process, Congress prevented the United States from adhering to the Havana Charter. The traditionally high tariff policy of the Republican party, the opposition both of the protectionists, who felt that the charter went too far, and of the liberals, who felt it did not go far enough toward free trade, and the opposition of business groups which opposed compromises on free trade and at the same time feared increased governmental involvement in trade management coalesced in a majority against America's own charter. After delaying for three years, the Truman administration finally decided in 1950 that it would not submit the Havana Charter to Congress where it faced inevitable defeat. Once the United States withdrew, the charter was dead.[8] Despite a prevailing norm of international cooperation, despite strong and persistent U.S. leadership, agreement on international control of trade proved elusive.

MULTILATERAL MANAGEMENT UNDER U.S. LEADERSHIP

While the demise of the Havana Charter did not preclude international trade management in the postwar era, it did mean that the management of this trade would be more limited than was originally envisaged. The ITO died and so did many rules of the Havana Charter, but the consensus on the need to establish an international trading order survived, embodied in GATT (General Agreement on Tariffs and Trade), which had been drawn up in 1947 to provide a procedural base and to establish guiding principles for the tariff negotiations then being held in Geneva. It was intended to be merely a temporary treaty to serve until the Havana Charter was implemented. But, because that charter was never ratified, GATT, by default, became the expression of the international consensus on trade.

GATT reflected the prevailing agreement on free trade. In the preamble, the contracting parties agreed to enter into

> reciprocal and mutually advantageous arrangements directed to the substantial reduction of tariffs and other barriers to trade and to elimination of discriminatory treatment in international commerce . . .[9]

The major rule for implementing free trade was the GATT principle of nondiscrimination. All contracting parties agreed to adhere to the most favored nation principle, which stipulated that

> any advantage, favour, privilege or immunity granted by any contracting party to any product originating in or destined for any other country shall be accorded immediately and unconditionally to the like product originating in or destined for the territories of all other contracting parties.[10]

The only exceptions to this general rule of equal treatment for all related to existing preferential systems and to future customs unions and free trade associations.

GATT also established an international commercial code with rules on such important issues as dumping and subsidies. The most important rule prohibited the use of quantitative restrictions, such as quotas, except for balance-of-payments reasons. Important areas which would have been regulated under the Havana Charter, however, were omitted from GATT. Provisions for economic development, commodity agreements, and restrictive business practices, for example, were not included. In addition, other topics not of great concern at the time, such as relations with state trading countries and access to supply, were left undeveloped in the code. These gaps were eventually to prove a major problem for the management of international trade.

In addition to establishing norms and principles, GATT provided a set of rules and procedures for what was to be the major method of trade management in the postwar period, multilateral trade negotiations. The preamble contained the commitment to enter into such negotiations, and the agreement provided the guidelines for such negotiations. The most important rule was reciprocity, the concept that tariff reductions should be mutually advantageous. While not part of the original GATT, the principal supplier procedure by which negotiations were to take place among actual or potential principal suppliers also became a negotiating rule of GATT.[11]

From a temporary treaty, GATT became not only an established commercial code but also an international organization with a secretariat and a director general to oversee the implementation of GATT rules and to carry out preparatory work for international trade conferences. GATT has also since evolved from a set of guidelines for trade negotiations to an institutional forum within which trade negotiations take place.[12]

While GATT provided the framework for achieving trade liberalization, the United States made that framework operate. Hull's vision of a prosperous and peaceful system based on free trade and on American leadership did not die with the Havana Charter. Indeed, with the coming of the Cold War, free trade took on new significance as a key to a prosperous West and to Western security in the face of Soviet aggression.

The importance of establishing a system of free trade among Western countries was used as the rationale for the Marshall Plan and for periodic congressional delegations of negotiating authority to the president.[13] American economic strength and the lure of foreign markets were a further reason for American interest in leading trade liberalization. Thus, just as it had stepped in to fill the gaps in Bretton Woods, so, when the Havana Charter and the ITO died, did the United States move in to head the trading system.

In the two decades following World War II, the United States led the system by helping Europe and Japan to rebuild production and by pushing for trade liberalization. In the early years, the Marshall Plan, or European Recovery Program as it was officially known, was the tool of American leadership in Europe. As we have seen, the United States played a key role in financing international trade and in encouraging long-term European trade competitiveness through the Marshall Plan. The United States also used the Marshall Plan as a lever to encourage regional trade liberalization in Europe. During the war and the immediate postwar period, significant barriers to trade had been erected throughout Europe, which accentuated the trade restrictions in effect since the 1930s. The United States encouraged regional liberalization within Europe, even though this conflicted with the larger U.S. goal of nondiscrimination on an international basis, and even though regional liberalization sometimes involved direct discrimination against the United States. The United States used its pivotal position to push actively for liberalization of trade and payments among Western European countries and in some cases to provide the funds for such liberalization.[14]

The United States also took an important leadership role with Japan. During the occupation, the supreme commander for the Allied forces and his administration directly controlled Japanese trade and the Japanese monetary system. And until the 1960s the United States helped the recovery and development in Japan by keeping the American market open for Japanese goods while at the same time accepting Japanese protectionist policies, many of which had been instituted under the occupation. The United States also supported Japanese membership in GATT and urged the Europeans, unsuccessfully, to open European markets to Japanese exports.[15]

Finally, the United States took an important role in multilateral trade negotiations, the principal form of trade management in the postwar period. The idea of creating a more open system through negotiations to remove tariffs and other trade barriers had originated with the U.S. Reciprocal Trade Agreements Act of 1934, which had led to a series of bilateral negotiations. Tariff reductions in these negotiations were based on reciprocity (i.e., mutual advantage), a system which satisfied important potential domestic political opposition to tariff reduction within the United States. The reductions negotiated bilaterally were broadened under the most favored nation agreements which the United States had with numerous countries under various commercial treaties.

This procedure of bilateral negotiations was expanded and broadened in the postwar period. A series of six multilateral trade negotiations were conducted by the members of GATT between 1947 and 1967. In the first five rounds, negotiations were carried out on an item-by-item basis. Principal suppliers negotiated agreements among themselves which were then multilateralized through the GATT commitment to nondiscrimination. As with the bilateral negotiations of the 1930s, reductions were reciprocal and mutually beneficial. The sixth multilateral negotiation, the Kennedy Round, used a new negotiating technique: linear tariff reductions. Item-by-item negotiations were abandoned and participants, instead, sought an overall reduction of tariffs by a certain percentage. This technique facilitated negotiations and enabled greater liberalization.

The United States, with the world's largest economy and a huge percentage of international trade, was the essential motivating force in these negotiations. Because the United States was in many cases one of the world's principal suppliers, its participation was required under GATT negotiating rules. Because the U.S. market was so important, there was little possibility of achieving reciprocity in tariff negotiations without the United States. Most importantly, without U.S. initiatives, the negotiations would probably never have taken place. American initiatives were responsible for the six major trade negotiations from Geneva in 1947 to the Kennedy Round which ended in 1967. American negotiators were important participants—mobilizing others, seeking compromises—in the actual negotiations.

Furthermore, throughout the 1940s and 1950s, the United States accepted limited benefits from trade negotiations. Although tariffs were reduced, according to the GATT principle, on a reciprocal and mutually beneficial basis, America's trading partners gained more than the United States. Because of European and Japanese exchange controls which persisted through the 1950s, the trade concessions had only a limited effect on U.S. exports. Because the United States did not impose controls, Europe and Japan gained immediate benefit from tariff reductions. The United States accepted such asymetrical benefits because of a commitment to European and Japanese recovery, because it expected to benefit from reductions when exchange controls were removed, and because it sought to maintain the momentum of establishing a freer trading system.

The system worked very well for the developed countries. Most quotas and exchange rate barriers were eliminated. Although for reasons of domestic politics restrictions remained in agricultural products, there was substantial liberalization of trade in manufactured products.[16] The rapid growth of trade was an important source of economic prosperity. The high point of this period of trade management was the negotiation of the Kennedy Round, which was culminated in 1967. The negotiations were long, difficult, and often precarious. States were unable to reach any significant agreement on agricultural trade. However, tariffs on nonagricultural products in the developed countries were reduced by about one-third.[17] After the Kennedy Round reductions tariffs on dutiable, nonagricultural products were reduced to an average of 9.9 percent in the United States, 8.6 percent in the six EEC (European Economic Community) states, 10.8 percent in the United Kingdom, and 10.7 percent in Japan.[18] But, just as the SDR negotiations were the high point of monetary cooperation and the Kennedy Round was the high point of trade cooperation, both were also the prelude to the erosion of the system.

By 1968 structural changes led to the resurgence of domestic political challenges to international management of trade. There were no new trade negotiations, and the system appeared to be unraveling.

FORCES OF CHANGE

As in the case of monetary relations, the important forces of change were increased interdependence, pluralism, and inflation with recession. In addition, because of the close connection of monetary and trade relations, the collapse of the monetary system worked as a force for change in international trade. Economic growth, trade liberalization, decreasing transportation costs, and the broadening horizons of businessmen led to a vast increase in trade among developed market economies after World War II.[19]

Trade in the Western system more than doubled between 1960 and 1969 and rose from 47 percent to almost 55 percent of total world trade.[20] Exports became a more important part of gross national product (GNP). From 1955 to 1970 the share of exports of goods and services in respective GNPs (at 1963 prices) increased from 8.1 percent to 14.1 percent for Japan and from 15.1 percent to 26.2 percent for the EEC (including intracommunity trade). Even in the United States, which remained much less dependent on trade than the other developed countries, the share of exports in America's GNP rose from 4.4 percent to 6.8 percent. For some nations the increase was dramatic. Italy's rose from 7.6 to 24.0 percent, and the Netherlands' rose from 38.6 to 63.1 percent.[21]

By making national economies more sensitive to external events and policies, interdependence provoked domestic opposition to free trade. Vulnerable economic sectors reacted against increased foreign competition. For example, as textile, steel, and electronics imports took a rising share of the American market, there was increased mobilization among domestic producers for protection in these sectors.

Interdependence also posed important problems for the method of trade liberalization. With the removal of tariffs and quotas on manufactured products, states had to reduce other trade barriers if they wished to continue the process of liberalization. The major remaining barriers to trade were nontariff barriers. Nontariff barriers include government procurement policies, customs procedures, health and sanitary regulations, national standards, and a broad range of other laws and regulations which discriminate against imports or provide assistance to exports. Industrial and regional policy, agricultural policy, and consumer and environmental protection are further examples of measures which have trade-distorting consequences. Because of the increasing desire of states to manage their economies and societies and because of the prohibition on the use of quotas and tariffs as a policy instrument, nontariff distortions to trade are on the rise.

The control of nontariff barriers is far more difficult than the regulation and removal of tariffs and quotas. Such policies are usually an integral part of national economic and social policies. Because they are often carried out for reasons other than trade protection, such policies have traditionally been considered within the national prerogative and not subject to international negotiation. International negotiation of such policies will not only challenge national policy control generally, but will further threaten to provoke domestic political opposition. Nontariff barriers also pose practical negotiating problems. The many different forms of nontariff barriers and the many different governmental bodies with authority over them preclude broad international negotiations such as those over tariffs. Reduction of nontariff barriers will require international agreements to coordinate and harmonize a broad range of policies. GATT offers few guidelines, and there exists little experience in such coordination and harmonization.[22]

Finally, and most importantly, interdependence made negotiations an inadequate form of trade management. Negotiations are crucial for seeking free trade and for harmonizing national and international interests in the pursuit of fair trade. But, in an era of both interdependence and the welfare state, periodic negotiations directed toward trade liberalization and adjustment cannot cope with the impact on national economies of foreign economic events and policies. With interdependence, greater and more constant consultation, cooperation, and even policy coordination are necessary to avoid intolerable disruptions of national and international economies.[23]

Increasing interdependence led to a serious questioning of the desirability of management for the purpose of reducing restrictions. The original economic rationale for free trade was increasingly questioned, and the political price of acquiring the advantages of free trade—the challenge to national management—seemed increasingly high.[24]

A second structural change was pluralism. The shift in economic and political power in the monetary system was paralleled in trade management. The clearest change has been the relative decline in the position of the United States and the rise in the position of Japan and the EEC. U.S. trade has declined as a percentage of total world trade. The huge and traditional (since 1893) U.S. balance-of-trade surplus began to erode and turned temporarily in 1971 to a balance-of-trade deficit. The traditional trade surplus with Japan turned into deficit in 1965; the traditional surplus with the EEC persisted throughout the 1960s but turned against the United States in 1972. This shift in the trading position of the United States gradually undermined America's ability and willingness to lead the system.

A crucial aspect of pluralism has been the emergence of the EEC as an independent system. Since 1958 the EEC has developed a customs union, with free internal trade in manufactured products, with a common external tariff on these goods, and with a common agricultural policy. The EEC is a dynamic and powerful trading bloc. Its trade with the rest of the world has grown more rapidly than U.S. trade, and intra–EEC trade has grown even faster. Community control of trade has been the primary tool for building an economically united and politically powerful Europe. But, in building a united Europe, the community has diverged from the GATT rules of nondiscrimination. Thus, it has been increasingly difficult to integrate EEC regional trade policy into the larger international system.

Yet another challenge to trade management was the breakdown of the monetary system. Monetary problems encouraged trade protectionism. Increasing crises after 1967 led to various trade measures designed to protect payments balances—exchange controls, exchange rate manipulation, special duties, capital controls—all of which undermined the norms of the GATT system.

Monetary breakdown also complicated the process of trade reform. In a fixed exchange rate system, negotiators had been able to estimate the impact of agreements on their trade and payments. Under floating rates such calculations became much more difficult. This problem of floating rates linked trade and monetary negotiations and complicated both. The Europeans and the Japanese, for example, asserted that they were unwilling to conclude trade agreements until international monetary reform had been carried out, whereas the United States opposed any monetary reform without assurances of a new trading order.

A final change affecting trade was the recession and inflation period of the 1970s. Postwar trade management took place during a period of unprecedented growth and stability. In an expanding world economy, countries—and political groups within countries—were able to perceive the positive advantages of cooperation and trade liberalization. Recession and inflation increased the possibility of disruptive national action and the possibility of management breakdown. In a time of economic crisis, there is great incentive to adopt beggar-thy-neighbor policies such as tariffs or export subsidies. When the oil crisis erupted, for example, and oil-induced deficits soared, there was a significant threat that consuming states would use trade restrictions to improve their balance-of-payments positions.

Finally, the emergence of double-digit inflation in 1973 added a new dimension to the problem of trade management. Before 1973 GATT and the process of trade negotiations concentrated on regulating and removing tariffs and other barriers to national markets. Now, suddenly, inflation created a new problem of trade: access to supplies. When inflation soared in the summer of 1973, the United States imposed export controls on a variety of items including soybeans and scrap metal to avoid domestic supply shortages and to dampen domestic price increases.

Numerous bills introduced in Congress in the ensuing months called for restrictions on other American exports. Just as states tried to export depression through import barriers in the 1930s, so the United States in the 1970s sought to export inflation through export controls.

The problem of export controls was accentuated when Arab oil producers instituted an embargo on oil going to the United States and the Netherlands and curtailed overall production to reduce supplies to other countries. Other Third World countries suggested that they might try similar methods to raise prices of their exports. The system, it became clear, needed new rules and structures to manage access to supplies and to avoid a new form of potential war, a war of export controls.[25]

PARALYSIS AND DRIFT

The changes in trade relations led to a paralysis of international management. After 1967 there were no new multilateral trade negotiations. In the vacuum created by the absence of negotiations, states followed policies which gradually eroded the system of leadership and the norms of cooperation developed in the postwar period. The EEC, Japan, and the United States all threatened to disrupt the system.

The attempt of the six and later the nine European states to build a common economic and political unit proved to be a major problem. The first goal of the EEC was to build a customs union with internal free trade and a common external tariff. Such customs unions had been specifically permitted as an exception to the GATT rules of nondiscrimination.[26]

Since the days of the Marshall Plan the United States had actively encouraged a European union as a way of strengthening the West. When it looked as if the EEC might increase trade discrimination, the United States, through the Trade Expansion Act of 1962 and the initiative for the Kennedy Round, sought to assure that European integration would remain open and nondiscriminatory. Although the success of the Kennedy Round suggested that Europe would remain committed to multilateralism and liberalism, by the late 1960s it seemed to the United States that Europe was moving in the opposite direction.

The community's Common Agricultural Policy (CAP), which blocked imports into the community and artificially stimulated competition in other markets, was a major problem. Since its implementation in 1966, CAP has been designed to maintain a politically acceptable level of farm incomes within the community through domestic price supports. But, to maintain artificially high internal prices, the EEC imposed a flexible external tariff on agricultural imports which assured that imported products would be more expensive than domestically produced products. This variable levy fluctuates to make up the difference between the community support price and the price of imports, so that imported products can only assume the slack that the EEC producers cannot fill. Another aspect of CAP is its lack of production controls. High price supports without production controls created huge food surpluses. So, to eliminate this surplus, the EEC gave export subsidies that were paid via the variable level on imports.

CAP is highly protectionist, especially toward the United States. Exports to the EEC account for a significant percent of U.S. agricultural exports. When the EEC was established, it imported 51 percent of U.S. poultry exports, 36 percent of soybean exports, 36 percent of feed grains exports, and 27 percent of cotton exports. Although overall U.S. exports to the community have been rising since the imposition of CAP, U.S. exports of protected items have fallen dramatically. For example, U.S. exports of grains and rice to the EEC in 1965–1966, before the imposition of the variable levy, totaled $708 million. In 1969–1970, after the imposition of the levy, these exports had dropped to $327 million. Similarly, the value of poultry and eggs exported to the EEC in 1965–1966 amounted to $32 million, whereas in 1969–1970 they amounted to $14 million.[27]

Despite its protectionist impact, the EEC has been unwilling to make any major revision in CAP. The United States attempted to put CAP on the agenda of the Kennedy Round before the system was installed, but the EEC refused. In the ensuing years, the community has consistently refused any significant concessions. Because agricultural interests have great economic and political power in Europe—just as they do in the United States and Japan—any concessions on agriculture would have posed domestic political problems in Europe. Concessions would also have threatened the very foundation on which the political contract of the EEC was built: the exchange of high agricultural prices for France in return for reduced tariffs and a large market for German-manufactured goods.[28]

Another problem created by the EEC has been the expansion of preferential trading arrangements, which were explicitly outlawed under the GATT rule of nondiscrimination. Beginning in 1958 with an agreement with the then French colonies in Africa, the EEC has negotiated preferential agreements with most of the Mediterranean Basin and much of Africa and even with some of the developed countries of Western Europe. The EEC has viewed such agreements as aid to underdeveloped countries and as adjustments for the discriminatory effects of CAP. Although the preferences have not had so great a trade diversionary impact as CAP—at least not for the developed market economies—the United States has viewed them as a crucial departure from the postwar agreement on nondiscrimination.

A third problem was created by the enlargement of the community to include the United Kingdom, Denmark, and Ireland. This expansion not only increased the size of the agricultural protectionist system and the existing preferential system, but also became a force for the extension of EEC preferences. Some of the European Free Trade Area (EFTA) countries, which for political reasons did not join the EEC, as well as many Commonwealth countries became linked with the EEC through preferential trade agreements.

By the late 1960s Japan was also creating trade problems. Although by 1968 that country had the world's third largest gross national product—after the United States and the Soviet Union—and had become one of the world's major trading powers, it remained to a great extent outside the trading order set up by the United States and Western Europe. Japan's philosophy and policy remained quite different from the norms and general practice of other members of the system. To Western Europe and the United States, it seemed that Japan followed a policy of protective economic nationalism justified perhaps in the dark days following World War II but clearly out of date by the 1960s. Despite a liberalization program begun in 1960, which removed significant foreign exchange barriers to trade and which began to eliminate the quantitative restrictions on many imports, Japan remained highly protectionist. Quantitative restrictions remained on many items including many agricultural products and raw materials and many supposedly infant industries such as computers, heavy electric generators, large heavy machinery, and automobiles. In addition, administrative regulations such as import licensing and import deposits also acted as barriers to trade. Finally, Japan insisted on maintaining an undervalued yen, which encouraged Japanese exports and, along with import restraints, enabled Japan to run large balance-of-trade surpluses.[29]

From the Japanese viewpoint, Western criticism of Japanese trade policy seemed both irrational and hypocritical. Because the doctrine of free trade had few intellectual roots and little domestic support in Japan, the Western commitment to liberalism seemed irrational. The Japanese opposed the excessive competition which they associated with laissez-faire and free trade and advocated instead harmony and cooperation through joint government–business management of the economy. The protectionist system established after World War II was thus not merely a temporary response to adverse circumstances but a policy with deep philosophical and historical roots. The continuance, albeit in modified form, of protectionism in the period following recovery was viewed as a valid approach to national growth and development.

Western demands for Japanese liberalization also seemed hypocritical to the Japanese who had faced significant restrictions on their exports to Europe and the United States. When Japan finally became a member of GATT in 1955, most European countries invoked Article 35, which allowed them to refuse MFN treatment to Japan and to continue to discriminate against Japanese imports. The United States did not use Article 35 against Japan. As Japan's trading vigor revived, however, the United States forced a series of "voluntary" export agreements on Japan, limiting the import of vast numbers of Japanese products into the American market. These restrictions, specifically directed at Japan, seemed more discriminatory to the Japanese than Japan's own broad, but universally applied, quantitative controls.

Finally, despite their economic resurgence, the Japanese retained the perspective of an economically insecure country. Despite large balance-of-payments surpluses, they continued to believe that the Japanese economy had a structural tendency to balance-of-payments disequilibrium and that foreign trade therefore had to be carefully controlled. Despite their economic strength, they continued to view liberalization as a means of economic domination which the powerful West wished to impose on a vulnerable Japan. In sum, from a Japanese viewpoint, their liberalization measures of the 1960s seemed rapid and in the spirit of integration into the international trading order, whereas, from the viewpoint of Europe and especially of the United States, Japan refused to adopt the free trade norms of the system and remained highly protectionist when the economic rationale for such protectionism had long disappeared.[30]

Finally, after the Kennedy Round, support for a multilateral free trade system began to wane in the United States, and American leadership became paralyzed. There were many reasons for this change in American attitudes and policy: specific threats to particular industries, general and increasing weakness of the American economy, the worsening of the U.S. balance of trade, and the feeling that the protectionist policies of the EEC and Japan were a source of U.S. problems.

Immediately following the Kennedy Round, spokesmen for vulnerable industries, such as textiles, steel, electronics, and shoes, began to put strong pressure on Congress to alleviate import competition.[31] Not only important sectors of industry but also labor, a traditional supporter of free trade, began to press for protection. As early as 1968 the AFL–CIO began to call for restrictions of U.S. trade, and in 1970 that organization officially shifted its policy from support for free trade to active lobbying for protection.

Congress responded immediately. In the months following the Kennedy Round, over one thousand restrictive trade bills were introduced calling for quotas on items ranging from electronic equipment to strawberries. In 1968 President Johnson introduced a trade bill which would have allowed continued U.S. participation in international trade negotiations. Because the president's authority to make international agreements expired with the Trade Expansion Act in June 1967, the bill granted limited authority to the president to make minor tariff adjustments. It also provided for the elimination of the American selling price (ASP), a nontariff barrier on chemical products, the elimination of which had been negotiated as part of a package settlement of the Kennedy Round. Finally, the bill liberalized criteria for adjustment assistance—aid available to industries and workers hurt by trade liberalization. Because of rising congressional protectionism, the Trade Expansion bill of 1968 never came to a vote. As a result a key part of the Kennedy Round agreement was not implemented, and the president was left without power to conclude even minor international trade agreements.

In 1969 President Nixon again attempted to obtain congressional authority for U.S. participation in trade negotiations by introducing a similar, limited trade bill. This time, protectionist forces launched a major drive for a protectionist trade bill. In 1970 Congress developed a bill which would have reversed postwar American trade policy. It would have imposed quotas—forbidden under GATT—on textiles and footwear and would have made protective tariff adjustment and adjustment assistance much easier to obtain.[32] The Trade Act of 1970 never came to a vote. Protectionism was averted by those in favor of free trade, but again at the price of presidential negotiating authority and the elimination of ASP.

It was not long, however, before Congress with powerful labor backing developed a new across-the-board protectionist trade bill, the proposed Foreign Trade and Investment Act of 1972, known as the Burke–Hartke bill.[33] Burke–Hartke, which increased the possibility of protectionist tariff adjustment and mandated extensive quotas on imports, was kept from a vote only after a massive campaign of opposition by the administration.

This rising protectionist mood of the country and of Congress had a restraining impact on the executive. The Johnson and Nixon administrations remained committed in principle to international negotiation and to the elimination of restrictive barriers to trade,[34] but, because the executive was forced to do battle with Congress to avoid protectionist legislation, the United States was unable to play a leadership role in the system. No longer could the president count on an assured majority for trade liberalization; no longer could he mobilize that majority as had earlier presidents by linking free trade with security and foreign policy. In an era of détente and what looked to Congress like European and Japanese obstreperousness, such appeals were ineffective. Trade liberalization thus ceased to be a dynamic plank in U.S. trade policy. Presidents Johnson and Nixon concentrated on a very limited policy of containing domestic protectionist forces, and containment sometimes meant capitulation.

From 1967 to 1975 the president of the United States did not have the authority to conclude trade agreements, and the process of trade negotiation ground to a halt. Furthermore, the president was forced by protectionist forces to take unilateral steps which undermined the system, the most important of which was a series of "voluntary" export controls. Under severe pressure from Congress and from its political constituencies, and preferring informal agreements to mandated quotas, the Johnson and Nixon administrations forced America's trading partners to agree to limit their exports to the United States. President Johnson, for example, concluded an agreement on steel exports with the Japanese and the Europeans, and President Nixon forced an agreement on textiles on the Japanese and other East Asian countries. In 1971, when the Japanese refused to conclude an agreement on textiles, President Nixon went so far as to request mandated quotas from Congress. The unilateral American approach to these agreements further undermined multilateral management and heightened the atmosphere of conflict characterizing trade relations.

GETTING TO TOKYO

By 1971, however, a limited policy of holding back protectionist forces was no longer acceptable to the Nixon administration. The American economy, with stagnant productivity, rising inflation, and the first trade deficit in the twentieth century, was approaching a crisis. Not only international economic harmony but also domestic economic welfare now seemed dependent on the revitalization of foreign trade. Thus in 1971 the Nixon administration decided to resume the initiative in international trade.

The thinking behind the change in policy and the new American initiative is reflected in the Williams and Peterson reports, two studies of international economic relations prepared for the Nixon administration in the first half of 1971 and released publicly later that year.[35] These studies reiterated the traditional commitment to free trade through multilateral international negotiations. More importantly, they recommended that the United States break the stalemate and initiate new multilateral negotiations on a broad range of problems including trade, international monetary problems, development of rules for foreign investment, and matters of burden sharing in defense. Both reports also advocated an aggressive U.S. negotiating policy. As the Williams report put it, the United States "should more than in the past use its bargaining power in the defense of its economic interests."[36]

The Nixon administration followed this prescription with a vengeance. In the spring of 1971 there were increasing statements from administration officials about a tough trade policy and increasing demands on Europe and Japan to cooperate in reestablishing a just trading order.[37] Then on August 15 President Nixon dropped his bombshell, the New Economic Policy. From the viewpoint of U.S. foreign trade, the policy was an assault on domestic economic problems, on the Congress, and on the other members of the Western economic system. It sought to deal with domestic sources of trade and monetary deterioration through wage and price controls and measures to encourage a rise in productivity. It sought to placate a protectionist Congress by an extremely aggressive stance toward American economic partners. And it sought to deal with those partners by imposing a 10 percent surcharge on dutiable imports and by demanding a realignment of currencies to reestablish the American balance-of-trade equilibrium.

The confusion created in the Western trading system by the August shock was accentuated in the process of negotiations which followed. Using the newly created weapons of inconvertibility and import surcharge, the United States went on the attack demanding major unilateral concessions from Europe and Japan: revisions of CAP, revisions of the EEC preference system, a halt in the expansion of EEC preferential agreements, and the lifting of Japanese restrictions. As part of the monetary negotiations, the United States demanded a permanent, assured trade surplus. The unilateral U.S. policy and the aggressive demands and threats led to significant conflict and confusion and threatened to provoke a destructive, retaliatory response.

Although the Europeans and Japanese rejected the U.S. demands for major unilateral concessions, they carried out no retaliatory measures and agreed to some minor but politically important concessions designed to appease protectionist forces in Congress. The United States, in turn, withdrew its demands for major concessions and agreed with the Europeans and Japanese to enter into multilateral trade negotiations to effect international trade reform. Thus the conclusion of the trade crisis of 1971, like the conclusion of the concurrent monetary crisis, was a standoff, an avoidance of further deterioration and a truce which provided breathing space for a revision of the system for managing international trade.

Trade reform, however, continued to be hampered by domestic constraints. The Nixon administration was constrained by the persistent strength of protectionist forces and specifically by the need to do battle with Burke–Hartke. The Europeans argued that they were unable to enter into multilateral talks until they had negotiated and carried out the entrance of the new EEC members. And the Europeans and the Japanese were leery about opening negotiations with the United States until Congress gave the president the authority to conclude a trade agreement.

At the same time, important forces were working for international cooperation. The Nixon administration supported new efforts. The Williams commission and the Peterson report, for all of their bellicosity, firmly urged a new series of multilateral negotiations. Important congressional groups were rallying against the protectionist trend and were receiving support from important interest groups.[38] In addition, there was recognition by Europeans and Japanese of the need to satisfy congressional concerns if there was to be a resumption of international management. As a result in 1972 the Europeans and Japanese negotiated bilateral agreements with the United States which removed some of the major political barriers to congressional approval of a liberal trade legislation. Finally, cooperation was taking place within international forums. Preparations were being made in GATT for new negotiations, and the OECD (Organization for Economic Cooperation and Development) was becoming an important forum for informal trade consultation and cooperation.[39] A high-level committee within the OECD, established at the initiative of the United States in 1971, was discussing proposals for trade and other economic reform, and the OECD generally was serving as a forum for policy discussions.[40] By late 1972 it was agreed to begin multilateral discussions in Tokyo in September 1973.

In March 1973 President Nixon submitted a sweeping trade bill, the Trade Reform bill, designed to satisfy a protectionist Congress and give the president powerful negotiating authority for the forthcoming trade talks. Under the bill the president was given greater authority than ever to conclude trade agreements: power to eliminate tariffs completely, to remove a broad range of nontariff barriers, to grant preferences for exports of underdeveloped countries, to grant most favored nation status to state trading countries, and to carry out new adjustment assistance programs. At the same time the president also gained authority to retaliate against the unfair trade practices of other states and to increase trade restrictions in case of domestic injury. The proposed Trade Reform Act was a significant departure in congressional delegation of power and was designed to be a powerful tool in the hands of the American president.

Domestic political conflict, however, delayed passage of President Nixon's trade bill for almost three years. Congress and the executive fought over the provision in the bill for most favored nation treatment for the Soviet Union and for Soviet access to U.S. government credits.[41] Passage was further delayed when Congress became increasingly distracted by Watergate and increasingly unwilling to delegate broad authority to President Nixon. When the formal opening of the new trade negotiations took place in 1973, the American president had no negotiating authority. Not until January 1975 did the Trade Act of 1974 become law,[42] and not until February of that year did serious trade negotiations begin.

TOKYO AND BEYOND

In September 1973 representatives of nearly one hundred countries met in Tokyo to begin the process of creating a new international trading order. In their declaration these countries committed themselves to continue the expansion and liberalization of world trade ". . . through the progressive dismantling of obstacles to trade and the improvement of the international framework for the conduct of world trade. . . ."[43] The Tokyo Round, begun officially that September and resumed after the passage of the U.S. Trade Act in February 1975, will continue the work of previous multilateral trade negotiations, but it will be far different from the six trade rounds which preceded it.

Earlier negotiations sought to lower quotas and tariff barriers primarily on nonagricultural products. Their goal was the implementation of GATT goals and rules. The Tokyo Round will continue tariff reduction but will go further to seek to regulate uncharted areas of international trade. It will seek not only to reduce barriers to trade but also to develop new guidelines and new mechanisms for trade management.

The working groups of the trade talks—the loci of actual negotiation—reflect the new focus of the trade talks. The tariff group will proceed with the traditional work of GATT and trade negotiations. The tropical products group and a group on improving GATT rules will confront special problems of trade with less developed countries.[44] Four other groups are directed to deal with the new problems of trade among developed countries. One group will seek to regulate and reduce nontariff barriers. The group, which has already categorized various types of nontariff barriers to facilitate negotiation, will begin by attacking four problem areas: quantitative restrictions, subsidies and countervailing duties, standards, and customs procedures.

The agricultural group will attempt to expand international management to trade in agriculture. In doing so, it will confront and attempt to reconcile two opposing views of the purpose and nature of international control in agriculture. The United States, because of its competitive advantage in agriculture, is a strong advocate of liberalization of agricultural trade, including the modification of the EEC's CAP.[45] The EEC, on the other hand, advocates not liberalization but rather the use of commodity agreements to stabilize world prices and long-term supply. It has also refused to negotiate on the fundamentals of CAP.[46]

The safeguards group will confront the problem, raised by growing interdependence and accentuated by recession and unemployment, of the greater vulnerability of many national industries to foreign competition and of the resultant increased political pressure for governments to take unilateral measures to protect threatened industries. GATT permits such safeguards but provides inadequate guidance for their regulation. The safeguards group will seek to determine under what conditions domestic measures such as subsidies or countervailing duties are permissible.

The sector group will examine the possibility of dealing with trade issues through a new industry-by-industry approach. Such a negotiating technique may enable negotiators to confront a number of different types of trade distortions which operate in a single industry.

Finally, although it has not yet been made a subject of a separate working group, the question of access to supply will most certainly be confronted during the Tokyo Round. The American Trade Act requires the consideration of the problem and public opinion, and political concerns suggest that it will be raised at the trade negotiations, probably in the context of other working groups.

The Tokyo Round will not only confront heretofore unregulated areas of international trade, it will also attempt to develop new forms of international management. The international regulation of NTBs, agriculture, safeguards, and export controls will require the harmonization of a complex set of national economic and social policies and laws.[47] Regulation of such policies, which have deep roots in national societies and economies, will require, first, the negotiation of mutually agreed international principles or guidelines which will expand and extend GATT rules to new areas.

To implement such an international code of conduct, there will have to be an agreement on sanctions against those who violate the established guidelines. Effective regulation will require mechanisms for frequent consultation to encourage implementation of the new guidelines in domestic policy, to deal with breaches of the rules and to cope with new problems that will most certainly emerge after the rules are written.

This last dimension is crucial. Limited control by international negotiation was sufficient when economies were relatively isolated. Interdependence and rapid economic change, however, have created new trade problems which cannot be controlled by periodic international negotiations. Inflation and recession or unexpected shocks such as the oil crisis of 1973–1974 cannot be regulated by the laborious GATT process or anticipated by even the most far-reaching rules. Greater flexibility and speed are now necessary to control trade. One solution to this institutional problem would be to establish a new international trade organization. An equally effective and politically more likely solution would be the expansion of cooperation and consultation within existing institutions such as GATT or the OECD or through informal contacts among public officials.

Whether the Tokyo Round will develop new rules and create new institutional capabilities is uncertain. The very fact that negotiations are taking place, however, suggests that a will to succeed—if not necessarily the ability—exists. The very process of negotiation, furthermore, may contain domestic pressure for disruptive action while the plans for reform go on.

NOTES

1. E. E. Schattschneider, *Politics, Pressures and the Tariff* (Englewood Cliffs, N.J.: Prentice-Hall, 1935). Congressional responsiveness to constituent interests is not necessarily a negative phenomenon in trade policy. See Robert A. Pastor, Legislative-Executive Relations and U.S. Foreign Trade Policy: The Case of the Trade Act of 1974. Prepared for delivery at the 1976 Annual Meeting of the American Political Science Association, Chicago, September 2-5, 1976.

2. The analysis in this chapter concentrates on trade relations among developed market economies. For issues involving underdeveloped countries, see Chapter 6 of this text; for East West trade issues, see Chapter 10.

3. See, for example, Richard N. Gardner, *Sterling-Dollar Diplomacy: The Origins and Prospects of our International Economic Order*, (New York: McGraw-Hill, 1969), p. 9.

4. Ibid., p. 102.

5. Ibid.

6. Ibid.; Clair Wilcox, *A Charter for World Trade* (New York: Macmillan, 1949). The trade charter was not exclusively an American idea; British planners were intimately involved in the process. See E. F. Penrose, *Economic Planning for the Peace* (Princeton, N.J.: Princeton Univ. Press, 1953).

7. See Gardner, *Sterling-Dollar Diplomacy*, Chaps. 8 and 17; Wilcox, *A Charter for World Trade*; Committee for Economic Development, Research and Policy Committee, *The United States and the European Community: Policies for a Changing World Economy* (New York: CED, November 1971).

8. Gardner, *Sterling-Dollar Diplomacy*, Chap. 17; William Diebold, Jr., *The End of the I.T.O.* (Princeton, N.J.: International Finance Section, Department of Economics and Social Institutions, Princeton University, 1952).

9. Kenneth W. Dam, *The GATT: Law and International Economic Organization* (Chicago: Univ. of Chicago Press, 1970), p. 391.

10. Ibid., p. 392.

11. Ibid., for an analysis of GATT.

12. Gerard and Victoria Curzon, "GATT: Traders' Club," in Robert W. Cox and Harold K. Jacobson et al., *The Anatomy of Influence: Decision Making in International Organization* (New Haven, Conn.: Yale Univ. Press, 1973), pp. 334-370.

13. For an excellent analysis of the process of making trade policy in the period, see Raymond A. Bauer, Ithiel de Sola Pool, and Lewis Anthony Dexter, *American Business & Public Policy: The Politics of Foreign Trade* (Chicago: Aldine, Atherton, 1972).

14. William Diebold, Jr., *Trade and Payments in Western Europe: A Study in Economic Cooperation, 1947-1951* (New York: Harper & Row, 1952); Robert Triffin, *Europe and the Money Muddle: From Bilateralism to Near Convertibility, 1947-1956* (New Haven, Conn.: Yale Univ. Press, 1957).

Two major programs grew out of the U.S. initiatives. The first was the liberalization of payments. Payments controls in the postwar period were major barriers to trade within Europe as well as to international trade. In 1948 the United States began to push for an intra-European payments scheme—a multilateral clearing union which would facilitate payments and thus trade within Europe. The European Recovery Administration and Paul Hoffman, its administrator, were strong advocates of the European Payments Union (EPU); they proposed the plan, became its advocates, and persuaded Congress to earmark funds for it. When the EPU finally came into existence in September 1950, it was backed in part by American funds. The second program which the United States encouraged was a liberalization of trade program within the Organization for European Economic Cooperation (OEEC). It actively encouraged the Europeans to remove quotas on trade between OEEC members, a goal achieved in the early 1950s.

The EPU and the OEEC trade liberalization, of course, were not simply U.S. programs foisted upon the Europeans. Europeans were to a great extent involved in the development of the programs. The OEEC scheme in particular was a European plan. But the United States acted as the catalyst, as the mover of the system. It was U.S. pressure that kept the Europeans moving forward.

15. Robert S. Ozaki, *The Control of Imports and Foreign Capital in Japan* (New York: Praeger, 1972), pp. 5–9; Warren S. Hunsberger, *Japan and the United States in World Trade* (New York: Harper & Row, 1964).

16. See, for example, Gardner Patterson, *Discrimination in International Trade: The Policy Issues, 1945–1965* (Princeton, N.J., Princeton University Press, 1966); Karin Kock, *International Trade Policy and the Gatt, 1947–1967*, Stockholm Economic Studies XI, (Stockholm: Almquist & Wiksell, 1969).

17. John W. Evans, *The Kennedy Round in American Trade Policy: The Twilight of the GATT?* (Cambridge, Mass.: Harvard Univ. Press, 1971), p. 282. For other studies of the Kennedy Round, see Ernest H. Preeg, *Traders and Diplomats: An Analysis of the Kennedy Round Negotiations under the General Agreement on Tariffs and Trade* (Washington, D.C.: Brookings Institution, 1970); Thomas B. Curtis and John R. Vastine, *The Kennedy Round and the Future of American Trade* (New York: Praeger, 1971).

18. Robert E. Baldwin, *Non-Tariff Distortions of International Trade*. Vashington, D.C.: Brookings Institution, 1970), p. 1. See, also, Ernest H. Preeg, *Traders and Diplomats*.

19. Richard N. Cooper, *The Economics of Interdependence: Economic Policy in the Atlantic Community* (New York: McGraw-Hill, 1968), pp. 59–80.

20. United Nations Conference on Trade and Development, *Review of International Trade and Development, 1970* (New York: United Nations, 1970), p. 45.

21. Organization for Economic Cooperation and Development, *Policy Perspectives for International Trade and Economic Relations*, Report by the High Level Group on Trade and Related Problems of the Secretary-General of Organization for Economic Cooperation and Development, (Paris: OECD, 1972), p. 18.

22. Robert E. Baldwin, *Non-Tariff Distortions of International Trade* (Washington, D.C.: Brookings Institution, 1970); William Diebold, Jr., *The United States and the Industrial World: American Foreign Economic Policy in the 1970s* (New York: Praeger, 1972), pp. 123–140; Stanley D. Metzger, *Lowering Nontariff Barriers: U.S. Law, Practice, and Negotiating Objectives* (Washington, D.C.: Brookings Institution, 1974).

23. Organization for Economic Cooperation and Development, *Policy Perspectives for International Trade and Economic Relations*, pp. 110–111.

24. For a criticism of free trade, see David P. Calleo and Benjamin M. Rowland, *America and the World Political Economy: Atlantic Dreams and National Realities*, (Bloomington, Ind.: Indiana Univ. Press, 1973), Chaps. 2, 6, 10.

25. See C. Fred Bergsten, *Completing the GATT: Towards New International Rules to Govern Export Controls* (British North-American Committee, 1974) and Chapter 10 of this text.

26. See Jacob Viner, *The Customs Union Issue*, Studies in the Administration of International Law and Organization, 10, (New York: Carnegie Endowment for International Peace, 1950).

27. Stanley Andrews, *Agriculture and the Common Market* (Ames, Iowa: Iowa State Univ. Press, 1973), p. 26.

28. Ibid., on the common agricultural policy; Organization for Economic Cooperation and Development, Agricultural Policy Reports, *Agricultural Policy of the European Economic Community* (Paris: Organization for Economic Cooperation and Development, 1974).

29. See, for example, Ozaki, *The Control of Imports and Foreign Capital in Japan*; Jerome B. Cohen, ed., *Pacific Partnership: United States–Japan Trade: Prospects and Recommendations for the Seventies* (Lexington, Mass.: Lexington Books, 1972); Philip H. Trezise, "U.S.–Japan Economic Relations," in *United States International Economic Policy in an Interdependent World*, Paper II, Papers submitted to the Commission on International Trade and Investment Policy and published in conjunction with the Commission's Report to the President (Washington, D.C.: Supt. of Documents, July 1971), pp. 183–194.

30. See, for example, Ozaki, *The Control of Imports and Foreign Capital in Japan*. Chap. 4; Hunsberger, *Japan and the United States in World Trade*; Yasuo Takeyama, "The

Outlook for U.S.–Japan Economic and Trade Relations," *Journal of International Affairs*, 28 (1974), 38–53.

31. See U.S. Congress, House Committee on Ways and Means, *Foreign Trade and Tariff Proposals*, Hearings, 90th Congress, 2d Sess. (1968).

32. For an analysis, see "The Trade Act of 1971: A Fundamental Change in United States Foreign Trade Policy," *Yale Law Journal*, 80 (June 1971), 1418–1455.

33. U.S., 92nd Congress, 1st Sess., Foreign Trade and Investment Act of 1972, S. 2592 and H.R. 10914. Introduced September 28, 1974 by Senator Vance Hartke and Representative James A. Burke.

34. See, for example, *Future United States Foreign Trade Policy*, Report to the President, submitted by the Special Representative for Trade Negotiations (Washington, D.C.: Supt. of Documents, January 14, 1969); Peter G. Peterson, *The United States in the Changing World Economy, Vol. 1: A Foreign Economic Perspective* (Washington, D.C.: Supt. of Documents, December 1971); Trezise, *United States International Economic Policy in an Interdependent World*, Paper II.

35. Peterson, *The United States in the Changing World Economy*.

36. Ibid., p. 294.

37. For example, see Statement by the Honorable William P. Rogers, Secretary of State, "Before the Opening of the Organization for Economic Cooperation and Development Ministerial Meeting, Paris, June 7, 1971." Department of State for the Press, June 7, 1971, No. 125.

38. For example, U.S. Congress, Senate Committee on Finance, *Trade Policies in the 1970s*, Report by Senator Abraham Ribicoff, 92nd Congress, 1st Sess. (March 4, 1971); National Planning Association, *U.S. Foreign Economic Policy for the 1970's: A New Approach to New Realities* (Washington, D.C., 1971); Committee for Economic Development, *The United States and the European Community*, November 1971.

39. On the Organization for Economic Cooperation and Development, see Henry G. Aubrey, *Atlantic Economic Cooperation: The Case of OECD* (New York: Praeger, 1967); Miriam Camps, "First World," *Relationships: The Role of the OECD* (New York: Council on Foreign Relations and Atlantic Institute for International Affairs, 1975).

40. For its conclusions, see Organization for Economic Cooperation and Development, *Policy Perspectives for International Trade and Economic Relations*.

41. See Chapter 11 of this text.

42. Trade Act of 1974, P.L. 93–618, 93rd Congress, 1st Sess. (Washington, D.C., 1975). The Act retained the essence of the Trade Reform bill but gave Congress a greater role in certain areas such as nontariff barriers.

43. Text of Tokyo Declaration, reprinted in Council on International Economic Policy, International Economic Report of the President, p. 112, (Washington D.C., 1974).

44. See Chapters 7 and 10 of this text.

45. For an argument in support of freer trade in agriculture, see D. Gale Johnson, *World Agriculture in Disarray* (New York: St. Martin's, 1973); D. Gale Johnson and John A. Schnittker, *U.S. Agriculture in a World Context: Policies and Approaches in the Next Decade* (New York: Praeger, 1974).

46. For a statement of the EEC point of view on the agricultural and other issues, see Stephen D. Cohen, *The European Community and the General Agreement on Tariffs and Trade* (Washington, D.C.: Information Service of the European Community, 1975).

47. On the idea of harmonization, see Harald B. Malmgren, *International Economic Peacekeeping in Phase II* (New York: Quadrangle Books, 1972), pp. 85–89; Matthew J. Marks and Harald B. Malmgren, "Negotiating Nontariff Distortions to Trade," *Law and Policy in International Business*, 7 (Spring 1975), 327–411.

4

The Multinational Corporation and the Absence of Management

Foreign direct investment is not a new phenomenon.[1] From the time men began to trade with one another, they set up foreign commercial operations. Foreign commercial investment reached a high point in the development of the large mercantile trading companies, such as the British East India Company and the Hudson's Bay Company. Beginning in the eighteenth century but more importantly in the nineteenth century, direct foreign investment in agriculture, mining, and manufacturing, as distinct from the earlier forms of commercial investment, developed. And by the early 1890s a large number of American manufacturers—Singer (the first large multinational corporation), American Bell, and Standard Oil, to mention but a few—had important manufacturing investments abroad. By World War I, according to one study, U.S. direct foreign investment amounted to an estimated $2.65 billion, 7 percent of the United States GNP (gross national product) of that time.[2]

In another sense, international investment is quite a new phenomenon. The nature and extent of international business have changed dramatically since World War II, creating a new and powerful form of international investment, the multinational corporation.

THE MULTINATIONAL CORPORATION

The group of international businesses lumped together as multinational corporations range from companies which extract raw materials to those which produce consumer goods, such as Coca-Cola, to those which manufacture computers. They differ significantly not only in what they do but in how they do it, their level of technology, their organizational structure, and the structure of the market for their products. Nevertheless, certain characteristics common to many multinational corporations can be used to describe this new phenomenon and to identify the problems it creates.

A multinational corporation is a firm with foreign subsidiaries which extend the production and marketing of the firm beyond the boundaries of any one country. Multinational corporations do not include large corporations—such as Lockheed or Grumman—which market their products abroad; they are firms which have sent abroad a package of capital, technology, managerial talent, and marketing skills to carry out production in foreign countries. In many cases multinationals' production is truly worldwide, with different stages of production carried out in different countries. Marketing also is often international. Goods produced in one or more countries are sold throughout the world. Finally, multinational corporations tend to have foreign subsidiaries in many countries. One analyst defined a multinational corporation as one with investments in six or more foreign countries and found that such firms accounted for 80 percent of all foreign subsidiaries of major American corporations.[3]

Multinational corporations are among the world's largest firms. In 1971 each of the top 200 multinationals had sales in excess of $1 billion. The top four multinationals had sales well over $10 billion each, and the largest—General Motors—had sales in 1971 of over $28 billion. The value added by each of the top ten multinational corporations in 1971 was over $3 billion, more than the GNP of over eighty countries. The value added of all the multinationals in the same year was estimated at roughly $500 billion, about one-fifth of world GNP (excluding the GNPs of centrally planned economies).[4] These corporate giants also tend to be oligopolistic. They are able to dominate markets because of their size, their access to financial resources, their control of technology, or their possession of a special differentiated product.[5]

Multinational corporations have important organizational characteristics. Foreign subsidiaries are directly owned by the parent either through sole ownership or through joint venture with public or private groups. Sole ownership has been the preferred scheme from the point of view of the enterprise because it allows maximum control.

Decision making for multinationls tends to be centralized, though management structures vary from company to company, and policy control emanates from the parent company when the international aspects of a firm's business become important. The classic pattern of the evolution of international investment has been from semiindependent foreign operations to the integration of international operations within a separate international division to the integration of international operations within the total company. As a result, key decisions involving foreign activities such as the location of production facilities, distribution of markets, location of research and development facilities, and long-range planning tend to be made by the parent company.[6]

Yet another organizational characteristic is the integration of production and marketing on an international scale. Production may take place in different stages in several different countries, and the final product may be marketed in still other countries. Integrated production and marketing reinforce the need for central decision making and central planning and are made possible by central control and central management.

Multinationals in many cases are mobile and flexible. Some are tied to specific countries by the need for raw materials or by a large capital commitment. Others, however, are able to shift operations across national boundaries for the purposes of company profits, markets, security, or survival. Mobility and flexibility are related to the central decision-making structure and to the vast resources of the company.

The centralized, integrated organizational structure reinforces the tendency of multinational corporations to make decisions with concern for the firm and the international environment and not with concern for the particular states in which it is operating. Their vast size, centralized organization, and integrated production and marketing are powerful resources which the firm can use to follow its international goals or policies.

The special characteristics of multinational corporations have placed them in potential conflict with states, and their international scope has been known to create political problems. Most importantly, multinational corporations may seek goals or follow policies that are valid from the firm's international perspective but which are not necessarily desirable from the national perspective. Policies and goals of multinational corporations may conflict with policies and goals of the states in which they operate. There is a related jurisdictional problem. Legally, multinational corporations have many different national identities and are therefore subject to many different jurisdictions. Because no one entity or country is responsible for overall jurisdiction and because jurisdiction is unclear in many specific cases, it is at times difficult for states to exert legal control over multinational corporations.

FORCE FOR CHANGE: THE SPREAD OF THE MULTINATIONALS

Despite its unique powers and its perspectives which may conflict with nation states, multinational corporations would not have emerged as a management problem had it not been for their phenomenal growth in the postwar era. The spread of multinational corporations and especially of U.S. multinationals has been a crucial characteristic of the contemporary world economy. From 1950 to 1966 the number of affiliates of U.S. multinational corporations rose from upwards of 7,000 to more than 23,000. The most rapid rise took place between 1957, when there were over 10,000 affiliates, and 1966, when there were over 23,000 (see Table 4-1). From 1960 to 1971 the stock of U.S.-owned direct investment measured by book value rose from $32.8 billion to $86 billion (see Table 4-2). Direct investment by other developed countries, though smaller than American investment, also rose dramatically. From 1960 to 1971 the stock of direct investment by West Germany rose from $758.1 million to $7.3 billion, that of the United Kingdom rose from almost $12.0 billion to $24.0 billion, and that of Japan from $289.0 million to $4.5 billion (see Table 4-2). By 1970 the value of international production had reached approximately $330 billion, more than the total exports of all market economies which amounted to $310 billion.[7]

Much of the growth of multinational corporations has taken place within the developed market economies. From the early 1950s to the early 1960s, outstanding direct U.S. investment in the world increased threefold, but direct U.S. investment in Europe increased more than ten times.[8] A similar trend occurred in Western European investment. Between 1958 and 1964, for example, new British investment in the EEC (European Economic Community) increased fivefold while new EEC investment in Britain increased almost eighteenfold.[9] By 1967 two-thirds of all foreign direct investment measured in book value was located in the developed market economies. Of this, 47.3 percent was invested in manufacturing, 23.6 percent in petroleum (primarily refining and distribution), 5.2 percent in mining and smelting, and 23.9 percent in miscellaneous other industries.[10]

By the 1960s foreign investment had come to play an important role in the economies of the developed states. Canada, which has traditionally had widespread and high levels of foreign investment, was the most extreme case. In 1967, 52 percent of Canadian manufacturing was owned by non-Canadians, 44 percent by Americans; 62 percent of petroleum and natural gas was foreign owned, 51 percent by Americans; 61 percent of mining and smelting was owned by foreigners, 51 percent by Americans.[11]

In Europe penetration is important although less extensive. In the United Kingdom, U.S. multinationals, which constitute almost 70 percent of all foreign investment, account for 13 percent of total manufacturing output, 9 percent of the labor force, and 20 percent of manufacturing exports. In Belgium, where half the foreign investment is American, foreign firms account for 25 percent of GNP, 33 percent of all sales, 18 percent of employment, and 30 percent of exports. Figures are lower for West Germany, Italy, and France.[12] Foreign control of high-technology industry in Europe is much greater than the general figures suggest.

Table 4-1 U.S. Multinational Corporations: Number of Foreign Affiliates by Area, 1950, 1957, and 1966

Area	1950		1957		1966		Average Annual Rates of Growth	
	Number	Distribution	Number	Distribution	Number	Distribution	1950–1957	1957–1966
Developed market economies	4,657	62.8%	6,105	59.4%	15,128	65.0%	3.9%	10.6%
Canada	1,961	26.4	2,765	26.9	4,360	18.7	2.9	5.2
Western Europe	2,236	30.1	2,654	25.8	8,611	37.0	2.5	14.0
European Economic Community	1,003[a]	13.5	1,225	11.9	4,063	17.5	2.9	14.3
United Kingdom	695	9.4	842	8.2	2,310	9.9	2.8	11.9
Israel	44	0.6	44	0.4	103	0.4	—	9.9
Japan	57	0.8	137	1.3	531	2.3	13.3	16.2
Southern hemisphere	359	4.8	505	4.9	1,523	6.5	5.0	13.0
Developing countries	2,760	37.2	4,048	39.4	7,718	33.2	5.6	7.4
Africa	175	2.4	270	2.6	683	2.9	6.4	10.9
Asia[b]	524	7.1	727	7.1	1,599	6.9	4.8	9.2
Western hemisphere	2,061	27.8	3,051	29.7	5,436	23.3	5.8	6.6
Unallocated	—	—	119	1.2	436	1.9	—	15.5
Total	7,417	100.0	10,272	100.0	23,282	100.0	4.8	9.5

[a]Excluding Luxembourg.   [b]Including Turkey and Oceania (other than Australia and New Zealand).

United Nations, *Multinational Corporations in World Development* (New York: United Nations, 1973), p. 143.

Foreign firms control very high (75–100 percent) or high (50–75 percent) shares of high-technology industries, such as computers and electronics, electrical machinery, oil refining, plastics, and transportation equipment.[13]

Several factors have contributed to the vast growth of the multinational corporation. Technology and organizational sophistication created the possibility of expansion. The development of communications, transportation, and techniques of management and organization have made possible centralization, integration, and mobility. The computer, telecommunications, and the development of corporate organization, which to a great extent came from the United States and were used by U.S. firms, have been an important factor in the dominance of U.S. corporations.

The managed but less restrictive international economic system provided a favorable setting for multinational expansion in the postwar

Table 4-2   Selected Developed Market Economies: Stock of Foreign Direct Investment, 1960–1971 (millions of U.S. dollars and percents)

Year	Japan	Federal Republic of Germany	United Kingdom	United States
Book Values				
1960	$ 289.0	$ 758.1	$11,988.2	$32,765
1961	$ 453.8	$ 968.7[a]	$12,912.1	$34,664
1962	$ 535.2	$1,239.6	$13,649.1	$37,149
1963	$ 679.2	$1,527.3	$14,646.2	$40,686
1964	$ 799.5	$1,811.7	$16,415.6	$44,386
1965	$ 956.2	$2,076.1	$16,796.5	$49,328
1966	$1,183.2	$2,513.2	$17,531.4	$54,711
1967	$1,458.1	$3,015.0	$17,521.1[a]	$59,486
1968	$2,015.3	$3,587.0	$18,478.8	$64,983
1969	$2,682.9	$4,774.5[a]	$20,043.2	$71,016
1970	$3,596.3	$5,774.5	$21,390.5	$78,090
1971	$4,480.0[a]	$7,276.9[a]	$24,019.0[a]	$86,001
Average Annual Rates of Growth				
1960–1965	27.0%	22.3%	7.0%	8.5%
1965–1971	29.4	23.2	6.1	9.7
1960–1971	28.3	22.8	6.5	9.2

[a]Exchange rate change.

United Nations, *Multinational Corporations in World Development* (New York: United Nations, 1973), p. 146.

era. The elimination of restraints on capital flows and trade provided the possibility for expansion of direct investment. Canadians and Europeans created incentives to attract foreign investment.[14] And, by having the greatest technological and financial resources, American firms were best able to take advantage of the international environment.[15]

Aside from a favorable setting for expansion, there were important incentives for individual firms to move abroad. Various theories have been developed to explain the motivation for the spread of multinational corporations. The product cycle theory argues that firms expand abroad in response to a threat to export markets. Firms develop new products and processes which they introduce abroad through exports. When their export position is threatened, they establish foreign subsidiaries in an attempt to retain their advantage. When the firm finally loses its advantage, it may move on to new products, attempt to create new advantages by altering the product, or seek lower-cost production sites in other countries.[16] The monopoly or oligopoly theory of foreign investment argues somewhat similarly that firms move abroad to exploit the monopoly power they possess through such factors as unique products, marketing expertise, control of technology and managerial skills, or access to capital.[17] Yet another theory posits that firms expand abroad to take advantage of foreign resources such as less expensive labor and technology or lower taxes and tariffs.[18]

The rapid growth of multinational corporations in Europe after 1955 is explained by a combination of favorable factors: the economic recovery of Europe, which provided an attractive market; the return to convertibility of European currencies, which made possible unrestricted repatriation of earnings and capital; greater political stability both internally and internationally; and the formation of the EEC, with its promise of a large market and its discrimination against third-party imports.[19]

It was the combination of the unique characteristics of multinational corporations and their phenomenal growth among developed market economies which posed international management problems. Multinational policy and interests came into potential conflict with national policy and interests in three areas: economic efficiency, growth, and welfare; national economic control; and the national political process.

EFFICIENCY, GROWTH, AND WELFARE

Modern governments have given high priority to the public policy goals of economic efficiency, growth, and improvement in the standard of living. In evaluating the impact of multinational corporations in developed market economies and determining management problems raised by multinationals, one must judge the effect of those firms on economic performance.

Proponents of multinational corporations argue that the new corporate form is a mechanism for increasing economic efficiency and stimulating growth. By transferring capital, technology, and know-how and by mobilizing idle domestic resources, multinational corporations, argue its advocates, increase world efficiency, foster growth, and thereby improve welfare.[20]

Critics of multinational corporations, on the other hand, argue that these international oligopolies may reduce efficiency and stifle growth. Because of the absence of competition, multinational corporations may be able to limit production, maintain artificially high prices, earn monopoly rents, and thus lower efficiency. They may actually hinder national growth by absorbing local capital instead of providing new capital, by applying inappropriate technology, and by employing expatriate, not indigenous, managers. And, point out the critics, global efficiency and growth do not necessarily maximize efficiency and growth for individual national economies.[21]

Unfortunately, much of the analysis and debate over the impact of multinational corporations remains theoretical. There are relatively few empirical studies of the impact of different multinationals on particular national economies. There are numerous reasons for the dearth of empirical analysis, including most importantly the lack of reliable data and the absence of an adequate theoretical framework to measure the impact of multinational corporations on national efficiency, growth, and welfare.[22]

Despite these limitations, some evaluation can be made from existing data. Most studies of the economic impact of multinational corporations in host developed market economies conclude that their overall effect is positive. One such case is Canada. Because of its vast penetration, foreign investment has been an important public issue in Canada and the subject of several major official and semiofficial studies and much private scholarly examination. All these studies have concluded that foreign investment has had a favorable impact on the Canadian economy.[23]

The Watkins report of 1968, which was critical of foreign investment, concluded that direct foreign investment, especially U.S. investment, was a key factor in Canadian economic development generally and an important factor specifically in capital formation, export promotion, and balance of payments. Furthermore, the Watkins report concluded, it was important that this investment was direct and not portfolio investment, for direct investment brought not only financial resources, but also a package of product, technology, management, and market access. The report noted that there were problems with direct foreign investment, that it may have stunted the domestic Canadian capital market and damaged the initiatives of local entrepreneurs, but it concluded that "[T]he host country typically benefits and often substantially from foreign direct investment."[24]

Similar conclusions were reached in a private study of foreign investment in France. The study found that foreign direct investment has been strategically important for the French economy. The major benefit was in the balance of payments, but foreign investment also increased the level of technology, of research and development and productivity, and of competition and, thus, of productivity. Foreign investment, this study argued, made the French economy more dynamic and competitive, particularly within the EEC.[25]

Conclusions regarding the economic impact of foreign investment in Great Britain have also been positive. One study of the United Kingdom estimated that foreign investment in Great Britain added a total of 2.0-2.5 percent a year to British GNP in the 1960s. Approximately 0.3 percent was added to British GNP by multinational firms locating in areas of above-average unemployment and using resources that otherwise would not have been used. Approximately 0.6 percent of the contribution to GNP was through the favorable impact on resource allocation and concentration in productive sectors. But perhaps the most valuable contribution came from the spillover effect, estimated at 0.5-1.0 percent of the GNP.[26] Another study by the same author cited numerous benefits to the British economy from foreign investment, including internal use of resources, research and development, capital, labor, competition, regional development, overall economic development, and the balance of payments.[27]

Despite indications of overall benefits from multinational corporations, however, such investment is not without costs for the host state. Costs arise because behavior which is rational for the corporation may be suboptimal for the host country. Several concerns emerge from public and private studies.[28] The fear of technological dependence is one. While access to advanced technology is one of the primary economic benefits of multinational corporations for host developed countries, the price of that access may be the stifling of domestic research and development. The concentration of research and development in the home state, primarily the United States, may discourage research and development activities in the host state and result in the subordination of the host to technology controlled from abroad. There is a related concern that host states may be paying excessive costs for imported technology because the monopoly control of technology by a multinational enables the parent to charge a monopoly rent for its use.[29] A similar concern arises regarding management skills. The transfer of managerial talent to host countries can be a source of efficiency and growth, but the use of foreign managers may also stifle indigenous managerial and entrepreneurial talent by denying nationals opportunities to use and develop their skills.

Yet another concern grows out of the oligopolistic character of multinational corporations. The entrance of foreign competitors may stimulate domestic competition and thus encourage efficiency, but it may also reduce competition and threaten existing domestic industries. Even such market dominance by multinational corporations may be beneficial if it brings with it new technologies and other economic efficiencies. But, if it does not introduce such improvements, it may decrease efficiency. Special concern is voiced by states when multinational corporations acquire existing national firms. Acquisition may give the firm access to capital, technology, and other resources and thereby improve its performance, but it may simply indicate a transfer of ownership adding no new efficiencies.

Some concern has been expressed regarding the import orientation of multinational corporations. The Gray report, for example, found that subsidiaries in Canada preferred to seek supplies and services within the company as opposed to within the country. This preference for importing from the parent may provide the highest quality goods and services, but it may retard the development of Canadian manufacturing and service sectors and thus limit the spillover effect that foreign investment has on the rest of the Canadian economy.[30] Other concerns have been voiced regarding export policy. While evidence suggests that multinational corporations have an equal or better export record than their domestic counterparts, the practice of restricting exports and limiting markets of individual subsidiaries is not unknown in multinational corporations. Finally, there is concern regarding the balance-of-payments impact of multinational corporations. With present data and methods, it is difficult to judge the entire payments ramifications of multinational corporations, but there is a feeling that the consequences may be negative in the long run.

In evaluating the problems created by the conflict between multinational corporations and host states over economic efficiency, growth, and welfare, one must go beyond economic analyses. Equally important is the way in which national elites view the impact of the multinational on the national economy. One study comparing elite attitudes in Britain, France, and Canada provides some insight.

A poll of national elites, national legislators, permanent government officials, labor union leaders, and heads of business firms in the three countries revealed that these groups felt that the economic impact—be it positive or negative—was a very important aspect of the influence of multinational corporations. The overall view of the multinational corporations was mixed but generally favorable. In Britain and France all but the union leaders were moderately but definitely favorable to multinational corporations. In Canada the reaction was more negative: all groups but businessmen had a negative view of the economic impact of foreign investment. Most of those polled in the three countries recognized important internal economic benefits on employment, capital, and skills. But they took a more negative view of the external impact—that is, the impact on the balance of payments.[31]

In sum, the economic impact of multinationals on the host economy seems generally positive, and elites generally perceive that positive impact. Yet there are real economic concerns in specific areas. The important issue for developed host countries is not whether foreign investment is economically worthwhile, but whether it is possible to increase the benefits and decrease the costs of direct foreign investment.

Until recently, examination of the effect of multinational corporations has focused on host states with the implicit assumption that the home state was the recipient of economic benefits. Recently, however, the assumption that multinational corporations are good for the home economy has come under fire. Some analysts and influential interest groups in the United States, particularly representatives of the AFL–CIO, argue that U.S. direct foreign investment has had a negative effect on the American economy by favoring foreign investment over foreign trade and production in the United States, by exporting jobs instead of goods, by allowing tax revenues to escape, and by impairing domestic economic development by sending capital abroad instead of using it at home.[32]

This viewpoint was reflected in the Burke–Hartke bill, which had strong labor backing. Burke–Hartke had important provisions which would have constrained U.S. foreign investment. It would have revised tax provisions, assessing foreign earnings in the year earned, not when repatriated, and repealing U.S. tax credits for foreign taxes paid by U.S. firms overseas. In addition, Burke–Hartke would have required U.S. corporations abroad to pay foreign workers the U.S. minimum wage and would have controlled the types of technology that could be exported from the United States. Although it was never passed, the bill suggests that home countries are also increasingly concerned about maximizing benefits and minimizing the costs of direct foreign investment.

NATIONAL ECONOMIC CONTROL

A second area of potential multinational–state conflict in developed countries is the interference of multinational corporations with national control of the economy. As developed states have sought increasingly to manage their economies to improve economic efficiency, growth, and welfare, the elite and the public have become concerned about external constraints on that control from multinational corporations.

The concern with national control emerges clearly in studies of elite and public attitudes toward foreign investment. In the comparative study of elite attitudes in Britain, France, and Canada, the loss of national control was seen as a crucial problem, especially when American firms were involved.[33] A study of Canadian attitudes revealed that the most adverse feeling toward multinational corporations involved the loss of control. Canadians generally perceive that there is a trade-off between the economic benefit of multinational corporations and their adverse effect on control over national affairs.[34]

The sense of lost control reflects, in part, an intangible feeling that, as a result of foreign investment, decisions crucial to the national economy are made outside the nation. The perception is not that these decisions are necessarily or always adverse, just that they are made elsewhere. The tendency of multinational corporations to centralize decisions in the parent suggests that the fears that decision making shifts from host to investing country are often justified. Interestingly, the intangible fear of loss of decision making is not related to the level of foreign investment. Canadians, who have a vast amount of foreign investment, are no more concerned than the English, who have much less. The French, with the lowest level of investment, on the other hand, evidence a high level of concern. The fear of lost control seems to be related more to different national expectations regarding the need for independence than to the actual threat to that independence.[35]

The fear of lost control of sensitive industries is particularly acute. Countries, including the United States, have always been concerned about foreign ownership of such sectors as communications, transportation, and finance. Increasingly, public officials feel that industries with a major influence on the economy, such as the automotive or petroleum industries, or those in the vanguard of scientific and technological development, such as computers or electronics, should remain under national control.[36] Yet these are precisely the industries dominated by multinational corporations.

While multinational corporations have often played an important role in achieving national goals, there is a concern that multinational corporations are less responsive to national economic planning than are domestically owned firms operating primarily in the national market.[37] The concern is, first, that activity rational for an international firm may not be in tune with that planned for the national economy and, second, that the multinational has the capacity to circumvent mechanisms for implementing national plans. Because multinational corporations have access to outside financing, they are not as dependent as domestic industry on national governmental finance and thus may not respond to governmental incentives to invest in certain industries or certain regions. Because they have fewer links with the national economy and polity, it is feared, they are less likely to cooperate voluntarily with national planning goals.

The Gray report, for example, expressed a concern that multinational corporations might interfere with the Canadian government's goal of increasing investment in manufacturing and discouraging overdevelopment of resource extraction. The report pointed out that

> foreign fabricating and manufacturing firms which integrate vertically backwards to obtain secure supplies of natural resources are less likely to respond to Canadian needs and economic capabilities as their *raison d'être* is shaped heavily by their committed investment elsewhere.[38]

In the 1960s the French were concerned that American multinational corporations, with their access to capital unavailable to French industry, were overinvesting in automobile production.[39]

Another concern is that multinational corporations may reduce the effectiveness of national monetary policy through their access to outside sources of funding. During a period of monetary restraint, multinational corporations may use external financing to follow expansionary policies, and, during periods of monetary expansion, they may use low interest rates to transfer funds abroad instead of using them locally. The Gray report, however, found that in Canada, the country with the greatest foreign investment and therefore the greatest disruptive potential, there was little interference with national monetary policy due to multinational corporations.[40] Another related concern is that, by their ability to move funds rapidly across national boundaries, MNCs may interfere with national exchange rate policy. A U.S. Treasury report suggested that, at least in 1971, such fears were ungrounded.[41]

A greater concern is that multinational corporations may evade national taxation. Through its central control of pricing, the multinational corporation can take profits in countries where taxes are low and avoid showing profits and paying taxes where taxes are high. Because transactions of subsidiaries of the same multinational are not arm's length transactions, that is, not determined by free market prices, the central decision-making unit can artificially fix the prices of those transactions. These so-called transfer prices can be manipulated to minimize taxes. A multinational can, for example, inflate the price of imports or decrease the value of exports among affiliated companies to minimize the earnings of a subsidiary in a high-tax country.

Another dimension of interference with national control is in what one author called the "national order."[42] Multinational corporations, it is charged, are less bound by national social codes and economic relationships. Thus, the links between business and government which exist in Europe and in Japan and which are a tool for national economic management may be more tenuous and less effective between national governments and multinational corporation management.

Another aspect of the national order is labor–business relations. It has been argued that American multinationals have followed labor policies inimical to national labor policies. It has been charged that they are more willing than national firms, for example, to discharge employees.

INTERFERENCE BY HOME GOVERNMENTS OF MULTINATIONALS

Another dimension of the problem of control is the threat not from the multinational itself but from the home government of the multinational to the host country, primarily the threat from the United States to the host countries of American multinational corporations. Such interference occurs when American laws are applied beyond U.S. borders through subsidiaries of the MNC.[43]

One area of American interference has been through extraterritorial application of American export controls. The Trading with the Enemy Act of 1917, the Export Control Act of 1949, and its successor, the Export Administration Act of 1969, have been used by the American government to control dealings of foreign affiliates of American corporations. The Trading with the Enemy Act empowers the president to regulate all commercial and financial transactions by Americans with foreign countries or nationals in time of war or national emergency. The act has been invoked in recent years to prohibit all trade with Cuba, China, North Korea, and North Vietnam. The Export Control and Export Administration acts give the executive the authority to "prohibit or curtail" all commercial exports including technical know-how to Communist countries from U.S. companies or their foreign subsidiaries. Because American courts hold the parent firm criminally liable for the acts of its foreign affiliates, there is great incentive for multinational corporations to cooperate with these U.S. regulations.

There have been cases in which the United States has blocked American subsidiaries' transactions abroad which were legal under the laws of the host country. It refused a license to a U.S.-owned Belgian company to export farm equipment to Cuba and forced a South African subsidiary of Ford-Canada to reject an order for armored trucks with gunmounts for the South African government. In one of the most famous and politically charged episodes, the U.S. government prevented IBM-France from selling equipment for the French space and nuclear programs to the French government by invoking obligations under the Non-Proliferation Treaty, which France had not signed.

The U.S. government, however, has not always prevailed. For example, in the case of Freuhof, an American firm manufacturing trucks in France, the United States was unable to block the company's sale of trailer trucks to a French company which planned to add truck cabs and sell them to the People's Republic of China. Resistance by the French government and French courts led the United States to withdraw its restriction. Numerous other cases suggest that the U.S. government is often willing to accede when foreign governments insist.[44] Furthermore, in recent years, as American policy has permitted greater trade with Communist countries, the incidence of host–home government conflict has decreased.

Another area of U.S. interference has been through antitrust legislation. The Sherman and Clayton acts seek to prevent restraint of competition both within the United States and in American import and export trade. And the U.S. courts have asserted a wide-ranging extraterritorial jurisdiction of these laws, including application to subsidiaries of American multinational corporations. The fact that a U.S. corporation is a parent of a foreign subsidiary has been held sufficient for jurisdiction by U.S. courts. On this basis, the American government has attempted to force, not always with success, disclosure of information by foreign subsidiaries. It has forced U.S. parents to divest themselves of foreign affiliates or to alter the behavior of their affiliates, even though that ownership or behavior was legal under host laws. American courts, for example, forced a U.S. beer company to divest itself of a subsidiary in Canada and obliged American parents to order subsidiaries to cease to operate in a radio cartel in Canada, even though this cartel had been approved by the Canadian government.

Finally there has been intervention through U.S. balance-of-payments policies. One measure taken by the U.S. government to improve its balance of payments in the 1960s was to reduce the net outflow of capital from the United States. Under the voluntary capital restraint program of 1965, the United States asked American corporations to limit new foreign investment in developed countries, to increase the amount of foreign investment financed by borrowing abroad, and to increase the return of earnings and short-term assets from foreign affiliates. In 1968 mandatory controls were imposed to require a reduction or moratorium in the level of investment flows from the United States to the developed states, with the exception of Canada. U.S. corporations cooperated with governmental controls, creating a serious impact on investment abroad, particularly in Europe where the policy threatened to dampen economic growth, hurt the balance of payments of European countries, and dry up local capital markets when American corporations, instead of borrowing in the United States, borrowed on local capital markets and competed effectively with European firms. The capital restraints were ended in the 1970s following the emergence of the float and the improvement in the American balance-of-payments position. It remains possible, however, that similar controls could be imposed in the future.

In conclusion, the potential for multinational corporations' disruption of national control is very real. However, considering the volume of transactions carried out by multinational corporations, the number of cases of clear and major threat to national control seem to be relatively small. Like the problem of the impact of the MNC on economic efficiency, growth, and welfare, the problem seems to be one of minimizing costs and maximizing benefits instead of rejecting the multinational as too costly for national independence.

MULTINATIONALS AND THE NATIONAL POLITICAL PROCESS

One final but important area where multinational corporations may interfere is in the politics of home and host states. As with any corporation in the home or host country, the multinational is a potentially powerful political force which can, and at times does, seek to shape law and public policy and which has an impact on the political environment. The nature and significance of the multinational corporation's impact on national politics in developed countries is an area which has not been sufficiently examined and about which little is known.

Still, there are several ways in which multinational corporations might attempt to influence politics in host countries. In the most extreme case it might overthrow an unfriendly government or keep a friendly regime in power. It might intervene in elections through legal or illegal campaign contributions or take action to support or oppose particular public policies. Finally, multinational corporations might influence the national political culture, that is, shape public political values and attitudes. In all of these actions the firm may act on its own, at the instigation of the home government, or with the support of the home government.[45]

In the case of Canada, the Gray report, which considered these possibilities, concluded that multinational corporations have little direct impact on Canadian public policy. The influence of foreign investment, according to that study, was in shaping alternatives available to Canadian decision makers. For example, because of the structure of Canadian industry and the fact that some firms are foreign controlled, public policy is limited in its efforts to rationalize industry.[46] The U.S. Senate Subcommittee on Multinational Corporations found that multinational corporations have engaged in legal and illegal payments in developed countries, but the subcommittee did not suggest just how such payments influenced public policy.[47]

Multinational corporations may also have an impact on public policy in the home state. One study of U.S. foreign policy found that the direct influence of any particular corporation is likely to be balanced by countervailing powers, even though corporate groups may shape policy. The most important influence, the study concluded, was the ability of business generally to shape the political consensus out of which American foreign policy is drawn. The predominance of the liberal approach to international economic relations would be an example of the intangible yet significant influence.[48]

A somewhat different view emerges from the hearings of the Senate Subcommittee on Multinational Corporations. These hearings suggest that multinational corporations at times become an important part of the dynamic of American foreign policy making, initiating demands, providing information, and at times cooperating in the execution of policy. Another impression which emerges is that multinational corporations at times follow policies independent of and perhaps in contradiction to official governmental policy.[49]

Another impact of multinational corporations on national politics is through their influence on social structure. One provocative study suggests that multinational corporations are altering both national and international class structures, creating new social, economic, and political divisions. According to the study, there is a new class structure emerging that consists of a transnational managerial class favoring a liberal international economic order; a large class of established labor, with secure employment and secure status in their local communities, which has been the primary object and beneficiary of social legislation and economic management; and a group of social marginals which has not been integrated into the new industrial society and which suffers the social costs of the system. The study finds that this new class structure, shaped by the multinational enterprise, will create new social conflicts not suited to control by presently established institutions.[50]

In conclusion, concern has risen in recent years, and, with that concern, conflict has been generated over the multinational corporation. The management of multinational corporations, however, has not become such a highly politicized and highly conflictual issue in the Western system as it has in the Third World. While there is a growing belief that multinational corporations must be managed to maximize benefits, there persists a general perception of the importance of international investment. As Prime Minister Pierre Trudeau of Canada put it,

> I don't worry over something which is somewhat inevitable, and I think the problem of economic domination is somewhat inevitable, not only of the

United States over Canada but perhaps over countries of Europe as well. . . . These are facts of life, and they don't worry me. I would want to make sure that this economic presence does not result as I say in a real weakening of our national identity. I use that general expression too. The way in which I do that is to try and balance the benefits against the disadvantages. It is obvious if we keep out capital and keep out technology, we won't be able to develop our resources and we would have to cut our standard of consumption in order to generate the savings to invest ourselves and so on. . . . Each country wants to keep its identity or its sovereignty, to speak in legal terms. It has to instantly make assessments, and when we make assessments it is to try and select those areas which are important for our independence, for our identity.[51]

MANAGEMENT OF MULTINATIONAL CORPORATIONS

Compared with the control of money and trade, international management of multinational enterprise has been extremely limited. One reason for the absence of an international order for investment is that multinational corporations have only recently emerged as a problem of international economic relations among developed market economies. The need for monetary and trade orders became clear as a result of the crisis of the 1930s, which was a crucial force behind the establishment of postwar management mechanisms. In investment, however, no such international crisis and no consensus have developed in the West. Consciousness about multinational corporations was not raised until the 1960s when these firms became important international economic phenomena.

Even when multinational corporations came to be seen as an international problem in the West, the extent of that problem was perceived as rather limited.[52] The fear of economic costs and of loss of national control have been balanced by the perception of very important economic benefits to be gained from foreign investment.

An important factor shaping these generally positive perceptions of multinational corporations is the dominant capitalist philosophy. According to this viewpoint, international investment, like international finance and trade, is economically rational and beneficial. The role of large corporations in politics is not seen as dangerous in countries where domestic corporations play such roles. This general receptivity to international capital shapes elite reactions to multinational corporations. It is interesting that the major dissent comes from the labor elites in the United Kingdom, France, and Canada. Furthermore, the two countries whose national policies evidence the greatest opposition to multinational corporations, France and Japan, are countries for which liberalism is not part of the national philosophical tradition.

Another reason for the limited perceived threat has been the power relationship between multinational corporations and governments of developed countries. In developed countries the multinational corporation is not perceived as a major threat to governmental power. While firms can influence economic performance and interfere with a nation's economic management, they cannot undermine the authority of these powerful, sophisticated governments. While multinational corporations control sensitive sectors, they do not, except in Canada, loom so large in the national economy that governments feel they must acquiesce to the strength of the multinational. Furthermore, Western governments possess not only the expertise—lawyers, accountants, economists, business experts—to regulate multinational corporations but the confidence that they can devise means for control.

Yet another reason for the limited perception of threat in the West is that virtually all developed states have their own multinational corporations. While American investment is clearly dominant, most other states have their own multinational corporations which are expanding throughout the West and the South. The position of the governments of developed market economies as both home and host moderates desires to restrict multinational corporations, for any restriction would limit national corporations.

A final important dimension of the limited threat and the lack of international control of multinational corporations is the absence of American concern and interest in such management. The American perception of a need for management, crucial in the development of international monetary and trade orders, has not existed in the field of international investment. The lack of perceived problems for the American political and economic systems, the dominant liberal ideology, and the political significance of the large multinational corporations in American politics prevented American leadership and even cooperation in the control of foreign investment.

NATIONAL MANAGEMENT

Most efforts to control multinational corporations in the present international system occur within the host country. Although policy in developed market economies has been receptive to foreign investment, there have been some attempts to regulate foreign corporations to maximize economic benefits and to minimize the loss of control.

The most important form of regulation is the control of initial capital investment. States have sought to restrict key sectors for national investment and to regulate the degree of foreign ownership or control in sectors open to foreign investment. While all countries have some form of key sector control—transportation, communications, and defense industries are commonly restricted industries—few of the developed market economies have comprehensive regulations or even a clear national policy regarding foreign investment.

Only Japan has consistently followed a comprehensive, restrictive policy.[53] In investment as well as trade, Japan's public philosophy and governmental policy differ from those of other Western countries. Since the Meiji period (1868–1912), when industrialization was carried out to maintain national independence from foreign incursions, Japan has deliberately restricted foreign investment. Postwar policy has been based on the Foreign Exchange Control Law of 1949 and the Foreign Investment Law of 1950, which provided governmental authority to screen all new foreign investment, with a view to limiting that investment, and to prevent the repatriation of earnings and capital of foreign investors. Governmental policy was highly restrictive. New foreign investment was limited to a few industries, and within those industries foreign ownership was limited to no more than 49 percent.

Policy regarding the purchase of existing industry was even more restrictive. Foreigners were limited to at most a 20 percent ownership of unrestricted industries and a 15 percent interest in the many restricted industries.

While restricting direct foreign investment, Japan sought to obtain the benefits of multinational corporations by separating the package of resources provided by the enterprise. Most particularly, Japanese firms purchased advanced technology through licensing agreements instead of acquiring technology through foreign control. As a result of these comprehensive, restrictive policies, foreign investment in Japan has been quite low (see Table 4-1).

From 1967 to 1971 and again in 1973, Japan carried out programs of liberalization of foreign investment. The number of restricted industries was reduced, and 100 percent ownership was permitted in some industries. Although foreign investment has increased, the role of foreign investment in the Japanese economy has not altered significantly. Many industries—those often the most attractive to foreign investment—remain closed, and government policy, while more open, continues to restrict the inflow of direct foreign investments.

Canada has also developed a policy for regulating the inflow of foreign investment.[54] The Canadian Foreign Investment Review Act of 1972[55] established a Foreign Investment Review Agency (FIRA) to screen new direct foreign investment in Canada. Unlike Japan, which defined restricted industries and numerical limits on foreign equity, the Canadian policy is to deal with foreign investment on a flexible case-by-case basis. The requirement for approval by the Review Agency is that the potential investor demonstrate positive benefits for Canada. Evaluation according to such criteria as the degree of Canadian participation, the effect on productivity and efficiency, and the effect on competition is highly discretionary. Furthermore, FIRA does not cover all foreign investment. Companies already established in Canada are exempt from review so long as their new investment remains within existing lines of investment. The review procedure, while hardly restrictive, seeks to encourage greater attention by new investors to Canadian concerns and interests.

Other states also screen new investment. Britain relies on ad hoc consideration of applications for new direct foreign investment. Investments which might create foreign dominance of an important economic sector, damage British research and development, interfere with official plans for industrial rationalization, or create excessive concentration are reviewed by appropriate ministries or agencies. British policy has been quite open, and restrictions have relied on commitments by new investors, not the rejection of investment. In the acquisition of Rootes Motor Company in 1967, for example, the United Kingdom required Chrysler to maintain a majority of British directors on the board, nominate a British director of Rootes to French Chrysler and Chrysler International, expand plants in Britain, and increase exports as condition for entry.[56]

France also screens new investment. Since 1967 all proposals for new direct foreign investment must receive prior approval from the Ministry of Finance. The ministry has the authority to require a temporary postponement of investment to allow further government study or to allow the investor to alter the project to meet government demands. It can also reject investment proposals. Like the United Kingdom, France has no formal statutory guidelines for evaluating foreign investment. In practice, judgments tend to favor investments which benefit employment, balance of payments, research and development, and exports; create new enterprises instead of acquiring existing firms; encourage French management at both the national and parent level; and fit in with governmental plans for industrial reorganization. While the French policy in the mid-1960s was restrictive, the general policy has been highly receptive to foreign investment.[57]

Aside from the control of initial capital investment, states have also attempted to manage the behavior of multinational corporations once established in their state. The ability to control multinational corporations' behavior is crucial to management, for it involves activities which challenge national economic performance and national control, such as transfer pricing, tax payments, labor policy, and research and development. Governments have made few attempts to regulate corporate behavior. Canada in 1966 provided a set of guidelines for foreign investment behavior, and France has reacted to worker layoffs by multinational corporations. The primary form of behavior control has been informal governmental pressure on firms to follow policies such as plant or export expansion. Regulation of multinational corporations' behavior has been hindered by the lack of study and analysis of the impact of foreign investment and by the limited incentive for regulation. In the future, as incentives to maximize benefits and minimize costs grow and as governmental sophistication and understanding of the multinational increase, new national regulation may emerge.

Governments have been more active in managing intervention by home governments of multinational corporations. Ad hoc reaction to such intervention is common. Thus in the Freuhof case France successfully opposed U.S. government demands for an export embargo, and the Canadian government obtained exceptions from the American capital restraints programs of 1965 and 1968. Recently, Canada enacted legislation requiring Canadian jurisdiction in antitrust action in Canada.

Finally, there have been few attempts in the major home country, the United States, to regulate MNCs. Concerns with balance-of-payments deficits led to capital control measures, Burke–Hartke reflected home concerns over export of jobs and the tax "loopholes" enjoyed by multinational corporations, and the investigation of the Senate Subcommittee on Multinational Corporations has revealed a broad range of foreign policy problems posed by the multinational. Growing American concern may lead to moves toward deconcentration, revision of tax provisions, control of transfer pricing, more stringent reporting requirements, and U.S. control of bribes and illegal payments by U.S. multinational corporations.[58]

Because developed market economies, with the exception of Japan, have been unwilling to restrict multinational corporations severely, many have sought to minimize their costs in other ways. Many states have sought to strengthen domestic industry. Such policies, as part of broader industrial policies, include governmental encouragement and support of industrial concentration and rationalization of national industry, research and development, maintenance of key industries or companies, development of national capital markets, and national managerial skills.[59] Methods include governmental financial assistance, tax preferences, government participation in industry, encouragement of mergers, financing of research and training programs, and "buy national" procurement policies. An example of governmental efforts to support national industry is the French and British support of national control in the computer industry. In 1966 the French government financed a new firm, Compagnie Internationale pour l'Informatique, and in 1967 the United Kingdom gave financial backing to the merger of three British firms into the International Computers.[60]

Another governmental support encouraging national industry to compete with multinational corporations or reduce the need for foreign investment is the Canada Development Corporation (CDC). Financed by the Canadian government, the CDC was set up in 1971 to invest seed money in new Canadian business, to provide capital for existing businesses threatened with foreign takeover, and to mobilize private Canadian investment behind Canadian corporations. The CDC has invested in both new and existing Canadian industry and has become involved in an attempt to capture control of existing foreign investment. In 1973—after a legal battle with the parent corporation—CDC purchased 30 percent of Texasgulf Incorporated, an American-owned natural resource corporation with the majority of its operations in Canada. Although the CDC did not obtain a controlling interest, it did obtain a degree of control through CDC directors on the board of Texasgulf. Nationalization through the market mechanism is a new technique for national control of multinational corporations.

Despite their expected growth and effectiveness, national solutions will remain limited by their inability to control the behavior of multinational corporations outside national boundaries. For this reason, interest in some broader form of management has been on the increase.

REGIONAL MANAGEMENT

One potentially important forum for multilateral management of multinational corporations is the EEC. A European solution figures prominently in the analysis of European critics of American multinational investment in Europe.[61] Two approaches for regional policy have been suggested: the development of community regulations on MNCs and the community's encouragement of European corporations which could balance American multinationals.

European regional management faces major obstacles.[62] There is no provision in the Treaty of Rome, which established the EEC, for control of non-EEC investment or for enforcement of an internal EEC industrial policy which might serve as a balance of foreign investment. Members of the community have consistently refused to delegate to the EEC any national authority for regulation or industrial policy. A French proposal in 1965 for community regulation of foreign investment was rejected by the other members who opposed a restrictive policy. A 1973 Commission of the Community proposal—for protecting employees in event of takeover and establishing community rules for stock exchange operations and the origins of funds for investment, international cooperation for supervising stock exchange operations, international assistance and cooperation in information, monitoring, tax recovery, transfer prices and license fees, and the collection of information—led nowhere.[63] A similar fate has confronted efforts at a common industrial policy. The commission has had little success in implementing an industrial policy to include the harmonization of national tax and corporate laws and support transnational mergers of European firms. Proposals for industrial policy, a European company, and a convention on the international merger of corporations have been blocked by national industrial policy and attempts to create "national champions."[64] EEC policy has been constrained by the lack of political will for a community policy in the member states.

INTERNATIONAL MANAGEMENT

International management of multinational corporations is virtually nonexistent. International regulations and agreements have tended to encourage the expansion of multinational corporations, not control their operations. Western international law developed before World War II provided important protection for foreign investment. The traditional law of prompt, adequate, and effective compensation in the case of nationalization and various patent and copyright conventions were designed for this purpose. Postwar agreements reinforced this general trend. IMF (International Monetary Fund) provisions on currency convertibility allow the repatriation of capital and earnings and thus facilitate the international flow of capital. GATT (General Agreement on Tariffs and Trade) tariff reductions facilitate international production and transfers within multinationals. And the OECD (Organization for Economic Cooperation and Development) Code of Liberalization of Capital Movements establishes the norms of nondiscrimination between foreign and domestic investors within a country, freedom of establishment, and freedom of transfer of funds.

While there has been some very marginal international regulation through various international agencies and international conventions whose authority covers certain aspects of multinational operations,[65] there has been little attempt to manage multinational corporations at an international level, and most of those attempts have failed.

One such abortive effort died with the Havana Charter.[66] The management of international investment had not been a part of the American scheme for a new postwar economic order. Ironically, in response to very strong pressure from American business groups, the U.S. delegation at Geneva in 1947 proposed a draft article on foreign investment. The article, intended to codify the prevailing Western liberal attitude on foreign investment and the rights of capital-exporting countries, provided for protection against nationalization and discrimination. Once the matter was placed on the negotiating agenda, however, its character quickly changed. The underdeveloped countries led by the Latin American states were able to redefine the proposed article to protect not capital exporters but capital importers. Provisions of the Havana Charter allowed capital-importing countries to establish national requirements for the ownership of existing and future foreign investment and to determine the conditions for future foreign investment. The inclusion of these investment provisions was a major reason for the opposition of U.S. business to the Havana Charter and for the eventual failure of the charter. GATT, its successor, contained no provisions for investment.

Throughout the 1950s and early 1960s, a do-nothing attitude prevailed. Attempts to develop international foreign investment law such as the United Nations' Economic and Social Council efforts in the 1950s and those of GATT in 1960 to restrict business practices surfaced but led nowhere.[67]

In the late 1960s as concern increased, more comprehensive proposals for a system of international management were developed. The most far-reaching proposals called for a body of international law under which multinational corporations would be chartered and regulated and for an international organization to administer these regulations.[68] It is unrealistic, however, to expect implementation of such a supranational plan in the present international system. International political will to delegate regulation to some supranational body simply does not exist in the Western system. Furthermore, the experience with the IMF and GATT suggests that regulation by international organization, in the present stage of development of the international system, is not an effective method for economic management. Formal and informal international consultation and cooperation are the primary mechanisms for international economic control.

More realistic proposals suggest a limited system of management, one of which advocates the development of a GATT for investment[69]—an intergovernmental General Agreement for the International Corporation to establish a set of accepted rules, consisting of a few fundamental concepts of substance and procedure on which there might be a general international consensus. Although the agreement would be a code of behavior, not a set of binding regulations, such rules might encourage the further development and application of international standards for foreign investment. The proposal further suggests the establishment of an agency which would investigate and make recommendations about the development of rules or their infringement, much as the GATT organization has done. Such an agency would not have compulsory authority, but it would have the power to publicize its findings and thus appeal to the constraints of public opinion.

The limited GATT resembles a recent agreement among the OECD countries. In 1976, in response to a great extent to pressure from underdeveloped countries as well as from developed countries, the developed market states agreed on a voluntary code of conduct for multinational corporations. An important factor leading to the OECD agreement was the new interest of the American government and American business in such an international code. Public revelations of corporate bribery and illegal political activity created domestic pressures for regulation of U.S. corporations. American business sought to deter congressional legislation and to internationalize any constraints placed on American firms through an international agreement.

The stated goal of the OECD code is to maximize the benefits of international investment. It suggests guidelines for corporate behavior such as greater disclosure of information, cooperation with laws and policies of host governments, refraining from anticompetitive behavior and improper political activities, respect for the right of employees to unionize, and cooperation with governments to develop voluntary guidelines for corporate behavior. As part of the multinational agreement, the OECD countries further agreed on guidelines for governmental policy regarding multinational corporations, including nondiscrimination against foreign corporations, equitable treatment under international law, respect for contracts, and government cooperation to avoid beggar-thy-neighbor investment policies. Finally, the developed countries agreed to establish consultative procedures to monitor and review the agreed upon guidelines. Although the OECD code is voluntary and its guidelines are often deliberately vague, it may serve as a first step toward the development and implementation of international norms.[70]

Another limited international solution was suggested by a United Nations' study of multinational corporations. In 1972 the issue of foreign investment and political intervention became highly politicized internationally as a result of reported American public and private intervention in Chilean politics. Pressures from Third World Countries led to U.N. hearings and a study by the Group of Eminent Persons.[71] The report of the group called for the gathering of information on multinational corporations and for greater cooperation among states to develop a code of conduct for multinational corporations and to reach international agreements on direct foreign investment.

As a result of these recommendations, two new organizations were established within the United Nations: a Center on Transnational Corporations to gather and generate information on multinational corporations and an intergovernmental Commission on Transnational Corporations to act as a forum for the consideration of issues relating to multinational corporations, to conduct inquiries, and to supervise the center. The commission might serve as a forum for the development of norms and principles for international investment and for negotiations toward the harmonization of various national policies regarding foreign investment. Because it is a large (forty-eight member) governmental and very public forum, however, it will probably create confrontation, politicization, and little management. The commission may well become a forum for the making and rejecting of demands rather than for real negotiation, bargaining, and management.

There may be greater potential for the center. To establish and enforce rules regarding multinational corporations, it is necessary to know how they operate and what effect they have on national economies. The dearth of such information has been an important obstacle to control. The gathering of information on multinational activity and on governmental regulation of multinational corporations will be important functions for the center. Another function will be the development of yet another code of multinational conduct which will be presented to the commission and which may expand and complement the OECD effort.

One final form of international management of multinational corporations involves not a unified and centralized order but, rather, a complex system of bilateral or perhaps multilateral negotiations among states possibly leading to a series of agreements on specific matters, possibly leading to methods for mediating conflicts. Conflict of national laws in such areas as taxation, antitrust regulations, patents, export controls, and balance-of-payments controls may be harmonized through such negotiation. In the area of taxation, for example, the OECD has developed a draft convention containing proposals on many issues of taxation. Although never implemented, the treaty has served as a guide for subsequent bilateral negotiations and treaties among developed market economies.[72]

Another possible bilateral approach might be the establishment of arbitration, adjudication, or simply consultation procedures which might accompany regulations or take the place of regulations when agreed rules cannot be established. It does not seem politically possible to delegate authority to some international arbitration commission. The World Bank has set up such an organization called the International Center for the Settlement of Investment Disputes, but very few nations—particularly the underdeveloped nations—have adhered to this organization, and few disputes have been submitted to it. It is possible, however, to create institutions or processes to which countries or companies and countries desiring a solution could turn. Such commissions exist in the socialist states to manage state-corporate disputes. Extensive bilateral consultations have been developed between the United States and Canada to deal with such problems as export controls and antitrust.[73]

In conclusion, international management of multinational corporations is in a rudimentary state of development. Despite international tension and national uneasiness regarding multinational corporations, the perception of a common interest in management does not exist in developed market economies or in the one country that might mobilize the system for common action—the United States. Until an international consensus for management develops, international control of multinational corporations will be nonexistent or ineffective. The future of management in the coming years is not with international order but with national regulation.

NOTES

1. Direct investment involves control as opposed to portfolio investment which involves capital movement but not control. This chapter focuses on direct investment in the developed market economies. See Chapter 8 for investment problems in North South relations.

2. Mira Wilkins, *The Emergence of Multinational Enterprise: American Business Abroad from the Colonial Era to 1914* (Cambridge, Mass.: Harvard Univ. Press, 1970), p. 201.

3. Raymond Vernon, *Sovereignty at Bay: The Multinational Spread of U.S. Enterprises* (New York: Basic Books, 1971), p. 11.

4. United Nations, *Multinational Corporations in World Development* (New York: United Nations, 1973), pp. 130-136.

5. See Stephen Hymer and Robert Rowthorn, "Multinational Corporations and International Oligopoly: The Non-American Challenge," in Charles P. Kindleberger, ed., *The International Corporation* (Cambridge, Mass.: M.I.T. Press, 1971), pp. 57 91.

6. Louis T. Wells, Jr., "The Multinational Enterprise: What Kind of International Organization?" in Robert O. Keohane and Joseph S. Nye, Jr., eds., *Transnational Relations and World Politics* (Cambridge, Mass.: Harvard Univ. Press, 1972), pp. 97 114; John M. Stopford and Louis T. Wells, Jr., *Managing the Multinational Enterprise: Organization of the Firm and Ownership of the Subsidiaries,* (New York: Basic Books, 1972).

7. United Nations, *Multinational Corporations in World Development,* p. 14.

8. Richard N. Cooper, *The Economics of Interdependence: Economic Policy in the Atlantic Community* (New York: McGraw-Hill, 1968), p. 82.

9. Ibid., p. 86.

10. United Nations, *Multinational Corporations in World Development,* p. 148.

11. *Foreign Direct Investment in Canada* (Ottawa: Information Canada, 1972), p. 20.

12. United Nations, *Multinational Corporations in World Development,* pp. 16 17.

13. Ibid., pp. 164 169.

14. For national incentives, see Jack N. Behrman, *National Interests and the Multinational Enterprise: Tensions Among the North Atlantic Countries* (Englewood Cliffs, N.J.: Prentice-Hall, 1970), pp. 13-28.

15. See Robert Gilpin, *U.S. Power and the Multinational Corporation: The Political Economy of Foreign Direct Investment* (New York: Basic Books, 1975), pp. 99 112; Samuel P. Huntington, "Transnational Organizations in World Politics," *World Politics,* 25 (April 1973), 342 347.

16. Vernon, *Sovereignty at Bay,* pp. 65 77.

17. See Stephen H. Hymer, The International Operations of National Firms: A Study of Direct Investment, Ph.D. dissertation (M.I.T., 1960); Charles P. Kindleberger, *American Business Abroad: Six Lectures on Direct Investment* (New Haven, Conn.: Yale Univ. Press, 1969), pp. 1 36.

18. See John Fayerweather, "International Transmission of Resources," in *International Business Management: A Conceptual Framework* (New York: McGraw-Hill, 1969), pp. 15-50.

19. Cooper, *The Economics of Interdependence,* pp. 89 91.

20. See Harry G. Johnson, "The Efficiency and Welfare Implications of the Interna-

tional Corporation," in Kindleberger, ed., *The International Corporation*, pp. 35–56; Kindleberger, *American Business Abroad*.

21. See Stephen Hymer, "The Efficiency (Contradictions) of Multinational Corporations," *American Economic Review*, 60 (May 1970), 441–448.

22. See John H. Dunning, "Multinational Enterprises and Nation States," in A. Kapoor and Phillip D. Grub, eds., *The Multinational Enterprise in Transition* (Princeton, N.J.: Darwin Press, 1972), pp. 402–410; Raymond Vernon, "A Program of Research on Foreign Direct Investment," in C. Fred Bergsten, ed., *The Future of the International Economic Order: An Agenda for Research* (Lexington, Mass.: Lexington Books, 1973), pp. 93–113.

23. See Royal Commission on Canada's Economic Prospects, *Final Report* (Ottawa: Queen's Printer, 1958); Task Force on the Structure of Canadian Industry, *Foreign Ownership and the Structure of Canadian Industry* (Ottawa: Privy Council Office, 1968); *Foreign Direct Investment in Canada*. For private studies, see Rudolph G. Penner, "The Benefits of Foreign Investment in Canada, 1950 to 1956," *Canadian Journal of Economics and Political Science*, 32 (May 1966); A. E. Safarian, *Foreign Ownership of Canadian Industry* (Toronto: McGraw-Hill, 1966). For a critical analysis, see Kari Levitt, *Silent Surrender: The Multinational Corporation in Canada* (New York: St. Martin's, 1970).

24. Royal Commission on Canada's Economic Prospects, *Foreign Ownership and the Structure of Canadian Industry*, p. 37.

25. Gilles Y. Bertin, "Foreign Investment in France," in Isaiah A. Litvak and Christopher J. Maule, eds., *Foreign Investment: The Experience of Host Countries* (New York: Praeger, 1970), pp. 105–122.

26. John H. Dunning, "Multinational Enterprises and Nation States," pp. 406–408.

27. John H. Dunning, "The Role of American Investment in the British Economy," *Political and Economic Planning, Broadsheet No. 508* (February 1969).

28. See Royal Commission, *Foreign Ownership and the Structure of Canadian Industry* and *Foreign Direct Investment in Canada*; United Nations, *Multinational Corporations in World Development*; Behrman, *National Interests and the Multinational Enterprise*, pp. 32–84; Jean-Jacques Servan-Schreiber, *The American Challenge* (New York: Atheneum, 1968).

29. On this point, see Harry G. Johnson, "The Efficiency and Welfare Implications of the International Corporation."

30. Royal Commission, *Foreign Direct Investment in Canada*, pp. 183–211.

31. John Fayerweather, "Elite Attitudes Toward Multinational Firms: A Study of Britain, Canada, and France," *International Studies Quarterly*, 16 (December 1972), 472–490.

32. See Cooper, *The Economics of Interdependence*, pp. 98–103; Gilpin, *U.S. Power and the Multinational Corporation*; Elizabeth Jager, "Foreign Trade and Investment Act of 1972," *Columbia Journal of World Business*, 16 (March–April 1972), 16–18; Nat Goldfinger, "A Labor View of Foreign Investment and Trade Issues," in *United States International Economic Policy in an Interdependent World*, Paper I, Papers submitted to the Commission on International Trade and Investment Policy and published in conjunction with the Commission's Report to the President (Washington, D.C.: U.S. Government Printing Office, July 1971), pp. 913–928. For a discussion of the negative impact on the U.S. of foreign regulations on multinational corporations, see C. Fred Bergsten, "Coming Investment Wars?," *Foreign Affairs*, 53 (October 1974), 135–152. For a rebuttal of critical charges, see U.S. Tariff Commission, *Implications of Multinational Firms for World Trade and Investment and for U.S. Trade and Labor*, 93rd Congress, 1st Sess. (1973).

33. Fayerweather, "Elite Attitudes Toward Multinational Firms," pp. 481–485.

34. John Fayerweather, *Foreign Investment in Canada: Prospects for National Policy* (White Plains, N.Y.: International Arts and Sciences Press, 1973), p. 20.

35. Fayerweather, "Elite Attitudes Toward Multinational Firms," pp. 483–484.

36. See, for example, French attitudes regarding sensitive industries, in Allan W. Johnstone, *United States Direct Investment in France: An Investigation of the French Charges* (Cambridge, Mass.: M.I.T. Press, 1965), pp. 32–34.

37. See Behrman, *National Interests and the Multinational Enterprise*, pp. 69–84.

38. Royal Commission, *Foreign Direct Investment in Canada*, p. 428.

39. Johnstone, *United States Direct Investment in France*, pp. 31–32.

40. Royal Commission, *Foreign Direct Investment in Canada*, pp. 243–251.

41. *The New York Times*, August 15, 1973, pp. 47ff.

42. Behrman, *National Interests and the Multinational Enterprise*, pp. 73–76.

43. For an excellent discussion of home government interference, see Behrman, *National Interests and the Multinational Enterprise*, pp. 88–127.

44. Ibid., pp. 104–113.

45. See similar possibilities outlined in Royal Commission, *Foreign Direct Investment in Canada*, pp. 301–306.

46. Ibid., pp. 305–307.

47. See U.S. Senate, 93rd Congress, 1st and 2nd Sess., and 94th Congress, 1st and 2nd Sess., *Multinational Corporations and United States Foreign Policy*, Hearings Before the Subcommittee on Multinational Corporations of the Committee on Foreign Relations (Washington: U.S. Government Printing Office, 1975).

48. Dennis M. Ray, "Corporations and American Foreign Relations," *The Annals*, 403 (September 1972), pp. 80–92.

49. See Chapter 8 of this text for a discussion of International Telephone & Telegraph; U.S. Senate, *Multinational Corporations and United States Foreign Policy*; Jerome Levinson, "The Transnational Corporation and the Home Country," in *Conference on the Regulation of Transnational Corporations*, February 26, 1976 (New York: Columbia Journal of Transnational Law Association, 1976), pp. 17–22.

50. Robert W. Cox, "Labor and the Multinations," *Foreign Affairs*, 54 (January 1976), 344–365.

51. In Fayerweather, *Foreign Investment in Canada*, p. 32.

52. See Chapter 8 for Southern perceptions.

53. See M. Y. Yoshino, "Japan as Host to the International Corporation," in Kindleberger, *The International Corporation*, pp. 345–369; Lawrence B. Krause, "Evolution of Foreign Direct Investment: The United States and Japan," in Jerome B. Cohen, ed., *Pacific Partnership: United States–Japan Trade: Prospects and Recommendations for the Seventies* (Lexington, Mass.: Lexington Books for Japan Society, 1972), pp. 149–176; Noritake Kobayashi, "Foreign Investment in Japan," in Isaiah A. Litvak and Christopher J. Maule, eds., *Foreign Investment: The Experience of Host Countries*, pp. 123–160.

54. For Canadian policies, see Fayerweather, *Foreign Investment in Canada*, pp. 136–168.

55. House of Commons of Canada, 29th Parliament, 1st Sess., 21 Elizabeth II, 1973, Bill C-132.

56. Dunning, *The Role of American Investment in the British Economy*, pp. 160–162.

57. Charles Torem and William Laurence Craig, "Developments in the Control of Foreign Investment in France," *Michigan Law Review*, 70 (December 1971), 285–336.

58. See Seymour J. Rubin, "Developments in the Law and Institutions of International Economic Relations: The Multinational Enterprise at Bay," *The American Journal of International Law*, 68 (April 1974), 484; Theodore C. Sorensen, "Improper Payments Abroad: Perspectives and Proposals," *Foreign Affairs*, 54 (July 1976), 719–733.

59. Behrman, *National Interests and the Multinational Enterprise*, p. 154.

60. Nicolas Jéquier, "Computers," in Raymond Vernon, ed., *Big Business and the State: Changing Relations in Western Europe* (Cambridge, Mass.: Harvard Univ. Press, 1974), pp. 214–219.

61. See Schreiber, *The American Challenge*.

62. See J. J. Boddewyn, "Western European Policies Toward U.S. Investors," *The Bulletin*, Nos. 93–95 (March 1974), 45–63; Raymond Vernon, "Enterprise and Government in Western Europe" in Vernon, ed., *Big Business and the State* (Cambridge: Harvard University Press, 1974), pp. 3–24; Behrman, *National Interests and the Multinational Enterprise*, pp. 161–172.

63. Commission of the European Communities, *Multinational Undertakings and Community Regulations* (Communication from the Commission to the Council, presented on 8 November 1973), Bulletin of the European Communities, Supplement 15/73.

64. See Commission of the European Communities, *Industrial Policy in the Com-*

munity, Memorandum from the Commission to the Council (Brussels: European Economic Community, 1970); Commission of the European Communities, *Proposed Statute for the European Company, Supplement to Bulletin 9-1970* (Brussels: European Economic Community, 24 June 1970); Commission of the European Communities, *Draft Convention on the International Merger of Sociétés Anonymes and Report on the Draft*, Bulletin of the European Communities, Supplement 13/73.

65. For example, the International Civil Aviation Organization, the International Labor Organization, and the World Health Organization.

66. See Clair Wilcox, *A Charter for World Trade* (New York: Macmillan, 1949), pp. 145-148.

67. United Nations Economic and Social Council, *Report of the Ad Hoc Committee on Restrictive Business Practices* (New York: United Nations, 1953); General Agreement on Tariffs and Trade, *Decisions of the Seventeenth Session*, Dec. 5, 1960, p. 17.

68. See George W. Ball, "Cosmocorp: The Importance of Being Stateless," *Columbia Journal of World Business*, 2 (November–December 1967), 25-30.

69. Paul M. Goldberg and Charles Kindleberger, "Toward a GATT for Investment: A Proposal for Supervision of the International Corporation," *Law and Policy in International Business*, 2 (Summer 1970), 295-323.

70. Organization for Economic Cooperation and Development, *International Investment and Multinational Enterprises* (Paris: Organization for Economic Cooperation and Development, 1976).

71. United Nations, *Multinational Corporations in World Development*; United Nations, *Report of the Group of Eminent Persons to Study the Impact of Multinational Corporations on Development and on International Relations* (New York· United Nations, 1974).

72. See Seymour J. Rubin, "The International Firm and the National Jurisdiction" and "Developments in the Law and Institutions of International Economic Relations," in Kindleberger, *The International Corporation*, pp. 179-204, 475-488.

73. See Isaiah A. Litvak and Christopher J. Maule, "Canadian-United States Corporate Interface and Transnational Relations," *International Organization*, 28 (Autumn 1974), 711-731; David Leyton-Brown, "The Multinational Enterprise and Conflict in Canadian-American Relations," *International Organization*, 28 (Autumn 1974), 733-754.

Part Three

The North-South System

5

The North–South
System and the
Possibility of Change

Management problems of the North–South system are quite different from those of the Western system. For the system of the developed market economies, the dilemma is whether it is possible to achieve the necessary international political capability to manage mutually beneficial international economic relationships. In the North–South system of dependence, the management dilemma is whether it is possible to achieve the necessary international political capability to *create* a system which is mutually beneficial for all.

In the Western system, control is facilitated by a perceived common interest in the system. In the North–South system there is no such perception of a common interest. The developed market economies feel that the system of dependence, although perhaps not perfect, is legitimate because it provides them with significant benefits which they believe extend to the system as a whole. Southern states feel that the system is illegitimate because they have not enjoyed its economic rewards. From their viewpoint, the system has hindered their economic development.

The management processes of the North–South system are also quite different from those of the Western system. In the West there is a relatively highly developed system of control, consisting of international organizations, elite networks, processes of negotiation, agreed norms, and rules of the game. Although power is unequally distributed in the West, all members have access to both formal and informal management systems. In North–South relations, in contrast, there is no well-developed system with access for all. The South has been regularly excluded from the formal and informal processes of system management. North–South relations are controlled by the North as a subsidiary of the Western system. Understandably, the North perceives this structure as legitimate, whereas the South perceives it as illegitimate.

Thus, the policy of the North has been to maintain the system of dependence, whereas the policy of the South has been to change it. It is the conflict between the powerful North seeking to preserve the status quo and the growing pressures for change from the South that is the key political dynamic of North–South international economic relations. The central political problem of the North–South system is whether it is possible for the South to change the system of dependence.

Southern efforts to alter the international economic system have focused on two obstacles to change: the present international market and management structure. A key problem is whether the existing economic system can be changed or whether it must be destroyed and replaced by an entirely new system capable of providing economic benefits for the South. The reform of management will be determined by the South's ability to influence the North, the North's ability and susceptibility to acquiesce to a modification of the system of management and the distribution of rewards, and the combined North–South capacity to reform the system or create a totally new one.

Three important schools of thought have offered different theories regarding the problem and the possibility of change: the liberal school, the Marxist–radical school, and the structuralist school.

THE LIBERALS

Liberal theories of economic development have been optimistic about the prospects for Southern development within the existing international market structure.[1] Indeed, according to the liberal school, contact with the developed market economies is an important means of promoting development. The major problems of development, in this view, are weaknesses in the various factors of production, especially capital and labor. Trade, foreign investment, and foreign aid are seen as crucial factors in overcoming these weaknesses.

Trade, according to liberal analyses, acts as an engine of growth. Specialization according to comparative advantage and international trade, it is argued, increases income. Specialization and trade in products particularly suited to the national factor endowment enable more efficient resource allocation and greater earnings. Such specialization is especially important for underdeveloped countries because they tend to have small domestic markets. The additional income may be translated into savings and may then be used to promote development through domestic expenditures for improvement of production or for import of necessary capital equipment.

This view also sees foreign trade as having an important indirect effect on development, by providing material goods necessary for development; disseminating technology, knowledge, managerial skills, and entrepreneurship; encouraging capital inflow through international investment; and stimulating competition.[2] Foreign investment is seen to bring in other important skills such as management and technology which increase productivity.[3]

And foreign aid from developed market economies, while not a market relationship, is believed to help fill resource gaps in underdeveloped countries by, for example, providing capital, technology, and education.

THE MARXISTS

Marxist theories take the opposite view of the international market system.[4] An equitable distribution of benefits, it is argued, cannot occur within the international capitalist system. Southern countries are poor and exploited because of their history as subordinate elements in the world capitalist system, and this condition will persist for as long as they remain part of that system. The international market is under the monopoly control of developed economies, and thus operates to the detriment of the underdeveloped countries tied to it. Quite simply, international market operations enable developed countries to extract the economic wealth of underdeveloped countries for their own use.

Trade between North and South is a process of unequal exchange, as control of the international market by developed capitalist countries leads to a declining price for the raw materials produced by the South and a rising price for industrial products produced by the North. Thus the terms of trade of the international market are structured against the South. In addition, international trade encourages the South to concentrate on backward forms of production which prevent development.

Foreign investment further hinders and distorts Southern development, often by controlling the most dynamic local industries and expropriating the economic surplus of these sectors via repatriation of profits, royalty fees, and licenses. According to many Marxist arguments, there is, in fact, a net outflow of capital from the South to the North. In addition, foreign investment contributes to unemployment by establishing capital-intensive production, aggravating uneven income distribution, displacing local capital and local entrepreneurs, adding to the emphasis on production for export, and promoting undesirable consumption patterns.

Another dimension of capitalist creation and perpetuation of underdevelopment is the international financial system. Trade and investment remove capital from the South and necessitate Southern borrowing from Northern financial institutions, both public and private. But debt service and repayment further drain Third World wealth. Finally, foreign aid serves to reinforce the distorted development of the Third World by promoting foreign investment and trade at the expense of true development and by extracting wealth through debt service. Reinforcing these external market structures of dependence, according to Marxist theory, are clientele social classes within the underdeveloped countries. Local elites which have a vested interest in the structure of dominance and a monopoly of domestic power cooperate with international capitalist elites to perpetuate the international capitalist system.

The result of international market operations and the existence of the clientele elite perpetuate dependence, so that any development under the international capitalist system is uneven, distorted, and at best partial.

THE STRUCTURALISTS

Structuralist analysis, like Marxist analysis, argues that the international market structure perpetuates backwardness and dependency in the South and encourages dominance by the North. Gunnar Myrdal, a leading structuralist theorist, argued that the market tends to favor the already well endowed and thwart the underdeveloped. Unregulated international trade and capital movements will accentuate, not diminish, international inequalities.[5]

The structural bias of the international market, according to this school, rests in large part on the inequalities of the international trading system. Trade does not serve as an engine of growth but actually widens the North–South gap. It does so, first, because of declining terms of trade for the South. Inelasticity of demand for the primary product exports of the less developed countries and the existence of a competitive international market for those products leads to a declining price for Third World exports. Second, the monopoly structure of Northern markets and rising demand for manufactured goods leads to rising prices for the industrial products of the North. Thus, under normal market conditions international trade actually transfers income from South to North.

International trade, it is also believed, has negative effects on national development for yet another reason. Southern economies' specialization and concentration on backward export industries do not fuel the rest of the economy as projected by the liberals. Instead, trade creates an advanced export sector which has little or no dynamic effect on the rest of the economy, and which drains resources from the rest of the economy. Thus trade creates a dual economy composed of a developed and isolated export sector and an underdeveloped economy in general.

Foreign investment, the second part of the structural bias, often avoids the South where profits and security are lower than in developed market economies. When investment does flow to the South, it tends to concentrate in export sectors thereby aggravating the dual economy and the negative effects of trade. Finally, foreign investment leads to a flow of profits and interest to the developed, capital-exporting North.

ECONOMIC CHANGE

The structuralist analysis of the international market is quite similar to the Marxist analysis and quite effective in pointing out weaknesses in the traditional liberal theory. There is an important point, however, at which the Marxist and structuralist theories diverge. Structuralist theory argues that the international capitalist system can be reformed, that the natural processes can be regulated. Although various theorists differ as to the preferred forms of such regulation—foreign aid, protection, access to Northern markets—they all believe that industrialization can be achieved within a reformed international market and that such industrialization will narrow the development gap.

Marxist theory, on the other hand, argues that the capitalist system is immutable. Developed market economies are unable to accept a reformed system. The only change possible is revolution: destruction of the international capitalist system and its replacement with an international socialist system. Two general explanations are offered for the inability of the North to accept reform.

One explanation rests on the argument that developed capitalist economies are unable to absorb the economic surplus or profits generated by the capitalist system of production.[6] Capitalist states are unable to absorb their rising surplus internally through consumption because worker income does not grow so fast as capitalist profits. To prevent unemployment and the inevitable crisis of capitalism resulting from overproduction and underconsumption, developed market economies invest excess capital in and export excess production to underdeveloped countries. Another way to absorb rising surplus and prevent the crisis of capitalism, according to some, is to invest in the military at home, which in turn leads to pressure for expansion abroad. All these forms of external expansion, it is argued, are functionally necessary for the system. They absorb economic surplus which if not absorbed would lead to the collapse of the capitalist system. Developed market economies need dominance, dependence, and imperialism.

A second explanation of the necessity of capitalist imperialism derives from the need for Southern raw materials.[7] Capitalist economies depend on Southern imports, and the desire to control access to those supplies leads to Northern dominance.

Arguments that dominance is necessary for the North do not withstand empirical examination. On the contrary, evidence suggests that the South is not necessary for the North and that underdeveloped countries, with perhaps a few exceptions, may be increasingly irrelevant for developed market economies.

First, the developed market economies seem structurally able to absorb their economic surplus. Certainly, developed economies have faced a critical problem of maintaining aggregate demand at acceptable levels. But it seems that these states have solved the problem internally through various policies which are part of the modern welfare state: income redistribution, fiscal and monetary policy, public social expenditures.

Second, foreign investment, especially in less developed markets, is not of vital economic importance for developed market economies, as the case of the United States, the major foreign investor, illustrates. Foreign investment is a relatively small percentage of total American investment. In 1972 U.S. foreign direct investment amounted to $94 billion, whereas total investment was in the trillions of dollars. Furthermore, the South does not constitute the major area of U.S. foreign investment and is, in fact, declining in importance. In 1972 underdeveloped countries accounted for 27 percent of all United States foreign direct investment, whereas developed market economies accounted for 68 percent; in 1960 U.S. direct foreign investment in the South accounted for 35 percent versus an investment of 61 percent in developed market economies.[8]

Moreover, it appears that income from underdeveloped countries is not of vital economic importance to the United States. In 1972, U.S. earnings on foreign investment were $8 billion versus gross domestic business earnings of $124 billion and gross national product of $1,155 billion. Although Southern investment is a small part of total foreign investment, earnings from underdeveloped countries do account for a significant percentage of total foreign earnings: in 1972 a little over $4 billion of the $8 billion total came from less developed countries Clearly, returns are greater in underdeveloped than in developed countries. Nevertheless, in 1972 Southern earnings accounted for only 3.4 percent of gross domestic business earnings and for an infinitesimal part of total GNP, and, importantly, 79.0 percent of these earnings came from investment in petroleum versus only 11.5 percent from nonpetroleum earnings in less developed countries.[9] In sum, U.S. investment and investment earnings in underdeveloped countries are significant but hardly crucial to the American economy as a whole.

Trade with the South is also not of crucial economic importance to the North and, like investment, is of decreasing significance. In 1960 exports of developed market economies to underdeveloped countries accounted for 13.8 percent of total world trade, whereas in 1969 they accounted for 11.0 percent. Similarly, exports from less developed to developed countries accounted for 15.5 percent of world trade in 1960 versus 13.3 percent in 1969.[10] According to one study actual market sales to underdeveloped countries do not exceed 3.0–3.5 percent of the output of American industry.[11]

Thus, the case for dependence as a necessary outlet for capitalist surplus does not seem sustainable. Underdeveloped countries do provide significant earnings for developed market economies and are important investment and export outlets, but they are not necessary for developed market economies and are in fact declining in importance for the North.

The second Marxist explanation of the necessity of Northern dominance rests on Northern dependence on Southern raw materials. Certain raw materials are critical to developed market economies, but raw materials in general are not so significant as Marxist theory suggests, and, in the areas where they are significant, raw material dependence may work to the detriment of the developed countries, not to their advantage.

The United States, and to a greater extent the Europeans and Japanese, depend on the import of certain important raw materials such as bauxite and alumina, chromium, copper, lead, manganese, nickel, phosphate, tin, tungsten, and zinc. In only a few cases, however, are the major suppliers of these materials Southern countries. Copper, iron ore, lead, manganese, phosphate, tin, and petroleum are examples.[12]

Furthermore, foreign dependence may often be more a matter of choice than of necessity, more a matter of price than of resource dependence. Substitutes or alternate sources of supply of many materials exist but are not being used because of cost considerations. Imports are used because they are cheaper, not because they are essential on a long-term perspective. The recent oil crisis demonstrates that, for even the most crucial raw materials, there are substitutes at a price and over a period of time.[13]

The raw materials argument, however, is the strongest case for Northern economic dependence on the South. The lower cost of Southern raw materials, in particular, enhances corporate profits. Yet recent events suggest that such dependence is the basis not for perpetual development of underdevelopment but for potential Third World bargaining power. The one area of Northern need for and profitability from the South may turn into the advantage of the South.

In conclusion, the arguments that dominance and exploitation of the South are necessary for the capitalist economies as a whole do not stand the empirical test. The South is important but not vital.

There is, however, a Marxist argument which contends that dependence, while not important for capitalist economies as a whole, is necessary for a particular class within those economies, specifically for the capitalist class that dominates that economy and polity.[14] According to these theories, capitalist groups, especially those managing multinational corporations, inevitably seek to dominate underdeveloped countries in their quest for profit. Because these groups control the governments of the developed states, they are able to use governmental tools for their own particular class ends.

To evaluate this theory, it is necessary to determine whether the capitalist class as a whole has a common interest in underdeveloped countries despite the fact that most capitalists do not profit, as has been shown, from foreign trade and investment. One theorist argues that the entire capitalist class has an interest in dominance and foreign expansion, including those capitalists having no relation to or profit from such expansion.[15] This is true, he argues, because there is a common interest in expansion because it serves to maintain the system as a whole. Yet the preceding analysis of the macroeconomic importance of the Third World suggests that underdeveloped countries are marginal and relatively more marginal now than in the last half century for the developed countries. Thus it is not possible to argue that the capitalist class as a whole has an interest in the South and in dominance because only a small percentage of that class profits from dominance and because the system itself is not dependent on dominance.

A stronger argument is that some powerful capitalists, such as the managers of multinational corporations, have a crucial interest in the South and in Northern dominance. Clearly, certain firms and certain groups profit from the existing structure of the international market. The crucial question is the role of these firms and these groups in Northern governmental policy. It seems clear that groups interested in Northern economic dominance play an important role in the politics of developed market economies and have an important impact on the foreign policies of those countries. The 1974 and 1975 investigations of the United States Senate Subcommittee on Multinational Corporations have revealed the crucial role of multinational corporations in American foreign policy in Chile and in the Middle East, for example.[16] As one radical theorist argued,

It is not necessary that the beneficiaries of imperialism dominate all policy making in order that the government be induced to undertake imperialist activities that serve particular class interests. It is only necessary that the beneficiaries exercise disproportionate influence in the sphere of foreign policy.[17]

But certain elements of the capitalist class need not inevitably dominate foreign policy in developed market economies. In the Middle East, for example, despite the vast importance of oil earnings and of petroleum, American foreign policy has not always reflected the interests of American oil companies.

On balance, then, dominance is important for the developed market economies and is especially important for certain groups within those economies. But dominance is neither necessary nor inevitable. There is a possibility of change. Under the right political circumstances, developed market economies can afford to respond to underdeveloped economies' demands. The system is exploitative now, but it is not necessarily and inevitably exploitative.

If, as it is argued, it is possible to change the system, the problem is to determine whether the underdeveloped countries can effectively make demands for such change in the management and the distribution of rewards and under what circumstances the North can be induced to respond. It is to that problem that the analysis of North–South relations in Chapters 6–9 is directed.

NOTES

1. For examples of liberal theory, see Gottfried Haberler, *International Trade and Economic Development* (Cairo: National Bank of Egypt, 1959); Ragnar Nurkse, *Equilibrium and Growth in the World Economy* (Cambridge, Mass.: Harvard Univ. Press, 1961); Gerald M. Meier, *International Trade and Development* (New York: Harper & Row, 1963). For a survey of the literature, see John Pincus, *Trade, Aid and Development: The Rich and Poor Nations* (New York: McGraw-Hill, 1967), pp. 89–146.

2. Haberler, *International Trade and Economic Development*, pp. 10–14.

3. Ragnar Nurkse, *Problems of Capital Formation for Underdeveloped Countries* (London: Basil Blackwell, 1953).

4. For examples of Marxist theory, see Paul A. Baran, *The Political Economy of Growth* (New York: Monthly Review, 1968); Arghiri Emmanuel, *Unequal Exchange: A Study of the Imperialism of Trade* (New York: Monthly Review Press, 1972); André Gunder Frank, *Capitalism and Underdevelopment in Latin America*, rev. ed. (New York: Monthly Review Press, 1969); André Gunder Frank, *Latin America: Underdevelopment or Revolution* (New York: Monthly Review Press, 1969); Pierre Jalee, *The Pillage of the Third World*, trans., Mary Klopper (New York: Monthly Review Press, 1968); Theotonio Dos Santos, "The Structure of Dependence," in K. T. Fann and Donald C. Hodges, eds., *Readings in U.S. Imperialism* (Boston: Porter Sargent, 1971), pp. 225–236; Thomas E. Weisskopf, "Capitalism, Underdevelopment and the Future of the Poor Countries," in Jagdish N. Bhagwati, ed., *Economics and World Order: From the 1970's to the 1990's* (New York: Macmillan, 1972), pp. 43–77.

5. See Gunnar Myrdal, *Rich Lands and Poor: The Road to World Prosperity* (New York: Harper & Row, 1957).

6. Paul A. Baran and Paul M. Sweezy, *Monopoly Capital: An Essay on the American Economic and Social Order* (New York: Monthly Review, 1966). These authors

define economic surplus as "the difference between what a society produces and the costs of producing it" (p. 9). For a critical analysis of the concept, see Benjamin J. Cohen, *The Question of Imperialism: The Political Economy of Dominance and Dependence* (New York: Basic Books, 1973), pp. 104–121.

7. See, for example, Pierre Jalee, *Imperialism in the Seventies*, trans., R. and M. Sokolov (New York: The Third World Press, 1972).

8. U.S. Bureau of the Census, *Statistical Abstract of the United States: 1974*, 95th ed. (Washington, D.C.: Government Printing Office, 1974), p. 781.

9. Ibid., pp. 373 and 781. This critical analysis of Marxist theory relies heavily on the analysis by S. M. Miller, Roy Bennett, and Cyril Alapatt, "Does the U.S. Economy Require Imperialism?." *Social Policy*, 1 (September–October 1970), 13 19.

10. United Nations Conference on Trade and Development, *Review of Trade and Development: 1970* (New York: United Nations, 1970), p. 45.

11. Miller et al., "Does the U.S. Economy Require Imperialism?"

12. U.S. Council on International Economic Policy, Critical Imported Raw Materials (Washington, D.C.: Government Printing Office, December 1974), pp. 24, 43, 45, 46.

13. Cohen, *The Question of Imperialism*, pp. 138 141.

14. See Arthur MacEwan, "Capitalist Expansion, Ideology and Intervention," *Review of Radical Political Economics*, 4 (Spring 1972), 36 58; Thomas E. Weisskopf, "Theories of American Imperialism: A Critical Evaluation," *Review of Radical Political Economics*, 6 (Fall 1974), 41 60.

15. MacEwan, "Capitalist Expansion, Ideology and Intervention."

16. U.S. Senate, *Multinational Corporations and United States Foreign Policy*, Hearings before the Subcommittee on Multinational Corporations of the Committee on Foreign Relations, 93rd Congress, 2nd Sess. (Washington: Government Printing Office, 1975).

17. Weisskopf, "Theories of American Imperialism," p. 51.

6

The Use of Aid

Foreign economic aid is frequently advocated by academicians and policy makers as a road to development. In the postwar period, public concessional funds for promoting development became a regular part of Northern foreign policies. Economic aid was used because it fitted well the desire of the developed market states to maintain the existing structure of international economic relations and at the same time to garner political influence in the developing world by responding to Southern desires for development. Aid, however, was a second-best solution for the South, for it involved neither a change in the management of North–South relations nor a meaningful redistribution of economic benefits.

AID IN THE EARLY POSTWAR ORDER

During the formative period of Bretton Woods, independent developing states attempted to make the postwar order a better environment for their economic development. At Bretton Woods, at Havana, and, finally, at the new United Nations, the less developed countries attempted to modify the projects and plans of the North to incorporate the goal of economic development. Development, they argued, was not just of interest to them, it was essential for realizing the postwar goals of international prosperity and peace.

The major effort of the developing countries in this early period was an attempt to modify the international trading system.[1] There were, however, some limited aid-related efforts. One such effort was an attempt to influence the statutes of the International Bank for Reconstruction and Development. As its name suggests, the IBRD had two purposes: the rebuilding of war-torn countries and the financing of further development of all IMF-IBRD members, developed and less developed.

Because of debt default in the interwar period, both developed and underdeveloped countries expected to have difficulty attracting private capital after the war. The World Bank was intended to deal with the confidence problem by guaranteeing private loans and providing funds for direct investment at market interest rates. The effort of the less developed countries, primarily the Latin American countries, at Bretton Woods was to ensure that development—meaning development for both industrial and developing countries—would have the same priority as reconstruction.[2] Another limited effort by the less developed countries was to include provisions in the Havana Charter for supporting World Bank loan applications and for aid in the form of nonremunerative capital loans.[3]

In these early years the North, and especially the Northern power in a position to transfer funds to the less developed countries, rejected aid as a route to development.[4] The United States in the immediate postwar years was not unconcerned with economic growth. Indeed, economic development was considered an integral part of the American plan for a postwar order built on economic prosperity and international peace. But, in the opinion of U.S. government officials, economic development did not require public international capital. Domestic efforts in Southern states and domestic, not external, capital, it was argued, would have to be the primary means of economic development. Such domestic efforts would be enhanced and the need for external capital reduced by trade liberalization. Expansion of trade would substitute for capital inflows.

While domestic efforts would have to be the main road to development, there would be, it was admitted, some need for external capital. However, this capital would have to be private. To promote development, Southern countries should stimulate the flow of such private capital. Trade liberalization would stimulate foreign private investment by improving export opportunities for that investment, and the creation of a favorable investment climate in underdeveloped countries would attract foreign capital. A favorable climate could be achieved by rejecting expropriation, following acceptable monetary and fiscal policies, and minimizing governmental competition with private business.

Finally, the United States recognized that in some cases public external financing might be appropriate. Such financing, however, would be limited in amount and would be offered on market or hard, not concession or soft, terms. Furthermore, according to the United States the flow of such financing to the South would have to await the fulfillment of a higher priority: European postwar reconstruction. Indeed, that reconstruction, it was argued, was important for Third World development because it would reopen European trade and European capital markets for the South.

Because of prevailing Northern views regarding aid and because of the weakness of the less developed countries in pressing for the few limited changes they sought regarding aid, no provision was made for public concessional funds to promote development in the postwar international economic order. The World Bank, the one international institution which might have provided aid for less developed countries, was unsuited for that task. In the end it was determined that the emphasis of IBRD activity would be reconstruction and not development.

Whereas the less developed countries had sought to establish development as the primary purpose, Europeans and especially the Soviet Union pressed for reconstruction as the major objective of the new organization. The articles of agreement theoretically gave equal weight to reconstruction and development but stressed that "special regard" be given by the bank to aiding countries which had suffered "great devastation from enemy occupation or hostilities."[5] Furthermore, the developed countries, which held the majority of stock in the bank and which thus controlled its policies, placed the emphasis on reconstruction in actual bank activity.[6]

The articles of agreement and their later interpretation by the bank's presidents and directors also set important limits on bank funds available for Southern economic development. The criteria for bank loans were such as to discourage many economically feasible loans. In keeping with the predominant Northern development philosophy, the bank was not to compete with private capital and, indeed, was to encourage the flow of private capital as the main source of external financing. The requirements that, except for extraordinary exceptions, only foreign exchange costs could be financed by the bank and that loans could be made only for specific projects limited the role of the bank in numerous development projects.

The terms of IBRD loans were also conservative. The bank made only hard loans. Interest rates reflected the market rate, and loans were to be repaid in hard currencies. The interest rate and the criterion that loans should be self-liquidating hampered flows to many of the poorest countries.

Other important restrictions, many not strictly economic, were placed on borrowers. The bank denied loans for such reasons as previous bad debts (which may have had no bearing on the ability of a country to repay the bank loan), governmental policies favoring state ownership of business, and other economic and political policies which the bank determined were unfavorable for economic development.

Finally, in keeping with Northern philosophy and with the tight capital situation of the time, funds available for even such restricted financing were limited. Total loans to developing countries in the period up to June 30, 1952, amounted to only $583 million.[7]

In the early 1950s the interest of less developed countries in aid increased. Growing public pressure for development, the failure to achieve international trade reform to encourage development, and the inadequacies of the IBRD led less developed countries to seek public concessional funds for economic development. Because they had been excluded from a voice in the postwar economic institutions, the less developed countries turned to the United Nations and to individual developed states in their quest.

It was in the United Nations—in the Economic and Social Council (ECOSOC) and its subcommittees, in the General Assembly and its subcommittees—that the less developed countries began to formulate and eventually to coordinate common demands for aid and for greater participation in the management of aid. Early efforts by the less developed countries in the United Nations consisted of ad hoc action in support of a public international agency to make soft loans and grants for Southern development.

The first major proposal for such an institutional change was made in a report in March 1949 by the Subcommission on Economic Development of the Economic and Social Council. The subcommission was critical of the World Bank's ability to "make a significant contribution to the massive investments required for economic development" and mentioned "the possibilities of opening up new sources of international finance under United Nations auspices."[8] The Indian chairman of the subcommittee went further and proposed a new international organization, the United Nations Economic Development Administration, financed by contributions from member governments which would make loans with liberal terms of repayment and with only nominal interest rates.

This proposal was rejected by the developed countries. Indicative of the Northern attitude was the response of the American expert of the subcommission to the proposal for an Economic Development Administration. The less developed countries, he said,

> should rely fundamentally on the International Bank for Reconstruction and Development for financing or collaborating in financing closely circumscribed types of projects to development not readily susceptible of implementation by purely private financing.[9]

Similar proposals put forward by the less developed countries were rejected by the developed countries. In 1951 a report of a committee of experts recommended the establishment of an International Development

Authority (IDA) to make grants for economic development. Despite unanimous Northern opposition, the underdeveloped countries were able to secure passage of a General Assembly resolution calling for the establishment of a special fund to make soft loans to underdeveloped countries. The resolution, however, made no specific provisions for such a fund and, in any case, carried no power over the North.[10]

In 1953 a committee of experts presented a plan for a Special United Nations Fund for Economic Development (SUNFED). This first SUNFED proposal called not only for soft loans for the South but also for Southern participation in the management of the fund. Representation on the executive board was not to be weighted according to financial contributions, as in the IBRD, but was to be divided between contributors and likely recipients. Both the soft loan and the management provisions were unacceptable to the North, which successfully opposed SUNFED.[11]

Less developed countries also appealed to individual Northern states, primarily to the United States, the only country in the early postwar years able to transfer significant resources to underdeveloped countries. At the end of the 1940s, the rhetoric of American foreign policy suggested that aid for development was a major aspect of American foreign policy. President Truman had announced in the famous "Point Four" of his inaugural address in 1949 that:

> We must embark on a bold new program for making the benefits of our scientific advances and industrial progress available for the improvement and growth of underdeveloped areas.[12]

And the International Development Act of 1950, which implemented Point Four, suggested that development assistance would become a major American foreign policy:

> It is the policy of the United States to aid the efforts of the peoples of economically underdeveloped areas to develop their resources and improve their living conditions.[13]

Despite this rhetoric, American policy regarding demands of the less developed countries, for bilateral aid closely resembled American responses in international forums: emphasis was to be on self-help; where capital was needed, it should be primarily private capital; where private capital was unavailable, external financing should be carried on primarily by the IBRD. In this period the United States carried out only two programs for economic aid. The Export-Import Bank gave market-term loans for financing of American trade, and the technical assistance program offered a small number of grants. In the 1950–1955 period, bilateral overseas development aid (i.e., public transfers of funds) from all of the developed market countries averaged $1.8 billion a year, and multilateral flows amounted to $100 million a year.[14]

THE TURN TO AID

Not until the second postwar decade did aid emerge as an important form of North-South economic interaction. Beginning in the mid-1950s as a result of several changes in the international system, Northern policies toward economic aid changed rather dramatically.

The first change was the emergence of less developed countries as increasingly active, albeit weak, actors in international relations. In the two decades following World War II, the nineteenth-century empires disintegrated and much of Africa and Asia achieved political independence. Following a compromise between the United States and the Soviet Union in 1955, new states were regularly admitted to the United Nations. By the end of the second postwar decade the United Nations had 122 members of which 87 were developing countries. Within the General Assembly and ECOSOC, the less developed countries began to form groups and make coordinated demands.

The major aid focus of the less developed countries was SUNFED. Although SUNFED was opposed by the North and especially by the United States, the Southern group refused to let the proposal die. Dissatisfied with the World Bank and with bilateral aid programs, they continued to press and maneuver for the adoption of their proposed organization. While SUNFED never came into being, the persistent efforts of the South helped to induce some changes. They led, first, to the establishment in 1959 of the United Nations Special Fund (UNSF) to finance through grants various preinvestment projects. Contributions to UNSF were voluntary and never approached even the very limited goal of $100 million. The pressure for SUNFED was also instrumental in important revisions in the World Bank system, specifically in the establishment of the International Finance Corporation (IFC) and the IDA.[15]

While the United Nations remained the primary focus for Southern pressure, another forum, a harbinger of things to come, developed at this time. This was the international conference of developing countries. The first such conference was held at Bandung, where twenty-nine Asian and African countries met in April 1955 to discuss their common problems. Although most of the discussion at Bandung centered on political problems, such as decolonization and nonalignment, various economic proposals also emerged. The major economic recommendations called for changes in trading relations, particularly for the establishment of commodity agreements to improve trade with the less developed countries. There were also recommendations for the establishment of a new financial aid institution and for the allocation by the World Bank of a greater part of its resources to Africa and Asia.[16]

In the process of discussing common political and economic problems at Bandung, the South took an important step in the development of a strategy toward the North. For the first time a large bloc of underdeveloped countries met in their own forum and away from institutions dominated by the North, where they concentrated on the attempt to achieve political and economic cooperation, to form a Southern group with specific and coherent views and demands.

Thus, from the mid-1950s the less developed countries were becoming more numerous, more outspoken, and somewhat more united and specific in their demands for international economic reform. But these changes alone did not lead the developed countries to turn to aid. The real change came when the South acquired political and security importance for the North. Demands for economic change were finally considered by the North not because the South made more noise or even more effective noise, but because the developed market economies began to perceive a threat to their traditional position of political dominance and security in the underdeveloped world.

The first and most important shift occurred in American policy, commencing in the early 1950s. Following the Communist's takeover of China in 1949 and the Korean conflict of 1950, the United States expanded its security interests to certain parts of the South, particularly to those states bordering the Soviet Union and the Chinese People's Republic and to certain Middle Eastern countries, and began a fairly significant military assistance program for aid to these Southern countries. While this aid concentrated on military assistance to bolster local armed forces, funds were also given for economic development designed to support local military capability.[17] Several important official and unofficial reports at this time developed the argument that there was a link between American security and Southern economic development.[18]

But it was not until the Soviet Union began to pose a threat in the Third World that the link between development and national security emerged as part of American foreign policy. During the Stalinist era the Soviet Union had little interest in the South. The only Soviet aid that flowed to the South had gone to local Communist parties. Following Stalin's death in 1953, however, the Soviet Union shifted its policy. In mid-1953 the Soviet Union announced that it would reverse its policy and contribute to the United Nations Expanded Programme of Technical Assistance (EPTA). At the same time, the Soviet Union began to negotiate a series of trade agreements with Southern countries to develop both business and political relations with the South.

In 1956, in a major statement, the Report of the Central Committee to the Twentieth Party Congress, Nikita Khrushchev announced a new Soviet policy in the Third World:

> These countries although they do not belong to the Socialist world system, can draw on its achievements in building an independent national economy and in raising their people's living standards. Today they need not go begging to their former oppressors for modern equipment. They can get it in the Socialist countries, free from any political or military obligations.[19]

In effect, Khrushchev announced that competition with the West was to be expanded to the less developed countries. Even before the Khrushchev speech the Soviet Union had begun to enter into aid agreements. In 1955 the Soviet Union concluded an arms agreement with Egypt and began negotiations for Soviet financing of the Aswan Dam. In that same year the Russians announced that they would build a steel mill in India. Syria, Indonesia, and Afghanistan also became the recipients of Soviet aid.[20]

Because of the new Soviet interest and activity in the South, Third World demands for development took on greater importance. The emerging Southern states became an area of competition in the Cold War. As in 1947–1949, when the Soviet Union appeared as a threat to the West in Europe, the United States reevaluated its previous policy; as it had with the Marshall Plan, the United States turned to a new program of foreign economic aid.

In 1956 and 1957 U.S. policy makers turned their attention for the first time to a serious consideration of foreign economic aid to developing countries. The result was the determination that economic assistance to the South could be a powerful tool in the Cold War. As one influential study put it,

> a comprehensive and sustained program of American economic assistance aimed at helping the free underdeveloped countries to create the conditions for self-sustaining growth can, in the short run, materially reduce the danger of conflict triggered by aggressive minor powers, and can, say in 2 to 3 decades, result in an overwhelming preponderance of societies with a successful record of solving their problems without resort to coercion or violence. The establishment of such a preponderance of stable, effective and democratic societies gives the best promise of a favorable settlement of the cold war and of a peaceful, progressive world environment.[21]

This conclusion was based on several calculations. There was the conviction that because of the widening Cold War the West had to respond to growing Southern demands for economic development. There was also a recognition that the postwar policy—economic development through trade liberalization supplemented by IBRD assistance—was economically ineffective and politically unacceptable to the less developed countries. The failure of past policy and the need to do something left two principal possibilities: the reform of international trade or the granting of foreign economic aid. Trade reform was the preferred solution of the less developed countries, but meeting the trade demands of the less developed countries would mean, in Western eyes, undoing the work of trade liberalization, which was a linchpin of the postwar economic order, and altering the advantages from trade which the North gleaned from that system.[22]

By comparison, economic aid seemed a relatively painless solution. According to economic analysis growth of the less developed countries was constrained primarily by insufficient capital investment, which was in turn constrained by insufficient savings and/or foreign exchange. External financial assistance, it was argued, would fill this resource gap and thus make growth possible. Capital assistance plus technical assistance to improve use of both domestic and external capital would enable the creation of conditions for self-sustaining economic growth.

This economic growth would have important political consequences. It would, according to one study, provide a constructive outlet for nationalism, encourage social progress, develop political leadership, and encourage confidence in the democratic process.[23] Finally, aid would serve American foreign policy by "help[ing] the societies of the world develop in ways that will not menace our security—either as a result of their own internal dynamics or because they are weak enough to be used as tools by others."[24] In sum, aid would lead to development, which would lead to political stability, which would lead to states' friendlier attitude toward the West.

The shift in American attitudes toward foreign aid was paralleled by a similar shift in the policies of other developed market economies, especially among the former imperial powers, France and the United Kingdom. Aid policies of these countries grew not out of the Cold War but out of the history of colonialism. Close cultural, economic, and political ties were established between metropole and colony during the years of the British and French Empires and were not necessarily severed at the time of independence. These historical connections plus the very real interest in maintaining a sphere of influence and of economic interest in the former colonies led in the late 1950s to the development of a policy of foreign aid by the former imperial powers.[25]

The principal result of the new link between aid and Northern foreign policy was the expansion of bilateral foreign aid programs. In the United States the Development Loan Fund (DLF) was established in 1958 with an appropriation of $300 million. By 1961 the DLF was allocated $600 million.[26] Then, after Vice-President Nixon was stoned and mobbed on a trip to Latin America in 1958 and after the Cuban Revolution of 1960, major new aid programs for Latin America were developed. In 1958 the United States reversed its long-standing opposition and agreed to the establishment of the Inter-American Development Bank. Of the bank's initial capital of $1 billion, $350 million was provided by the United States.[27] In 1960 President Kennedy proposed an Alliance for Progress, a vast program of economic aid to Latin America. Between 1961 and 1969, $4.8 billion net was sent from the United States to Latin America.[28] Overall annual American aid increased from $2.0 billion in 1956 to $3.7 billion in 1963.[29]

The United States was also active in pressuring the other developed market economies to increase financial flows to the South. The United States publicly urged a greater role for Europe and Japan in foreign aid and supported the creation of a Development Assistance Committee within the OECD (Organization for Economic Cooperation and Development) to concern itself with aid policies.[30] While much smaller in total amounts, British and French aid increased significantly in this period. British aid doubled from $205 million in 1956 to $414 million in 1963. French aid rose from $648 million in 1956 to $863 million in 1963.[31] And, as aid giving increased in the North, foreign aid interests grew in importance within national bureaucracies. The creation of the U.S. Agency for International Development, the French Ministry and then Secretariat for Cooperation, the British Ministry for Overseas Development, and other similar institutions in other Northern states established a permanent place for advocates of foreign aid within Northern decision-making processes and helped establish foreign aid as a regular form of international economic and political interaction.

The shift in national policy was reflected in a shift in international aid. In 1956 with U.S. support the IBRD members created the subsidiary International Finance Corporation (IFC), designed to give hard loans for private investment in underdeveloped countries without the government guarantee required for IBRD loans. With $100 million in subscribed capital it was designed to invest in equity shares of corporations, provide loans, underwrite public issues, act as a broker bringing foreign and domestic partners together, and as an entrepreneur. The IFC, like the Bank, remained firmly in Northern and especially American hands.

In 1958, at the initiative of the United States, the lending capacity of the IBRD was increased from $10 to $20 billion. As the developed market economies recovered and could borrow in capital markets on their own credit, the IBRD shifted its flow of funds to developing countries.

In 1960, also at U.S. initiative, the International Development Association (IDA) was established, with initial capital of almost $700 million, as a separate institution closely integrated with the World Bank. A major innovation in international aid giving, it makes soft loans, at low interest rates and for long terms, for economic development in Third World countries. Criteria for IDA loans were made less stringent than for IBRD loans. IDA, however, remained under the firm control of the developed countries. In 1960 IDA and the World Bank accounted for 7 percent of net official aid commitments from OECD countries and multilateral agencies. By 1970 they accounted for 18 percent.[31]

In conclusion, because of the Cold War and the resistance of the developed countries to economic restructuring in the second postwar decade, amounts of foreign aid increased and aid became institutionalized both within national policy making and in international organization. But aid altered neither the distribution of wealth nor of power.

THE FAILURE OF AID

Aid did not transform the South and therefore had little impact on North–South relations. In most cases, aid simply became a new feature of economic dependence. It did not necessarily lead to growth. The simple link between aid and economic growth postulated in theory and policy was proven incorrect. Aid seemed to have contributed to growth in certain countries such as Pakistan, Korea, and Taiwan where there had been massive aid inflows. In such countries aid was a major percentage of total investment, a source of financing crucial imports, and the source of important technological improvements. Even in these success cases, however, aid was important because other factors—effective private initiatives and mineral development—were operative.[32] In some countries such as Mexico and Thailand, growth took place without significant aid.[33] And, in other countries such as India, foreign aid had little impact on economic growth.[34]

Furthermore, Southern growth, when it did occur because of aid and other factors, was quite limited. The underdeveloped countries as a group achieved an increase of 5.1 percent in GNP in the period 1960 to 1970. However, because of a rapidly rising population, the actual increase in per capita GNP for these years was only 2.5 percent. Performance in the first years of the 1970s was similar. Although an overall growth rate of less than 5.5 percent was reached, per capita growth was only 2.5 percent. Furthermore, most of the Third World did not experience even this rate of growth. A few rapidly growing, upper-income Third World countries accounted for most of Southern growth. These rapidly growing states, such as Brazil, Mexico, Taiwan, and South Korea, were bridging the development gap, but most of the Third World remained on the other side of the widening chasm. Over half of the total population of the Third World inhabited countries where per capita rate of growth of GNP was less than 1.5 percent, and, staggeringly, 46.0 percent of the total population of the South experienced a decline in per capita income.[35]

Relative growth performance was even more discouraging. Quite simply, the gap between rich and poor was widening. According to one study the gap between North and South increased from almost $1,500 per capita in 1960 to nearly $2,000 in 1967.[36] A United Nations study of performance in the first years of the Second Development Decade predicted that the gap would increase from $2,500 in 1970 to $3,715 by 1980.[37]

Finally, the increase of per capita GNP did not always coincide with development of the economy as a whole, self-sustaining growth, and social welfare.[38]

Despite an increase in GNP, important structural barriers to development remained and, indeed, were often aggravated by the growth process. Despite the initial successes of the Green Revolution, which, for example, led to increasing wheat and rice production, most Southern agricultural structures such as land ownership and the use of improved technology remained unchanged. Agricultural output increased by only small percentages and was unable to keep up with population growth.[39] Another structural problem was the dual economy, the development of a modern dynamic sector alongside the traditional, undeveloped and stagnant, sector. Aid and other development factors seem in many cases to have affected only a part of the economy. Unemployment was associated with economic dualism. Increased output in the developed sector resulted largely from increased application of capital and not from increased employment. Thus, the dynamic sector has been unable to absorb the increased work force which has resulted from population increases.[40] The massive unemployment in the Third World—an estimated 20 percent of the entire male labor force in the developing world without work was not helped by the developed sector.[41]

The belief that aid would lead to a take-off into self-sustaining development was in most cases mistaken. Even the most optimistic reports concluded that self-sustaining growth was not possible in the twentieth century while some less optimistic analysts questioned that timetable.[42] Thus Southern countries could expect to continue to depend on aid for many years to come.

Finally, growth often did not lead to social welfare. Growth seemed to aggravate the unequal distribution of income in much of the South, where national income remained or became even more concentrated in the hands of a few. In Brazil, for example, per capita GNP in real terms grew 2.5 percent per year from 1960 to 1970, but the share of income received by the poorest 40 percent of the population declined from 10 percent in 1960 to 8 percent in 1970. At the same time the share of the richest 5 percent grew from 29 percent to 38 percent.[43] While income distribution was essentially an internal problem of less developed countries, aid seemed to have little impact on equity.

Various explanations have been offered for the failure of aid. One school which includes most of the Southern countries argues that aid quantities have been insufficient and that aid policies have been misguided. The North, it is said, has given only relatively small amounts of aid because it has no real interest in altering the North–South system. Furthermore, inefficiencies such as aid tying and the financing of only foreign exchange costs hinder the effectiveness of that small amount of aid. And aid strategies employed in the 1950s and 1960s which emphasized industrialization at the expense of agricultural development accentuated unemployment and social dislocations.[44] Another variant of the argument that aid has failed because of bad policies places the blame on the less developed countries. Criticisms of improper policies among the less developed countries range from such areas as economic controls and an emphasis on industry at the expense of agriculture to corruption and mismanagement of aid.[45]

Other critics contend that, by its very nature, aid cannot encourage development. Some argue that aid cannot affect the primary determinants of development which are social, political, and economic factors in Southern states. As one critic argued,

> People's economic qualities and attitudes, their values, objectives and motivations, their social and political institutions, together with natural resources and external market opportunities are the major determinants of development . . . . Foreign aid is relatively ineffective as an instrument of development because, even at the best of times, it cannot affect these underlying determinants of development favourably to any great extent . . .[46]

Those who take this view argue that the United States made a grave error in equating aid to developing countries with aid to Western Europe under the Marshall Plan. The European Recovery Program was a success because large financial transfers fell on the fertile social, economic, and political soil of Western Europe. Some critics go so far as to argue that aid has a negative effect on development. Aid, it is said, perpetuates inefficiencies or stifles national savings and entrepreneurship.[47]

Radical critics contend that aid cannot encourage development because it is designed to perpetuate and increase underdevelopment. In their view aid stunts agriculture, encourages trade and investment dependence, and reinforces the dominance of exploitative Southern elites.[48]

While there is insufficient data to directly link foreign economic assistance to the accentuation of dependence in trade and investment, it is clear that the development policies of most Northern states have tended to reinforce economic links with the South. The United States, for example, has used aid to discourage the expropriation of existing investment. The Hickenlooper amendment to the Foreign Assistance Act provides that U.S. aid should be withheld in the event of nationalization or expropriation without a prompt, adequate, and effective compensation. The United States has also encouraged new foreign investment by providing information, sharing the costs of investment surveys, and guaranteeing such investment against risk. U.S. aid also supports trade links by encouraging the use of U.S. goods, especially through tied aid, and by discouraging the development in some cases of competing industry.[49]

Aid in many cases reinforced the political links of dependence. It provided access to the North for economic decision making in the South. The granting of aid and the conditions placed on that aid provided important tools for influencing economic policies in recipient countries. The United States, for example, placed increasing economic conditions on aid which shaped monetary and fiscal policy, investment policy, and international economic policy such as exchange rate and nationalization policy. Through the supervision of aid projects, the U.S. aid bureaucracy became increasingly involved in decision making in recipient countries.[50] A similar pattern occurred with French aid to the former French colonies in sub-Saharan Africa. Financial and technical assistance provided by France played a key role in the governmental operation, functioning of the economy, and economic development in recipient countries.[51] Such economic influence occurred in multilateral aid programs as well. The World Bank, for example, has used its aid to encourage debt settlement and support private investment in the South.[52]

Aid also reinforced North–South dependence by providing the North with political leverage in the South. Aid was used to support preferred internal and external policies of recipient governments; withdrawal or threatened withdrawal of aid has been used to express disapproval or opposition to internal and external policies. This type of influence applied more importantly to bilateral aid and was an explicit purpose of such aid.

The various ways in which the United States has used aid to attempt to influence policy and political developments in recipient countries are a good catalog of the ways aid is used by the North. The United States has given emergency support in economic crises as a way of supporting new regimes (Dominican Republic 1962, Brazil 1964), bolstered old regimes faced with financial crises (Iran 1961, Colombia 1962), given relief to relieve politically threatening unemployment situations (Peru 1961, Honduras 1963), and backed candidates in elections (Chile 1964, 1971). It has demonstrated opposition through the election mechanism by withholding aid in the case of military coup, or to discourage such a coup, or even to change the composition of a government (Vietnam 1963). Aid has been used to promote such foreign policies as the granting of base rights and support in conflicts with the Soviet Union.[53]

Although aid created a new tool for Northern dominance, aid did not always increase Northern bargaining power. The degree of Northern dominance through aid varied not only with some "objective" measurement of Northern influence but also with the eye of the beholder. Donors often felt that aid was given for altruistic reasons and without political strings; alternately, donors often felt that aid was given for political reasons but that its effect was nil or even counterproductive. Recipients, on the other hand, often felt that aid constituted not influence but intervention in national policy.[54]

STAGNATION AND DECLINE OF AID

The effectiveness of aid as a strategy for development had yet another limitation: it depended on continuing Northern goodwill. Most economic assistance was bilateral assistance, and even multilateral institutions and programs depended on continued Northern support. If the North, for one reason or another, determined that it no longer had reason to transfer resources to the South, there was little the South could do about it. The South discovered this vulnerability in the mid-1960s, when the North became increasingly disillusioned with aid and indifferent to the South.

The North's disillusionment developed, in part, because aid did not fulfill the Northern expectations that it would lead to economic development, political democracy and stability, and loyalty in the Cold War. Clearly, aid did not work from an economic point of view. It also did not work from a political point of view. The presumed link between aid and political development favorable to the West was also proven inaccurate. Aid led neither to democratic government nor to political stability. Indeed, instability and a resultant threat seemed to increase not decrease with development.[55] And aid did not necessarily win friends and influence people. While Southern countries perceived aid as a tool of dependence, Northern states perceived unruly and ungrateful Third World recipients flouting Northern policies and biting the hand that fed them.

As the 1960s wore on, the political and military significance of the South declined, and the perceived threat to Northern interests diminished. The major reason for the decline in Southern political and military importance was the end of the Cold War. After 1962 the strategic relationship between the United States and the Soviet Union began to stabilize, and superpower conflict began to moderate. As a result, "winning" or "losing" Third World allegiances gradually came to seem less important to each side. In addition, both sides discovered that it was difficult if not impossible to win friendship through economic assistance. The South began to look less suitable as a testing ground for rival forms of political and economic organization. Thus the United States and the Soviet Union decided that winning such friendships in many cases simply did not matter.

The Europeans came to similar conclusions, for somewhat different reasons. While France retained an important interest in sub-Saharan Africa for prestige and economic benefit, the significance of that region for French security disappeared, and its role in French foreign policy generally declined. Similarly, as Britain cut military commitments east of Suez and moved toward a more European-oriented foreign policy, the political and security motivations for aid to the Commonwealth declined. Thus, as one aid expert from the Third World put it, "The enemy today in the richer countries is not so much disenchantment as indifference."[56]

Finally, foreign aid cost too much. As the assumption linking aid and economic development dissolved, the cost of aid and its duration expanded. In the face of such costs and of domestic economic problems in the West, the political consensus for aid further disintegrated.[57] As military expenditures for Vietnam increased and as balance of payments worsened, U.S. development aid declined. In 1973 U.S. overseas development aid fell to a postwar record low of $2.97 million.[58] The other developed market economies increased aid slightly, but, as economic problems emerged in their countries, foreign aid also fell victim.[59]

The Northern interest in aid giving was thus short-lived. The goal of the United Nations Development Decade—that developed countries give 1 percent of their national income—was never reached, and aid as a percentage of national product actually declined. To be sure, there was an increase in total aid from developed market economies in the third postwar decade. Total aid from members of the OECD increased from $6.6 billion in 1968 to $9.4 billion in 1974.[60] But this increase was more than offset by several factors.

A rising rate of inflation and several currency realignments meant that, despite the absolute increase in dollar amounts, there was no real increase in aid. In fact, in constant value terms, the real volume of aid declined by 7 percent from 1965 to 1974. Aid from the major donor, the United States, declined from $3.5 billion in 1967 to $3.0 billion in 1973, but in real resource value (constant 1967 dollars) it declined from $3.5 billion to $2.0 billion.[61] Aid was also increasingly tied. Aid recipients had to purchase goods from donors and employ donor shipping and insurance at costs often significantly above competitive world market prices. Estimated costs of tying aid in individual countries frequently exceeded 20 percent.[62]

The South was also increasingly burdened with debt service. After

1960 the net transfers of aid to underdeveloped countries were significantly undermined.[63] From 1965 to 1969 the rise in service payments on the official and officially guaranteed debt of eighty less developed countries exceeded the rise in gross flows of new capital aid. As a result, the net transfer of resources declined slightly during this period.[64] During the 1960s the public external indebtedness of these eighty countries grew at an average annual rate of 14 percent, and service payments grew at an average annual rate of 9 percent.[65]

Finally, aid was unevenly distributed. Individual Northern donors retained sufficient political, strategic, and economic interests in individual Southern countries and Southern regions to maintain significant aid programs. The United States continued aid to Korea, Vietnam, Laos, Israel, and Jordan. France maintained aid to former colonies in sub-Saharan Africa, and Britain continued aid to certain Commonwealth members. Less developed countries having special ties with developed states received a disproportionate share of total bilateral aid flows. For example, they accounted for only 3 percent of the population of the South, but they received 28 percent of bilateral aid commitments for the period 1969–1972.[66]

The failure of aid to alter dependence and the decline in aid transfers led to Southern disillusionment. A few Southern states, especially Tanzania and Burma, rejected aid and turned to other self-help policies.[67] In most of the Third World, the primary emphasis was given to the goal of trade reform and to control over foreign investment and raw materials.[68] The less developed countries, nevertheless, attempted to reform economic aid.

To press for trade and investment reform and to improve aid, the less developed countries sought to form a united Southern bloc to improve their bargaining position with the North. Organized unity and common demands, it was hoped, would compensate for increasing irrelevance. Building on the experience of common action in the United Nations and in Third World forums such as the Bandung conference, the Southern states gradually developed an institutionalized Third World bloc, the Group of Seventy-Seven, to confront the North with common demands for changes in the international economic system.[69]

The South sought to increase the volume of aid and to improve its quality. Less developed countries pressed the Northern states through the United Nations Conference on Trade and Development (UNCTAD) to commit themselves to transfer first 1.0 percent and then 0.7 percent of their respective GNPs. Proposals were made and urged on the North to improve the terms of aid by increasing the soft loan and grant element, increasing the duration of loans, easing the debt burden, and untying aid.[70] The Southern bloc also sought to obtain participation in aid management and thereby increase Southern control over aid. Various proposals were developed and presented to the North which would limit Northern control by increasing the multilateral component of aid and by making aid transfers more automatic.

The principal scheme to change aid management was to relate international monetary reform to development finance. Proposals were made to link the creation of SDRs (Special Drawing Rights) with the transfer of resources to developing countries. The essence of such plans was to inject SDRs into the system by allocating them not to developed but to underdeveloped countries. The South was most interested in proposals which called for the allocation of a large share of new SDRs directly to the underdeveloped countries, or to IDA, or to regional development banks.[71] In 1965 a report of an UNCTAD Group of Experts led to the adoption of the link as a development goal of the South and UNCTAD. The report pointed out that the link would be an automatic and formally institutionalized aid-giving process. It would thus avoid the decision-making process of developed market economies which had turned against development finance. Furthermore, it would bypass the Northern argument that aid was becoming too costly from a balance-of-payments viewpoint. By avoiding the balance-of-payments costs of aid, the link would increase aid flows.[72]

None of these Southern aid proposals met with any meaningful response from the North. The North accepted the goal of aid transfers of 0.7 percent of GNP and eventually agreed to ease the terms of aid. These agreements, however, were viewed by the North as goals, not obligations, and in most cases were not met. Furthermore, the North firmly resisted all link proposals.

Southern unity, it was clear, could not provide an alternative to real bargaining power with the North. Despite increasingly desperate and extreme Southern demands, the North remained unmoved. As one study put it,

> In some ways the greatest political problem in economic development and in North-South relations in the next decade will arise from the lack of political importance of the poor countries to the rich countries. . . . The danger is not that the rich will depend on the poor in the next decade, but that they may ignore them.[73]

TOWARD A FOURTH WORLD: CRISES OF THE 1970s

The consequences of being ignored by the North abruptly increased in the 1970s. Three crises—in food, energy, and Northern growth—created a new threat to the South and a new need for foreign economic aid.

As has been noted, a crucial structural problem of underdevelopment virtually untouched by aid was agriculture. Southern food production was unable to keep up with a rapidly expanding population. The Green Revolution, which had raised high hopes in the 1960s, had little impact on most of Southern agriculture. While there had been great success in expanding wheat and rice production in the South, there had been little advance in other products—coarse grains, starch roots, and pulses—which are the staple diet in most developing countries. Furthermore, the increased production in wheat and rice depended on very precarious factors such as irrigation, provision of seed and fertilizer in the right time and quantity, training in the use of new techniques, and the development of a market.[74] In addition, the emphasis on rapid industrialization, stressed in the 1960s, left the agricultural sector less productive than before.

Increasingly, the South experienced a new form of dependence on the North for crucial food imports to meet the gap between production and necessary consumption. Gross cereal imports of the South rose from 12 million tons between 1949 and 1951 to 36 million tons in 1972.[75] Such imports strained Southern balances of payment. The South simply did not have enough foreign exchange to meet the rising need for food imports. Thus, food shortages and nutritional deficiencies as well as food dependence became a major characteristic of Southern underdevelopment. The Northern potential leverage from food dependence was profound.

Despite growing food dependence, the Southern food situation did not reach crisis proportions until 1973. The limited increases in per capita production in the South were compensated by major increases in Northern production, and international food aid helped fill the supply and foreign exchange gap. But after 1972 the political economy of food was drastically altered. A decline in world food production was caused by draught and floods. Resultant shortages plus increased Russian purchases and misguided farm policies in major Northern food-producing countries led to the end of food surpluses, a drastic decline in world food stocks, and an equally drastic rise in world food prices.[76] These changes led to severe food shortages and balance-of-payments crises for many Southern states. The cost of grain imports of all developing countries which had been $3.7 billion in 1971 and $3.8 billion in 1972 rose to $7.4 billion in 1973 and to $12.4 billion in 1974.[77]

In the past, food shortages and payment difficulties had been alleviated by Northern aid. In the 1950s and 1960s the granting of food aid was relatively painless for the North due to high levels of production and low prices. Indeed, the American food aid program—PL 480 or Food for Peace—had served only secondarily as an aid program and primarily as a way of disposing of U.S. surpluses generated by price support programs. But by the 1970s such aid was more costly, of less political interest, and hence less available. As stocks fell and prices rose, the volume of food aid was sharply reduced. In 1972, for example, the real value of all food aid was estimated at $1.13 billion. In 1973, when agricultural production was dropping in the South and when the import bill was soaring, the real value of food aid had dropped to $553 million.[78] Although it did not occur, the less developed countries also faced the possible use of access to food as a political weapon.

The second crisis to affect the South in the 1970s was that of oil and energy. The increase in the price of oil, from $1.80 per barrel in 1971 to $11.65 in 1974, posed a vital threat to Southern development. The most obvious effect of the rising prices of oil and such crucial oil-related products as petrochemical fertilizers was a balance-of-payments crisis for nonoil-producing Southern states. Some of the more developed Southern states—those such as Turkey, Korea, Brazil, and the Phillipines which are bridging the development gap—will probably be able to manage this new burden if Northern capital markets remain open to them. Although the balance-of-payments burden will be onerous for such states—for example, the additional cost of oil for Korea in 1974 represented 20 percent of total imports, for Turkey it represented 19 percent, and for Brazil 16 percent[79]—these countries have relatively strong reserve, balance-of-payments, and export positions. Thus, they should be able to attract foreign investment and foreign loans, even though reliance on foreign financing will increase problems of debt and debt service.[80]

Prospects for the majority of the South, however, are grim unless they receive significant foreign aid. Those most severely threatened are states with per capita incomes of less than $200 per year, growing food import needs, limited access to international capital markets, and the greatest dependence on foreign aid. The burden of increased energy costs was and will continue to be onerous for them. For example, the increased cost of oil represented 26 percent of Senegal's imports in 1974, 24 percent of India's, and 20 percent of Ethiopia's.[81] The burden on foreign exchange will force a curtailment of imports crucial for development and for survival, whereas the decrease in energy consumption will mean a decrease in overall production and consumption which are already precariously low. Unable to turn to private capital markets, they will be forced to forego imports and decrease energy consumption unless they receive foreign aid.[82]

The final crisis for the South was recession and inflation in the North. Northern inflation significantly increased the import bill for the South. Southern development in the 1960s depended greatly on the expansion of exports to Northern markets. The slowdown in the developed market economies has had and will continue to have a detrimental effect on Southern exports. Depending on the actual decline in Northern growth rates, growth of Southern exports in the coming decade could decline by as much as 30–40 percent.[83] Such a decline has the same potential impact as additional costs for food and energy imports: curtailment of development programs, reduction of production, and restriction of consumption. Even a modest decline in developed country growth rates, a safe prediction for the 1970s, will substantially reduce growth levels in developing countries.[84]

The increased import bills and the decline in export earnings caused by the crises of the 1970s have created a new and urgent need for external capital. To maintain the minimum growth objective of 6 percent of the United Nations Second Development Decade, the South will need vast new amounts of capital, much of which must be aid. According to conservative estimates of the World Bank, the developing countries needed an additional $2.6 billion of external capital in 1974 and another $6.8 billion in 1975. In 1974 the bank also estimated that of these amounts $0.8 billion of concessional funds would be required for 1974 and $2.1 billion for 1975 and that much of the remainder would have to be supplied at below market rates. In the period 1976 to 1980, according to World Bank projections, the South will need an estimated $10–12 billion of additional external capital per year of which $4–5 billion must be on concessional terms.[85]

Because of these new needs, the South has increased the level and intensity of its aid demands. In virtually all international forums—the United Nations, the IMF and IBRD, the World Food Conference of 1974, and special sessions of the United Nations General Assembly—the South has raised a unified cry for increased aid to deal with the new international economic disorder.

The ability of the South to obtain public concessional funds for development will be determined by three factors. The first determinant will be the South's ability to link demands for aid to larger demands for a new international economic order. The call for the new order was issued at a special session of the United Nations General Assembly in the spring of 1974. Following the heady success of the oil-producing states in raising oil prices, the South demanded a major reform of the international economic system, including greater and more effective aid flows and participation in management. The Declaration and Action Programme on a New International Economic Order called for a link between SDR allocation and development finance, the implementation of the 0.7 percent of GNP goal established by the United Nations, and greater participation of less developed countries in IBRD and IDA decision making.[86]

A strategy of linking aid to the New International Economic Order will depend on the South's ability to present a unified front in bargaining with the North. Despite the common plight of dependence and underdevelopment, Southern unity has been plagued by important cleavages such as different levels of development, different political ideologies, and different ties with Northern countries. Ironically, the action of the oil-producing states—which has posed a severe threat to the South—has also served as a force for Southern unity and cooperation. The ability of a unified OPEC (Organization of Petroleum Exporting Countries) to increase the threat to and to achieve significant rewards from the North has demonstrated the potential effectiveness of Southern unity in bargaining with the North. It also created, at least temporarily, a solidarity of interest in the South. The spectacular success of the oil producers has led to a spurt of Southern admiration and a sense of Southern solidarity. Common action at the United Nations special sessions in 1974 and 1975 and unity in the negotiations regarding a producer-consumer conference on raw materials are examples of this new unity.

Crucial to the unity and bargaining strength of the South will be the adherence to the bloc of the oil-producing states. These countries have the potential to pose a serious threat to the North by withholding petroleum, and, without their cooperation, Southern unity, as in the past, will be of little use. There are signs that the oil-producing states, or at least some of them, are willing not only to adhere to the bloc but also to play a leadership role in encouraging Southern solidarity and uniting Southern development demands with raw material threats. The role of Algeria in the United Nations and in producer-consumer negotiations is an example of this potentially important leadership.[87]

Another determinant of future aid will be the ability of the nonoil less developed countries to obtain aid from the new rich, the oil producers. The old poor may be able to appeal to the new rich on the basis of Third World solidarity. The history of common action and shared problems may serve to make the oil producers more receptive to Southern demands. Because some of the major oil producers are unable to absorb their new wealth, they may find it relatively easy to assist in development finance. The attempt to obtain aid from the new oil rich has been an important strategy of the South. In part, it explains the absence of Southern reaction to the increase in oil prices which threaten to devastate their economies. The North also looks to the oil producers as sources of development finance. The IMF and IBRD schemes, for example, have been based in part on acquiring financing from members of OPEC.

Some of the hopes of both South and North have been borne out. In 1974 OPEC members transferred approximately $2.2 billion in grants and concessions to nonoil-producing countries, or 1.8 percent of their GNP as compared with transfers of only 0.33 percent by the OECD countries. Another $2.6 billion was transferred to these countries on nonconcessionary terms, including nearly $2.0 billion in World Bank bonds and subscriptions to the Asian Development Bank, the Inter-American Bank, and the African Development Bank.[88]

There are, however, important limits on OPEC aid. Despite the importance of oil producer transfers, they in no way meet the balance-of-payments problems of the less developed countries let alone the development concerns. Furthermore, aid from oil producers has been concentrated in a small handful of countries. The major surplus countries are, with the exception of Iran, Arabic and have given their aid primarily to Middle Eastern states. In 1974, for example, Egypt, Syria, and Jordan received $1.2 billion of the total $2.2 billion of aid, whereas African countries received only $45 million and India and Sudan received only $300 million.[89] Other forms of balance-of-payments relief are unlikely. An attempt by OPEC member Nigeria, for example, to offer oil at a lower price to its beleagured fellow African states was squashed by OPEC. Many states hit hard by the oil crisis cannot reasonably expect aid from the oil producers except as that aid is the result of subscriptions to international organization.

A final determinant of aid flows will be Northern attitudes. If, as in the 1950s, external factors cause a shift in Northern attitudes toward the South, aid might increase. One possible change would be a crisis of conscience growing out of the recognition of the desperate plight of the South. Such a moral regeneration will certainly have an impact on temporary relief measures such as food aid and some balance-of-payments assistance for the poorest of the Southern states. But moral responsibility, as the history of aid demonstrates, is a weak reed on which to base demands for resource transfers. It might lead to temporary relief in crisis situations, but such reactions are usually ephemeral and clearly not the basis for any major shift in aid.

A more important change in Northern attitudes is the new concern in the North for international economic management. The food crisis, the energy crisis, and economic recession have affected the North as well as the South. While economic disorder in the North has been less severe—higher prices and reduced growth rates as opposed to starvation and the collapse of development—it has created a new common interest in expanding international control over market forces. Thus the North has a self-interest in food management, in energy management, and in the reversal of economic recession through international cooperation. Such management may benefit the South and, in some cases, might require the inclusion of certain states of the South in management. Depending on how these leading Southern states define their relation to the other less developed countries, the South may benefit not so much from its specific demands as from the recognition that the problems which the South faces are also faced, albeit somewhat differently, by the North.

There have been some signs of a shift in Northern policy, whether due to anticipated threats, to a moral crisis, or to some larger interest in management. Several short-term crisis management actions have been taken. The IMF has established two facilities to deal with balance-of-payments crises growing out of increased energy costs. The oil facility established in 1974 was a temporary loan fund to help finance balance-of-payments deficits caused by increases in the costs of petroleum and petroleum products. The facility loaned funds at an interest rate of approximately 7¾ percent to both developed and underdeveloped states. Approximately $2.0 billion of loans were made in 1974, and another $3.5 billion was made available for 1975. Most of the money for the facility was borrowed from oil-producing states.[90] The IMF has also established a facility to subsidize interest rates on oil facility loans for the poorest Southern states. Other crisis management programs have been various national food aid programs which attempt to meet the crisis in various underdeveloped countries. All these programs are temporary emergency measures directed at survival, not at systematic reform or even aid reform.

More permanent reforms in aid giving have been suggested. The World Bank has authorized a Third Window (the first two being the IBRD and IDA) to increase funds available for development and to provide loans at rates midway between the IBRD market rates and IDA's nominal rates. The concessional interest rate will be made possible by an Interest Subsidy Fund (ISF). The lack of contributions by the United States and other developed states to the ISF has curtailed early expectations for the Third Window.[91] IDA plans to seek a larger replenishment of funds. And the IMF is setting up a fund for the underdeveloped countries by selling part of its gold subscription. Other proposals include an international investment trust managed by the IFC to offer incentives for investment in Southern states by providing guarantees for such investment and an International Fund for Agricultural Development.[92]

It remains to be seen whether these more important reforms will be adopted. Despite important forces for change and despite some signs of a new Northern receptiveness to such programs for international resource transfers, there are equally important forces working against these transfers. The continuing political irrelevance and the economic weakness of the nonoil-producing South as well as the important demands on Northern resources due to internal economic crises in the North will work against major reform. The North may be willing to undertake emergency, crisis management measures but will very likely be unwilling to agree to major changes.

In conclusion, while the crises of the 1970s will probably lead to increases in aid to the Third World, such flows will only prevent deterioration, they will not encourage a major spurt in economic development. There are few signs of movement toward reform in the nature of aid flows or of a change in management of aid toward greater Southern participation and no suggestion that aid in the 1970s and 1980s could do more for Southern development than aid in the 1960s and 1970s. Some

Third World states—Brazil, Taiwan, and South Korea—will cross the development gap, but most will fall behind. The result of the recent economic disorder, thus, will most likely be not the end of Third World dependence but the creation of a new and more miserable Fourth World.

NOTES

1. See Chapter 7 of this text.
2. Henry J. Bitterman, "Negotiation of the Articles of Agreement of the International Bank for Reconstruction and Development," *The International Lawyer*, 5 (January 1971), 59 88.
3. Clair Wilcox, *A Charter for World Trade* (New York: Macmillan, 1949), p. 142; Williams Adams Brown, Jr., *The United States and the Restoration of World Trade: An Analysis and Appraisal of the ITO Charter and the General Agreement on Tariffs and Trade* (Washington, D.C.: Brookings Institution, 1950), pp. 97 104, 152 158.
4. The following analysis is based on David A. Baldwin, *Economic Development and American Foreign Policy, 1943-1962* (Chicago: Univ. of Chicago Press, 1966), pp. 16 22.
5. In Edward S. Mason and Robert S. Asher, *The World Bank Since Bretton Woods* (Washington, D.C.: Brookings Institution, 1973), p. 23.
6. Ibid., pp. 22 23.
7. Ibid., p. 176. For International Bank for Reconstruction and Development lending policies, see Mason and Asher, pp. 150 190 and Baldwin, *Economic Development and American Foreign Policy, 1943-1962*, pp. 29 50.
8. Cited by Mason and Asher, *The World Bank Since Bretton Woods*, p. 382.
9. Ibid., p. 383.
10. Ibid., pp. 91 92.
11. See John G. Hadwen and Johan Kaufman, *How United Nations Decisions Are Made* (Dobbs Ferry, N.Y.: Oceana Publications, 1962), Chap. 5.
12. "The Inaugural Address of the President," U.S. Department of State, *The Bulletin*, 20 (January 30, 1949), 125.
13. In Goran Ohlin, *Foreign Aid Policies Reconsidered* (Paris: Organization for Economic Cooperation and Development, 1966), p. 16.
14. Ibid., p. 66.
15. On SUNFED, see Hadwen and Kaufman, *How United Nations Decisions Are Made*, On the Special Fund, see "The United Nations Special Fund," An Explanatory Paper by the Managing Director (New York: United Nations Special Fund, 1959). For a discussion of IFC and IDA, see page 140.
16. "Final Summary of the Asian-African Conference," *Report on Indonesia*, 6 (June 1955).
17. See *Military Assistance and the Security of the United States, 1947-1956*, a study prepared by the Institute of War and Peace Studies of Columbia University in U.S. Senate, Foreign Aid Program, Compilation of Studies and Surveys under the direction of the Special Committee to Study the Foreign Aid Program, 85th Congress, 1st Sess., 1957, pp. 903 969.
18. See *Report to the President on Foreign Economic Policies* (Washington, D.C., 1950); International Development Advisory Board, *Partners in Progress, A Report to the President* (March 1951); Advisory Committee on Underdeveloped Areas, *Economic Strength for the Free World* (May 1953); U.S. Mutual Security Agency, Advisory Committee on Underdeveloped Areas, *Economic Strength for the Free World: Principles of a U.S. Foreign Development Program*. A Report to the Director for Mutual Security (Washington, D.C., 1953).

19. In Robert S. Walters, *American and Soviet Aid: A Comparative Analysis* (Pittsburgh, Pa.: Univ. of Pittsburgh Press, 1970), p. 30.

20. See Marshall I. Goldman, *Soviet Foreign Aid* (New York: Praeger, 1967), pp. 60 167; Walters, *American and Soviet Aid*, pp. 26 48.

21. U.S. Senate, *Foreign Aid Program*, p. 20.

22. See Chapter 7 of this text.

23. Max F. Millikan and W. W. Rostow, *A Proposal: Key to an Effective Foreign Policy* (New York: Harper & Brothers, 1957), pp. 34 38.

24. Ibid., p. 39. For an analysis of the role of aid in political development, see Robert A. Packenham, *Liberal American and the Third World: Political Development Ideas in Foreign Aid and Social Science* (Princeton, N.J.: Princeton Univ. Press, 1973).

25. For an excellent summary, see Ohlin, *Foreign Aid Policies Reconsidered*, pp. 27 36. See, also, Teresa Hayter, *French Aid* (London: Overseas Development Institute, 1966); Overseas Development Institute, *British Aid—A Factual Survey* (London: Overseas Development Institute, 1963 1964).

26. Baldwin, *Economic Development and American Foreign Policy, 1943–1962*, p. 204.

27. Ibid., p. 202.

28. Jerome Levinson and Juan de Onis, *The Alliance That Lost Its Way: A Critical Report on the Alliance for Progress* (Chicago: Quadrangle Books, 1970), p. 139. This study is a critical analysis of Alliance for Progress.

29. Organization for Economic Cooperation and Development, *Flow of Financial Resources to Less-Developed Countries 1956–1963* (Paris: Organization for Economic Cooperation and Development, 1964), p. 19.

30. Organization for Economic Cooperation and Development, *Flow of Financial Resources to Less-Developed Countries, 1956–1963*, p. 32.

31. See Mason and Asher.

32. Pearson, *Partners in Development: Report of the Commission on International Development* (New York: Praeger, 1969), pp. 48 52; Irving Brecher and S.A. Abbas, *Foreign Aid and Industrial Development in Pakistan* (Cambridge, Mass.: Harvard University Press, 1972); Gustav F. Papanek, *Pakistan and Development: Social Goals and Private Incentive* (Cambridge, Mass.: Harvard Univ. Press, 1967); Irma Adelman, ed., *Practical Approaches to Development Planning: Korea's Second Five-Year Plan* (Baltimore, Md.: Johns Hopkins Press, 1969); John D. Montgomery, *The Politics of Foreign Aid: American Experience in Southeast Asia* (New York: Praeger, 1962), pp. 96 99; Neil H. Jacoby, *U.S. Aid to Taiwan* (New York: Praeger, 1966).

33. Roger D. Hansen, *Mexican Economic Development: The Roots of Rapid Growth* (Washington: National Planning Association, 1971).

34. See Lawrence Veit, *India's Second Revolution: The Dimensions of Development* (New York: McGraw-Hill, 1976).

35. United Nations Conference on Trade and Development, *The Second United Nations Development Decade: Trends and Policies in the First Two Years* (New York: United Nations, 1974), pp. 68 70.

36. Richard Jolly, "The Aid Relationship: Reflections on the Pearson Report," in Barbara Ward, Lenore d'Anjou, and J.D. Runnalls, eds., *The Widening Gap: Development in the 1970s* (New York: Columbia Univ. Press, 1971), p. 283.

37. United Nations Conference on Trade and Development, *The Second United Nations Development Decade*, p. 68.

38. On the meaning of development, see Gerald M. Meier, *Leading Issues in Economic Development: Studies in International Poverty*, 2nd ed. (New York: Oxford Univ. Press, 1970), pp. 5 9.

39. United Nations Conference on Trade and Development, *The Second United Nations Development Decade*, p. 82.

40. Ibid., pp. 81 85; Meier, *Leading Issues in Economic Development*, pp. 430 439.

41. Statement for the Economic and Social Council by the President of the International Bank for Reconstruction and Development on 27 October 1969, in United Nations Conference on Trade and Development, *The Second United Nations Development Decade*, p. 82.

42. See Jolly, "The Aid Relationship: Reflections on the Pearson Report."

43. Robert S. McNamara, Address to the United Nations Conference on Trade and Development, Santiago, Chile, April 14, 1972 (Washington, D.C.: International Bank for Reconstruction and Development, 1972), pp. 4-7.

44. See Pearson, *Partners in Development*, pp. 168 193; John Pincus, *Trade, Aid and Development* (New York: McGraw-Hill, 1967), pp. 295 348; *The Charity of Nations: The Political Economy of Foreign Aid* (New York: Basic Books, 1973). See Chapter 7 of this text for a discussion of the problem of emphasizing industry at the expense of agriculture.

45. See Harry G. Johnson, *Economic Policies Toward Less-Developed Countries* (New York: Praeger, 1967), pp. 67 78.

46. Peter Bauer, "UNCTAD and Africa," in Meier, *Leading Issues in Economic Development*, p. 282.

47. Ibid., pp. 280-284; Milton Friedman, "Foreign Economic Aid: Means and Objectives," in Gustav Ranis, ed., *The United States and the Developing Economies* (New York: Norton, 1964), pp. 24 38.

48. See Samir Amin, "Development and Structural Change: African Experience," in Ward, *The Widening Gap*, pp. 312 333; Susanne Bodenheimer, "Dependency and Imperialism," in K. T. Fann and Donald C. Hodges, *Readings in U.S. Imperialism* (Boston: Porter Sargent, 1971), pp. 155 181; Denis Goulet and Michael Hudson, *The Myth of Aid: The Hidden Agenda of the Development* Reports (New York: International Documentation North America, 1971).

49. See Joan M. Nelson, *Aid, Influence and Foreign Policy* (New York: Macmillan, 1968), pp. 69-90.

50. Ibid., pp. 69-85. Howard Wriggins, "Political Outcomes of Foreign Assistance: Influence, Involvement, or Intervention?," *Journal of International Affairs*, 22 (1968), 220 225; Andrew M. Scott, *The Revolution in Statecraft: Informal Penetration* (New York: Random House, 1965), pp. 73-80.

51. See Hayter, *French Aid*; Joan Edelman Spero, "France and Francophone Africa: The Study of A Dependency Relationship," Ph.D. Dissertation (Columbia University, 1973).

52. For a highly critical study of the World Bank, see Teresa Hayter, *Aid as Imperialism* (Harmondsworth, Eng: Penguin Books, 1971).

53. Nelson, *Aid, Influence and Foreign Policy*, pp. 69-120.

54. Wriggins, "Political Outcomes of Foreign Assistance," p. 217-220.

55. Samuel P. Huntington, *Political Order in Changing Societies* (New Haven, Conn.: Yale Univ. Press, 1968), pp. 1-92.

56. I. G. Patel, "Aid Relationship for the Seventies," in Ward, *The Widening Gap*, p. 308.

57. See Samuel P. Huntington, "Foreign Aid for What and for Whom," *Foreign Policy*, 1 (Winter 1970-1971), 161-189; Samuel P. Huntington, "Does Foreign Aid Have a Future?," *Foreign Policy*, 2 (Spring 1971), 114-134.

58. Organization for Economic Cooperation and Development, *Development Cooperation 1974 Review*, p. 133.

59. Ibid., pp. 125-134.

60. Ibid., p. 14.

61. Ibid.

62. Pearson, *Partners in Development*, pp. 172-175.

63. Ibid., pp. 153-167.

64. United Conference on Trade and Development, *Debt Problems of Developing Countries* (New York: United Nations, 1972), p. 1.

65. Ibid., p. 3.

66. Organization for Economic Cooperation and Development, *Development Cooperation 1974 Review*, p. 167.

67. See "The Policy of Self-Reliance: Exerpts from Part III of the Arusha Declaration of February 5, 1967," *Africa Report*, 12 (March 1967), 11-13; Henry Bienen, "An Ideology for Africa," *Foreign Affairs*, 47 (April 1969), 545-559.

68. See Chapters 7 and 8 of this text.

69. See Chapter 7 for a discussion of the development of Group of Seventy-Seven.

70. United Nations Conference on Trade and Development, *Towards a New Trade Policy for Development* (New York: United Nations, 1964), pp. 79–89; United Conference on Trade and Development, *Towards a Global Strategy of Development* (New York: United Nations, 1968), pp. 32 44.

71. See Y. S. Park, *The Link Between Special Drawing Rights and Development Finance* (Princeton, N.J.: Princeton University, Department of Economics, International Finance Section, September 1973).

72. United Nations Conference on Trade and Development, *International Monetary Issues and the Developing Countries*, Report of the Group of Experts (New York: United Nations, 1965).

73. Robert O. Keohane and Joseph S. Nye, "World Politics and the International Economic System," in C. Fred Bergsten, ed., *The Future of the International Economic Order: An Agenda for Research* (Lexington, Mass.: Lexington Books, 1973), p. 156.

74. See Organization for Economic Cooperation and Development, *Development Co-operation 1974 Review*, pp. 61 114.

75. Ibid., pp. 65 66.

76. See Fred H. Sunderson, *The Great Food Fumble* (Washington, D.C.: Brookings Institution, 1975).

77. Roger D. Hansen et al., *The U.S. and World Development: Agenda for Action 1976* (New York: Praeger, 1976), p. 156.

78. Organization for Economic Cooperation and Development, *Development Co-operation 1974 Review*, p. 87.

79. Ibid., p. 19.

80. Ibid., pp. 19 20.

81. Ibid., p. 20.

82. Ibid., pp. 20 21.

83. International Bank for Reconstruction and Development, International Development Association, *Additional External Capital Requirements of Developing Countries: An Analysis by the Staff of the World Bank Group*, March 1974, processed, p. 9.

84. Ibid., pp. 2, 6 9; International Monetary Fund, *Annual Report 1975* (Washington, D.C.: International Monetary Fund, 1975), p. 21.

85. International Bank for Reconstruction and Development, *Additional External Capital Requirements of Developing Countries*, p. 3.

86. "Declaration and Action Programme on the Establishment of a New International Economic Order," in Guy F. Erb and Valeriana Kallab, ed., *Beyond Dependency: The Developing World Speaks Out* (New York: Praeger, 1975), pp. 193–194.

87. See Roger D. Hansen, "The Political Economy of North-South Relations: How Much Change?," *International Organization*, 29 (Autumn 1975), 921–948.

88. Maurice J. Williams, "The Aid Programs of the OPEC Countries," *Foreign Affairs*, 54 (January 1976), 317–318 and 322.

89. Ibid., p. 321.

90. International Monetary Fund, *Annual Report 1974*, Washington, D.C., 1974), pp. 52–53, 122–126; International Monetary Fund, *Annual Report 1975*, pp. 53–56, 90–95.

91. See Trilateral Commission, "OPEC, The Trilateral World, and the Developing Countries: New Arrangements for Cooperation, 1976–1980," *The Triangle Papers*, 7 (1975).

92. See Global Consensus and Economic Development, address by Secretary Kissinger Prepared for Delivery at the Seventh Special Session of the United Nations General Assembly, U.S. Department of State, *The Bulletin*, 73 (September 22, 1975), pp. 425–441.

7

Trade Strategy

Most Southern economies are highly dependent on trade with the North. Export earnings constitute a large percentage of GNP, and imported goods are crucial for development. Yet many less developed countries believe that the international market and trade management system established by and for the North have deprived them of many of the benefits of trade and have excluded them from its political management. Therefore, since World War II underdeveloped countries have tried several strategies in an effort to modify the international trading system and to achieve the goals of development and independence.

EXCLUSION AND SELF-ISOLATION FROM THE POSTWAR TRADING ORDER

After World War II the independent Southern states fought to include their interests in the new postwar international trading order. The economic development of the South was not a major concern of wartime and postwar economic planning. The American and British governments, largely responsible for planning a new trading order, paid little attention to the special development goals and needs of the South in constructing the new trade system. The postwar planners argued that Southern interests coincided with Northern desires to create a system based on free trade. Indeed, the North argued, the liberalization of international trade would provide a major stimulus for Southern development and would obviate the need for significant economic assistance. Freer trade, according to the North, would lead to the most efficient and profitable use of national factors of production, it would increase national income and foreign exchange earnings, and it would attract foreign private capital.[1]

Southern states felt quite differently. In their view, the system proposed by the North served the interests of the powerful industrial states and offered little hope for Southern development. The South argued that free trade threatened their new policies for development through national industrialization and protection from foreign competition. This policy was based on the infant industry argument that protection was crucial to encouraging the development of an industry that was appropriate for a country's factor endowment but which could not develop without temporary protection from external competition. Protection from foreign competition for an initial stage would allow the domestic producer to attain optimum size and economies of scale within the domestic market. Once the infant stage was completed, protection could be removed and free trade resumed.[2] What the less developed countries sought was the right to use protection but at the same time participate in the fruits of greater access for their exports to the markets of the developed states.

Thus in the postwar negotiations the independent underdeveloped countries tried to modify the free trade system proposed by the North. The less developed countries, for example, opposed the proposed ban on the use of import quotas and on the establishment of new preferential trading systems and sought freedom to use such measures for development. They also made proposals to exempt commodity agreements from free trade rules. They wanted to be able to establish agreements among producers and consumers or among producers only to stabilize commodity prices and to assure minimum prices. These Southern proposals were opposed by the North as exceptions to free trade and as a threat to the very nature of the liberal trading system which the North, and especially the United States, sought to establish.[3]

Because the North wanted to obtain the approval of the less developed countries for the new trade charter, the South was in a position to have access to Northern negotiations, and its bargaining position to make demands on the North was better than it had ever been before or would be for a long time after. As a result, while the South did not achieve significant reform of the North's free trade system, it did achieve some limited modifications.

A new chapter on economic development not in the original Northern drafts was included in the Havana Charter. Under very specific and limited conditions, underdeveloped countries were released from a full commitment to free trade. With prior approval of the ITO (International Trade Organization) and/or the parties to trade agreements involved and following highly restrictive guidelines, states could obtain exceptions to bans on import controls, establish regional preference systems to promote economic development, and enter into commodity agreements.

Not only did the Havana Charter recognize in some degree the special problems of underdeveloped countries and their need for special treatment, the institutional structure of the ITO also created the possibility for Southern participation in management. Despite Northern dominance, the South had access to the major decision-making bodies of the ITO. Furthermore, the provisions for economic development in the charter might have been a basis for injecting the concerns of less developed countries in the management of trade. Consideration of these demands, of course, would have depended on the application and interpretation of the charter by the developed countries, but the Havana system left room, albeit limited, for interpretations favorable to Southern demands and created an institutional base for making of those demands.[4]

The potential integration of the concerns of less developed countries in the regulating of international trade ended, however, with the death of the Havana Charter. GATT (General Agreement on Tariffs and Trade), which replaced the charter as the constitution of the new trading order, excluded the interests of the underdeveloped countries. The original GATT agreement was designed only as an interim measure and included none of the provisions for development which the South had fought to include in the Havana Charter. There were no provisions for development cooperation, for commodity agreements, for preferential trading systems for the South, or for the use of restrictions to further development. Only one article dealt with the special problems of the South. It authorized a country to use nondiscriminatory quantitative restrictions to assist economic development or reconstruction. Such exceptions, however, required prior approval from the contracting parties—which meant the North—were limited in duration, and required annual reporting. In practice, such restrictions made the article virtually useless.[5] Finally, the demise of the Havana Charter left the underdeveloped countries without the ITO, which provided an institutional base for possible future integration of their trade demands.

Not only the exclusion of development and institutional provisions from the GATT but the GATT negotiating process as well systematically excluded the interests of the South from the international management of trade. The bargaining position of the South at the various tariff negotiations was hurt by the free trade rules of GATT. The nondiscrimination or most favored nation principle, which stipulated that a trading concession between any two countries be extended to all contracting parties on an equal basis, eliminated the possibility of preferential trading agreements for developmental purposes. The GATT rule of reciprocity provided that all trade concessions had to be mutual. But the South with its small markets had little to exchange for concessions in its favor and was thus crippled in bargaining.

The South was also hurt by the GATT device of negotiation among principal suppliers. Under GATT practice, trade concessions were negotiated among importing countries and principal suppliers of any particular item. Many products of interest to the underdeveloped countries were left out of GATT negotiations because there were no principal suppliers. In other cases, when the underdeveloped countries were the principal suppliers, they were unable to put products or issues of interest to them on the agenda because the South represented only a minority of GATT membership and GATT power. The principal supplier rule tended to exclude agricultural products and cascading tariffs from tariff negotiations.

The underdeveloped countries were also disadvantaged by their bargaining weakness. Because they lacked the staff to sustain difficult and sophisticated trade negotiations with the powerful developed countries, their interests were not adequately represented. Recognizing these biases, many underdeveloped countries chose not to join GATT or not to participate in the international trade negotiations sponsored by GATT. Underdeveloped countries entered into few trade agreements and received few benefits from the negotiating process by which trade was managed.[6]

Excluded from GATT, the underdeveloped countries directed their limited attempts to revise the trading system to other forums: the General Assembly, ECOSOC (Economic and Social Council), the United Nations regional commissions and their trade commissions, and the Food and Agricultural Organization.[7] Efforts to reform the international trading system through international management, however, were not the primary strategy of underdeveloped countries in this period. Isolated from the management system, they then sought to insulate themselves from adverse conditions of the international market. During the first postwar decade, the trade policy followed by many Southern states was an inward-looking policy of industrialization through import substitution. The goal of this policy was national development insulated from the international market.

The desire of the South to isolate itself from the international market may be traced back to the interwar and wartime experience. The collapse of commodity prices and a rising external debt after 1929 crippled the South's import capacity. The inability of the North to supply necessary manufactured products during the war further encouraged the South to be wary of dependence on foreign markets and foreign supplies and to prefer a policy of self-sufficiency. This historical experience was reinforced by political independence which increased the desire for economic development and economic independence. Protection had historically been a route to development in the North, and, it was hoped, protection from external competition would help Southern industrialization and development as well. Import substitution also appealed to underdeveloped countries as a way of improving balance of payments by decreasing imports.[8]

Thus after World War II many underdeveloped countries, particularly those in Latin America, either continued the protection introduced before or during the war or established new protectionist barriers in an attempt to develop an internal market for domestic production. Very high rates of protection were assured through tariffs, quantitative controls, and multiple exchange rates.[9] Protection encouraged the development of local industry by providing an assured market and by channeling domestic savings into industry through increased industrial profits. Import substitution meant isolation on the export as well as on the import side from the international market. Although exports were not deliberately discouraged, little emphasis was given in this period to the promotion of production for export. One effect of the emphasis on import substitution and industrialization, as we shall see, was to damage Southern exports.[10]

MOTIVES FOR CHANGE

By the late 1950s it was becoming clear that the Southern strategy of isolation from the international trading system was a failure. It led neither to development nor to independence and may have actually aggravated the negative impact of international trade on the South. Increasingly dissatisfied with the operation of the international market and with the exclusion from management, and often unable or unwilling to carry out domestic reforms to further economic development, the underdeveloped countries began to look for a new trade strategy.

The first reason for a change in strategy was the worsening economic situation of the South. Import substitution had not provided an answer. It had, indeed, fostered some industrialization, but at an excessively high price. Despite significant efforts, industrial production still accounted for only a small percentage of GNP. Although some of that production was efficient, too often new industry was inefficient and high in cost. Furthermore, capital-intensive production methods and policies such as favoring profits over wages and discouraging traditional labor-intensive industry meant that new industry did not contribute to employment.

Industrialization through import substitution also had a negative effect on the other sectors of the economy. Agriculture in particular paid a high price, for that was the sector to finance industrialization. New investment in agriculture was limited; real earnings declined as industrial profits rose; income inequalities between agriculture and industry were aggravated. As a result of these economic dislocations, people began to leave the countryside for the town, but the new industry in the cities could not absorb the burgeoning urban population. Thus unemployment and income inequalities increased further.

Finally, import substitution did not help the balance of payments. High-cost domestic manufactures could not meet international competition and thus were not exported; increased factor costs and an overvalued currency hurt traditional agricultural exports. Furthermore, import substitution did not decrease imports but, rather, changed the composition of those imports. Instead of importing finished products, Southern countries now imported raw materials, parts, capital goods, and greater amounts of agricultural products.[11]

Import substitution and isolation from the international market therefore were coming to be seen as a dead end. Domestic reform was difficult and politically risky. Thus governments of many Southern states concluded that their international trade and economic development policy would have to be based, instead, on export expansion. Export growth, it came to be felt, could maximize efficiency of production and increase earnings and foreign exchange available for development, much as the liberals had always argued. According to the less developed countries, however, such expansion and such benefits could not occur without a restructuring of the international trading system, for that system prevented export growth.

First, argued the less developed countries, there was a long-term deterioration in the South's terms of trade.[12] The prices of raw materials exported by the underdeveloped countries were declining in relation to the prices of manufactured products imported by the less developed countries from the developed countries. Because of trade unions and monopoly markets in the developed market economies, it was argued, increased productivity in manufacturing in the North was absorbed by higher wages and profits and did not lead to a fall in the price of manufactures. On the other hand, in the less developed countries, because of unemployment and the absence of labor organization plus the existence of a competitive international market for Southern raw materials, increased productivity in primary products led not to increased wages or profits but to a decline in prices. The terms of trade also turned against the South because of an inelastic demand in the North for primary products. An increase in production of raw materials led not to an increase in consumption but to a decline in price. Finally, prices of Southern products tended to fall because of the development of synthetics and substitutes—for example, nylon replacing cotton—in the North.

The structural decline in terms of trade for primary producers was aggravated by Northern protectionist policies. According to the South, the development of competitive, mechanized Northern agriculture through protectionist systems, the development of domestic mineral extraction under protectionist national security policies, and Northern taxes on tropical foodstuffs all accentuated the declining position of commodity exports.

Another problem of the international market, according to the South, was the inherent instability of commodity prices. Fluctuations in prices and thus in export earnings, in their view, hindered investment and disrupted development planning.

Finally, the South felt that its real potential to export manufactured products was constrained by Northern dominance of the international market. The head start of the North which gave the developed countries established positions in international markets as well as Northern protection prevented the expansion of Southern manufactured exports.

The South was particularly critical of a myriad of Northern protectionist measures, for example, the practice of imposing a higher tariff on intermediate or finished products than on raw materials. Such "cascading" tariffs meant that the effective rate of protection of the finished product was much higher than the nominal rate. The impact of differential tariffs was to favor the import of raw materials from less developed countries, to discourage the import of processed or semiprocessed products, and thus to discourage the development of Southern industry. Unusually high tariffs or import quotas were imposed on many Southern manufactures such as textiles, footwear, and leather goods which competed effectively with Northern industries.

Where there were no tariff or quantitative restrictions, the North often forced restrictive export agreements on Southern states obliging them to control the amount of their exports.[13] Nontariff barriers such as health standards, labeling requirements, and customs procedures posed difficult hurdles for Southern states with their lack of marketing expertise and experience.[14]

These constraints on exports with the less developed countries were reflected in the South's declining role in international trade. The Southern share of world exports dropped from 31.6 percent in 1950 to 21.4 percent in 1960. In the same period the trade of developed market economies grew from 60.4 percent of total world exports to 66.8 percent and the socialist states went from 8.0 percent of total world exports to 11.8 percent. In the 1950–1960 period, exports of the developed countries grew 8.7 percent, whereas those of underdeveloped countries grew only 3.5 percent.[15]

Dissatisfaction with the operation of the international market and with Northern policy led to increasing Southern dissatisfaction with exclusion from the management of the international trading system. As noted earlier, the free trade principles of GATT and the bias of the GATT negotiating system against the South excluded less developed countries from trade benefits. As long as the South followed import substitution and deemphasized international trade, such exclusion was important but not critical. But, when the South began to seek to expand its trade, exclusion from management became unacceptable.

In the latter half of the 1950s, Southern pressure for a change in the GATT system increased. The number of independent Southern states grew. At Bandung and the United Nations and within GATT itself, the old and new Southern states pressed for greater consideration of their problems. By that time the developed countries could no longer deny the reality of the declining position of the South in world trade and the failure of their earlier predictions that free trade would lead to development. In addition, pressure for Northern consideration of the Southern trade problem was coming from the Soviet Union.

As has been noted, in the mid-1950s the Soviet Union was developing a new interest in and new ties with the Third World through aid and trade programs. In 1956, and then in 1958, the Soviet Union proposed the holding of an international conference on trade and the creation of a world trade organization outside GATT. The North opposed any change in GATT dominance of trade management and persuaded the South to reject the Soviet proposal in favor of reform within GATT. But, as a result of rising Southern concern, the crisis of Southern balance of payments, and the challenge from the Soviet Union, the North felt it could no longer ignore the Southern problems.

In 1957 the contracting parties of GATT appointed a panel of experts to examine the problems of Southern trade. The report of this panel, the Haberler report, published in 1958, reached some of the same conclusions that other economists and the Southern states themselves were reaching regarding their trade problems. The panel focused on export trade in primary products and pointed out several problems: Northern trade barriers, the deterioration in the price of less developed countries' exports, and Southern import-substitution policies. Only slight reference, however, was made to the problem of exports of Southern manufactured products.[16]

The Haberler report led in 1958 to the GATT Programme for the Expansion of International Trade. Three new committees were established within GATT, one of which was to deal with the problems of Southern trade, particularly with Southern exports of primary products and manufactured goods, and to make recommendations to the Northern states for the expansion of Southern export earnings. The committee's recommendations, however, remained recommendations and were not adopted as policy by the North. Commodity protectionism and discrimination against Southern manufactures continued. The lack of leadership interest and the barriers to change posed by well-organized interest groups in the North meant that the developed market economies were unwilling to go beyond the gesture of studying Southern problems.[17]

Dissatisfaction with GATT increased. Many newly independent Southern states had joined the organization in the hope that the new interest in the South would lead to policy change. Beginning in 1961 they and the other Southern states took their demands for policy change to the GATT ministers. Twenty-one underdeveloped countries within GATT demanded that a new Programme of Action drawn up by them be adopted by the contracting parties. By 1963 a six-point program that was in fact accepted by most contracting parties called for a standstill on tariff and nontariff barriers for exports of Southern states, elimination of quantitative restrictions inconsistent with GATT rules, duty-free entry for tropical products, elimination of customs duties on primary products important for the less developed countries' trade, reduction and elimination of customs tariffs on semiprocessed and processed Southern exports, and reduction by the North of internal taxes and revenue duties on products produced primarily or wholly in Southern states. The new program, however, proved to be a set of goals, not a policy commitment. No timetables were accepted for the implementation of the program by the North, and the EEC (European Economic Community) stated strong reservations.[18]

Thus the less developed countries, increasingly frustrated with the trends of trade and with the structure of management, turned to a new strategy. The South was coming to the conclusion that the way to modify the system was not through modification of GATT from within but through an assault from without.

UNITY AND CONFRONTATION

The Southern strategy of the 1960s was one of unity and confrontation. Beginning in 1961 the South formed a loose coalition and then a united front to press the North for change in trade management and in the operation of the international trading system. In Third World conferences and in United Nations forums where the South commanded a majority, the underdeveloped countries pushed through their demands in the form of declarations, recommendations, and resolutions on trade and other economic reform.

The first Southern demand was for an international conference on trade and development, and the first attempt to unite the South behind such a demand came at the Belgrade Conference of nonaligned countries in September 1961. At this conference, composed primarily of African and Asian countries, President Tito of Yugoslavia proposed the holding of a world conference within the United Nations framework to consider economic problems of importance to the South. The Declaration of the Belgrade Conference invited all countries concerned to convene such an international economic conference. At the General Assembly session of

1961, the Southern states proposed and, despite Northern opposition, succeeded in passing a resolution which called on the United Nations to consult the member governments regarding the holding of a conference on international trade and the possible agenda of such a conference.

The development of the Southern front and the demand for an international conference underwent a major advance at the Conference on Problems of Developing Countries held at Cairo in July 1962. For the first time several Latin American states joined the Asian and African nations in a unified Southern attempt to formulate a joint policy and a joint demand on the developed countries. The Cairo conference issued an influential declaration calling for a conference to deal with the problems of international trade, primary commodities, and economic relations between developing and developed countries.

Faced with the persistence and growing unity of the South plus increasing Southern numerical control of the General Assembly, the North realized that it could no longer prevent the holding of a United Nations conference on trade and development. Largely as a result of the united action of the Cairo conference, the North abandoned its policy of opposition and agreed to a decision of the United Nations Economic and Social Council (ECOSOC) in 1962 to convene UNCTAD (the United Nations Conference on Trade and Development). In that same year the General Assembly endorsed the ECOSOC decision with an almost unanimous vote. Southern unity and numerical strength in the United Nations thus succeeded in calling the first UNCTAD in Geneva in 1964.[19]

The Southern strategy of bloc confrontation turned next to achieving the goal of trade reform through UNCTAD. To establish a common front, the loose coalition of the pre-UNCTAD period was consolidated in the more formal and organized Group of Seventy-Seven. Based on the precedents of common action in the U.N. and in the Third World conferences, the group began as seventy-seven cosponsors of the Joint Declaration of the Developing Countries made to the General Assembly in 1963. In this declaration the Southern bloc, for the first time, spelled out its common goals for trade reform. According to the declaration,

> The existing principles and patterns of world trade still mainly favour the advanced parts of the world. Instead of helping the developing countries to promote the development and diversification of their economies, the present tendencies in world trade frustrate their efforts to attain more rapid growth. These trends must be reversed.[20]

What the South wanted was to make international trade:

> a more powerful instrument and vehicle of economic development not only through the expansion of the traditional exports of the developing coun-

tries, but also through the development of markets for their new products and a general increase in their share of world exports under improved terms of trade.[21]

To that end they offered a series of general goals for UNCTAD: the improvement of institutional arrangements including, if necessary, the establishment of new machinery and methods; the progressive reduction and early elimination of all barriers and restrictions impeding Southern exports, without reciprocal concessions on their part; increased exports of primary products both raw and processed to the developed countries and stabilization of prices at fair and remunerative levels; the expansion of markets for exports of less developed countries' manufactures and semimanufactures; more adequate financial resources at favorable terms to enable developing countries to increase imports of capital goods and industrial raw materials essential for development; better coordination of aid and trade policies; and improvement in Southern invisible trade, especially a reduction of shipping and insurance costs.[22]

Following the joint action for the 1963 declaration, the Group of Seventy-Seven, which retained its original name but which eventually came to include nearly one hundred states, developed as a permanent political group representing Southern interests. Group unity has been based on the perception of a common interest in altering the international economic system and on the perception that unity will enhance bargaining power with the North and thus the achievement of their development goals. As the Southern states themselves put it,

> This unity has sprung out of the fact that facing the basic problems of development they have a common interest in a new policy for international trade and development . . . . The developing countries have a strong conviction that there is a vital need to maintain, and further strengthen, this unity in the years ahead. It is an indispensable instrument for securing the adoption of new attitudes and new approaches in the international economic field.[23]

Group unity has been maintained by internal decision-making procedures. All proposals are cleared by the group before they are presented for negotiation with the developed countries, and all proposals must be unanimously endorsed by all group members. The group coordinates policy through numerous meetings and conferences preceding and during periods of negotiation with the North.[24]

An important force in maintaining the united Southern front has been the establishment of UNCTAD as a permanent organization with a secretariat. The secretariat and its secretary-general have reinforced the perception of common interest by providing a doctrine which defines that common interest and common dilemma and which serves as an important basis for united action. The doctrine of UNCTAD has been the work to a great extent of its first secretary-general, Raul Prebisch, and reflects his structuralist analysis of North–South relations.

According to the doctrine, the world is divided into a center, or developed countries, and a periphery, or underdeveloped countries. The operation of the market works against the underdeveloped countries because of the long-term structural decline in Southern terms of trade and because of Northern protectionist policies which discriminate against Southern exports. As a result the South is faced with "a persistent tendency toward external imbalance," what Raul Prebisch called the trade gap. Unless measures are taken to counteract the structural bias against the South and to fill the trade gap, argues UNCTAD, the underdeveloped countries will not be able to meet the United Nations development goal of 5 percent annual growth.

According to UNCTAD doctrine, what is needed is a redistribution of world resources to help the South: international trade and other North–South economic relationships must be restructured to provide for a transfer of resources from North to South, and the responsibility for such transfers rests with the North.[25]

Aside from providing a doctrine which defines the common Southern interest, UNCTAD has also served Southern unity by providing important technical services. UNCTAD studies provide the South with the information necessary to confront the North in bargaining. UNCTAD proposals in many cases have provided the basis for the formation of Southern proposed resolutions and recommendations. At times the secretary-general has even acted to conciliate differences within the Group of Seventy-Seven. As a result of these various forces for Southern unity, the Group of Seventy-Seven has been able to make joint proposals, to delegate common spokesmen and negotiators for dealing with the North, and to vote as a group in UNCTAD.[26] Southern unity within UNCTAD has gradually, through the Group of Seventy-Seven, spread to other forums: the IMF (International Monetary Fund), the Environmental Conference, the Conference on the Law of the Sea.

THE LIMITS OF UNCTAD

The strategy of a united Southern front led to some limited successes. It improved the Southern bargaining position vis-à-vis the North, it led to the creation of UNCTAD, and it made possible some modifications in the international trading system. But Southern unity and UNCTAD have not altered the management of trade or the operation of the international market in a significant way.

One problem with the strategy has been the difficulty in maintaining Southern unity. Many cleavages—political and ideological, differing levels of development, and different relations with Northern states— divide the South. While there has been no problem reaching agreement on common general goals, these other differences make it difficult to reach agreement on specific, short-term policies. For example, preferences for Southern manufactures in Northern markets tend to benefit the more developed Southern countries at the expense of the less developed Southern countries. Regional preferences of the EEC with the associated developing states have also been a point of controversy between states affiliated with the community and those not affiliated. More recently, the cleft between oil-producing and oil-consuming states has proved a potential threat to common Southern policy. Because the Group of Seventy-Seven has no institutional structure and no strong leadership, it has proved particularly difficult to resolve internal conflict.

The cleavages in the Group of Seventy-Seven hinder the formulation of common policy in several ways. They prevent the development of very specific programs for bargaining with the North. Disagreement on details of a preference scheme, for example, hampered negotiations with the North, and conflict on details of the link proposal have prevented the development of a Southern blueprint for monetary reform. Cleavages also tend to lead either to the escalation of demands or to the acceptance of the lowest common denominator of agreement, both of which weaken Southern bargaining. Agreement on the most extreme positions politicizes conflict and confrontation with the North and prevents serious bargaining. The acceptance of the lowest common denominator weakens Southern demands.[27]

The impact of Southern cooperation was also weakened by a united front of opposition from the developed countries. The developed market economies disagreed among themselves on many central issues such as trade preferences and commodity prices. Nevertheless, the developed countries did agree on other issues such as opposition to the creation of a powerful UNCTAD and a desire to deal with trade issues in GATT. Furthermore, the demands of the less developed countries surpassed what even the more flexible developed countries were willing to concede. Thus, the Group of Seventy-Seven faced a wall of Northern opposition. Combined with Southern unity, Northern opposition has made UNCTAD a forum for conflict more than for cooperation.[28]

Perhaps most importantly, the Southern strategy has been hampered by the inability to pressure the North. Unity and confrontation are effective only if the South can withhold something that the North wants or needs. But until recently the South had very little with which to threaten the North.

The marginal economic importance of the South, its declining importance as an area of superpower competition, and its own internal divisions made it possible for the North to defeat or weaken the resolutions proposed by the South. More importantly, even when the South forced through resolutions or recommendations, the North, possessing the material and political resources necessary to implement such recommendations or resolutions, was able to ignore them or refuse to cooperate.

The history of UNCTAD negotiations on three principal demands made by the South reveals the failure of the Southern strategy of unity and confrontation. The three demands, found in the Joint Declaration of 1963 and the Prebisch report for UNCTAD I, are a change in institutional structure, improvement in the export of Southern manufactures, and improvement in Southern commodity trade.

The goal of institutional change has been a major success of the Group of Seventy-Seven.[29] Despite persistent opposition from the North, the unified South was able to push through the 1964 Geneva session the establishment of UNCTAD as a permanent organization within the framework of the United Nations General Assembly. UNCTAD consists of the conference, which meets every four years; the Trade and Development Board, which serves as the standing committee of the conference and which meets twice yearly; four permanent committees, which meet at least once a year; and the secretariat with a secretary-general nominally subordinate to the United Nations but with significant de facto autonomy.

The institutionalization of UNCTAD has been an important step toward Southern participation in management and Southern modification of the international trading system. UNCTAD has become a major forum for the expression of Southern demands. It is the avenue by which proposals of the Group of Seventy-Seven are channeled into the system and the means by which the North is confronted with Southern concerns. Because the South has an automatic majority, UNCTAD resolutions favor the point of view of the less developed countries. These resolutions can serve as pressure on the North for concrete action. For this reason one analyst has called UNCTAD a pressure group for the poor nations.[30] Also, as has been discussed, UNCTAD enhances Southern unity and the effectiveness of Southern demands by actively supporting Southern interests.

The formation of UNCTAD as a permanent organization has also had an impact on institutional change in GATT.[31] As Southern pressure for institutional change emerged in the early 1960s, the developed countries sought to maintain the dominance of GATT in trade management. Recognizing that GATT had not been sufficiently responsive to Southern needs and concerns, the North argued that GATT was flexible and could be adapted to meet Southern interests without the formation of a new and potentially rival structure such as UNCTAD. In response to early proposals for institutionalization and to the actual establishment of UNCTAD in 1964, the contracting parties agreed to add a new section on trade and development to the GATT agreement.

The new Part IV, which came into operation in 1965, was an attempt to make up for the failure of GATT to include the economic development section of the Havana Charter. Part IV called on states to refrain from increasing trade barriers against products of special concern to less developed countries and to give high priority to the reduction and elimination of such barriers. It called also for a standstill on internal taxes on tropical products. Part IV makes certain exceptions to the free trade rules for the less developed countries. It eliminates the rule of reciprocity in trade negotiations for developing countries and provides for the establishment of commodity agreements to stabilize and assure more equitable prices. Finally, the new section calls for joint action to promote trade and development, which was the basis for the establishment of a Trade and Development Committee in GATT to work on the elimination and reduction of trade barriers.

Although these institutional changes have provided an important first step for Southern participation in trade management, they have not gone much beyond providing a forum for the articulation of Southern demands and a means of improving the formulation of those demands. While the South sought an institution which could make and implement decisions, the North insisted on a much weaker structure. Thus, UNCTAD cannot compel its members to take action: it can only make proposals. Although these proposals create public pressure on members to comply, there is no way to oblige members to do so. The South must rely on the political willingness of the North to implement programs.

The commitment to action under Part IV of GATT is similarly limited. Qualifications make the section nonbinding, an expression of a goal and a series of recommendations but not a commitment to take action. Measures are to be adopted "to the fullest extent possible," and exceptions are granted "when compelling reasons, which may include legal reasons, make it impossible."[32]

The continued resistance of the developed countries was evidenced during the Kennedy Round negotiations in GATT. While the less developed countries did derive some benefit from the reduction of tariff barriers on manufactured products, the South was generally dissatisfied with the results of this first trade negotiation which followed the implementation of Part IV. Restrictions against Southern manufactures remained higher than the norm, especially for such products as iron and steel, textile products, and clothing, which are of special interest to the underdeveloped countries. Despite some advances such as reductions on tropical products, agricultural protectionism remained intact. Despite the reduction of some tariff barriers, quantitative restrictions and nontariff barriers continued to limit Southern exports generally.[33]

As has been demonstrated time and again, UNCTAD and GATT recommendations are insufficient to prod the North into action. The inability of the South to change Northern policy is revealed in the case of Southern demands for a scheme for general preferences and for commodity arrangements.

One of the principal demands of the Group of Seventy-Seven in UNCTAD was for the expansion of industrial exports of developing countries.[34] Such expansion, it was argued, could not be achieved alone by the free trade approach of eliminating obstacles to exports. It would also be necessary to carry on the active promotion of less developed countries' industrial exports by granting them preferential access to Northern markets. A preference system would offer lower tariffs to less developed countries than to developed countries. It would help Southern industries overcome the problem of high initial costs and, by opening larger markets, would enable them to lower their costs and eventually to compete in world markets without preferences.[35]

The demand for a general system of preferences has achieved some success. At UNCTAD I, the preference proposal met with opposition from the United States and with mixed response from other developed countries. The United States argued that preferences would have little positive effect on the trade gap and that they would have the severe negative consequences of undermining the free trade system by encouraging new discriminatory practices and uneconomic production and by hindering efforts to decrease tariff barriers generally. Other Northern states are more sympathetic. The United Kingdom, West Germany, Holland, and Denmark supported in principle a general preferential scheme, whereas France and Belgium supported a limited preferential system among certain countries. With the United States adamantly opposed and the others divided, UNCTAD I merely referred the issue to the Trade and Development Board.

Progress was made between UNCTAD I and II in 1968. The Group of Seventy-Seven continued its pressure, reinforced by the failure of the Kennedy Round negotiations to reduce barriers to Southern manufactured exports. The North discussed the issue in the OECD, but no progress was made until 1967 when the United States changed its position. Increasing U.S. isolation from the views of both North and South, the proliferation of exclusive EEC preferences, which the United States viewed as worse than a general preference scheme, and the pressure of Latin America led to the change in American policy. As a result, agreement was reached at UNCTAD II in New Delhi on the principle of establishing a preferential scheme. A Special Committee of Preferences was set up to continue negotiations and to develop a specific plan. Agreement was expected by 1969.

Negotiations, however, bogged down following UNCTAD II. There were conflicts both within the Northern and Southern groups and between them over which products would receive preferences, over the size of the preference, over exceptions and safeguards, and over a general scheme versus special schemes. By 1970 agreement was reached on a scheme to be introduced in 1971, but once again there were delays. Finally, in 1975 with the passage of the U.S. Trade Reform Act, all developed countries had instituted preferential schemes.

The systems which emerged, however, were not those that the less developed countries had sought. The underdeveloped countries preferred a permanent system by which all developed states would provide unrestricted or duty-free access for all industrial exports including processed and semiprocessed agricultural products and raw materials of all developing states. International consultation in their plan was to be required prior to exemption of any product from the Generalized System of Preferences (GSP) or any use of an escape clause. Existing reverse preferences and special preferential systems were to be phased out. Finally special provisions were to help the less developed developing countries who stood to gain fewer benefits from the GSP.[36]

The Northern preference schemes differ in crucial ways from these Southern proposals. Because the North was unable to agree on a common general system, individual states adopted similar but different schemes. The preferences granted are temporary, and their application is limited by important quantitative restrictions. The major schemes are subject to ceiling limitations on the quantity or value of any particular import receiving preferences. Preferential treatment applies up to a ceiling for any particular product or, in the American scheme, for a product coming from any individual country. Imports above the ceiling are subject to normal tariff rates. Thus there is, in effect, a quota on the amount of imports receiving preferential treatment. In addition, the number of products covered by preferences has been severely limited. Many of the products excluded from preferential treatment are those such as textiles and leather goods in which the South enjoys a comparative advantage.[37] The United States program, for example, excluded textiles and apparel articles subject to textile agreements, watches, import-sensitive electronic articles, import-sensitive steel articles, certain footwear, import-sensitive glass products, and any other article that the president determines is import sensitive.[38]

In addition, the developed countries have reserved the right to refuse to grant preferences to any state they choose, although only the United States has actually taken such action. The U.S. scheme makes several exclusions. It denies preferences, for example, to all members of OPEC (Organization of Petroleum Exporting Countries) and any state which is "party to any other arrangement of foreign countries" or which "participates in any action pursuant to such arrangement the effect of which is to withhold supplies of vital commodity resources from international trade or to raise the price of such commodities to an unreasonable level . . . ." A country which has nationalized, expropriated, or otherwise seized ownership or control of U.S. property or which has repudiated or nullified a contract or agreement with a U.S. citizen or entity without prompt, adequate, and effective compensation may also be excluded, as may all Communist countries and countries which refuse to cooperate with the United States in the control of drug trafficking.[39]

The preference schemes make no special provisions for the less developed developing countries and provide for unilateral application of safeguards by the developed countries without prior consultation. Finally, it remains unclear as to just who will benefit from even these limited preferences. Ironically, the success of GATT in general trade liberalization tends to eliminate the difference between preferential treatment and general treatment and to wipe out the advantages of preferences. Thus, the adoption of GSP represents more of an apparent rather than a real victory for the South.[40]

Until recently the story of commodity schemes was shorter and even less successful.[41] Commodity arrangements are of great interest to the South because they represent a huge percent of Southern exports and foreign exchange earnings. The problems of commodity trade are numerous: price fluctuations, which affect foreign exchange earnings for development; Northern protectionism and discriminatory tax policies; and competition from synthetics and substitutes. Southern proposals to UNCTAD have covered numerous commodity problems and issues: commodity agreements to stabilize prices and to establish remunerative

Table 7-1   Dependence on Selected Mineral
Imports from Underdeveloped Countries,
1973 (as a percentage of consumption)

	United States	Japan	Western Europe
Bauxite and aluminum	67.0%	47.0%	22.0%
Chrome	31.0	38.0	38.0
Copper	51.0	49.0	57.0
Iron ore	34.0	44.0	30.0
Lead	25.0	16.0	16.0
Manganese	68.0	21.0	42.0
Nickel	7.0	88.0	2.0
Phosphates	—	39.0	67.0
Tin	94.0	90.0	85.0
Tungsten	61.0	96.0	58.0
Zinc	11.0	32.0	16.0

Council on International Economic Policy, *International Economic Report of the President*, (Washington, D.C., March 1975), pp. 161–162.

and equitable prices; compensatory finance schemes to ease earnings fluctuations; the liberalization of Northern protection against Southern commodities; and aid for products facing competition from substitutes and synthetics. Quite simply, until the oil crisis and its aftermath, there was virtually no action in any of these areas. The North successfully resisted virtually all commodity restructuring.[42]

Thus by the beginning of the 1970s, it was clear that the strategy of the 1960s, like that of the 1950s, had failed. Southern unity and confrontation without the stick of a credible threat to the North proved to be weak tools for bargaining with the North. The UNCTAD "victories" had led to only minor revisions in Southern dependence. The Group of Seventy-Seven was unsuccessful because it was unable to pressure the developed countries to bargain seriously with them. The result was increasing frustration and hostility from the underdeveloped world.

COMMODITY POWER: TOWARD A NEW STRATEGY?

In the early 1970s there were several changes that seemed to offer the South an opportunity to pose a serious threat to the North. Suddenly, it seemed possible for the underdeveloped countries, through their control of vital raw materials, to bargain effectively with the North.

For several reasons, the North was becoming more dependent on some raw material imports from the South (see Table 7-1). While overall consumption was rising, high-grade Northern supplies of many materials were being depleted, and extraction in the North was becoming increasingly expensive. Supplies in underdeveloped countries, in contrast, were plentiful and production costs relatively low. The result was a rising share of imports from less developed countries in total consumption (see Table 7-1).

Northern demand for Southern raw materials was accentuated by the boom and inflation in the developed market economies. An economic boom in the developed countries at the end of the 1960s and beginning of the 1970s led to a surge in Northern demand for raw materials from the underdeveloped countries. Inflation and the uncertainties of floating exchange rates led to a shift of speculative funds into commodities, further increasing demand. The resultant price inflation and supply shortages in commodities in the early 1970s vividly demonstrated Northern dependence on Southern raw materials (see Figure 7-1). Price and supply became a public political issue in the developed countries through their impact on national economic health and on developed country consumers.

Figure 7–1 Export Price Trends

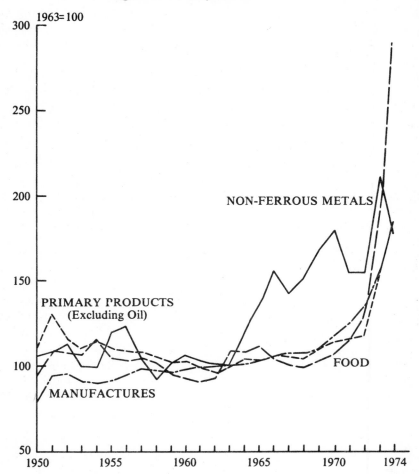

U.S. Council on International Economic Policy, *Critical Imported Materials: Special Report*, December 1974, p. 7.

While increasingly concerned about price and availability of supply, the North was decreasingly able or willing to assure such supply through political and military action. Political control was undermined by the end of colonialism and the declining influence of the West in Third World governments resulting from hostility to the North. In addition, changing public attitudes and the risk of escalation constrained military action to protect Northern economic interests.[43] Finally, economic troubles and conflict undermined the ability of the North to mount a joint economic, political, or military action in case of supply problems.

At the same time, other factors were increasing the South's ability to control access to its raw materials. New, skilled cadres in many Southern states were acquiring knowledge and expertise in the raw materials industry and in world commodity market conditions and operations.[44] Increased national control over raw material production facilitated the control of supplies. Moreover, as frustration with the North increased, the South's political leaders were increasingly willing to use these new skills to manipulate raw material supply.

Crucial to increasing the North's perception of dependence and the South's sense of increased control was the example of the manipulation of supply by OPEC, which demonstrated to both developed and developing countries that Southern producers of raw materials could pose a serious threat to the North by withholding or threatening to withhold supplies of raw materials. It also demonstrated to the South that a unified Northern response to or Northern retaliation for such action was not inevitable.[45]

Southern states are aggressively using the commodity weapon to press the North for a restructuring of the international economic system. (On commodity cartels, see chapter 9.) The Group of Seventy-Seven at Third World Conferences in 1974, 1975, and 1976 developed a coordinated program for a New International Economic Order (NIEO). At special sessions of the United Nations General Assembly in May 1974 and September 1975, at the regular assembly session of fall 1974, and at UNCTAD IV in May 1976, the Southern bloc pressed these demands on the North. The Declaration and Action Programme on the Establishment of a New International Economic Order adopted in May 1974 by a Special Session of the General Assembly reflected the new sense of power of the Third World. In that declaration, the underdeveloped countries proclaimed that

> the present international economic order is in direct conflict with current developments in international political and economic relations. . . . The developing world has become a powerful factor that makes its influence felt in all fields of international activity. These irreversible changes in the relationship of forces in the world necessitates the active, full and equal participation of the developing countries in the formulation and application of all decisions that concern the international community.[46]

The Third World program for the New International Economic Order as reflected in the various recommendations presented by the underdeveloped countries touches all areas of international economic interaction.[47] Aid proposals called for Northern commitment to the transfer of 0.7 percent of GNP as set by the second United Nations Development Decade, a greater flow to emergency funds designed to deal with the food, energy, and recession–inflation crises, a renegotiation of the less developed countries' debt, and the implementation of the link in monetary reform. Foreign investment recommendations called for the right of expropriation, greater Northern control of multinational corporations, more effective application of technology by foreign investors, and improvement in ways of transferring technology to less developed countries.[48]

A key element of the NIEO proposals was trade. The South called for trade reform with particular vehemence and directed much of its diplomatic activity at trade issues. The Group of Seventy-Seven called for a reduction in Northern tariff barriers on a nonreciprocal basis, for improvement in the preference schemes implemented by the developed countries, for more effective adjustment assistance in the developed countries to ease the cost of greater less developed countries imports and to defuse political opposition, and for international commodity agreements. A very important aspect of the Southern program was the proposed integrated commodity program developed by the Group of Seventy-Seven with the help of the UNCTAD secretariat. As presented at the fourth UNCTAD conference held in Nairobi, Kenya in May 1976, the proposal called for a single international agency and a common fund of $6 billion to support the price of ten commodities.[49]

The ability of the less developed countries to use the commodity weapon to make such changes in the old economic order will depend in part on Southern unity in bargaining with the developed countries. If the Third World can link its various potential commodity threats and, in particular, if the oil threat can be linked to other Third World demands, the South stands a much better chance of forcing the North to make concessions.

Important forces, however, threaten to divide the South. Cleavages arising from its heterogeneity continue to plague the Group of Seventy-Seven. The different impact of the energy, food, and recession crises on the different Southern states and the domestic problems these crises create may undermine the perception of a common interest in joint action and may encourage states to concentrate on national or regional problems to the detriment of Southern unity.

Nevertheless, the South has demonstrated a surprising degree of cohesion in its demands for a new international economic order, and in its actions at the United Nations, the preparatory producer–consumer conference, UNCTAD IV and the IMF. The learning experience of the Group of Seventy-Seven has facilitated Southern solidarity and effectiveness. Over a decade of common action in international forums has given the group an understanding of how to bargain jointly with the North. Members now develop their positions early and come well prepared for international negotiations. An important force for unity and strength has been the emergence of OPEC leadership. Some oil producers, Algeria in particular, have been willing and able to mobilize a common Southern front and to link the oil issue with other Third World issues. OPEC states helped to organize the group at the United Nations special sessions and demanded a linkage between oil and other Third World issues at the Conference on International Economic Cooperation (CIEC).[50]

Another determinant in the new commodity strategy is the maintenance of the threat to the North. There is great disagreement among experts about the nature of the raw material threat. Some see long-term structural changes in the international economy and a resultant permanent commodity threat.[51] Some view oil as the exception and commodity power as a short-term phenomenon based on temporary shortages.[52] This study in analyzing commodity cartels suggests that some Southern states have the motivation and perhaps the short-run capability to disrupt the economies of the developed North.[53]

The powerful Northern states are becoming aware of that motivation and capability. France, with a tradition of economic planning and an acute sense of vulnerability to supply interruption, was the first major Northern state to endorse the idea of a new international economic order. At the sixth special session of the United Nations General Assembly, France pressed for the organization and international management of raw material markets.[54] In the fall of that year, France proposed a producer–consumer dialogue as an alternative to the American policy of confrontation.

The EEC has also demonstrated a new flexibility. The Lomé Convention, signed in February 1975 by the community and the forty-six associated African, Caribbean, and Pacific (ACP) states, contains the germ of a new international economic order. Lomé increased aid to the ACP states and gave them a greater voice in aid management. The agreements provide for preferential access for ACP products to EEC markets without reciprocal advantages for EEC products. They also create a compensatory finance scheme to stabilize the export earnings of the associated states from 12 key commodities.[55]

In May 1975 at a meeting of the Commonwealth Heads of Government in Jamaica, Prime Minister Harold Wilson of the United Kingdom unfolded a new British policy, "a new deal in world economies, in trade between nations and the terms of that trade."[56] Mr. Wilson's proposed new deal included a general international commodity agreement, specific commodity agreements, stabilization of export earnings, and consideration of indexing prices of raw materials and manufactured products.

While European (and Japanese) policy was moving toward some accommodation to Southern demands, the United States remained opposed to a new North–South dialogue to revise the economic order. Long the supporter of the free market, more self-sufficient, and thus less vulnerable to external supply control, the United States felt that other Northern states were reacting too quickly and with too much panic to the threat of commodity power. In the view of U.S. policy makers, there was no major threat from any but the oil-producing states. Eventually, when the Third World oil consumers recognized that OPEC was damaging their economies, they would turn on the oil producers. Eventually the short-term factors which led to temporary Northern vulnerability would disappear and commodity prices would fall. With time also the panicky Europeans and Japanese would realize that there was no threat. According to the United States, the West should not allow oil power to be linked with other issues, and, above all, the developed market economies should not make precipitous bargains with the South based on a temporarily unfavorable situation.

Thus, the United States was willing to discuss oil and energy issues but was opposed to any broad consumer–producer negotiations which would link energy to other issues of the new international economic order. When the oil producers and the other less developed countries insisted on such a linkage at a preparatory producer–consumer conference in April 1975, the United States refused to agree, and the meeting collapsed.[57]

In May 1975, however, the United States altered its position. The U.S. had learned at the preparatory conference that Third World solidarity was not as ephemeral as it had thought. As Undersecretary of State Charles W. Robinson put it,

> "We expect the OPEC–LDC [less developed countries] bloc under OPEC leadership to be a strong and vocal force in future international fora.[58]

The United States also discovered the importance of OPEC leadership when the producers threatened to raise their prices significantly at their September 1975 meeting if the United States did not respond to the broader demands for a new international economic order. Another reason for the change was a sense of confidence in consumer solidarity. The coordination of policy by the Northern states at the preparatory conference demonstrated to policy makers the success of their strategy of uniting the once disparate developed countries.[59] Finally, despite that unity the United States also discovered that the Europeans and Japanese were prepared to move ahead to make deals with Third World states if the United States continued to drag its feet.

At a speech in Kansas City in May 1975, Secretary of State Kissinger announced that the United States was now willing "to discuss new arrangements in individual commodities on a case-by-case basis" and to "propose that the World Bank explore new ways of financing raw material investment in producing countries."[60] Then in September 1975 at the seventh special session of the United Nations General Assembly, Secretary Kissinger announced an American program for achieving a new international economic order. It included new trade preferences and benefits for Southern exports, a proposal for a compensatory finance scheme, programs to improve the access of Third World states to private capital markets, a series of institutes and funds to transfer technology to and to develop new technology appropriate for the South, and new international rules governing multinational corporations.[61]

Whether the Kissinger speech signalled a real or a rhetorical change remains to be seen. On the one hand, the reform of policy was tenuous. Most of the details of the Kissinger proposal had not been worked out. Important Treasury officials opposed many of the Kissinger proposals, especially the greater willingness to discuss commodity agreements. On the other hand, the United States has cooperated in the creation of an improved compensatory finance scheme within the IMF and of an IMF trust fund through which the underdeveloped countries will receive the profits from the sale of one-sixth of the fund's gold. It signed commodity agreements in tin and coffee (although it refused to sign a cocoa agreement), and at long last it instituted its preference scheme for Southern exports.

THE PROCESS OF NEGOTIATION

Recent policy declarations and programs indicate a greater flexibility on the part of the North. They do not constitute a revolution in the international economic order. The ability of the underdeveloped countries to bargain for that new order will be tested in a series of negotiations in various international forums in the years ahead.

One such forum is UNCTAD. Held in 1976, UNCTAD IV clearly demonstrated the new unity and offensive strategy of the South. Less developed countries formed a united and well-prepared front against the disunited developed countries. And this unity and preparation enabled the Group of Seventy-Seven to reject a proposal by the United States for an International Resources Bank which the less developed countries viewed as a maneuver against their commodity program and to oblige the developed countries to agree to attend a conference to be held by March 1977 to discuss the international regulation of key commodities. The less developed countries also made some advances in the discussion of debt rescheduling.

Nevertheless, UNCTAD IV also demonstrated the limits of the conference as a negotiating forum. Much of the time was spent with North and South in conflict. The North rejected the commodity program; the South rejected the American proposal for a resources bank. The statement on the commodity program specifically recognized differences of view over objectives and modalities of commodity agreements and in any case entailed only an agreement by the developed countries to attend a conference. There seemed little likelihood that the developed countries would be cooperative at such a conference. Most—especially West Germany and the United States—remained opposed.

Following UNCTAD IV statements from U.S. policy makers, particularly officials in the Treasury, emphasized that the United States felt it had in no way committed itself to the idea of a comprehensive commodity program. Thus, as in the past, UNCTAD was an ineffective bargaining forum. Bloc organization led to polarization of positions. Publicity further politicized conflict and hindered serious bargaining. In addition, the North has never viewed UNCTAD as an appropriate forum for negotiation. As long as UNCTAD cannot impose decisions, it will remain ineffective for more than pressure politics.

The Conference on International Economic Cooperation (CIEC) is another forum.[62] This producer consumer conference, composed of group representatives, began meeting in December 1975 and was to last a year. Discussions are taking place in CIEC's four commissions on energy, raw materials, finance, and economic development. The limited membership and the technical nature of the commissions may diffuse conflict and facilitate negotiation and agreement. On the other hand, the separation of energy from other issues may hinder the Southern strategy of linkage, and CIEC, because of its limited membership and limited lifespan, may not be able to impose a common program. Thus in the end CIEC may be more useful for generating ideas and for putting pressure on the North than for reaching specific agreements.

Another avenue for North–South bargaining is GATT. The developed countries have evidenced an interest in discussing international commodity management in the multilateral trade negotiations. Developed market economies have been increasingly concerned about price stability and access to supplies of raw materials. Because of inflation the fluctuation of commodity prices, once an issue of interest only to underdeveloped countries, has become a concern of developed countries as well. Access to supply has also recently emerged as a principal issue of international trade in the North. Export controls such as the U.S. embargo on soybeans and scrap metal have been imposed by the North in an effort to moderate domestic prices; export controls have been used by primary producers such as OPEC in an effort to increase prices. Furthermore, GATT is the preferred negotiating forum for the North and one which would allow the North to separate energy and other commodity issues. As a result, it seems certain that the North will make a concerted effort to develop new agreements and new rules on access in the multilateral trade negotiations.[63]

This concern with price stability and access may enable the South to negotiate effectively in multilateral trade negotiations for the first time since World War II. Developing states may be able to trade price and access commitments for such Northern assurances as a fair price for raw materials or increased access to Northern markets for Southern manufactures. Also as a result of this new bargaining power, the South has evidenced interest in the GATT trade negotiation forum. Furthermore, it seems that many Southern representatives recognize the advantages of the private, off-the-record GATT negotiations for real bargaining as opposed to the public political posturing with little economic payoff of UNCTAD, or even the CIEC.

Yet another forum for North–South bargaining is the bilateral or regional one. If discussions in the various multilateral forums mentioned above do not lead to agreement, North–South bargaining may deteriorate into bilateral or regional deal making. Concessions may be offered on a limited basis providing assurance for a few but threatening to break down the larger system of international trade which has developed since World War II. For example, the Europeans, feeling more vulnerable than the United States to supply interruptions, might be tempted to make a separate arrangement with several Southern states. Thus the special relationship between the associated developing states and the EEC might be expanded and solidified. Such a system might lead to a series of economic blocs, for example, a European–African bloc or a U.S.–Latin American bloc.

Whatever the forum, North–South discussions will focus on various new forms of international trade management and income redistribution through trade. Several forms of commodity management will most certainly be discussed. One possibility is one or more international commodity agreements (ICAs) among producers and consumers of particular products. ICAs control the fluctuation of price and assure a minimum and/or maximum price for producers. They may be designed to stabilize the price or to increase it. ICAs may be of three types or combinations thereof: buffer stock schemes such as that of the International Tin Agreement, whereby price is managed by purchases or sales from a central fund at times of excessive fluctuation; export quotas such as those used by the International Coffee Agreement, whereby price is managed by assigning production quotas to participating countries to control supply; and multilateral contracts, in which importing countries contract to buy certain quantities at a specified low price when the world market falls below that price and whereby exporting countries agree to sell certain quantities at a fixed price when the world market price exceeds the maximum.

ICAs face several problems. A major stumbling block is the different goals of producers and consumers. Producers would like to use ICAs to raise prices; consumers would be willing to consider their use to stabilize prices. Accommodating these opposite goals will prove difficult but probably not impossible. More difficult are various practical problems of commodity management. Agreements in the past have been plagued by such problems as temptations to cheat when prices rise, variations of price and supply among different qualities of the same commodity, encouragement of the use of substitutes, the difficulty of imposing drastic production or export reductions, and the high cost of financing buffer stocks. Moreover, some critics argue that ICAs are inefficient, encouraging waste and the misallocation of resources. Others point out that ICAs help only a few developed countries and may actually hurt others faced with higher prices due to ICAs.[64]

One way of avoiding some of the constraints of ICAs while accomplishing their goal is through compensatory finance. Such schemes attempt to stabilize or to increase earnings of less developed countries not by price manipulations, but by compensating Southern states when the price of a commodity leads to a decline in export earnings. This is accomplished through a fund to compensate countries for shortfalls in export earnings.

One such compensatory finance scheme was instituted by the IMF in 1963 and was greatly expanded in 1975. Another compensatory finance scheme in operation is that created by the EEC under the Lomé agreement. This scheme establishes a fund to pay the associated ACP states compensation when the market price for certain commodities falls below a certain level. For the wealthier associated states compensation takes the form of an interest-free loan, whereas for the poorest states compensation takes the form of a grant.[65]

Several possibilities for expanding international management also exist in the area of access to supplies. Negotiation on access to supplies would represent a radical change in trade management. The concern of GATT and of postwar international trade negotiations has been access not to supplies but to markets. This emphasis reflects the concern of the postwar policy makers to correct the sins of import restriction of the interwar period. Thus, while GATT established important rules for the restrictions on access to markets, it made few restrictions on access to supplies, and even those few restrictions were weakened by actual practice. Quantitative export controls could be imposed in case of domestic scarcity or to conserve exhaustible resources. GATT also permitted export controls through nonquantitative measures such as export duties or taxes.[66] Moreover, the many trade negotiations focused on issues of market access. Now, however, because of both Northern and Southern export controls, access to supply has become a major trade issue.

One approach to regulating access to supply would be the negotiation of a broad set of rules and enforcement procedures similar to the rules and procedures for access to markets. One proposed set of rules would stipulate when export controls can be used, would limit their duration and would establish a legal basis for consumer response and an international framework for complaints and management.[67] In return for agreement on such additions to GATT, the South might be able to extract some concessions from the North. The development of such a broad set of rules, however, is difficult, for it requires a broad consensus (both between Northern consumers and Southern producers and between Northern producers and consumers) and the ability to agree on specifics which probably do not exist.[68]

A more likely solution might be the exchange of commitments between producers and consumers. Southern producer states might trade an agreement on assured supplies in return for a Northern consumer agreement of assured access to Northern markets or for Northern participation in commodity or compensatory finance agreements.

Whether commodity agreements and/or access agreements will emerge from a new round of trade negotiations remains unclear. What does seem clear, however, is that revolution is not imminent. Negotiations will be long and difficult. New areas of management are being approached. The charting of such areas will require a significant learning process; agreement on specifics will be difficult, piecemeal, long in coming. However, as in the case of trade negotiations among developed market economies, the process of negotiation—if indeed it is negotiation and not simply the statement and restatement of conflicting positions—will in itself be important. It will indicate an attempt to move from confrontation to consultation and negotiation. It may also signify an attempt to move from "free trade" of the postwar order to "fair trade" of the new economic order. If a step in this direction is the result, the international economic system will have achieved a major transformation.

NOTES

1. Clair Wilcox, *A Charter for World Trade* (New York: Macmillan, 1949), p. 141.

2. Economic Commission for Latin America. *The Economic Development of Latin America and Its Principal Problems* (Lake Success, N.Y.: United Nations, 1950): Economic Commission for Latin America, *Theoretical and Practical Problems of Economic Growth* (New York: United Nations, 1951). For an interesting recent debate on inward- versus outward-looking trade policies, see Paul Streeten, ed., *Trade Strategies for Development: Papers of the Ninth Cambridge Conference on Development Problems*, September 1972 (New York: Wiley, 1973), pp. 51–102.

3. Wilcox, *A Charter for World Trade*; Williams Adams Brown, Jr., *The United States and the Restoration of World Trade* (Washington, D.C.: Brookings Institution, 1950), pp. 97–104, 152–158.

4. Wilcox, pp. 140–167; Brown, pp. 178–180, 203–211, 217–222.

5. Only four underdeveloped countries Ceylon, Cuba, Haiti, and India sought and obtained permission to impose quantitative restrictions under Article XVIII. The limitations imposed by the contracting parties, however, destroyed much of the benefit of their use. Article XVIII was revised in 1955 to provide a greater possibility for withdrawal or modification of concessions previously made and to enable the use of quantitative restrictions for balance-of-payments reasons. But, once again, the many safeguards included rendered it of little use to the South. Sidney Wells, "The Developing Countries, GATT and UNCTAD," *International Affairs*, 45 (January 1969), 65 67; Karin Koch, *International Trade Policy and the GATT, 1947–1967* (Stockholm: Almquist & Wiksell, 1969), pp. 227 232.

6. Steffan B. Linder, "The Significance of GATT for Underdeveloped Countries," in *Proceedings of the United Nations Conference on Trade and Development*, 5 (1964), 502 532.

7. Diego Cordovez, "The Making of UNCTAD: Institutional Background and Legislative History," *Journal of World Trade Law*, 1 (May June 1967), 253 254.

8. Ian Little, Tibor Scitovsky, and Maurice Scott, *Industry and Trade in Some Developing Countries: A Comparative Study*, Published for the Development Centre of the Organization for Economic Co-operation and Development, Paris (London: Oxford University Press, 1970), pp. xvii xxii, 1 29. For an example of the economic argument underlying import substitution policies, see Gunnar Myrdal, *An International Economy*, 1969 ed. (New York: Harper & Row, 1956), pp. 275 284.

9. Although not permitted under GATT, the South was able to follow protectionist policies under IMF rules, which allowed quantitative restriction for balance-of-payments reasons, or under GATT waivers or because they were not members of GATT.

10. Little et al., *Industry and Trade in Some Developing Countries*, pp. 1 29. For the Latin American experience with protection, see Economic Commission for Latin America, *The Process of Industrial Development in Latin America* (United Nations: New York, 1966), pp. 21 35.

11. For the limits of import substitution, see Little et al., ibid.; United Nations Conference on Trade and Development, *Toward a New Trade Policy for Development, Report by the Secretary-General* (New York: United Nations, 1964), pp. 21 22.

12. The argument here is that of Raul Prebisch: see United Nations Conference on Trade and Development, *Toward a New Trade Policy for Development*. For a summary of Prebisch's argument and the arguments of the critics of the theory of declining terms of trade, see A. S. Friedeberg, *The United Nations Conference on Trade and Development of 1964: The Theory of the Peripheral Economy at the Centre of International Political Discussions* (Rotterdam: Rotterdam Univ. Press, 1969), pp. 33 67. For a more recent challenge, see reports of a United Nations study in *The New York Times*, May 25, 1975, p. 1.

13. One of the most flagrant examples of restrictive export agreements is the Long-Term Arrangement Regarding International Trade in Cotton Textiles, which was negotiated in GATT. The North, in particular the United States, forced the underdeveloped exporters (as well as Japan) to agree to "voluntarily" limit their cotton textile exports with the threat that the alternative – national import quotas imposed by national legislatures would be worse.

14. For the Southern view of trade barriers, see United Nations Conference on Trade and Development, *Towards a New Trade Policy for Development*; United Nations Conference on Trade and Development, *Towards a Global Strategy of Development* (New York: United Nations, 1968). For other analyses, see Harry G. Johnson, *Economic Policies Toward Less Developed Countries* (New York: Praeger, 1967), pp. 78 110; John Pincus, *Trade, Aid and Development: The Rich and Poor Nations* (New York: McGraw-Hill, 1967), pp. 177 194.

15. Economic Commission for Latin America, *Economic Survey 1969* (New York: United Nations, 1969), pp. 61, 62.

16. *Trends in International Trade: A Report by a Panel of Experts* (Geneva: The Contracting Parties to the General Agreement on Tariffs and Trade, October 1958). The experts were Roberto de Oliviero Campos, Gottfried Haberler, James Meade, and Jan Tinbergen.

17. Koch, *International Trade Policy and the GATT, 1947 1967*, pp. 235 239.

18. Ibid., pp. 239-244.

19. For a history of events leading up to UNCTAD I, see Cordovez "The Making of UNCTAD"; Friedeberg, *The United Nations Conference on Trade and Development of 1964*; Charles L. Robertson, "The Creation of UNCTAD," in Robert W. Cox, ed., *International Organisation: World Politics* (London: Macmillan, 1969), pp. 258-274.

20. United Nations General Assembly, 18th Session, Official Records: Eighteenth Session, Supplement No. 7 (A 5507), p. 24.

21. Ibid.

22. Ibid., p. 25.

23. In Branislav Gosovic, *UNCTAD, Conflict and Compromise: The Third World's Quest for an Equitable World Economic Order Through the United Nations* (Leiden, Netherlands: A. W. Sijthoff, 1972), p. 271.

24. Ibid., pp. 286-291, for decision making in the Group of Seventy-Seven.

25. For the role of the secretariat see Joseph S. Nye, "UNCTAD: Poor Nations' Pressure Group," in Robert W. Cox and Harold K. Jacobson, *The Anatomy of Influence: Decision Making in International Organization* (New Haven, Conn.: Yale Univ. Press, 1973), pp. 348 349. For a statement of the UNCTAD doctrine, see United Nations Conference on Trade and Development *Towards a New Trade Policy for Development* and *Towards a Global Strategy of Development*.

26. For an analysis of the Group of Seventy-Seven, see Gosovic, *UNCTAD, Conflict and Compromise*, pp. 271 292.

27. Ibid., pp. 279 286, on Southern cleavages.

28. Ibid., pp. 293 301, for the Northern bloc within UNCTAD. There is also a group composed of the socialist states of Eastern Europe.

29. On the institutional question generally see Cordovez, "The Making of UNC-TAD"; Gosovic, *UNCTAD, Conflict and Compromise*, pp. 173 266.

30. Nye, "UNCTAD: Poor Nations' Pressure Group."

31. On the addition of Part IV generally, see Kenneth W. Dam, *The GATT: Law and International Economic Organization* (Chicago: Univ. of Chicago Press, 1970), pp. 236-244.

32. Ibid., p. 239.

33. United Nations Conference on Trade and Development, *The Kennedy Round, estimated effects on tariff barriers: report by the Secretary General of UNCTAD*. Parts I and II (New York: United Nations, 1968). International Bank for Reconstruction and Development and International Development Agency, *Annual Report 1968*, pp. 33 34.

34. For a history of the issue of preferences see Gosovic, *UNCTAD, Conflict and Compromise*, pp. 65-93. For a study of U.S. policy, see Ronald I. Meltzer, *The Politics of Policy Reversal: The American Response to the Issue of Granting Trade Preferences to the Developing Countries, 1964-1967*, unpublished Ph.D. dissertation, (Columbia University, 1975).

35. United Nations Conference on Trade and Development, *Towards a New Trade Policy for Development*, pp. 65 75.

36. Gosovic, *UNCTAD, Conflict and Compromise*, pp. 65 93.

37. United Nations Conference on Trade and Development, *Proceedings of the United Nations Conference on Trade and Development, Third Session* (13 April to 21 May 1972), Vol. II, Merchandise Trade (New York: United Nations 1973), pp. 104 140; Tracy Murray, "How Helpful Is the Generalised System of Preferences to Developing Countries?," *Economic Journal*, 83 (June 1973), 449 455.

38. U.S. Code, *Congressional and Administrative News, 93rd Congress, Second Session 1974*, Vol. 2 (St, Paul, Minn.: West Publishing Company, 1975), pp. 2398-2399.

39. Ibid., pp. 2395-2396.

40. Murray, "How Helpful Is the Generalised System of Preferences to Developing Countries?"

41. For a history of the commodity issue see Gosovic, *UNCTAD, Conflict and Compromise*, pp. 93-114. For recent developments see Chapters 9 and 10 of this text.

42. Gosovic, *UNCTAD, Conflict and Compromise*, pp. 99 101.

43. See Klaus Knorr, "The Limits of Economic and Military Power," *Daedelus*, 104 (Fall 1975), 229-243.

44. See Chapter 8.

45. See Chapter 9.

46. Declaration and Action Programme on the Establishment of a New International Economic Order, in Guy F. Erb and Valeriana Kallab, *Beyond Dependency: The Developing World Speaks Out* (Washington, D.C.: Overseas Development Council, 1975), p. 186.

47. Ibid., pp. 165–236, for some of these statements. For a summary which this analysis uses, see Roger D. Hansen, "The Crisis of Interdependence: Where Do We Go from Here?" in Roger D. Hansen, ed., *The U.S. and World Development: Agenda for Action 1976* (Washington, D.C.: Overseas Development Council, 1976), pp. 45–47.

48. See Chapter 8.

49. The mechanisms for increasing and stabilizing prices were to include buffer stocks, a common fund for financing such stocks, multilateral purchase and supply agreements for particular commodities, and compensatory finance.

50. On the Conference on International Economic Cooperation, see Chapter 9.

51. See, for example, C. Fred Bergsten, "The Threat from the Third World," *Foreign Policy*, 11 (Summer 1973), 102–124 and "The New Era in World Commodity Markets," *Challenge*, 17 (September–October 1974), 34–42; Donella H. Meadows et al., *The Limits to Growth: A Report for the Club of Rome's Project on the Predicament of Mankind* (New York: Universe Books, 1972).

52. See, for example, Stephen D. Krasner, "Oil Is the Exception," *Foreign Policy*, 14 (Spring 1974), 68–84; Raymond Mikesell, "More Third World Cartels Ahead?," *Challenge*, 17 (November–December 1974), 24–27.

53. See Chapter 9.

54. Remarks by Foreign Minister Michel Jobert before the sixth special session of the United Nations General Assembly, April 10, 1974, Ambassade de France, Service de Presse et d'Information.

55. *Lomé Dossier*, reprinted from *The Courier*, 31 special issue, March 1975, (Brussels: Commission of the European Communities, 1975). See, also, Isebill V. Gruhn, "The Lomé Convention: Inching Towards Interdependence," *International Organization*, 30 (Spring 1976), 240–262.

56. Speech on world trade in commodities, delivered by Prime Minister Harold Wilson to the Commonwealth heads of government meeting in Kingston, Jamaica, 1 May 1975 (British Information Service, Policy and Reference Division, 33/75), p. 1.

57. See "Department Discusses Preparatory Meeting of Oil Producing and Consuming Nations," statement by Charles W. Robinson, Under Secretary for Economic Affairs, U.S. Department of State, *The Bulletin*, 72 (May 26, 1975), 688–689.

58. Ibid., p. 690.

59. Ibid.

60. "Strengthening the World Economic Structure," address by Secretary Kissinger, U.S. Department of State, *The Bulletin*, 72 (June 2, 1975), 717; see, also, "The Global Challenge and International Cooperation," address by Secretary Kissinger at Milwaukee, U.S. Department of State, *The Bulletin*, 73 (August 4, 1975), 149–157.

61. "Global Consensus and Economic Development," address by Secretary Kissinger prepared for delivery at the seventh special session of the United Nations General Assembly, U.S. Department of State, *The Bulletin*, 73 (September 22, 1975), 425–441.

62. On CIEC, see Chapter 9.

63. See, for example, Senator Walter F. Mondale, "Beyond Detente: Toward International Economic Security," *Foreign Affairs*, 53 (October 1974), 1–23.

64. Johnson, *Economic Policies Toward Less Developed Countries*, pp. 137–149.

65. Ibid., pp. 149–152; Friedeberg, *The United Nations Conference on Trade and Development*, pp. 130–146; Marion Bywater, "The Lomé Convention," *European Community*, (March 1975) pp. 5–7; address of Secretary of State Kissinger to seventh special session of the General Assembly, *The Bulletin*, 73 (September 22, 1975).

66. Frieder Roessler, "GATT and Access to Supplies," *Journal of World Trade Law*, 9 (January/February 1975), 27–30.

67. C. Fred Bergsten, *Completing the GATT: Toward Rules to Govern Export Controls* (Washington: British North American Committee, November 1974).

68. Roessler, "GATT and Access to Supplies."

8

Managing the Multinational Corporation

Multinational corporations have become a problem in the management of Western interdependence. Concern over their management in the underdeveloped world, however, is much greater than in the developed countries.[1] Multinational corporations have far greater power in the South than in the North, and there is evidence to suggest that the costs of multinationals' power have been far greater in the underdeveloped world than in the developed world.

POWER: THE LOCAL ECONOMY

The importance of foreign investment in the South varies from country to country. In some states it is relatively insignificant, whereas in others it plays a key role. Multinational corporations have tended to concentrate in a few underdeveloped countries. Five countries alone Argentina, Brazil, Mexico, Venezuela, and Nigeria account for 35 percent of all private foreign investment in the South. Eleven other countries—Libya, the British West Indies, Jamaica, Panama, Trinidad, Tobago, Iran, Saudi Arabia, India, Indonesia, and Malaysia—account for another 27 percent.[2] In these countries, in particular, foreign investment possesses considerable power.

The power of multinational corporations grows out of their structural position within the relatively small and underdeveloped economies of many Southern states.[3] Because much of the gross national product of underdeveloped states still comes from the agricultural and service sectors, multinational corporations play a relatively small part in total GNP. But foreign investment often accounts for important percentages of the total stock of local investment, local production, and sales.[4]

More importantly, foreign investment dominates key industries in Southern states. Historically, Northern firms controlled the South's raw materials, long the key to development. Multinationals, for example, controlled oil in the Middle East, copper in Chile and Zambia, and bauxite in Jamaica and Guyana. Although less developed countries in some cases have increased national control over these raw materials,[5] Northern firms retain control over a vast amount of Southern primary products, and investment from the North has grown in this sector.

A second and more recent sector of Northern control is in manufacturing. Since World War II underdeveloped countries have sought to expand their industrial sector as a primary means of development and have provided incentives for investment in manufacturing. It has often been multinational corporations and not national businesses which have taken the lead in these new growth sectors. Foreign investment is growing most rapidly in manufacturing—more rapidly than the Southern manufacturing sector as a whole—and is thus moving to dominate the new Southern industry.

Foreign firms represent a significant percentage of the largest and most powerful firms in Southern economies. Foreign investment in the Third World tends to be found in industries which are dominated by a small number of large firms. For example, U.S. foreign investment is found in such highly concentrated industries as petroleum, copper, aluminum, chemicals, transportation, food products, and machinery.[6] The large firms which dominate such industries have greater power to control supply and price than firms in more competitive industries. Thus, the oligopolistic structure of foreign investment means that significant economic power is concentrated in the hands of a few large foreign firms.

These characteristics of multinational corporations in Southern economies—their important share of the overall economy, their dominant position in key industries, the predominance of oligopolistic firms—mean that foreign firms are in a position to make decisions which have an important impact on the level and direction of development of Southern host economies. Furthermore, when local dominance by multinationals is combined with other characteristics of multinational corporations, the stage is set for vast potential corporate power in less developed economies. The integration of powerful local subsidiaries into huge international firms which are often worldwide oligopolies and the centralization of decision making in the parent firm mean that many decisions crucial to the development of Southern economies are not even made locally by the foreign firm but are made in board rooms in Detroit or New York.

The extent of corporate power in Southern economies can be understood by looking at two countries in which foreign investment plays a key role: Mexico and Brazil.[7] These Latin American states are among the top five recipients of foreign investment.[8] The pattern of foreign investment and its relationship to the economies of these two states reflects the constraints on decision-making characteristic of many less developed countries.

In both Mexico and Brazil foreign investment plays a pivotal and growing role in the economy. In Mexico multinational corporations produced 23 percent of the total gross domestic product in manufacturing in 1970, up from 18 percent in 1962.[9] In 1972 multinational corporations accounted for 28 percent of all Mexican sales, up from 20 percent in 1962.[10] In Brazil in 1969 foreign multinationals controlled 42 percent of all assets in the manufacturing sector and 34 percent of all assets in industry. Foreign multinationals together produced an estimated 50 percent of all local sales in Brazil in 1970.[11] And U.S. multinationals alone accounted for 20 percent of all Brazilian sales in manufacturing in 1970, up from 13 percent in 1966.[12]

In both countries foreign control has been greatest in the largest firms and certain key industries. In Mexico 50 percent of the largest 300 industrial firms and 61 percent of the largest 100 firms were foreign controlled in 1972.[13] Foreign control is particularly predominant in the most technologically advanced and capital-intensive industries in Mexico: for example, in nonelectrical machinery (95 percent), transportation (79 percent), and chemicals (68 percent).[14] These industries are also the fastest growing and the most profitable.[15] Finally, foreign investment is found in highly concentrated industries. Multinational corporations accounted for 71 percent of all manufacturing sales in highly concentrated industries.[16]

The situation in Brazil is similar. In 1972, 40 percent of the 300 largest manufacturing firms and 59 percent of the top 100 manufacturing firms were foreign owned.[17] Foreign control is concentrated in the most advanced and most dynamic growth industries: chemicals (69 percent), transportation (84 percent), and machinery (74 percent).[18] It is also centered in highly concentrated industries. In 1968 foreign firms owned at least two of the top 4 firms in 66 industries which account for 44 percent of all manufacturing production in Brazil.[19]

Finally, studies indicate that foreign-owned firms in Mexico and Brazil are highly integrated with the international corporation. Local subsidiaries are owned directly by the parent, depend on the parent for finance, and do most of their trading with the parent corporation.[20]

The picture which emerges from a study of Mexico and of Brazil is one of great multinational power. The predominant position of foreign investment in the local economy combined with the integration of foreign-owned firms in the larger international multinational network means that decisions crucial for economic development in Mexico and Brazil are being made outside those two countries.

POWER: LOCAL GOVERNMENT

Such a situation of economic dominance, however, need not inevitably mean the removal of decision making from national control. Theoretically, Southern governments could assert the control necessary to retain decision making at home. Host state laws could be passed to regulate multinational corporations, and host governments could impose restrictions on multinational corporations when investment agreements are negotiated. To impose such controls Southern governments could use the one important bargaining advantage they possess: control over access to their territories.[21] Control over access to resources which the multinational wants—to local raw materials, local labor, and local markets—could be used by Southern states to impose controls on foreign investors.

In practice, however, the bargaining advantage of control over access has proved a weak tool for the South. One of the major problems is that the multinational, too, has control over resources which less developed countries want for development. The South's desire for the benefits of direct foreign investment—for example, the ability to develop a valuable raw material deposit or the possibility of expanding industrialization through new factories—poses an important dilemma for those countries' policy makers. On the one hand, officials want to regulate multinationals to maximize national benefits and to minimize national costs. On the other hand they do not want to make regulation so restrictive that it will deter potential investors.

Related to the dilemma of the desire to regulate and the fear of overregulating is the problem of uncertainty.[22] Before a foreign investment is actually made, potential investors are uncertain about the eventual success of the operation and about its final cost. For example, a corporation proposing to explore for and develop oil in an underdeveloped country cannot be certain of its ultimate course of action until prospecting has been carried out and extracting capability is developed, that is, determining whether oil will be discovered and at what price. Similarly, a corporation proposing to manufacture sewing machines for a local foreign market may not be able to determine the ultimate potential of that market and the final costs of production. Another risk faced by the corporation is the risk of political instability in Third World host states and the uncertainty of the effect of political change and possible turmoil on investment. For foreign investors, such uncertainties serve to reduce the attractiveness of the local factors of production and the local market and thus weaken the hand of the host country.

Another factor weakening the bargaining power of the less developed countries is the absence of competition for investment opportunities. The availability of alternate sources of raw materials and cheap labor elsewhere can diminish the bargaining ability of any one Southern state. At times, the oligopolistic nature of multinational corporations—the fact that a few companies dominate the industry and that those companies often collaborate with each other to decrease competition—can weaken the hand of the underdeveloped countries.[23]

Furthermore, even if a country resolves the dilemma in favor of regulation, there remain important constraints on the ability of the country to carry out regulatory policies. One Southern problem has been that of skill. Southern governments have been unable to control multinational corporations and retain decision-making power at home because they have lacked the skilled manpower necessary to draft and enforce laws and to negotiate agreements to regulate foreign investment. Without skilled lawyers, accountants, and specialists in the particular businesses which the state seeks to regulate, Third World governments are no match for the multinational corporation.

Another governmental problem has been the multinationals' ability to intervene in the domestic political process of the host state, to further corporate, as opposed to host government, interests. Multinational corporations are potentially able to use their resources in both legal and illegal political activities in host countries. Tactics such as public relations activities, campaign contributions, bribery, and economic boycott are available to the corporation. In their ability to intervene in domestic politics, multinational corporations are, in one sense, no different from national corporations; the problem they pose is not in the area of foreign investment but in their ability as private corporations to influence government.

There are, however, several characteristics of multinational corporations which distinguish them from national corporations and which make their participation in host politics a problem for Southern states. Because multinational corporations are foreign owned, they are not considered legitimate participants in the national political process. Their interests may not necessarily be those of the host state; their policies may in varying degrees reflect their own corporate interests or the interests of their home state. For these reasons, numerous states have barred foreign firms from political activities. Political participation by multinational firms carries the connotation and, at times, the reality of a challenge to national sovereignty.

In addition, multinational corporations bring unusually vast resources to their political activities. Their significant financial resources and the international structure of the corporation are potentially powerful political tools.

Multinational corporations also derive great potential power from their relationship to the government of their parent corporations. Investment in Southern states tends to be highly concentrated according to home country. U.S. investment, for example, is predominant in Latin America, whereas French investment is dominant in the former French colonies in sub-Saharan Africa.[24] In the home country, these giant corporations often play a powerful political role. The ability of the multinational to pressure its home government to take certain actions and follow specific foreign policies to influence host governments adds to the imbalance between Third World governments and multinational corporations.[25]

In sum, because of their powerful position within Third World economies and vis-à-vis Third World governments, multinational corporations can affect economic efficiency and welfare and influence politics in Southern host countries. The crucial question then, is, How have these corporations used their power?

EFFICIENCY, GROWTH, AND WELFARE

Proponents argue that foreign investment has a positive impact on Southern economic development.[26] Such investment fills important resource gaps in underdeveloped countries and improves the quality of factors of production. One of the most important contributions, it is argued, is capital. Multinational corporations bring otherwise unavailable financial resources to the South through the capital of the firm and the access of the firm to international capital markets. Figures indicate that an important part of the flow of capital to underdeveloped countries comes from foreign investment. Between 1970 and 1973 direct investment represented 26 percent of total bilateral flows from North to South. Such investment is also a major area of expansion of capital flows to the South. Also between 1970 and 1973 direct investment grew 75 percent, whereas public foreign aid (grants and loans) only grew 25 percent.[27]

Multinational corporations also contribute crucial foreign exchange earnings to the underdeveloped world through their trade effect. First, the unique marketing skills of the multinational corporations and their competitive products, it is argued, generate exports and thus increase the foreign exchange earnings of host countries. Furthermore, the manufacture for the local market of products which otherwise would have been imported also saves precious foreign exchange.

A second crucial resource gap filled by the multinational, according to proponents of foreign investment, is technology. Multinational corporations allow Southern states to profit from the sophisticated research and development carried out by the multinational and make available technology which would otherwise be out of the reach of underdeveloped countries. Thus technology improves the efficiency of production and thus encourages development.

Third, say proponents, foreign investment improves the quality of labor in the South. It provides needed managerial skills which improve production; it creates jobs and trains workers.

Supporters argue, finally, that multinational corporations have a positive impact on welfare as well as on efficiency of production. The creation of jobs, the provision of new and better products, and programs to improve health, housing, and education for employees and local communities, it is argued, improve the standard of living in the Third World.

This positive view of the role of multinational corporations in growth, efficiency, and welfare has come under increasing attack. A growing number of empirical studies now suggest that, at best, policies adopted because they are optimal for the multinational are not necessarily optimal for the subsidiary or the host state and that, at worst, the multinational exploits underdeveloped countries and perpetuates dependence.[28]

Multinational corporations, argue these critics, do not bring capital to the South, and multinational corporations do not bring in as much foreign capital as proponents suggest. Financing of foreign investment is done largely with host country, not foreign, capital.[29] For example, between 1958 and 1968, U.S. manufacturing subsidiaries in Latin America obtained 80 percent of all financing locally, through either borrowing or subsidiary earnings.[30]

The fact that multinational corporations obtained most of their financing locally has other detrimental effects. Because of their strength, multinational corporations often have preferred access to local capital sources and are able to compete successfully with and thus to stifle local entrepreneurs. In addition, such local financing is often used to acquire existing nationally owned firms.

One study of the Mexican economy revealed that the 43 percent of U.S. multinational corporations entered Mexico by acquiring existing firms and that 81 percent of these firms were formerly owned by Mexicans.[31] And in Brazil 33 percent of U.S. multinational corporations began operations in Brazil by acquiring local firms. In the late 1960s and early 1970s, acquisitions accounted for 50 percent of new multinational affiliates in Brazil, 63 percent of which were formerly owned by Brazilians.[32]

Some critics argue that foreign investment in underdeveloped countries actually leads to an outflow of capital. Capital flows from South to North through profits, debt service, royalties and fees, and manipulation of import and export prices. Such reverse flows are, in and of themselves, not unusual or improper. Indeed, the reason for investment was to make money for the firm. What certain critics argue, however, is that such return flows are unjustifiably high. Profits in underdeveloped countries are substantially higher than profits in developed market economies. The average return on book value of U.S. direct foreign investment in developed market economies in the period 1965–1968 was 7.9 percent, whereas average returns in developing countries was 17.5 percent.[33]

Furthermore, argue the critics, profits represent only a small part of the effective return to the parent. A large part of the real return comes from licensing fees and royalties paid by the subsidiary to the parent for the use of technology controlled by the parent. In 1972 the payment by foreign affiliates for the use of technology accounted for 30 percent of total dividend income and for 60 percent of all income from manufacturing received by U.S. parent corporations.[34] Critics do not argue that subsidiaries should not pay the parent for research and development costs incurred by the parent which eventually benefit the subsidiary. What the critics contend is that subsidiaries in underdeveloped countries pay an unjustifiably high price for technology and bear an unjustifiably high share of the research and development costs. The monopoly control of technology by the multinational corporation enables the parent to exact a monopoly rent from its subsidiaries.[35] And the parent chooses to use that power and to charge inordinately high fees and royalties to disguise high profits and avoid local taxes on those profits.

Yet another mechanism of capital outflow—of disguising profits and evading taxes—is trade. A large volume of trade of multinationals' subsidiaries in underdeveloped countries is intracompany trade. In many cases subsidiaries located in less developed countries are actually obliged by agreements with the parent to purchase supplies from and to make sales to the parent.[36] The parent is able to manipulate the price of such intracompany imports and exports—the transfer price—to benefit the firm. Critics of multinational corporations argue that firms have used this transfer price mechanism to underprice exports and overprice imports and thereby to remove capital from the South.[37] In one study of an extreme case, it was shown that overpricing of pharmaceutical imports into Colombia amounted to $3 billion.[38]

The negative effects of such decapitalization would be limited if in the process of removing capital multinational corporations made a significant contribution to local development. Critics argue that the contribution of multinational corporations is limited or negative. Technology, it is argued, is not the great boon for the South as proponents of multinational corporations suggest. The high cost of technology has already been mentioned. Another criticism is that the importation of technology stunts the development of local technological capabilities.[39] Yet another problem is the appropriateness of technology. Although some foreign investment has entered the South to take advantage of abundant Southern labor and thus has contributed to employment, some multinational corporations bring advanced capital-intensive technology developed in and for developed countries which does not contribute to solving the problem of unemployment in underdeveloped states.[40]

Critics also argue that multinational corporations do not benefit Southern labor. They make only a limited contribution to employment, and they stunt local entrepreneurs by competing successfully with them in local capital markets by acquiring existing firms and by using expatriate managers instead of training local citizens.[41]

Finally, the trade benefits of multinational corporations, according to critics, are severely limited by restrictive business practices. Written agreements between parent and subsidiary often include clauses restricting exports and requiring subsidiaries to produce only for the local market. Management policy often similarly limits subsidiary production and marketing.[42]

In sum, argue the critics, multinational corporations create a distorted and undesirable form of growth. Multinational corporations often create highly developed enclaves which do not contribute to the development of the larger economy. These enclaves use capital-intensive technology which employs few local citizens; acquire supplies from abroad, not locally; use transfer prices and technology agreements to avoid taxes; and send earnings back home. In welfare terms the benefits of the enclave accrue to the home country and to a small part of the host population allied with the corporation.

Not only does the enclave not contribute to local development, say the critics, it often hinders it. In other words, the enclave economy develops at the expense of the local economy and thus of local welfare. It absorbs local capital, removes capital from the country, destroys local entrepreneurs, and creates inappropriate consumer demands which distort production away from economically and socially desirable patterns.

In conclusion, the economic impact of foreign investment in underdeveloped countries is quite different from its impact in developed market economies. The effect of foreign investment varies from country to country, from firm to firm, from project to project. But evidence suggests that multinational corporations at best do not make as great a contribution to Southern host countries as they might and that in some cases they have a negative impact on Southern development.

NATIONAL POLITICAL PROCESS

Evidence also suggests that multinational corporations have intervened in important ways in political processes in host states. Multinational corporations have taken both legal and illegal actions within host states to favor friendly governments and oppose unfriendly governments, to obtain favorable treatment for the corporation, and to block efforts to restrict corporate activity. They have engaged in such legal activities as contributing to political parties, lobbying with local elites, and carrying out public relations campaigns.[43] They have also engaged in illegal activities: illegal contributions to political parties,[44] bribes to local officials,[45] and refusals to comply with host laws and regulations.[46] They have also used such extralegal methods as international boycott to pressure an unfriendly government.[47]

Multinational corporations have also used their power in the politics of the home state to obtain foreign policies favorable to corporate interests. They have helped shape the liberal world vision which the U.S. government has sought to implement since World War II and which has favored foreign direct investment. They have worked for specific legislation such as the Hickenlooper amendment, which enables the U.S. government to cut off aid to any country nationalizing U.S. investments without compensation, and the Overseas Private Investment Corporation, which ensures foreign investment in many Southern countries.[48] This legislation protects foreign investment and tends to link the interests of the corporation with the foreign policy interests of the United States. At times, corporations have gone beyond legislation to seek governmental support for their opposition to unfavorable regimes in host countries.[49]

Not only have corporations sought to shape home government policy, they have also served as tools of that policy. Such corporate activity ranges from providing cover for intelligence operations to serving as a conduit for foreign aid. For example, the decision by the U.S. government in 1950 to allow oil companies to exempt royalty payments from American taxes was a device used by the executive to transfer aid to Middle Eastern oil-producing states at a time when such aid would not have been approved by Congress.[50]

One of the most notorious examples of multinational interference in host country politics and one which vividly demonstrates the multiple political threat posed by multinational corporations was the intervention of the International Telephone & Telegraph Company in Chile in the early 1970s. From 1970 to 1972 ITT actively sought, first, to prevent the election of Salvadore Allende as president of Chile and, once Allende was elected, to seek his overthrow. In the process, ITT not only resorted on its own to a variety of illegal or extralegal activities but also sought to involve the U.S. government in both open and clandestine activities against Allende and was solicited by the U.S. government to serve as an agent of its policy.

ITT's principal investment in Chile and the main reason for its political intervention was in Chiltelco, a profitable telephone company valued by ITT at $153 million.[51] ITT had done well in Chile and had maintained good relations with various Chilean governments. And, although it seemed likely that Chile would eventually nationalize Chiltelco, ITT expected, under agreements with the Chilean government, to be compensated for the book value of the company.[52]

ITT's hopes for compensation for Chiltelco dimmed in 1970, the year that presidential elections were held in Chile. The popular President Eduardo Frei, with whom ITT had maintained good relations, could not succeed himself, and it seemed that Salvadore Allende, the Marxist candidate who had campaigned on a platform of nationalization,[53] might become the next president of Chile. ITT, worried that Allende's election would lead to the nationalization without compensation of Chiltelco, determined to intervene to prevent his election.

The first documented step in this intervention was an attempt to block Allende by supporting conservative candidate Jorge E. Alessandri in the popular election of September 1970. Alessandri was considered a strong candidate and had, through his brother-in-law Arturo Matte, close contacts with ITT. ITT proposed to funnel money to Alessandri. John McCone, former director of the CIA and a member of the board of directors of ITT, arranged a meeting between Harold Geneen, the president of ITT, and William V. Broe who was in charge of the CIA's Clandestine Service for the Western Hemisphere. At a meeting in July 1970, Geneen offered to assemble a substantial election fund for Alessandri and to have that fund controlled and channeled by the CIA. According to Broe, he refused McCone's offer, but the agency and the corporation agreed to keep in contact about developments in Chile.[54]

It is not known whether ITT found another conduit, though some actions certainly were taken; for example, the corporation pumped funds to conservative newspapers opposed to Allende.[55] In any case, ITT's efforts to swing the popular election to Alessandri failed. Allende emerged as the leader in the popular vote with 36.3 percent of the votes, whereas Alessandri received 34.9 percent and the Christian Democratic candidate Radomiro Tomic trailed with 27.8 percent.

Under the Chilean constitution, if no candidate receives a majority of the popular vote, the presidency is determined by a vote of the Congress seven weeks after the popular election. The ITT intervention was now directed at swinging the congressional elections from Allende to Alessandri.[56] The directors and President Geneen decided that ITT would spend up to $1 million to block Allende.[57]

Just what that money was to be used for is suggested by a memorandum sent from ITT agents Bob Berellez and Hal Hendrix in Latin America to the home office in New York. The memorandum stated that financial and other support had already been offered to Alessandri[58] and suggested other actions such as continuing direct assistance for conservative newspapers which opposed Allende, radio and television propaganda against Allende, support for a family relocation center for wives and children of key persons involved in the anti-Allende campaign, and propaganda in Europe and Latin America against Allende.[59] The recommendations, it seems certain, were adopted as company policy. Also adopted as policy was an all-out effort to persuade the American government to take action in cooperation with ITT to block Allende. McCone offered Henry Kissinger, the president's assistant for national security affairs, and Richard Helms, director of the CIA, $1 million to support a plan to block Allende.[60] Similar offers were made by a lesser ITT figure, Jack Neal, to officials on Kissinger's staff and in the State Department.[61] The offers were turned down.

At this point an interesting development occurred. The CIA in the person of Broe sought ITT's support for a plan to block Allende by causing economic disruption in Chile.[62] Although the intentions of the CIA were unclear, it seemed that the agency sought to cooperate with foreign banks and corporations to cause economic chaos and thus political instability in Chile by such measures as stopping credits and delaying shipments. Such measures would, it was hoped, lead to a right wing victory in the congressional elections or to military intervention. ITT rejected the plan as "unworkable" but went so far as to solicit the opinion of other corporations involved in Chile for the CIA.[63]

Once again, ITT and the U.S. government could not stop Allende. On October 24, 1970 the Chilean congress elected him President of Chile. Now, ITT moved into the third stage of intervention, advocacy of the overthrow of Allende. Following the October election, ITT urged a policy of economic and political disruption on the U.S. government and on its fellow multinational corporations.[64] Most outrageous was a memorandum dated October 21, 1971, one year after Allende's election, sent by William Merriam of ITT to Peter Peterson, the head of the Council for International Economic Policy, urging an eighteen point program of disruption designed to foment an uprising against Allende. Included in the program were restricting public and private credit, boycotting Chilean copper, delaying fuel delivery and shipments of small arms and ammunition, and instituting an anti-Allende propaganda campaign and CIA activity.[65]

Just what independent policies ITT followed and what role ITT played in U.S. policy toward Allende in the post election period are as yet unknown. In March 1972 Jack Anderson published information revealing ITT's attempts to overthrow Allende, and Anderson's revelations led to a Senate inquiry which revealed the extent of ITT's intervention. On the next day the Allende government broke off negotiations with ITT regarding compensation for Chiltelco. On September 11, 1973, Allende was overthrown by a military coup.

The intervention of ITT into Chilean politics may not be an

example of typical behavior of multinational corporations in Southern states; certainly, many or even most multinational corporations do not pursue such ruthless and persistent politics of intervention. But there are enough examples of such intervention to suggest that multinational corporations are in a position to exercise significant political influence and often use that position to favor whatever the company perceives its corporate interest to be. In that sense, multinational corporations have posed serious threats to the autonomy of Southern political processes.

FORCES OF CHANGE

The abuse of power by multinational corporations is not a new phenomenon. Yet most Southern governments have encouraged foreign investment and placed few restrictions on the operation of foreign investors in their states. In recent years, however, many Southern governments have criticized multinational corporations, and some have altered their open door policies. The reasons for this change are to be found in the improvement in the bargaining position of these states.[66]

There has been a change in the attitude of ruling elites toward foreign investment, in part as a response to new public pressures. The forces of modernization—of economic change and rising expectations— have led to the political mobilization of many new groups.[67] Business, labor, students, peasants, and even government bureaucrats are now making major demands which are shaping the attitudes of governments toward multinational corporations.

One such demand is for economic and political independence. The multinational corporation is a convenient and logical target of new nationalist criticism.[68] As such nationalist sentiment developed in the late 1950s and 1960s, it became an important force in altering elite attitudes.[69] In the 1970s exposés of political intervention by multinational corporations in Southern politics further outraged Southern publics and led to a new spurt of antimultinational opinion.

The ITT scandal has played an important catalytic role in public mobilization against multinational corporations. The initial revelations by columnist Jack Anderson led to a U.S. Senate inquiry into multinationals in general which has revealed multiple other instances of their intervention in politics.[70] Publicity about ITT and Chile also led to a unified Southern outcry against multinational corporations and to a United Nations investigation of these entities.[71]

Modernization and political mobilization have also led to another type of public demand which affects multinational corporations. These are demands for improved economic welfare, housing, transportation, and jobs. To satisfy these new pressures and to preserve their own political power, Southern elites have turned to the multinational corporation. In the view of ruling elites, the multinational is a potential resource for fulfilling public demands.[72] Southern ruling elites, many of them heading unstable and vulnerable governments, have been very responsive to these new public pressures and have in turn used them to their own best advantage. Opposition to multinational corporations has become a politically useful and a politically potent platform for Southern elites.

Another factor in changing elite attitudes has been the new critical economic analysis. Until recently most respectable economic analyses argued that multinational corporations were a positive force in development. The new data demonstrating the detrimental effects of foreign investment has shaped the perceptions of important elites. As one critic of MNCs put it,

> serious and competent economists can make a strong case against a permissive attitude toward private foreign investment and thus bring respectability even to attitudes originally based upon an unthinking, emotional reaction.[73]

A second change has occurred in Southern skills. An important determinant in changing host power has been what one analyst has called the host country learning curve.[74] Motivated by the desire and the political necessity of controlling foreign investment, host states seek to develop the skills and expertise necessary to manage foreign investment. Third World countries gradually train cadres possessing the legal, financial, and business skills necessary to monitor and operate multinationals' subsidiaries. Such has been the case, for example, with the copper industry in Chile and with the oil industry throughout the world. An uptrend in the learning curve has enabled Southern states to use and generate data about multinational corporations' operations, to write effective laws to control multinational corporations, to administer these laws, and, in some cases, to operate firms if and when they are nationalized.

Another dimension of changing Southern bargaining power is decreasing uncertainty. Analysts have pointed out that a distinction must be made between the bargaining position of a host country vis-à-vis a potential investor and the bargaining position vis-à-vis an investor who has made a significant and successful investment in a host country.[75] When a country is seeking investment, it is in a weak bargaining position. Foreign investors are uncertain about the success of the potential operation and about its final cost. To overcome these uncertainties and to attract investment, host countries must follow permissive policies regarding investment. But, once a foreign investment is made and is successful, the bargaining relationship changes, and the power of the host country increases. The host country now has jurisdiction over a valuable multinational asset. As uncertainty decreases, host governments come to regret and resent earlier permissive policies and agreements. The success of the operation leads host governments to seek revision of permissive agreements with foreign investors while the financial commitment and financial interest of the company weaken its bargaining position and its ability to resist new terms for operation.

Another factor of change is increasing competition for investment opportunities in the South. The increasing numbers of foreign investors and countries with major multinational corporations means that Southern states have more alternatives in choosing foreign investors. These alternatives are important at the level of individual investment, allowing greater competition and thus better terms for host countries. They are also important in that they allow Southern states to avoid the concentration of investment from one traditionally dominant Northern home state. Thus, for example, Japanese multinationals have emerged as an alternative to U.S. firms in Latin America, and U.S. companies have in turn emerged as an alternative to French firms in Africa.[76]

Finally, increasing Northern dependence on Southern raw materials may improve the bargaining strength of the South: the perceived vulnerability of developed market economies to interruptions of supply and to shortages of raw materials, as demonstrated in 1973 and 1974 by the rise in the price of raw materials and by the OPEC (Organization of Petroleum Exporting Countries) supply interruption, may prove to have been the bellwether of a crucial shift in North–South bargaining.[77]

LESS DEVELOPED COUNTRIES' MANAGEMENT OF FOREIGN INVESTMENT

These forces of change have led to new Southern attempts to manage foreign investment. As discussed earlier, efforts at international management of the multinational corporation have been few and futile. Because both home and host governments are unwilling to give up any regulatory powers, international cooperation and regulation have been limited to establishing forums for publicity and institutions to gather information. Despite the apparent enthusiasm of the underdeveloped countries for the attempt by the United Nations Center on Transnational Corporations to develop an international code of conduct, little can be expected of such efforts. The real effort to control multinational corporations has and will come at the national level or perhaps, as in the attempt of the Andean Common Market (ANCOM), at the regional level.[78]

The most publicized Southern attempts to manage multinational corporations have been nationalizations of local subsidiaries. Peru's military government, for example, nationalized the International Petroleum Corporation, various banks, and the fishmeal and fish oil industry.[79] Chile and Zambia have taken over the copper industries.[80] Many oil-producing states have already nationalized or are in the process of nationalizing the oil industry.[81]

Nationalization, while highly visible, is not the major method of Southern management or the prevailing trend of Southern attempts at control. Most underdeveloped countries still seek foreign investment and the potential economic benefits associated with that investment. What more and more of them are attempting, however, is to ensure that foreign investment will bring those benefits to their economies at minimum cost and thus contribute to, not detract from, economic development.[82]

Potentially far more important than well-publicized nationalizations are the enactment in recent years of new foreign investment regulations, the adoption of new economic policies regarding foreign investment, and the creation of new bureaucratic structures to administer these new laws and policies. The goals of these new attempts at management have been to control foreign investment—to decrease overall participation in the local economy, to increase governmental control, and to increase the host country share of the economic rewards—while at the same time to attract foreign capital, technology, and skills for national development.

A broad range of regulatory techniques and positive incentives have been used to meet these goals. One important means of control has been regulation of the entry of new investment or the expansion of existing investment. New investment laws limit the sectors in which foreign investment is permitted. Banking, communications, transportation, and public utilities are commonly reserved for national ownership. In the ANCOM Uniform Code on Foreign Investment, reserved sectors are closed not only to new but also to existing foreign investment. Foreign firms operating in reserved sectors must offer at least 80 percent of their shares for sale to national investors.[83]

Restrictions are also placed on the amount of equity that foreigners may hold in local companies. Mexico's foreign investment code of 1972, for example, limits foreign equity and management control in new ventures to 49 percent.[84] ANCOM requires that all new and existing foreign-owned companies which wish to qualify for ANCOM's duty-free trade must agree to divestment provisions. They must gradually sell control over a fifteen- or twenty-year period.[85]

Through these sectoral and equity restrictions governments are encouraging new forms of foreign participation—joint ventures, licensing agreements, management contracts, and turnkey arrangements—to replace total or majority ownership. The goal is to "unbundle" the foreign investment package, to separate technology, managerial skills, and market access from equity and control.

Regulations are also placed by host states on acquisitions. Several states are now moving to prevent the takeover of nationally owned firms by multinational corporations. Mexico, for example, requires prior authorization before allowing a foreign investor to acquire 25 percent of the equity or 49 percent of the stock of a nationally owned firm and gives Mexican investors a chance to make the purchase in place of the foreigner.

Another means of control being attempted by a few underdeveloped countries is regulation of multinationals' behavior after entry. Some countries, including those in ANCOM, place restrictions on profit and capital repatriation. Others, such as Mexico, supervise technology and licensing agreements.[86] Some countries are now requiring registration and greater disclosure of such information as capital structure, technology used and restrictions on its use, and reinvestment policies.[87]

A third control technique relies not on restrictions but on positive incentives. Inducements such as tax advantages or exemptions from import restrictions have been used to encourage companies to invest in new fields or to use new technologies, to invest in export industries and in less developed regions of the country, and to increase sectoral competition. Brazil has relied on such positive tools of public policy to manage multinational corporations.[88]

A fourth technique is support of state-owned industry. In many industries with high barriers to entry, government-owned enterprise is the only visible national alternative to foreign investment. In both Mexico and Brazil, for example, state-owned corporations have been formed in such important basic industries as petroleum, steel, finance, utilities, and transportation.[89] An interesting new version of the countervailing force is the recent attempt by a new multipurpose Latin American organization, Sistema Economico Latinoamericano, to form Latin American multinational corporations. In industries such as nuclear energy or raw materials where national capabilities—capital, markets, and research and development—are limited, multilateral cooperation among less developed countries to form either state-owned or semipublic multinational entities may provide an alternative to direct foreign investment.[90]

A final method of control has been the producer cartel.[91] Various exporters of raw materials—particularly oil, copper, and bauxite—have attempted to manage multinational corporations by cooperating to increase prices as well as the national share of profits and national ownership. Until now, only OPEC, the oil producers' cartel, has used this technique successfully.

Actual attempts to manage the multinational corporation through nationalization or through new laws and policies vary from country to country and within countries from industry to industry. Variations in some cases depend on the specific characteristics of internal politics: past history or foreign investment behavior, prevailing ideologies, and the extent of mobilization among certain groups. But policy is not determined solely by local politics. Two key determinants are more universal: the level of development of a country and the "age" of the particular investment.

One analyst has suggested that raw material concession agreements pass through four stages,[92] which may be adopted to explain the variation of investment policy within the South. First, at the time when host countries are seeking foreign investment and when their bargaining position is weak, they follow permissive policies to attract investment; open door policies such as tax incentives and exemptions from import restrictions are commonly used. Then, once the foreign investment has been successful, governments begin to oblige the investor to submit to laws of general application such as tax, land use, and labor practices laws. Third, to improve national economic benefits, governments seek to improve linkages between foreign investment and the local private economy; at this stage they may oblige foreign investors to use local suppliers or to train local manpower. Finally, the government seeks to take over some of the ownership prerogatives of the corporation; it seeks actual ownership of equity or becomes involved in the process of business decision making on such matters as price or supply.

Many underdeveloped countries are still in the early stages of this cycle. Most of Central America and sub-Saharan Africa and much of Asia (Hong Kong, Malaysia, Singapore, Taiwan) are still seeking to attract foreign investment or are merely applying laws of general application.[93] They impose few restrictions and offer numerous incentives.

Other more developed countries are now attempting to create linkages with the local economy: Brazil, the Philippines, Indonesia, Pakistan, Ghana, and Nigeria. These states generally welcome foreign investment but place certain restrictions such as limits on foreign equity in certain sectors, prior approval mechanisms, and requirements on use of local supplies.

Finally, there are Mexico, the six ANCOM members, Argentina and India, states which are in the last stage of the cycle and are seeking to acquire ownership and/or decision-making control of foreign corporations. It is these countries which have passed laws controlling entry and regulating behavior of multinational corporations. These countries are relatively well developed, have had a long experience with many foreign investments, and are thus higher up in the learning curve. They have the ability to draft and to attempt to enforce strict regulations of foreign investment.

In all stages there are important variations for certain industries. Some countries in the earlier stages—such as many Arab oil producers—impose significant restrictions on raw material or public service investments. Such investments are also subject to greater control in countries farther along the cycle. This different treatment exists because these tend to be the oldest investments, ones in which significant national learning has taken place. They are also politically sensitive investments, linked in the first case to a wasting national patrimony and in the second to a service vital for national sovereignty and security.[94]

On the other hand, countries farther along the cycle may follow open door policies for certain new industries. ANCOM, for example, permits, and certain members have taken advantage of, exemptions of certain industries from sectoral and equity requirements. Mexico is expected to relax its equity requirements for firms which export or invest in less developed regions.

New laws and new policies, however, are necessary but not sufficient indicators of increased Southern control. Important constraints on the actual ability of states to manage multinational corporations remain. One such constraint is the expertise and information needed for the effective administration of new investment regulations. As has been noted, some states have acquired a certain level of expertise in monitoring and regulating foreign investment. They have also established bureaucratic structures responsible for implementing the new laws and are seeking new information on which to base their control. But it remains to be seen whether the new national cadres and bureaucratic structures are a match for the multinational, as such firms continue to possess the resource of manpower and access to information about company activities which enable them to minimize the effects of regulation.

Yet another administrative problem is the ability to ensure real transfer of decision making from the multinational to the host state or its nationals. Many subsidiaries, although subject to national regulation and even ownership, continue to depend on the parent for supplies, capital, technology, and markets. This integration of the subsidiary into the larger international structure of the firm remains a crucial barrier to the actual enforcement of new laws and policies.[96]

Another constraint lies in the ability of multinational corporations to intervene in local political processes or to attempt to involve home governments in their cause. When Honduras imposed a tax on banana exports, for example, United Brands (formerly United Fruit) bribed an official of that government to reduce the tax.[97] And, remember, it was in response to proposed nationalization that ITT carried out its nefarious schemes.

A final uncertainty regarding the actual impact of new laws and policies rests in the attitudes of ruling elites in Southern states. Despite public pressure and overt changes in attitudes and policies of these elites, their real commitment to regulate foreign investment remains to be tested. Furthermore, it remains to be seen who will benefit from the management of multinational corporations. Will ruling elites combine the regulation of multinational corporations with policies of redistribution of national income? Or, will such regulation merely benefit and increase the power and wealth of a small part of the population of the South? Will the management of the multinational lead not only to a new international economic order but to a new national order as well?

NOTES

1. The terms foreign investment and the multinational corporation have been used interchangeably in this chapter. Because much, though not all, foreign investment in underdeveloped countries is made by multinational corporations, this usage should not interfere with the analysis made and the conclusions reached.

2. Organization for Economic Cooperation and Development, *Stock of Private Investment by Member Countries of the Development Assistance Committee in Developing Countries—End 1972* (Paris: Organization for Economic Cooperation and Development, 1974), pp. 4–5.

3. For a similar analysis of two countries, see Richard S. Newfarmer and Willard F. Mueller, *Multinational Corporations in Brazil and Mexico: Structural Sources of Economic and Noneconomic Power*, Report to the Subcommittee on Multinational Corporations of the Committee on Foreign Relations, 94th Congress, 1st Sess. (Washington, D.C.: 1975).

4. See, for example, Raymond Vernon, *Sovereignty at Bay: The Multinational Spread of U.S. Enterprises* (New York: Basic Books, 1971), p. 22.

5. See chapter 9.

6. Newfarmer and Mueller, *Multinational Corporations in Brazil and Mexico*, pp. 25–27; United Nations Conference on Trade and Development, *Restrictive Business Practices: The Operations of Multinational Enterprises in Developing Countries, Their Role in Trade and Development*. A Study by Raymond Vernon (New York: United Nations, 1972), p. 3.

7. These examples were chosen because of and information used is based largely on a unique study by Newfarmer and Mueller, *Multinational Corporations in Brazil and Mexico*.

8. Organization for Economic Cooperation and Development, *Stock of Private Investment*.

9. Newfarmer and Mueller, *Multinational Corporations in Brazil and Mexico*, pp. 55–56.

10. Ibid., p. 57.
11. Ibid., p. 111.
12. Ibid., p. 113.
13. Ibid., p. 53.
14. Ibid., p. 54.
15. Ibid., pp. 80–94.
16. Ibid., p. 61.
17. Ibid., p. 107.
18. Ibid., p. 108.
19. Ibid., p. 114–117.
20. Ibid., pp. 73–80, 125–131.
21. For an analysis of control over access, see Samuel Huntington, "Transnational Organizations in World Politics," *World Politics*, 25 (April 1973), 333–368.

22. See Raymond Vernon, "Long-Run Trends in Concession Contracts," *Proceedings of the American Society for International Law*, Sixty-First Annual Meeting (Washington, D.C., 1967), pp. 81–90; Theodore H. Moran, *Multinational Corporations and the Politics of Dependence: Copper in Chile* (Princeton, N.J.: Princeton Univ. Press, 1974), pp. 157–162.

23. This applies particularly to collusion by the major international oil companies. See Chapter 9.

24. Organization for Economic Cooperation and Development, *Stock of Private Investment*, p. 8; Joan Edelman Spero, "Dominance-Dependence Relationships: The Case of France and Gabon," Ph.D. dissertation (Columbia University, 1973), pp. 162 204.

25. See Dennis M. Ray, "Corporations and American Foreign Relations," in David H. Blake, ed., *The Annals of the American Academy of Political and Social Science: The MNC* (Philadelphia, Pa.: 1972), pp. 80–92.

26. See, for example, Harry G. Johnson, "The Efficiency and Welfare Implications of the International Corporation," in Charles P. Kindleberger, ed., *The International Corporation: A Symposium* (Cambridge, Mass.: M.I.T. Press, 1970), pp. 35 56; Lester B. Pearson, *Partners in Development: Report of the Commission on International Development* (New York: Praeger, 1969), pp. 99–123; United Nations Conference on Trade and Development, *The Role of Private Enterprise in Investment and Promotion of Exports in Developing Countries*, report prepared by Dirk U. Stikker (New York: United Nations, 1968); Herbert K. May, *The Effects of United States and Other Foreign Investment in Latin America* (New York: Council for Latin America, 1970).

27. Organization for Economic Cooperation and Development, *Development Cooperation: Efforts and Policies of the Members of the Development Assistance Committee, 1974 Review*, report by Maurice J. Williams (Paris: Organization for Economic Cooperation and Development, 1974), p. 117.

28. Leading critics include Celso Furtado, for example, *Obstacles to Development in Latin America* (Garden City, N.Y.: Doubleday, 1970); Stephen Hymer, for example, "The Multinational Corporation and the Law of Uneven Development," in Jagdish N. Bhagwati, ed., *Economics and World Order: From the 1970s to the 1990s* (New York: Macmillan, 1972), pp. 113–140; Ronald Müller, for example, *Global Reach: The Power of the Multinational Corporations* (New York: Simon and Schuster, 1974), written with Richard J. Barnet; Constantine V. Vaitsos, for example, *Intercountry Income Distribution and Transnational Enterprises* (Oxford: Clarendon Press, 1974).

29. Sidney M. Robbins and Robert Stobaugh, *Money in the Multinational Enterprise: A Study of Financial Policy* (New York: Basic Books, 1972), pp. 63–71; R. David Belli, "Sources and Uses of Funds of Foreign Affiliates of U.S. Firms, 1967-68," *Survey of Current Business*, (November 1970), 14–19; Grant L. Reuber, *Private Foreign Investment in Development* (Oxford: Clarendon Press, 1973), p. 67.

30. Ronald J. Müller, "Poverty is the Product," *Foreign Policy*, 13 (Winter 1973–1974), 85–88.

31. Newfarmer and Mueller, *Multinational Corporations in Brazil and Mexico*, pp. 67–72.

32. Ibid., pp. 121–125.

33. United Nations, *Multinational Corporations in World Development* (New York: United Nations, 1973), p. 187.

34. Newfarmer and Mueller, *Multinational Corporations in Brazil and Mexico*, p. 17.

35. See Johnson, "The Efficiency and Welfare Implications of the International Corporation"; Walter A. Chudson, *The International Transfer of Commercial Technology to Developing Countries* (New York: United Nations Institute for Training and Research, 1971).

36. Constantine V. Vaitsos, *Intercountry Income Distribution and Transnational Enterprises*, pp. 42–43.

37. Ibid., pp. 44–54.

38. Ibid., p. 47.

39. Constantine V. Vaitsos, "Foreign Investment Policies and Economic Development in Latin America," *Journal of World Trade Law* 7 (November–December 1973), 639;

Albert O. Hirschman, *How to Divest in Latin America and Why, Essays in International Finance*, November 1969 (Princeton, N.J.: International Finance Section, Dept. of Economics, Princeton University, 1969), pp. 5 6.

40. International Labor Organization, *Multinational Enterprises and Social Policy* (Geneva: International Labor Organization, 1973), pp. 52 53.

41. Ibid., for an analysis of various issues involved in labor policy.

42. United Nations, *Multinational Corporations in World Development*, p. 195; Vaitsos, *Intercountry Income Distribution and Transnational Enterprises*, pp. 54 59; United Nations Conference on Trade and Development, *Restrictive Business Practices* (New York: United Nations, December 1969), pp. 4 6.

43. For an interesting case study, see Adalberto J. Pinelo, *The Multinational Corporation as a Force in Latin American Politics: A Case Study of the International Petroleum Company in Peru* (New York: Praeger, 1973).

44. Gulf Oil, for example, contributed $4 million illegally in South Korea, *The New York Times*, May 17, 1975, p. 1.

45. Bribes have been made, for example, by United Brands in Honduras for favorable tax treatment (*The New York Times*, April 10, 1975, p. 1) and in arms and airplane sales, such as those of Northrop Corporation in Saudi Arabia and Brazil (*The New York Times*, June 6, 1975, p. 41 and July 1, 1975, p. 39).

46. See, for example, Piñelo, *The Multinational Corporation as a Force in Latin American Politics*, pp. 17–25.

47. The control of international markets, for example, made possible the boycott by the major international oil companies of Iranian oil in 1951–1953 which contributed to the overthrow of Premier Mossadegh.

48. On the Overseas Private Investment Corporation, see U.S. Senate, 93rd Congress, 1st Sess., *The Overseas Private Investment Corporation, A Report to the Committee on Foreign Relations, United States,* Subcommittee on Multinational Corporations, October 17, 1973 (Washington, D.C.: U.S. Government Printing Office, 1973); U.S. Senate, 93rd Congress, 1st Sess., *Multinational Corporations and United States Foreign Policy*, Hearings Before the Subcommittee on Multinational Corporations of the Committee on Foreign Relations, Part 3 (Washington, D.C.: U.S. Government Printing Office, 1973).

49. See, for example, accounts of the role of the United Fruit Company in the United States overthrow of President Arbenz of Guatemala, in Richard J. Barnet, *Intervention and Revolution: The United States in the Third World* (New York: World Publishing, 1968), pp. 229–232; David Wise and Thomas B. Ross, *The Invisible Government* (New York: Random House, 1964), pp. 165–183; U.S. Senate, Committee on Foreign Relations, Subcommittee on Multinational Corporations, 93rd Congress, 1st Sess., *The Overseas Private Investment Corporation, A Report with Additional Views* (Washington, D.C., 1974).

50. See, for example, U.S. Senate, *Multinational Corporations and United States Foreign Policy*, Part 8 for information on rulings on the 1950 Aramco tax decision.

51. U.S. Senate, *Multinational Corporations and United States Foreign Policy*, Vol. 1, pp. 211–212.

52. Ibid., p. 210.

53. Ibid., p. 458.

54. Ibid., pp. 244–247. According to Mr. McCone's testimony when he was the director of the CIA, a similar offer was made in 1964 to him to support the candidacy of Eduardo Frei but was refused.

55. Ibid., p. 127.

56. The plan was in fact more complicated. Mr. Alessandri was to be elected but then was to resign and call for new elections in which Mr. Frei would be eligible to run and, it was hoped, would emerge victorious.

57. U.S. Senate. *Multinational Corporations and United States Foreign Policy*, pp. 101 102.

58. Ibid., Vol. 2, p. 613.

59. Ibid., pp. 614–615.

60. Ibid., Vol. 1, p. 102.

61. Ibid., p. 460.

62. Ibid., p. 172.

63. Ibid., pp. 174–177.

64. Ibid., pp. 44–45.

65. Ibid., p. 41.

66. See Vaitsos, "Foreign Investment Policies and Economic Development in Latin America," for another analysis of this change.

67. Samuel P. Huntington, *Political Order in Changing Societies* (New Haven, Conn.: Yale Univ. Press, 1968).

68. For an analysis of economic nationalism, see Harry G. Johnson, "A Theoretical Model of Economic Nationalism in New and Developing States," *The Political Science Quarterly*, 80 (June 1965), 169–185. See criticism by Vaitsos, "Foreign Investment Policies and Economic Development in Latin America," p. 632.

69. See, for example, Richard L. Sklar, *Corporate Power in an African State: The Political Impact of Multinational Mining Companies in Zambia* (Berkeley, Calif.: Univ. of California Press, 1975).

70. See U.S. Senate, *Multinational Corporations and United States Foreign Policy.*

71. See United Nations, *Multinational Corporations in World Development* and *Report of the Group of Eminent Persons to Study the Impact of Multinational Corporations on Development and on International Relations* (New York: United Nations, 1974).

72. Theodore H. Moran, *Multinational Corporations and the Politics of Dependence: Copper in Chile* (Princeton, N.J.: Princeton Univ. Press, 1974), pp. 164–166.

73. Edith Penrose, "The State and the Multinational Enterprise in Less-Developed Countries," in John Dunning, ed., *The Multinational Enterprise* (London: Allen & Unwin, 1971), p. 230. For role of the new economic analysis in Chile, see Moran, *Multinational Corporations and the Politics of Dependence*, pp. 57–88.

74. Moran, *Multinational Corporations and the Politics of Dependence*, pp. 163–167.

75. Raymond Vernon, "Long-Run Trends in Concession Contracts"; Moran, *Multinational Corporations and the Politics of Dependence*, pp. 157–162.

76. Organization for Economic Cooperation and Development, *Stock of Private Investment*, p. 8.

77. See *Declaration and Action Programme on the Establishment of a New International Economic Order* (New York: United Nations General Assembly Resolutions, May 1974); *Charter of Economic Rights and Duties of States* (New York: United Nations General Assembly Resolution, December 1974); *The Daker Declaration and Action Programme of the Conference of Developing Countries on Raw Materials* (February 1975); "Solemn Declaration of the Algiers Conference of the Sovereigns and Heads of State of the OPEC Member Countries (March 1975)," in Guy F. Erb and Valeriana Kallab, eds., *Beyond Dependency: The Developing World Speaks Out* (Overseas Development Council, 1975), pp. 185–236.

78. Even ANCOM resolutions must be enacted nationally.

79. On International Petroleum Corporation, see Pinelo, *The Multinational Corporation as a Force in Latin American Politics.*

80. Moran, *Multinational Corporations and the Politics of Dependence;* Sklar, *Corporate Power in an African State.*

81. For oil and other minerals, see Raymond F. Mikesell, ed., *Foreign Investment in the Petroleum and Mineral Industries: Case Studies of Investor-Host Country Relations* (Baltimore, Md.: Johns Hopkins Press, 1971).

82. For a discussion of the cost-benefit problem, see Pierre Uri, "The Role of the Multinational Corporation," with comments by C. Fred Bergsten and Gerry Helleiner, in Helen Hughes, ed., *Prospects for Partnership: Industrialization and Trade Policies in the 1970s* (Baltimore, Md.: Johns Hopkins Press, 1973), pp. 69–100.

83. Members of ANCOM are Bolivia, Chile, Colombia, Ecuador, Peru, and Venezuela. Bolivia, Colombia, Ecuador, and Peru have chosen not to apply these divestment regulations. On ANCOM, see Dale B. Furnish, "The Andean Common Market's Common Regime for Foreign Investments," *Vanderbilt Journal of Transnational Law*, 5 (Spring 1972), 313–339.

84. On Mexico see Frank M. Lacey and Lic. Maclovio Sierra de la Garza, "Mexico—Are the Rules Really Changing?," *International Lawyer*, 10 (Summer 1976) 560–588.

85. On divestment, see Hirschman, *How to Divest in Latin America and Why.*

86. Lacey and Garza, "Mexico—Are the Rules Really Changing?," pp. 572–573.

87. See, for example, Business International Corporation, *Investment, Licensing and Trading Conditions Abroad: Peru* (Business International, 1973).

88. See, for example, Business International Corporation, *Investment, Licensing and Trading Conditions Abroad: Brazil* (Business International, 1973).

89. Newfarmer and Mueller, *Multinational Corporations in Brazil and Mexico*, pp. 55, 112, 150.

90. Simón Alberto Consalvi, "The Latin American Economic System: Turning Point for Regional Economic Integration," *Venezuela Now*, 1 (March 15, 1976), pp. 71–73.

91. See Chapter 9.

92. Vernon, "Long-Term Trends in Concession Contracts."

93. See Business International Corporation, *Investing, Licensing and Trading Conditions Abroad* for these and others.

94. See Mikesell, ed., *Foreign Investment in the Petroleum and Mineral Industries.*

95. Business International Corporation, *Investing, Licensing and Trading Conditions Abroad: Mexico* (Business International, 1974).

96. See, for example, Newfarmer and Mueller on Mexico, in *Multinational Corporations* in Brazil and Mexico, p. 59.

97. *The New York Times*, April 10, 1975, p. 1. The revelation of this finding by the Securities & Exchange Commission led to a coup in Honduras.

9

Oil and Cartel Power

At a time when it seemed that the South was becoming less important to the North and that frustration and anger were to be the lot of the underdeveloped countries, a ray of hope suddenly emerged. In 1973 Southern oil-exporting states dramatically reversed a system of dependency and increased not only their economic rewards but also their political power. The OPEC (Organization of Petroleum Exporting Countries) strategy, that of a producer cartel, became the new hope of the underdeveloped countries.

THE DEPENDENCY SYSTEM OF INTERNATIONAL OIL

The international oil system which was overturned by the producers was from its earliest days dominated by a small number of international oil companies.[1] These were the "seven sisters," five American (Standard Oil of New Jersey now known as Exxon, Standard Oil of California, Mobil, Gulf, and Texaco), one British (British Petroleum), and one Anglo–Dutch (Royal Dutch-Shell).

This international oil oligopoly began before World War I in the United States with the Standard Oil trust and then spread throughout the world. A few companies, following the Standard Oil model, gained control of the domestic oil industry by the development of vertical integration, in this case, that is, by controlling all the supply, transportation, refining, and marketing operations. Vertical integration was reinforced by control of technology for exploration and refining.

In the late nineteenth century the large oil companies began to move abroad, and, with their vast resources, they obtained control of foreign supplies on extremely favorable terms.[2] However, their comfortable position was, in the years after World War I, threatened by ruinous competition. So, to preserve their dominance, the international oil companies adopted the familiar oligopolistic strategy of cooperation: to control supply, the seven sometimes shared sources through joint ventures and sometimes divided up sources by explicit agreements; to control their markets, they agreed to divide markets, fix world prices, and discriminate against outsiders.[3]

The home governments of the seven sisters played a supporting role in these efforts. The Northern imperial powers' political dominance of oil-producing regions facilitated oil company activities. Indonesia, for example, was controlled by the Dutch, the Middle East and North Africa by the British and the French, and Venezuela, somewhat less directly, by the United States. Aside from providing a favorable political and military environment, governments often took specific actions to support oil companies owned by their nationals. Under the San Remo agreement with the French in 1920, the British government attempted to restrict the oil rights in Mesopotamia to British and French companies. And, later, the U.S. government was of great assistance to American oil companies in Venezuela and subsequently supported American companies in Iraq and in the Persian Gulf at the expense of the British.

Faced with a few mammoth oil companies which controlled technology and market access, cooperated with each other, and operated with the strong backing of their powerful home governments, underdeveloped countries were forced to bargain from a position of weakness. And, when the power of the companies was added to the uncertainty about the success of oil ventures and to the availability of alternative sources of supply, that bargaining relationship became even more distorted. As a result, in return for the payment of a small fixed royalty to host governments, the international oil companies obtained control over the production and sale of much of the world's oil.[4]

There was some evolution in this system in the decade following World War II. One important change, the impact of which was not felt until much later, was the emerging dependence of the developed market economies on imported oil. In the 1950s relatively inexpensive oil became the primary source of energy for the developed world. Western Europe and Japan, with no oil supplies of their own, soon became huge importers of oil; in the United States, oil consumption soon outdistanced even vast domestic production so that, by the end of 1950, the United States was a net importer of oil.

More evident in the early postwar era was a change in the attitude of host governments. Growing nationalism and awareness of the development gap engendered a more aggressive attitude toward the seven sisters, and decreasing uncertainty over the success of oil ventures and states' dissatisfaction with the terms of agreements negotiated under a very asymmetrical bargaining relationship engendered even more aggressive policies. In these years host governments succeeded in revising concession agreements negotiated before the war; first was Venezuela during the war, then Saudi Arabia in 1950, and, finally, the other Middle Eastern producing states renegotiated agreements with the companies. They redefined the basis for royalty payments and instituted an income tax on foreign oil operations. They also established what at the time was considered to be a revolutionary principle: that new royalties and taxes combined would yield a fifty-fifty division of profits between the companies and their respective host governments.[5] As a result, the profits accruing to host governments increased significantly. The per barrel payment to Saudi Arabia, for example, went from $0.17 in 1946 to $0.80 in 1956–1957.[6]

Despite these important changes in Northern dependence and the Southern share of profits, the seven sisters continued to control the international oil system: they controlled almost all the world's oil reserves outside the Communist states, they controlled production at the wellhead, they dominated refining and transportation, and they controlled marketing. By these means they were thus able to manage the price of oil.

This continuing dominance of the seven sisters was based in part on their ability to preserve their oligopoly power. The incursion of competitors in upstream operations, that is, in crude oil production, was blocked by the majors' control through concession agreements of many oil-rich areas and by the long lead times inherent in finding and developing oil in territory unclaimed by the majors. Outsiders were also deterred from competing with the seven sisters downstream, that is, in the refining, transportation, and marketing operations. Not having their own crude oil supplies, competitors had to purchase oil from the majors. But, because the majors tended to take their profits at the upstream level, thus charging a high price for crude oil as compared with final product, there were small profits for downstream operations, which discouraged the entrance of competitors.

The ability of the oil oligopoly to manage the price of oil to their advantage was facilitated by the nature of the demand for oil. The demand for petroleum is highly inelastic, at least in the short run. Because there are no readily available substitutes and because it is difficult to decrease consumption, an increase in the price of oil does not significantly decrease the demand for oil. Thus, if companies can maintain a higher price for oil, they will not necessarily lose in appreciable sales volumes and so will continue to reap high profits. By controlling the supply of oil, companies could thus assure a high price.

This is exactly what the seven sisters succeeded in doing. They retained control of supply by keeping out competitors, and they cooperated among themselves to restrict that supply by a series of cooperative ventures: joint production and refining arrangements, long-term purchase and supply agreements, joint ownership of pipelines, and some joint marketing outside the United States. They also refrained from price competition.

Interestingly, maintaining prices at a level above that which would have prevailed under competitive conditions met with little resistance from the developed countries. European opposition to lowering the price of oil was squelched by a desire to protect the domestic coal industry, as lower oil prices would have increased oil consumption and thus have threatened the coal industry and coal miners, both important political groups. American opposition was balanced by a concern for the domestic oil industry as well as by the political power of the five American sisters.[7] American oil was much more costly than foreign oil, and the domestic producers needed protection from lower international prices to survive. Thus the interests of the domestic and the international American oil companies, both powerful political forces in the United States, supported a price which was high in terms of the cost of production.[8]

Finally, the dominance of the seven sisters was backed by political intervention, from the industry as well as from their home governments. One extreme example of such intervention took place in Iran in the early 1950s. In the period of renegotiation of concession agreements after World War II, the government of Iran sought a new agreement with the Anglo-Iranian Oil Company (A.I.O.C., the predecessor of British Petroleum). When company–government talks broke down in 1951, the Iranian government of Premier Muhammed Mossadegh nationalized the A.I.O.C. assets in Iran. The British government became actively involved as an advocate of the company, of which it was a part owner. The British represented the company in negotiations and went so far as to impose a financial and economic embargo on Iran and to threaten military intervention. The British embargo, combined with an embargo on Iranian oil by the international majors, placed severe economic and political constraints on Mossadegh's government, accentuating the already existing internal political conflict over the role of the Shah. The United States at first sought to mediate between Britain and Iran. But, when numerous efforts failed and when Iran rejected a final offer which the United States considered reasonable and fair, the United States turned against Mossadegh. In August 1953 the opponents of Mossadegh, including the Shah with assistance from the CIA, overthrew Premier Mossadegh. A new concession was soon negotiated, and the political pressure from the oil companies and the consumer governments ended.[9]

FORCES OF CHANGE

Several important changes, however, eventually altered the power of the international oil companies and led first producing and then consuming states to alter their dependence on the seven sisters.[10]

Changes occurred initially in the oligopolistic structure of the international oil industry. Competition increased in refining and marketing as an increasing number of refineries were built by private and public companies. At the same time competition for concessions to explore for and produce crude oil increased. Beginning in 1954, when smaller American firms with the support of the American government joined the new Iranian consortium, new companies became active on the international oil scene. Companies which had little or no international business—private American, European, and Japanese firms and French and Italian state-owned companies—began to seek concessions in existing and new oil-producing regions. They went to Algeria, Libya, and Nigeria, and they were successful. In 1952 the seven majors produced 90 percent of crude oil outside North America and the Communist countries, but by 1968 they produced only 75 percent.[11]

Changes also took place in the company control of pricing. Increased competition for supplies meant increased production. By the end of the 1950s, the growth in production outdistanced the growth in consumption. The seven sisters, no longer able to restrict supply, were unable to maintain the price of oil at the old level.

Aggravating the increasing supply were U.S. quotas on the import of foreign oil. These quotas were instituted in 1958 ostensibly to protect national security. Protection of the American market from lower-priced foreign oil was necessary, it was argued, to ensure domestic production and national self-sufficiency.[12] In fact, such protection also conveniently served the economic interests of the domestic American producers, which could not have survived without protection, as well as the interests of the five American internationals that also owned domestic sources of supply.[13] The effect of the quotas was to cut off the American market for the absorption of the new supplies produced abroad. As a result, in 1959 and 1960 the international oil companies lowered the posted price of oil, the official price on which taxes are calculated. This act was to be a key catalyst for producer government action against the oil companies.

While changes in the structure of the international oil industry were undermining the dominance of the seven sisters, changes in oil-producing states were improving their bargaining position vis-à-vis the companies. The same factors which generally improved the position of host countries vis-à-vis foreign investors operated in the oil-producing states: changing elite attitudes, improved skills, decreasing uncertainty, and increasing alternatives.

The importance of the increase in alternatives was evidenced in the concessions negotiated by the new international oil companies. The emergence of these new participants increased the alternatives available to producer states and therefore increased the bargaining power of host governments. Producer states were thus able to obtain larger percentages of earnings and provisions for relinquishment of unexploited parts of concessions.[14] As a result of these renegotiations, oil-producing governments increased their earnings and began to accumulate significant foreign exchange reserves. For example, from 1964 to 1970 the total official reserves of the major oil-exporting countries (Algeria, Indonesia, Iran, Iraq, Kuwait, Libya, Nigeria, Saudi Arabia, Trinidad and Tobago, and Venezuela) increased from $2.87 billion to $5.17 billion and in 1971 the figure jumped to $8.18 billion. Furthermore, these reserves were concentrated in a few countries, particularly Libya and Saudi Arabia.[15] Monetary reserves meant that the important oil producers could afford the short-term loss of earnings that might result from an embargo or production reduction carried out in an effort to increase the price of oil or to seek other concessions from the companies and the consuming states.

Cooperation also improved the bargaining position of the host governments. What precipitated this cooperation were the price cuts of 1959 and 1960. Because their tax receipts are determined by price, the oil-exporting countries were greatly upset by these unilateral actions. So, in September 1960, five of the major petroleum-exporting countries—Iran, Iraq, Kuwait, Saudi Arabia, and Venezuela—met in Baghdad to discuss the oil company action. At that meeting the five decided to form OPEC to protect the price of oil and the revenues of their governments.[16] In its first decade OPEC expanded its membership from five to thirteen members who accounted for 85 percent of world oil exports.[17] Despite the dominance of OPEC members in the world oil market, the new organization had little success in bargaining with the oil companies. The ability of OPEC to influence price or government revenues depended on the ability of the various members to cooperate to reduce production and thus to force a price increase. Although OPEC tried, it was unable to agree on production reduction schemes. It was not until the 1970s, when other conditions became favorable, that OPEC would emerge as a powerful and effective tool of the producer states.

A final and critical change in the international political economy of oil was the altered position of the Western consuming countries. As their reliance on oil as a primary source of energy grew and as internal sources of supply in the United States declined, the developed market economies became increasingly dependent on foreign oil, especially on oil from the Middle East and North Africa (see Table 9–1). By 1972 Western Europe derived almost 60 percent of its energy from oil, almost all of which was imported. Oil supplied 73 percent of Japan's energy needs, and virtually all of that oil came from abroad. Even the United States was becoming vulnerable. By 1972 the United States used oil for 46 percent of its energy and imported almost one-third of that required oil.

For Western Europe and Japan, the Middle East and North Africa became the overwhelmingly important source of oil imports. In 1972, 80.4 percent of Western European oil imports and 78.9 percent of Japan's imports came from this region. By 1972 even the United States relied on the Middle East and North Africa for 14.9 percent of its oil imports. The developed market economies had become increasingly vulnerable to the threat of supply interruption or reduction. And this vulnerability was accentuated by the declining political influence of these countries' governments in the oil-producing regions and by the absence of individual or joint energy policies to counter any manipulation of supply.

As can be seen, in the 1960s and early 1970s major modifications gradually developed in the bargaining position of the three major actors in the international oil system. The position of the oil companies and of the developed market economies was significantly weakened, whereas the position of the producing states, especially those in the Middle East and North Africa, was significantly strengthened.

THE PROCESS OF CHANGE: FROM NEGOTIATION TO UNILATERAL POWER

Only minor changes occurred in the power structure of international oil in the 1960s. But, through a series of concessions, the oil-producing states succeeded in increasing their governments' revenues. The posted price of oil was never again lowered, but then it was never raised in this period to the pre-1959 level. And the oil-producing states gradually developed their ability and their experience in cooperation.[18]

The major changes in the system began in 1970. In the 1970s the oil-producing states—especially the Arab oil producers—developed a strong bargaining position vis-à-vis both the companies and the consuming states. Favorable international economic and political conditions plus internal cooperation enabled them, first, to take control of prices and, then, to assume actual ownership of oil investment.

The catalyst for future change was the Libyan government's action against the oil companies in 1970.[19] With Libyan oil supplying 25 percent of Western Europe's total oil imports,[20] Libya had significant advantages

Table 9-1 Energy Consumption and Oil Consumption and Imports in United States, Western Europe, and Japan, 1962 and 1972

	1962			1972		
	United States	Western Europe	Japan	United States	Western Europe	Japan
Totals (millions of barrels per day)						
Energy consumption (oil equivalent)	23.27	13.96	2.25	35.05	23.84	6.58
Oil consumption	10.23	5.24	0.96	15.98	14.20	4.80
Oil imports[a]	2.12	5.19	0.98	4.74	14.06	4.78
Middle East/ North Africa[b]	0.34	3.80	0.72	0.70	11.30	3.78
Other	1.78	1.39	0.26	4.04	2.76	1.00
As % of Total Energy Consumption						
Oil consumption	44.0%	37.5%	42.7%	45.6%	59.6%	73.0%
Oil imports[a]	9.1	37.2	43.6	13.5	59.0	72.6
Middle East/ North Africa[b]	1.5	27.2	32.0	2.0	47.4	57.4
Other	7.6	10.0	11.6	11.5	11.6	15.2
As % of Total Oil Consumption						
Oil imports[a]	20.7%	99.0%	102.1%	29.7%	99.0%	99.6%
Middle East/ North Africa[b]	3.3	72.5	75.0	4.4	79.5	78.6
Other	17.4	26.5	27.1	25.3	19.4	20.9
As % of Total Oil Imports						
Oil imports[a] Middle East/ North Africa[b]	16.0%	73.2%	73.5%	14.9%	80.4%	78.9%
Other	84.0	26.8	26.5	85.1	19.6	21.1

[a]Imports are gross rather than net; that is, exports are not deducted. Thus, they exclude product exports from West European refineries. For Japan, excess of imports over consumption arises because of small quantities of product exports, refinery losses, and (presumably) independent construction of the two series. By showing gross rather than net imports, the degree of foreign dependence is slightly overstated. The overstatement matters, if at all, only in the case of Western Europe.
[b]Includes negligible quantities from West Africa in 1962.

Joel Darmstadter and Hans H. Landsberg, "The Economic Background," in "The Oil Crisis: In Perspective," *Daedaelus*, 104 (Fall 1975), 21.

in its bargaining relationship with the corporations. Libyan oil was also important to certain independent oil companies which relied heavily on Libyan oil for their European markets and whose vulnerability separated them from the majors in Libya and thus prevented a common company bargaining position. Libya's bargaining position was further strengthened by its significant official foreign exchange reserves.

After the radical government of Colonel Mu'amar Qahdafi came to power in a coup in September 1969, it demanded negotiations with the oil companies for an increase in the posted price of and the tax on Libyan oil. Furthermore, when the talks stalled, the Libyan government threatened to nationalize the companies and cut Libyan oil production. As its first target the government selected the vulnerable Occidental Petroleum, which relied totally on Libya to supply its European markets and would have lost these markets without Libyan oil. Production reductions were imposed on Occidental in June and August 1970. In September Occidental capitulated, and the other companies were forced to follow.

The Libyan settlement was a harbinger of things to come. It provided for an immediate increase of $0.30 in the posted price of oil, an increase to $2.53 for Libyan crude, and for an increase of $0.02 a year until 1975 when the posted price would be $2.63. There was, in addition, an increase of approximately 5 percent in the income tax on oil. The Libyan contest with the oil companies had an important demonstration effect on the attitudes of other oil-producing states. It revealed the vulnerability of the companies and the unwillingness of the Western consumers to take forceful action in support of the companies. It also led to a major conceptual change in the minds of oil producers by demonstrating that government revenues could be raised not only by increasing exports but also or instead by increasing price.

In December 1970 the OPEC countries met in Caracas and passed resolutions calling for an increase in the posted price of oil and in host country income taxes on that oil. The companies in return sought to stem the tide. Their hope was to avoid a producer policy of divide and conquer and to enter into negotiations with all oil-producing countries to obtain a long-term, stable agreement on price and tax increases.[21] The governments of the oil-consuming states—although increasingly concerned about the trends in host–company relations—continued to allow the companies to manage relations with the oil producers.[22]

Negotiations between OPEC and the oil companies began in Teheran, Iran in January 1971. When negotiations bogged down in February, the countries threatened to enact changes unilaterally and to cut off oil to the companies. The threat forced the companies to settle. The agreement at Teheran provided for an increase in the posted price of Persian Gulf oil from $1.80 to $2.29 per barrel (see Figure 9-1). To account for expected inflation, the agreement provided for an increase of 2.5 percent annually in this price. In addition, government royalties and taxes rose from 50 percent to 55 percent. In return, the companies received a five-year commitment on price and government revenues. In April 1971 a similar agreement, but with a higher price, was reached with Libya at Tripoli.

Barely four months later, when President Nixon announced the inconvertibility of the dollar and the 10 percent surcharge, a fundamental pillar on which the five-year agreements were based collapsed. Because the price of oil is stated in dollars, the real value of the Teheran and Tripoli agreements was altered when the value of the dollar was changed. After the Smithsonian agreement, the oil producers demanded a new agreement to account for international monetary changes. In January 1972 in Geneva an agreement was negotiated which provided for an increase in the posted price of oil and a continuing adjustment to account for exchange rate changes. The price of Persian Gulf oil then rose to $2.48.

Figure 9-1 Changes in Posted Price of Crude Oil in Saudi Arabia,[1] Iran,[2] and Libya[3] 1970–1974

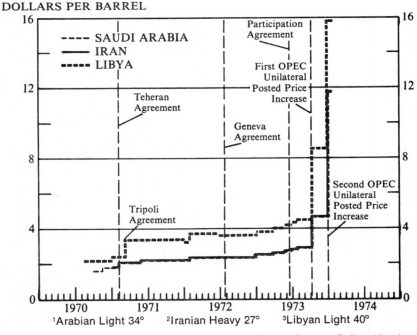

DOLLARS PER BARREL

¹Arabian Light 34°   ²Iranian Heavy 27°   ³Libyan Light 40°

Source: *Multinational Corporations and United States Foreign Policy.* Hearings before the Subcommittee on Multinational Corporations of the Committee on Foreign Relations, Part 5, U.S. Senate, 93rd Congress, 1st and 2nd sess., p. 288.

Despite this modification, the five-year period of stability sought by the companies—promised, they thought, at Teheran and Tripoli—proved ephemeral. No sooner had the issue of price and revenue been settled than the new issue of participation emerged. In 1972 OPEC called for a new conference to discuss nationalization. The companies resisted. OPEC, they argued, had no right to demand a reordering of the international oil system before 1975. But OPEC insisted that the question of participation was a totally new subject and therefore was not covered by Teheran and Tripoli.

Thus negotiations were held, and an agreement was reached in December 1972 among Saudi Arabia, Qatar, Abu Dhabi, and the companies which provided a framework for the producing governments to negotiate with the oil companies in acquiring ownership of the companies operating in their states. Ownership would start at 25 percent and rise gradually to 51 percent of control by 1982.[23] Individual states then entered into negotiations with the oil concessionaires.

The final negotiation between oil producers and oil companies took place in October 1973. Despite significant achievements, the oil producers remained dissatisfied. The rising demand for oil in the consuming countries surpassed existing capacity[24] (see Figure 9–2). Resulting oil shortages drove up the market price of oil. However, because the posted price was fixed by the five-year agreements, it was the oil companies and not the oil producers who benefited from the rise in the price. Another reason for dissatisfaction was the fact that companies were making bids for new government-owned oil at prices above those of the Teheran and Tripoli agreements. Finally, increasing inflation in the West, the second devaluation, and the downward float of the dollar undermined the real value of earnings from oil production. Despite a second adjustment of prices to reflect monetary changes, the countries remained dissatisfied.

The conditions creating discontent also created the possibility for alleviating that discontent. Economic conditions were highly favorable to OPEC. Rapidly rising demand and shortages of supply meant that the developed market economies were highly vulnerable to supply interruption by even one significant producer and were therefore in a weak bargaining position on price. In September 1973, when OPEC summoned the oil companies for negotiations, they came. Negotiations began on October 8 in Vienna. The oil producers demanded substantial increases in the price of oil, the companies stalled, and on October 12 the companies requested a two-week adjournment of talks to consult with their home governments.

The adjournment, it turned out, was not for two weeks but forever. Political as well as economic conditions now enhanced the bargaining position and escalated the demands of the most powerful of the oil producers: the Arab states. The fourth Arab–Israeli war had begun on

Figure 9-2 World Crude Oil Spare Capacity and Demand (excluding Communist countries)

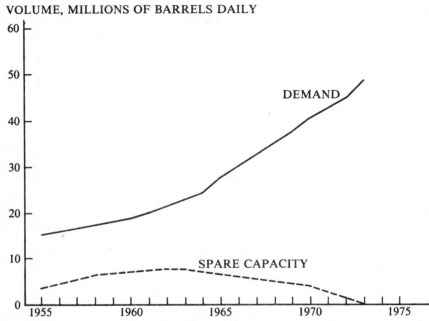

VOLUME, MILLIONS OF BARRELS DAILY

Source: *Multinational Corporations and United States Foreign Policy.* Hearings before the Subcommittee on Multinational Corporations of the Committee on Foreign Relations, Part 5, U.S. Senate, 93rd Cong., 1st and 2nd sess., p. 212.

October 6, just two days before the Vienna talks began. A common interest in supporting the Arab cause vis-à-vis Israel and supporters of Israel in the consuming states was an important force for unity of the Arab members of OPEC in their economic confrontation with the companies and the consumers. On October 16 the Organization of Arab Petroleum Exporting Countries (OAPEC) unilaterally increased the price of their crude oil—to $5.12.[25] Other oil producers followed with comparable price increases. On December 23, OPEC unilaterally raised the price of Persian Gulf oil to $11.65 to take effect January 1, 1974.

The actions of October and January demonstrated that, henceforth, on issues of price the producers need not negotiate with the companies or with the consuming states; they possessed the power to dictate terms unilaterally. Since the fall of 1973, oil prices have been determined by the OPEC members acting as a producer cartel. Producers have negotiated among themselves to determine the posted price of oil and have then imposed that price on consumers. OPEC members have instituted production reductions to manipulate supply conditions and thus to maintain price, the same technique used by the seven sisters in an earlier era. Crucial to this program of maintaining price by reducing supply has been the role of the major reserve countries and large producers: Saudi Arabia and Kuwait have been willing to support the cartel by themselves, absorbing a large part of the production reductions necessary to maintain price.[26]

The oil companies have not been able to resist the transfer of power from company to host government. The monopoly control of oil by OPEC, the unity of the producers, and tight market conditions have prevented the companies from having any leverage. Furthermore, the companies have little incentive to resist. They have been able in most cases to pass price increases along to consumers and thus have not suffered financially from the loss of control over price.

Producers have asserted their power not only on questions of price but also on issues of ownership. The participation agreement proved to be as fleeting as those in Teheran and Tripoli. The new sense of power over price was quickly translated into a desire for immediate and total equity control. All the major oil-producing states have now signed agreements with the oil companies providing for immediate majority or total national ownership of subsidiaries located in those states.

Thus the international oil companies have lost their powerful position as managers of the international political economy of oil. It would be wrong, however, to think that they have disappeared. Although no longer the arbiters of supply and price, although no longer the owners of oil concessions, the seven sisters and their many smaller relatives still play a vital role in the international oil scene. As holders of technology and markets, they are needed by the newly powerful producer governments. As their holdings are nationalized, their role is becoming that of a vitally necessary service contractor to producer states. Still, it is a far cry from the days when the companies divided up the producing regions among themselves and obtained control of the world's oil for a song.

With the decline of the companies, Northern consumer governments attempted to counter the power of the producers.[27] But the consumers, unlike the producers, were unable to agree on a common policy. The United States sought to form a countercartel to destroy OPEC. U.S. policy makers reasoned that unified opposition to OPEC and the threat of economic or military retaliation would undermine producer solidarity and lead to a decline in oil prices. To this end, the United States pressed Western Europe and Japan to attend a consumer conference and to develop a united policy. The conference, held in Washington in February 1974, demonstrated the inability of the consumers to agree on a common strategy. While the Americans argued for unity and resistance, the Europeans and Japanese—far more dependent on foreign sources of oil, far less interested in support for Israel, and somewhat fearful of U.S.

dominance—opposed a countercartel and argued for cooperation with the producers. The only common effort to emerge from the conference was an agreement to establish an International Energy Agency (IEA) to work on an emergency oil-sharing scheme and a long-term program for the development of alternate forms of energy.

After the Washington conference, the United States, the Europeans, and the Japanese went their own ways. The United States sought to destroy producer unity and to divide the rest of the Third World from OPEC by continuing to press for consumer unity and the development of the IEA. The Europeans sought special bilateral political and economic arrangements with the oil producers and resisted consumer bloc strategies. France, the strongest opponent of the American approach, refused to join the IEA and urged instead a producer–consumer dialogue.

In late 1974 a compromise was reached between the United States and France. The United States obtained grudging French acceptance of the IEA, although France refused to join, and France obtained grudging American support for a North–South dialogue. After some delays and conflicts, CIEC (the Conference on International Economic Cooperation) finally commenced in December 1975.[28] The conference constituted a recognition, if not a total acceptance, by the United States and the other consumers that they could not alter the power of the producer states over the price of oil and that what they could seek at best was some conciliation and coordination of common interests.

OTHER OPECs?

The success of the oil producers led to a revolution in the thinking of Southern raw material producers. Suddenly, it seemed that producer cartels could bring the end of dependence. Producer organizations in copper, bauxite, iron ore, bananas, and coffee were either formed or took on new life after October 1973. The Third World issued a call for producer associations. In April 1974 at a special session of the United Nations General Assembly, the less developed countries demanded the establishment of a new international economic order which was to include Northern support for the functioning and aims of producer associations.[29] In December 1974 the Third World pressed through the General Assembly a Charter of Economic Rights and Duties of States which included an article on the right of the South to form producer associations and the duty of the North to "respect that right by refraining from applying economic and political measures that would limit it."[30]

To determine whether producer cartels are a realistic strategy or yet another exercise in futility, it is necessary to review the reasons for the oil producers' success and thereby to develop a model for effective producer action.

Several market factors set the stage for OPEC's success. The demand for oil imports is high. Oil and, specifically, oil imports play an important and growing role as a source of energy in the North (see Table 9–1). Until North Sea oil becomes available, Europe and Japan will remain virtually totally dependent on foreign sources for oil. Even the once self-sufficient United States has become increasingly dependent on oil imports. The demand for oil and oil imports is also price inelastic. There are no readily available substitutes for petroleum, and there is no way significantly to decrease consumption. Thus an increase in the price of oil does not lead to a significant decrease in demand.

Supply factors also favored OPEC. The supply of oil is price inelastic, that is, an increase in its price does not lead to the rapid entrance of new producers into the market. Large amounts of capital and many years are required to develop new sources of oil. In addition, supply inelasticity was not relieved by stockpiles of oil. In 1973 the developed countries did not have oil reserves to use even in the short run to increase supply and alleviate the effect of supply reductions.

Finally, at the time of the OPEC price increases, there were extremely tight supply conditions in the international market for oil. Rapidly rising demand in the consuming countries was not matched by rising production (see Figure 9–2). As a result, a small number of important producers or even one major producer were in a position to influence price by merely threatening to limit supply.

This economic vulnerability of consumers set the stage for OPEC action. A number of political factors, however, determined whether such action would take place. An understanding of the behavior of interest groups helps to explain the ability of the oil producers to take joint action to raise the price of oil.[31]

First, there is a relatively small number of oil-exporting countries. OPEC's thirteen members control 85 percent of world oil exports; seven Arab producers control 54 percent of world exports.[32] Common political action is more likely when the number of participants is so limited, as the small number maximizes all members' perception of their shared interest and the benefits to be derived from joint action.

The oil producers were also helped by the experience of over a decade of cooperation. OPEC encouraged what one analyst has described as "solidarity and a sense of community."[33] It also led to experience in common action. In the period 1971–1973 the oil producers tested their power, saw tangible results from common action, and acquired the confidence to pursue such action.

Confidence was reinforced by the significant monetary reserves of the major producers. The reserves minimized the economic risks of attempting some joint action such as reducing production or instituting an embargo. The reserves were money in the bank which could be used to finance needed imports if the joint effort to raise the price of petroleum was not immediately successful. According to one analyst, it enabled the oil producers to take a "long-term perspective," to enter into common policies in the first place, and to avoid the later temptation of taking advantage of short-term gains by cheating.[34]

The common political interest of the Arab oil producers in backing their cause in the conflict with Israel reinforced their common economic interest in increasing the price of oil. The outbreak of the 1973 war greatly enhanced Arab cohesiveness and facilitated the OAPEC decision of October 16 to raise oil prices unilaterally.

Group theory suggests, however, that perception of a common interest is often insufficient for common action. A leader or leaders are needed to mobilize the group and to bear the major burden of group action. Leadership has been crucial in common oil producer action. In 1973 the initiative of the Arab producers in unilaterally raising prices made it possible for other producers to increase their prices. Since 1973 the willingness and ability of Saudi Arabia and Kuwait to bear the major burden of production reductions enabled the producers to maintain the new higher prices.[35]

Producer action was facilitated by the nature of the problem. Manipulation of price was relatively easy because it was a seller's market. Given the tight market, it was not necessary to reduce supply significantly to maintain a higher price. Ironically, the international oil companies also facilitated joint producer action. Producing nations were able to increase price by taxing the oil companies. The companies acquiesced because they were able to pass on the tax to their customers.[36] Producing nations were also able to reduce supply simply by ordering the companies to limit production. Increasing governmental control of the companies facilitated the institution of these reductions.

Finally, producer success was assured by the absence of countervailing consumer power. The weakness of the corporations and the consumer governments was demonstrated by the Libyan success in 1970 and by subsequent negotiations beginning with Teheran. The disarray and acquiescence of the oil companies and the oil-consuming governments in 1973 sealed the producing nations' success. Particularly important was the inability of the developed market economies to take joint action—in contrast to the group action of the producers—to counter the cartel.

Several factors suggest that in the short term, and perhaps in the medium term, some producer cartels might succeed. In the near term economic conditions are propitious for many commodities, particularly for those on which consuming states are highly dependent (see Table 7–1). The United States, for example, relies on imports of bauxite, tin, bananas, and coffee. Western Europe and Japan, less well endowed with raw materials, depend also on imports of copper, iron ore, and phosphates. The disruption of supply of many of these commodities, particularly critical minerals, would have an important disruptive effect on the developed market economies.

In addition, over the short and medium term, demand for and supply of these commodities is price inelastic. With few exceptions, a price increase for these materials would not be offset by a decrease in consumption, which would lead to an increase in total producer revenues. Similarly, when supply is price inelastic, a rise in price will not immediately lead to the emergence of new supplies, as it takes time and money to grow new crops and exploit new mineral sources. It should be noted that for some critical raw materials an inelasticity of supply can be cushioned by stockpiles, and developed countries have accumulated such supplies for strategic reasons. Nevertheless, while stockpiles can serve to resist cartel action over the short term, not all commodities can be stockpiled, and stockpiles in many commodities are generally insufficient to outlast supply interruptions that persist for more than a few months.[37]

In the long run, however, demand and supply are more elastic and thus less conducive to successful cartel action. A rise in price above a certain level will generally lead to a shift in demand to substitutes. Aluminum will be substituted for copper; coffee will be replaced by tea. With time it is also possible to develop new sources of supply for most commodities. New coffee trees can be planted; new mineral resources including vast resources in the seabed can be exploited. Of course, some of these new supplies may be relatively more expensive, as new production will often have to rely on costly technologies and on lower-quality ores. So, it should be noted, new production may undermine a cartel, but it may have little effect on price.

Because of the long-term elasticity of demand and supply, the successful survival of a cartel generally depends on two complex factors. First, producers have to manage price so that it does not rise above a level which would encourage use of substitutes. Such management requires sophisticated market knowledge and predictive ability. Then, too, because the threshold price may be lower than the preferred price for many producers, agreement on joint action may be quite difficult to achieve. Second, and equally difficult, the supply response from other producers must be managed. Unless a producer association can control this response, any cartel will necessarily fail in time.

Tight market conditions favor producers over the short term. As demonstrated by the oil action, a seller's market facilitates cartel action by enabling one or a small number of producers to raise prices, as occurred in 1973–1974. At that time the simultaneous economic boom in the North and uncertain currency markets which encouraged speculation in commodities led to commodity shortages and dramatic price increases. Developed countries were particularly vulnerable to threats of supply manipulation, and producer countries were in a particularly strong position to pose such threats. For example, Morocco in phosphates and Jamaica in bauxite took advantage of this situation to raise prices.

Should similar conditions recur, other such producer action might succeed as long as market conditions remained favorable. Some argue that such conditions are cyclical and short-term and that producer gains would thus be short-lived.[38] Without such tight markets, producers would have to turn to more difficult techniques of supply management such as buffer stocks or production controls.[39] Others have argued, however, that such conditions are very likely to develop more frequently and perhaps even permanently because of a structural change in the world economy in which the demand for raw materials is growing rapidly while supplies are decreasing in quantity and quality.[40]

In addition to these economic factors, several political conditions also favor producer action, again primarily over the short run. For many commodities—for example, bauxite, copper, phosphates, bananas, cocoa, coffee, natural rubber, and tea—a relatively small number of Southern producers dominate the export market, and a number of these producers have formed associations with the goal of price management.

Several recent political developments make producer cooperation more likely. One is a new sense of self-confidence. The OPEC experience has suggested to other producers that, through their control of commodities vital to the North, they may possess the threat they have long sought. Thus many Third World states now feel that they can risk more aggressive policies toward the North.

Another new development stems not from confidence but from desperation. The simultaneous energy, food, recession, and inflation crises have left most Southern states with severe balance-of-payments problems.[41] Some states may feel that they have no alternative to instituting risky measures which might provide short-term economic benefits but which will probably prove unsuccessful or even damaging in the long run.

Reinforcing economic desperation is political concern. Political leaders, especially those in the Third World, tend to have short-run perspectives, as maintenance of their power may depend on achieving short-term gains despite inevitable long-run losses.[42] However, this argument is directly opposite to the OPEC model for a successful producer cartel, wherein monetary reserves enabled the producing nations to take a long-term perspective, to risk short-term losses for long-term gains. In other cases, producers with huge balance-of-payments deficits may be moved to risk long-term losses for short-term gains. And, as has been argued, short-term maximization of revenues may in fact be rational action for the long-term view; that is, if producers feel that their short-term profits will be sufficient to achieve economic diversification and development, they may rationally pursue short-term gains.[43]

The emergence of leaders in some producer groups is yet another new development. Jamaica's unilateral action in raising taxes and royalties on bauxite production and Morocco's unilateral action to raise the price of phosphate have altered the conditions for other bauxite and phosphate producers.

Finally, cooperation can sometimes be facilitated by the nature of the task of managing price and supply. In such commodities as bauxite and bananas, vertically integrated oligopolistic multinational corporations can be taxed according to the OPEC formula. In these and other commodities, production control is facilitated by increasing governmental regulation or ownership of production facilities.

Despite this clear political potential for cooperation, however, there remain major problems of joint action. While many commodities are supplied by a small number of producers, these producers often find they have more in conflict than in common. The copper producers, for example, are divided on political as well as economic differences. Moreover, while the foreign exchange crisis may encourage cooperation, it also may facilitate consumer resistance. Producing nations that have no reserves and that rely on the export of one commodity for the bulk of their foreign exchange earnings are not in a position to endure long concerted corporate or consumer government resistance. Furthermore, the temptation to take short-term profits from concerted action at the expense of longer-term gains is greater in situations of balance-of-payments crisis. And, while the task of price management may be easy in some cases, as when there is a leader and when multinational corporations are present, such advantages do not exist for many commodity-producing nations.

Perhaps one of the greatest barriers to producer cartels is the task of managing supply. Few countries have a large enough share of production and large enough reserves to engage in the kind of leadership role played by Saudi Arabi and Kuwait. No one country or small group of countries is able to bear the burden of supply reduction for the entire commodity group.

In the absence of tight markets, then, supply can only be controlled through buffer stock schemes or through export or production reductions—methods that are politically complex and economically costly. Many commodities are perishable and hence cannot be stored in a buffer stock, whereas other commodities require enormous buffer stocks and vast financing to maintain prices. Export and production reductions are equally difficult to accomplish. Export reduction without production controls poses the same problems of storing and financing as buffer stocks. And agreements to reduce production are difficult to achieve— even OPEC has never been able to agree on a prorationing scheme—and may be costly in terms of employment.

B'AUXITE, BANANAS, AND COPPER

The potential benefits as well as the problems of producer cartels may perhaps be better understood by a brief examination of condition in three commodity-producing organizations which have attempted to increase prices: bauxite, which was and is likely to continue to be a success; bananas, which failed but has some potential for success; and copper, which was a failure and is likely to remain so.

In May 1974 Prime Minister Michael Manley of Jamaica announced a plan to increase his country's revenues from bauxite production by 250 percent and to alter the relationship between Jamaica and the six huge multinational companies which owned, produced, processed, and marketed Jamaican bauxite.[44] The prime minister asked Parliament to increase taxes and royalties on bauxite production and to base the new royalties and taxes not, as before, on the tonnage of bauxite extracted but, rather, on the price of aluminum ingots. To prevent the companies involved from shifting production out of Jamaica, the prime minister asked that aluminum companies be required to maintain production levels established by the Jamaican government or to pay taxes on that level whether or not it was actually maintained. Finally, to increase governmental control of the industry, the prime minister asked Parliament to authorize him to open negotiations with the six companies to establish governmental ownership of bauxite lands and to move toward government ownership of production facilities. Parliament approved the prime minister's program in June 1974. The six aluminum companies protested that Jamaica was violating binding contracts and appealed to the International Center for Settlement of Investment Disputes of the World Bank. But they eventually acquiesced and negotiated new long-term agreements with Jamaica providing for increased government revenues and governmental participation in ownership. Following the Jamaican action, other bauxite exporters—the Dominican Republic and Surinam—demanded and, so far, have obtained similar revenue increases.

The Jamaican action was successful for several reasons. Consuming states are highly dependent on bauxite imports. Demand for bauxite has risen rapidly—at an average of 9.2 percent per year from 1963 to 1973[45]—and much of that demand is met by imports. None of the six largest consuming states produces more than 50 percent of its bauxite needs, and most produce very little.[46] The United States, for example, imports 90 percent of its bauxite consumption, and half of that comes from Jamaica.[47]

Furthermore, bauxite demand is price inelastic, in large part because the price of bauxite is only a small percentage of the price of aluminum, and most of the price relates to processing costs. Thus an increase in the price of the raw material does not lead to a major increase in the price of the finished product or, in turn, to a significant decrease in consumption. Supply is also price inelastic over the short and medium term, as vast amounts of capital and many years are needed to develop new sources.

The structure of the market also favored Jamaica. Bauxite is sold primarily among subsidiaries of the large vertically integrated multinational corporations, so the price is subject not to the market but to negotiation. If a producing country can develop bargaining advantages, it can renegotiate the price in its favor.

The vulnerability of the multinational aluminum corporations enabled Jamaica to do just that. The companies had oriented their production facilities around the particular type of bauxite coming from Jamaica, had become dependent on Jamaican supplies in time of a tight market, and had made major capital investments in Jamaica.[48] They were vulnerable to supply disruption and thus to Jamaican demands. Moreover, because of their oligopolistic market positions, they, like the oil companies, could pass on the increased price to consumers without the fear of losing market shares.

Jamaica was thus in a position to move independently against the companies, and she had important incentives to do so. Higher prices for food grain and petroleum had increased Jamaican import costs by almost 32 percent, or $183 million, between 1973 and 1974.[49] As one of Jamaica's leading newspapers put it,

> The decision has to be regarded as one of national emergency rather than political expediency or ideology; world terms of trade have changed so drastically and mercilessly against countries like Jamaica that the situation morally approximates a legal right to cancel a contract because of acts of God or enemies of States.[50]

Other producers are now emulating Jamaica. The question is whether they can maintain the new higher price over the long term. One problem is the availability of substitutes such as steel and plastics. However, because bauxite represents only a small percentage of the price of aluminum, there is room for a significant price rise without a major threat of substitution. The greatest problem relates to elasticity of supply. Bauxite is found in many countries, many of which, like Brazil and Australia, are capable of and interested in expanding production. Aluminum can also be extracted from clays other than bauxite which are found in abundance throughout the world. The use of nonbauxite clays becomes cost efficient, however, only at very high bauxite price levels.

Thus, the problem for Jamaica and other producers is to control new bauxite production. To this end, in March 1974, Jamaica and nine other countries—Surinam, Guyana, the Dominican Republic, Haiti, Ghana, Guinea, Sierra Leone, Yugoslavia, and Australia—established the International Bauxite Association with the stated goals of fair and reasonable profits for member countries, increased processing in producer states, and greater national ownership of bauxite resources.[51]

Important factors that encourage their success include the fact that together these few countries control much of the world's bauxite exports; they benefit from high import dependence of consuming countries, from inelasticities of demand and supply, and from the vertical integration of the industry and the absence of a free market; several of the key producers—Jamaica, Surinam, and Guyana—have geographical and ethnic ties; and, perhaps, most importantly, Jamaican leadership has demonstrated the benefits of cooperative action.

In many ways the situation of the banana producers resembles that of the bauxite exporters.[52] Banana production is highly concentrated, with five countries accounting for 64 percent of world banana exports— Ecuador (21 percent), Costa Rica (15 percent), Honduras (13 percent), Panama (8 percent), and the Philippines (7 percent)—and the consuming countries are totally dependent on imports. Furthermore, the demand for bananas is price inelastic in the near term and under certain conditions in the long term, largely because, like bauxite, the price of the raw material is only a fraction of the price of the retail product. Temperature-controlled transportation, refining, and distribution account for most of the cost of bananas.[53] Thus a significant increase in the price of bananas does not lead to an equal increase in the retail price of bananas. If the price is not raised to such high levels that consumers turn to substitutes, demand remains inelastic in the long run. Finally, supply is also inelastic in the short run.

Also as with bauxite, multinationals play a key role in the banana industry. Bananas are sold to subsidiaries of the same multinational corporation which owns and operates the banana plantations. These oligopolistic vertically integrated multinational corporations are dependent on these sources of supply and are vulnerable because of expensive investments in transportation and refrigeration. Finally, because of their oligopolistic market position, the companies can pass on price increases to consumers without fearing loss of markets to competitors.

The banana-producing countries have attempted to take advantage of these favorable conditions. In March 1974 the Central American banana-producing countries and Colombia formed the Union of Banana Exporting Countries (UPEB) and agreed to impose an export tax of $1.00 on each box of bananas. The effort failed. Only four countries— Colombia, Costa Rica, Honduras, and Panama—actually imposed a tax, only Panama imposed the agreed $1.00 duty, and soon all reduced the duty significantly.

There were several reasons for the failure of UPEB (Union des Paises Exportadores de Banana). The multinational banana companies— United Brands, Standard Fruit, and Del Monte—fought back viciously. They challenged the tax in local courts and refused to pay the government until the courts determined the legality of the duty. They stopped exports, cut production, destroyed crates of bananas, laid off workers, threatened not to reinvest after the hurricane in Honduras, and, in Honduras, resorted to bribery to obtain a tax reduction.[54]

Another problem was the refusal by Ecuador, the largest producer and the country with the greatest ability to expand its production, to join UPEB. Ecuador argued that the tax was not viable without concurrent production reductions and that, in any case, as an oil producer it did not suffer from the oil price increase which was UPEB's justification for its tax. While Ecuador most probably acted out of self-interest, its decision did serve to point out the important long-run problem of excess supply. Although the demand for bananas has grown, supply has grown even more rapidly. Without some form of supply control, UPEB price rises would collapse. Because bananas are perishable, the form of control would have to be production reductions. Yet these are politically difficult to achieve.

A third raw material group which has sought to carry out an OPEC strategy is the association of copper producers, CIPEC (Conseil Intergouvernemental des Pays Exportateurs de Cuivre). In June 1974 the group, which was formed in 1967, resolved "to control the declining price of copper on world markets."[55] To that end the Intergovernmental Council of Copper Exporting Countries (CIPEC), in November 1974, announced that its members would restrict monthly exports of copper by 10 percent and would not increase inventories of refined copper. In April 1975 the export reduction was increased to 15 percent. All to no avail. Copper prices continued to decline.

At first, several market factors seem to favor CIPEC. Although the United States supplies 83 percent of its own copper needs through mining and recycling scrap, Europe imports 93 percent and Japan 90 percent of their respective total consumption.[56] Furthermore, import dependence is increasing. World copper consumption has risen rapidly and with it imports have also risen. In 1950, for example, imports accounted for 41.1 percent of industrial world consumption, whereas in 1973 imports accounted for 51.5 percent of consumption.[57]

Demand is also price inelastic, at least in the short run. Because there are no readily available, adequate substitutes for copper, producers can increase their total earnings by increasing the price. Supply is also inelastic in the short run because of the cost and time involved in bringing new production on line. Moreover, copper stockpiles are usually quite limited.[58]

Several political factors are also conducive to CIPEC success. CIPEC's four original members—Chile, Peru, Zambia, and Zaire—control 53 percent of world exports of copper. If other Third World producers joined, CIPEC would account for almost two-thirds of world exports.[59] Some movement toward expansion is taking place. In 1975 Indonesia became a full member, and Australia and Papua New Guinea became associate members. Mauritania has applied for associate membership. In addition, because the governments of the major members of CIPEC control all or a majority of production and all of the marketing of copper, they are in a position to carry out policies to control supply. Furthermore, as has been noted, in 1974 and 1975 the countries did agree to and did carry out export reductions of 15 percent.

Despite these favorable conditions, CIPEC has little chance of increasing the price of copper. In the long run demand for copper from CIPEC is highly elastic. New sources of raw copper are available.[60] One of the most important and potentially threatening sources is from deep-sea nodules. Unless any price increase of copper is relatively modest, new supplies will be developed. Also, unless any increase is limited, substitutes such as aluminum and plastics will be used.

Finally, the demand for copper is highly income elastic; that is, an increase in the growth rate of the developed countries leads to a significant increase in the demand for copper, whereas a decline in growth leads to a significant decline in demand. This elasticity was demonstrated by the rise in price of copper during the economic boom of 1973–1974 and its precipitous drop during the recession of 1974–1975.[61] For producers, this means that, except in times of boom in the developed market economies, copper is and will be in surplus supply. Thus, if producers wish to raise or even stabilize prices, they must develop schemes which will absorb huge quantities of copper or prevent its production in the first place. Limited reductions such as the 15 percent export cutbacks of 1974–1975 are insufficient.

It is this problem of developing effective schemes to manage supply which confronts CIPEC. One scheme which CIPEC has considered is a buffer stock. Under such a program a central agency would buy copper when the price fell below an agreed upon floor and would sell when it rose above that floor. However, because supply is generally significantly in excess of demand, a buffer stock program would be prohibitively expensive—one estimate suggested a minimum cost of $2 billion,[62] a sum clearly beyond the capabilities of CIPEC. Moreover, outside financing from, for example, IMF (International Monetary Fund) or OPEC, does not seem likely, as IMF offers assistance only to producer–consumer groups and OPEC has shown little interest in financing CIPEC.

Another alternative would be to reduce production, but this would also be difficult to accomplish, since non-CIPEC producers would not agree to such reductions and would take advantage of any price rises achieved by CIPEC reductions to increase their sales. One potential producer is the United States, which, given its position to mine the ocean floor, could disrupt the market. Furthermore, CIPEC members themselves are not interested in production reductions. Because copper production is labor intensive, any reduction would lead to unemployment and, possibly, to social unrest and political problems for producer governments. It is probably for this reason that the export reductions of 1974 and 1975 were not matched in most countries by production reductions.

Even if CIPEC could agree on how to reduce production or how to finance a buffer stock, its members would have difficulty in agreeing on a common price, as production costs differ from country to country. Thus what looks like a low price for one producer would provide respectable profits for another.[63]

Finally, there are no common political interests to serve as an incentive for common CIPEC action. Indeed, there has been political conflict among the members. Zambia broke diplomatic relations with Chile after the 1973 coup. And since the coup Chile has been a reluctant member of CIPEC; it does not wish to antagonize the United States, its political supporter in an unfriendly world and one of its major creditors. In sum, CIPEC has little short- or long-term chance of success in its goal of increasing copper prices.

THE MEANING OF COMMODITY POWER

There is a possibility that producers might attempt joint action to increase the price of commodity exports, if only out of sheer frustration and even against all rational calculations. Some of these efforts may succeed; most will fail. Even if they fail, however, such producer action may have a disruptive effect on the economies of the developed states, as well as on other Third World states.

The possibility of irrational producer action and the disruptive potential of such action may provide a bargaining tool for the South.[64] From the OPEC experience, Northern countries have learned of the costs of commodity disruption, and, from the efforts of Jamaica, UPEB, CIPEC, as well as other producers, they have learned that Southern states can attempt cartel strategies. As a result, indications are that the Northern states are at long last considering that it may be in their interest to bring the less developed countries into the system they have so long managed by and for themselves.

NOTES

1. The following analysis of the international oil oligopoly is based largely on accounts in Morris A. Adelman, *The World Petroleum Market* (Baltimore, Md., Johns Hopkins Press, 1972); J. E. Hartshorn, *Politics and World Oil Economics: An Account of the International Oil Industry in its Political Environment*, rev. ed. (New York: Praeger, 1962 and 1967); Edith T. Penrose, *The Large International Firm in Developing Countries: The International Petroleum Industry* (Cambridge, Mass.: M.I.T. Press, 1969); Anthony Sampson, *The Seven Sisters: The Great Oil Companies and the World They Made* (New York: Viking Books, 1975); Federal Trade Commission, *International Petroleum Cartel*, Staff Report to the Federal Trade Commission submitted to the Subcommittee on Monopoly of the Select Committee on Small Business, U.S. Senate, 82nd Congress, 2nd Sess. (Committee Print No. 6) (Washington, D.C., 1952).

2. See Zuhayr Mikdashi, *A Financial Analysis of Middle Eastern Oil Concessions: 1901–1965* (New York: Praeger, 1966); Charles Issawi and Mohammed Yeganeh, *The Economics of Middle Eastern Oil* (New York: Praeger, 1962), pp. 24–40.

3. In 1928, for example, Shell, Standard Oil, and Anglo-Persian (the predecessor of BP) concluded the "As Is," or "Achnacarry," agreement to divide world markets and determine world prices, and in that same year a group of British, Dutch, American, and French companies agreed to divide up much of the old Ottoman Empire in the Red Line agreement. Also important was the basing-point pricing system which established a common price at several locations, or basing points, and standard, not actual, freight charges from the basing point to the destination. This system prevented low-cost producers from expanding their market share by reducing prices. See Penrose, *The Large International Firm in Developing Countries*, pp. 180–183.

4. See Mikdashi, *A Financial Analysis of Middle Eastern Oil Concessions: 1901–1965*; Issawi and Yeganeh, *The Economics of Middle Eastern Oil*; Gertrude G. Edwards, "Foreign Petroleum Companies and the State in Venezuela," in Raymond F. Mikesell et al., *Foreign Investment in the Petroleum and Mineral Industries* (Baltimore, Md.: Johns Hopkins Press, 1971), pp. 101–128; Franklin Tugwell, *The Politics of Oil in Venezuela* (Stanford, Calif.: Stanford Univ. Press, 1975); Donald A. Wells, "Aramco: The Evolution of an Oil Concession," in Mikesell, *Foreign Investment in the Petroleum and Mineral Industries*, pp. 216–236.

5. Wells, "Aramco: The Evolution of an Oil Concession."

6. Adelman, *The World Petroleum Market*, p. 207.

7. See, for example, Robert Engler, *The Politics of Oil: Private Power and Democratic Directions* (Chicago: Univ. of Chicago Press, 1961).

8. This interest later led to support for an oil import quota system imposed in 1958 and designed to protect the American market from cheap foreign oil.

9. Benjamin Shwadran, *The Middle East, Oil and the Great Powers* (New York: Council for Middle Eastern Affairs, 1955), pp. 103–152; J. C. Hurewitz, *Middle East Politics: The Military Dimension* (New York: Praeger, 1969), pp. 281–282.

10. See Penrose, *The Large International Firm in Developing Countries*, pp. 248–263; Adelman, *The World Petroleum Market*, pp. 196–204.

11. Mira Wilkins, *The Maturing of Multinational Enterprise: American Business Abroad from 1914 to 1970* (Cambridge, Mass.: Harvard Univ. Press, 1974), pp. 386–387.

12. See, for example, Joan Edelman Spero, "Energy Self-Sufficiency and National Security," in Robert H. Connery and Robert S. Gilmour, eds., *The National Energy Problem*, Proceedings of the Academy of Political Science, 31 (December 1973), 123–136.

13. See, for example, Engler, *The Politics of Oil*.

14. See footnote 4.

15. International Monetary Fund, *Annual Report of the Executive Directors for the Fiscal Year Ended April 30, 1972* (Washington, D.C.: International Monetary Fund, 1972), pp. 31–32.

16. For a history of the Organization of Petroleum Exporting Countries, see Zuhayr

Mikdashi, *The Community of Oil Exporting Countries: A Study in Governmental Cooperation* (Ithaca, N.Y.: Cornell Univ. Press, 1972).

17. Zuhayr Mikdashi, "The OPEC Process," *Daedalus*, 104 (Fall 1975), 203. The new members were Abu Dhabi, Algeria, Libya, Qatar, the United Arab Emirates, Nigeria, Ecuador, Indonesia, and Gabon.

18. Mikdashi, *The Community of Oil Exporting Countries*, pp. 196–207.

19. On evolution of events in Libya, see U.S. Senate Committee on Foreign Relations, *Multinational Corporations and United States Foreign Policy: Multinational Petroleum Companies and Foreign Policy*, hearings before the subcommittee on Multinational Corporations, 93rd Congress, 1st and 2nd Sess., Part 5 (Washington, D.C., 1974).

20. Organization for Economic Cooperation and Development, Oil Committee, *Oil Statistics: Supply and Disposal 1970* (Paris: Organization for Economic Cooperation and Development, 1971), p. 27. There were several reasons for the powerful Libyan position in the European market. Transportation of oil from Libya was much cheaper and safer than transportation of oil from the Persian Gulf, which, with the closing of the Suez Canal, required a long trip around Africa. Furthermore, in 1970 there had been a decline in the supply of oil from Nigeria due to the civil war and the pipeline which carried Saudi oil to the Mediterranean had been cut in Syria. Finally, Libyan oil was low in sulfur and therefore desirable for environmental reasons.

21. See U.S. Senate, *Multinational Corporations and United States Foreign Policy.*

22. There was some consultation by the developed market states. The U.S. Department of Justice issued a waiver to oil companies under antitrust law enabling them to cooperate in bargaining to resist unreasonable demands for higher prices. See U.S. Senate, *Multinational Corporations and United States Foreign Policy*, Part 5, pp. 145–173. President Nixon then sent Undersecretary of State John N. Irwin to the Middle East to encourage governments to enter into joint negotiations with the companies. Secretary Irwin, however, capitulated to the demand of the Shah of Iran for separate negotiations.

23. Kuwait signed the agreement, but the national assembly did not ratify it.

24. For the reasons, see Joel Darmstadter and Hans H. Landsberg, "The Economic Background," *Daedalus*, 104 (Fall 1975), 15–37.

25. The Organization of Arab Petroleum Exporting Countries, was formed by three conservative Arab states, Kuwait, Libya, and Saudi Arabia, in 1968. It was expanded in 1970 to include Algeria, Abu Dhabi, Bahrain, Dubai, and Qatar.

26. See Mikdashi, "The OPEC Process."

27. See Wilfrid L. Kohl, "The United States, Western Europe and the Energy Problem," *Journal of International Affairs*, 30 (Spring/Summer 1976), pp. 81–96.

28. See Chapter 7 of this text.

29. Guy F. Erb and Valeriana Kallab, eds., *Beyond Dependency: The Developing World Speaks Out* (New York: Praeger, 1975), p. 189.

30. Ibid., p. 206.

31. The following analysis is to a great extent influenced by the theory of collective action developed by Mancur Olson, *The Logic of Collective Action: Public Goods and the Theory of Groups* (Cambridge, Mass.: Harvard Univ. Press, 1965 and 1971).

32. James W. Howe and the Staff of the Overseas Development Council, *The U.S. and World Development: Agenda for Action 1975* (New York: Praeger, 1975), p. 236.

33. Mikdashi, *The Community of Oil Exporting Countries*, pp. 196–207.

34. Stephen D. Krasner, "Oil Is the Exception," *Foreign Policy*, 14 (Spring 1974), 78–79.

35. "World Production in Low Gear," *Petroleum Economist*, 43 (January 1976), 7.

36. See Raymond Mikesell, "More Third World Cartels Ahead?," *Challenge*, 17 (November–December 1974), 24–26 on the OPEC method of taxing multinational corporations.

37. See U.S. Council on International Economic Policy, *Special Report: Critical Imported Materials*, (Washington, D.C., December 1974), p. 22.

38. Ibid.

39. See Chapter 7.

40. C. Fred Bergsten, "The New Era in World Commodity Markets," *Challenge*, 17 (September–October 1974), 34–42; Donella H. Meadows et al., *The Limits to Growth: A*

Report for the Club of Rome's Project on the Predicament of Mankind (New York: Universe Books, 1972).

41. See Wouter Tims, "The Developing Countries," in Edward R. Fried and Charles L. Schultze, eds., *Higher Oil Prices and the World Economy: The Adjustment Problem* (Washington, D.C., The Brookings Institution, 1975), pp. 169–195.

42. John E. Tilton, "Cartels in Metal Industries," *Earth and Mineral Sciences*, 44 (March 1975), 41–44.

43. Harry G. Johnson, *Economic Policies Toward Less Developed Countries* (New York: Praeger, 1967), pp. 136–162.

44. The six are the Aluminum Company of America, Alcan Aluminum Ltd., Reynolds Metals Company, Kaiser Aluminum and Chemical Corporation, Anaconda Company, and Revere Copper and Brass Company.

45. Anthony Edwards, *The Potential for New Commodity Cartels: Copying OPEC, or Improved International Agreements?*, QER Special No. 27 (London: The Economist Intelligence Unit, September 1975), p. 41.

46. Ibid.

47. U.S. Council on International Economic Policy, *Critical Imported Materials*, p. A–2. Figures are for 1973. The crucial position of Jamaica in the American market is based on its large production—it is the world's largest producer after Australia and is the largest exporter in the Third World—the low-cost transportation of Jamaican bauxite to American markets, and the low-cost production in Jamaica.

48. See statement of Hon. Thomas O. Enders, assistant secretary of state for economic and business affairs, in *Outlook for Prices and Supplies of Industrial Raw Materials*, hearings before the Subcommittee on Economic Growth of the Joint Economic Committee, 93rd Congress, 2nd Sess., July 25, 1974, p. 180.

49. James W. Howe, *The U.S. and World Development*, p. 238.

50. *The Christian Science Monitor*, May 21, 1974, p. 2.

51. *The New York Times*, March 19, 1974, p. 60.

52. This discussion involves Latin American producers. The other producers, former British and French colonies, have special agreements with developed countries which guarantee markets and provide price supports and financial aid. See Edwards, *The Potential for New Commodity Cartels*, p. 37.

53. Ibid., p. 36.

54. Ibid., pp. 36–37, for example.

55. K. W. Clarfield et al., *Eight Mineral Cartels* (New York: *Metals Week*, McGraw-Hill, 1975), p. 57.

56. U.S. Council on International Economic Policy, *Critical Imported Materials*, p. 43.

57. Joseph C. Wyman, *Perspective on Copper* (New York: The Research Group of Reynolds Securities, Inc., February 1975), p. 6.

58. Edwards, *The Potential for New Commodity Cartels*, p. 53.

59. Mikesell, "More Third World Cartels Ahead?," p. 28.

60. Copper scrap now provides 44 percent of total U.S., 38 percent of West German, and 35 percent of Japanese consumption. Further recycling possibilities are limited. See Edwards, *The Potential for New Commodity Cartels*, p. 52.

61. This rise and drop was aggravated by the Japanese accumulation of stocks to hedge against shortages in the boom period and the sales of these vast stocks during the economic recession.

62. *Eight Mineral Cartels*, p. 97.

63. See interview with Sir Ronald Prain in *The London Times*, October 9, 1974, p. 15.

64. On the use of irrational behavior as a strategic move, see Thomas C. Schelling, *The Strategy of Conflict* (New York: Oxford Univ. Press, 1960), pp. 130–131.

Part Four

The East-West System

10

East-West Economic Relations

It was neither desired nor expected by planners constructing the new international economic order between 1943 and 1947 that the East would not be part of the postwar system.[1] Although the Soviet Union had, between the wars, been separated from the international economic system by the West's diplomatic reserve and by Stalin's autarkic development policy, the Soviet Union was never completely isolated. From the time of the revolution until the early 1930s, when the collapse of world trade led to a collapse of trade with the West, the Soviet Union carried on an important trade relationship with the developed countries and with the United States in particular.[2] Soviet imports of Western raw materials and of Western technology in this period made an important contribution to Soviet growth,[3] and U.S.–Soviet economic interaction revived during the war years through U.S. lend-lease assistance.

Some doubted the interest in or ability of the Soviet Union to join the liberal multilateral system envisioned by the postwar planners.[4] American officials, however, actively sought the participation of the Soviet Union in the postwar economic order. Postwar peace, in their view, depended in large part on international economic prosperity and harmony. Soviet participation in the international economic order would encourage harmony, and trade with the Soviet Union would create demand for U.S. products, thereby encouraging prosperity. Thus the United States pressed for Russian adherence to the Bretton Woods agreements and seriously considered giving a $10 million loan to the Soviet Union for postwar recovery.[5]

The participation of Eastern Europe in the postwar economic order was not questioned by Western planners. The countries of Eastern Europe had been closely integrated with the West, especially Western Europe, in the interwar period. In 1938, for example, some 60–65 percent of Eastern Europe's imports came from Western Europe, one-fourth of which came from Germany alone. In the same year 60 percent of East Europe's exports went to Western Europe of which 22–23 percent went to Germany.[6]

Planners expected the states of Eastern Europe to be liberated from German domination and to rejoin the international economic system. Czechoslovakia and Poland, which had been on the side of the Allies during the war, were invited to attend the international monetary and trade conferences. The United Nations Relief and Rehabilitation Administration was created in 1943 to assist Eastern and Southern Europe to recover after their liberation.[7] Even as late as 1947, the states of Western Europe in estimating the aid they would need from the United States decided to assume "a substantial and steady resumption" of trade of principal goods with the East.[8]

Nevertheless, the economic relationship between the capitalist countries of the West and the Communist countries of the East became one of independence and, for most of the postwar era, of confrontation. The Cold War led to an effort on both sides to separate the economies of East and West and to use that separation as a tool of political confrontation. The Soviet Union refused to join the Western economic order and, with the new Communist states of Eastern Europe, created a separate economic system. The Western states sought for political and military reasons to isolate the Communist economies and to integrate those of the developed market states. As Joseph Stalin put it,

> The disintegration of the single, all-embracing world market must be regarded as the most important economic sequel of the Second World War and of its economic consequences. . . . China and European people's democracies broke away from the capitalist system and, together with the Soviet Union, formed a united and powerful socialist camp confronting the camp of capitalism.[9]

THE CREATION OF AN EASTERN ECONOMIC BLOC

The creation of a separate Eastern economic system was part of the Soviet Union's postwar policy of dominance in Eastern Europe.[10] The Soviet Union had four principal goals in Eastern Europe in the first postwar decade, all of which were related to the formation of a separate economic system. The Soviet Union's ideological purpose was to advance world revolution and the spread of communism.

According to Marxist theoreticians, the formation of a separate Eastern economic bloc would deepen the crisis of world capitalism and speed its inevitable demise. The denial of Eastern markets would accentuate the West's economic problems unsolved since the Great Depression and reinforced by the war. Stalin stated that denying the Eastern markets to the West would contract Western export possibilities, create idle industrial capacity, and lead to the inevitable internal economic and political collapse of capitalism.[11] The formation of a separate socialist bloc would isolate the East from the coming economic chaos in the West and would enhance socialist economic development. A self-sufficient and independent Eastern bloc was thus possible and desirable.[12]

The Soviet Union's military goal in Eastern Europe was to prevent Germany or other "hostile" Western powers from controlling Eastern Europe, thereby posing a threat of military invasion to the Soviet Union. Related to the historical fear of invasion from Germany was the political goal of establishing friendly regimes, that is, Communist regimes, in the states bordering the Soviet Union. Economic control and isolation were tools for reinforcing Russian political and military control and for avoiding capitalist influence in the region.

Finally, the Soviet Union sought access to the resources of Eastern Europe—raw materials and capital equipment—which could be used to rebuild the Soviet Union after the war and later to further its economic development. Russian control of Eastern European development policies and foreign trade would enable the Soviet Union to extract needed goods on favorable terms from these states.

Through wartime diplomacy, military occupation, and coups d'etat, the Soviet Union established Communist satellite regimes in all the states of Eastern Europe.[13] The Soviet Union in cooperation with national Communist leaders restructured the economies of Eastern Europe, introducing state ownership of the means of production, central planning, and the Russian model of economic growth based on self-sufficiency and all-around industrialization.[14] The Soviet Union also sought to build a socialist international economic system centered on the Soviet Union, with a high level of mutual interaction internally and a low level of interaction with the West.

The Soviet Union refused to join the new international economic institutions created by the West and prevented those satellites which were eligible and which evidenced an interest from participating in Western institutions. Although the Soviet Union participated in the Bretton Woods conference, it refused to ratify the Bretton Woods agreements and become a member of the IMF (International Monetary Fund) and the IBRD (International Bank for Reconstruction and Development).[15]

Czechoslovakia and Poland, the only two states of the East to join the fund and the bank, withdrew in 1950 and 1954, respectively.[16]

Although invited, the Soviet Union refused to attend the preparatory meetings and the international negotiations which led to the Havana Charter. Of the Eastern states, only Czechoslovakia and Poland participated in the Havana negotiations but did not ratify the charter. None were contracting parties of GATT (the General Agreement on Tariffs and Trade).[17] The Soviet Union rejected the American offer of aid under the Marshall Plan and refused to allow Poland and Czechoslovakia, the two Eastern states offered Marshall Plan aid, to accept U.S. aid and join the OEEC (Organization for European Economic Cooperation), the European organization established to coordinate European use of Marshall Plan funds.[18]

In place of the Western institutions, the Soviet Union established the Council for Mutual Economic Assistance (Comecon). This economic organization, whose members included the Soviet Union and the states of Eastern Europe (except Yugoslavia), was established in 1949 as the Eastern response to the Marshall Plan. As stated in the communique issued at the time of its formation, the purpose of Comecon was to reinforce Eastern economic cooperation in isolation from the West. The communique argued that Eastern economic isolation was caused by the West not by the Soviet Union:

> As a result of . . . [developing] economic relations and the implementation of economic co-operation between the countries of people's democracy and the USSR, conditions have been created to accelerate the restoration and development of their national economies. . . . [T]he Governments of the United States of America, of Great Britain, and of certain western European states . . . boycotted trade relations with the countries of people's democracy and the USSR because these countries did not consider it appropriate that they should submit themselves to the dictatorship of the Marshall Plan, which would have violated their sovereignty and the interests of their national economies. In the light of these circumstances . . . [and to] establish . . . wider economic co-operation between the countries of people's democracy and the USSR, the conference considered it necessary to create the Council for Mutual Economic Assistance.[19]

Comecon sought technical cooperation and joint planning, but its main purpose was to coordinate bloc trade. A series of bilateral trade agreements between the Soviet Union and the satellite countries reinforced Comecon trade coordination.

Not only institutional affiliation but economic flows as well were redirected in the new Eastern order: the East had formed a separate trading system. While in the interwar period the vast majority of Eastern European trade was with countries of the West, by 1953 that vast majority had switched to the Eastern bloc. In 1938, 10.0 percent of Eastern exports went to Eastern countries including the Soviet Union, 68.4 percent went to Western Europe, 4.4 percent to the United States and Canada, and 5.1 percent to Latin America. By 1953 Eastern trade had been reoriented to the bloc: 64.0 percent of Eastern exports went to Eastern countries, 14.4 percent to Western Europe, 0.6 percent to the United States and Canada, and 0.5 percent to Latin America.[20]

Comecon and the bilateral trade agreements between the Soviet Union and the satellite countries were an important means for redirecting the trade away from the West and toward the bloc. Another tool was the Soviet Union's access to the planning process of the satellite countries. The economic system which existed in the Soviet Union and which was adopted in Eastern Europe was that of state ownership and central planning. Under market systems as in the West, the allocation of resources—decisions about what to produce, how to produce it, and to whom to distribute it—is determined by and large by private supply and demand. Under a centrally planned system, such decisions are made by a central state planning organization.

Through its political and military power, the Soviet Union was able to shape the economic plans of Eastern Europe in the direction it preferred. Plans were prepared with the assistance of Soviet economic advisers by hand-picked economists trained in the Soviet Union.[21] Through access to the planning process, the Soviet Union was able to compel Eastern European states to produce and export those products desired by the Soviet Union. Through long-term trade agreements, the Soviet Union obliged Czechoslovakia, for example, to emphasize production of heavy machinery, equipment, and arms instead of following the original Czech plan for more diversified, less trade-oriented production.[22]

The reorientation of trade tended to benefit the Soviet Union in the first postwar decade, and evidence suggests that it was able to negotiate extremely favorable prices for its imports and exports.[23] One notorious example was the Polish–Soviet agreement on coal, under which Poland agreed to deliver large quantities of coal to the Soviet Union at a very favorable price.[24]

Yet another form of Soviet redirection of trade was the reparations imposed on former Axis countries. In East Germany the Soviet Union unilaterally dismantled factories and claimed goods from current production for the Soviet army and the Soviet economy. The total value of these transfers has been estimated at $18 billion. In Hungary, Romania, and Bulgaria, the Soviet Union also dismantled factories and claimed goods from current production, the total value of which has been estimated at close to $2 billion.[25]

Financial ties were also redirected from West to East. Eastern European currencies were made inconvertible.[26] The nationalization of foreign investment disrupted private capital flows. The Soviet Union and most of the satellites were not eligible for IMF or IBRD assistance, and they rejected Marshall Plan aid. External financial relations oriented to the Soviet Union provided some credit for Eastern Europe, primarily credits for the purchase of raw and other materials and investment credits for the purchase of equipment from the Soviet Union.[27]

Finally, investment ties, such as they were, were restructured. After the war, as reparations, the Soviet Union acquired numerous German industrial enterprises operating in Hungary, Romania, and Bulgaria, former allies of Germany. When the entire private sector was eliminated and replaced by state-operated and -controlled companies, Soviet investments were not seized. The Soviet Union operated these enterprises primarily as joint companies with the local national government. These companies enjoyed preferential status in such areas as taxes and access to foreign exchange and raw materials. Furthermore, they often offered preferential prices to the Soviet Union. Because of their powerful and preferential position, they became a source of intrabloc conflict and were liquidated after 1954.[28]

WESTERN ECONOMIC WARFARE

While the Soviet Union deliberately created a separate economic system, Western economic warfare accentuated the isolation of the East.

Economic warfare was part of the West's Cold War policy. By early 1947, following the establishment of Communist regimes in the Soviet-occupied states of Eastern Europe, Soviet pressure on Iran and Turkey, the outbreak of civil war in Greece, and political instability in Western Europe, U.S. policy makers concluded that earlier hopes for postwar cooperation with the Soviet Union were unrealistic. The East's rejection of Marshall Plan assistance, the coup in Czechoslovakia, and the Berlin blockade of 1948 confirmed the U.S. view that the Soviet Union was a permanent political and military threat to the West.

The United States and the other Western countries adopted numerous policies to deal with the Soviet threat. One policy, as we have seen, was the building of an economically strong and united West through the European Recovery Program, the establishment of a strong international monetary system, and the development of freer multilateral trade. Another policy was to develop Western military strength through NATO and the stationing of American troops in Europe. Yet another way of meeting the Communist threat was to deny the Soviet Union and its allies resources which would enhance their military capability and political power. A strategic embargo and credit restrictions were used to block the flow of these resources to the East.

The Western strategic embargo began in full force with the passage of the U.S. Export Control Act of 1949.[29] This act, which remained in force for twenty years, authorized the president to "prohibit or curtail" all commercial exports[30] and to establish a licensing system in the U.S. Department of Commerce to regulate exports to Communist countries. As part of the licensing system, the Commerce Department established a commodity control list of embargoed items. Any product which had military applicability or which would contribute to the military or economic potential of a Communist state was placed on the restricted list.[31] At the height of East–West tension in Korea, 1,000 items were embargoed by the United States.[32]

The United States sought, with mixed success, to impose its strategic embargo on other Western states. In 1949 under U.S. pressure, a Coordinating Committee (Cocom), which had no binding authority, was set up to discuss and, the United States hoped, to coordinate Western strategic embargo lists. Cocom succeeded in drawing up an international list of restricted items for its fifteen members.[33]

There was, however, significant conflict between the United States and its allies over the list, largely because the United States adopted a much broader definition of "strategic goods" than did the Europeans or Japanese. For the United States, the strategic embargo was intended to impair not only Eastern military strength but Eastern political and economic power as well. The U.S. embargo therefore was directed at military capability in its largest sense, that is, at nonmilitary goods which would enhance economic performance and development as well as at military goods.[34] On the other hand, because the Europeans and Japanese had a greater economic stake in trade with the East than the United States, they tended to feel that a broad embargo would simply encourage greater Eastern solidarity without hindering military and political capability. Thus they advocated a more limited definition of strategic goods, namely, those with direct military implications.[35] As a result of allied resistance, the international list was always less comprehensive than the U.S. control list.

To overcome European resistance to American embargo policy, the U.S. Congress passed the Mutual Defense Assistance Control Act of 1951.[36] The so-called Battle Act authorized the president to deny all U.S. military, economic, and financial assistance to any country which knowingly permitted the shipment of strategic goods to Communist countries. Although it caused significant resentment in Europe, the act was an effective tool which the United States used to encourage compliance from countries receiving Marshall Plan aid.

By the mid-1950s, however, the Europeans no longer relied upon American assistance, and, moreover, the Cold War seemed less virulent following the death of Stalin and the end of the Korean conflict. The

United States could no longer resist pressures from its allies to relax the restrictions on exports to the East. Cocom lists were shortened in 1954 and in 1958 when they came to reflect more closely the European definition of "strategic goods." Interestingly, the relaxation of the Cocom list did not completely eliminate Atlantic conflict over embargo policy. The attempt by the U.S. government to impose embargo controls on subsidiaries of U.S. multinational corporations in Europe continued to be a source of tension within the West.[37]

The United States also sought to deny the East financial resources. The major legislative basis for such control was the Johnson Debt Default Act of 1934, passed as an effort to compel countries including the Soviet Union and many others to repay debts incurred during World War I. The Johnson act prohibited private persons or institutions from extending credit to a foreign government in default on obligations to the United States. Although the Johnson act was not originally intended as an anti-Communist measure, it came to be directed at Communist countries. Following World War II, the act was amended to exempt members of the IMF and the World Bank, that is, virtually all states except those in the East. Only Yugoslavia which was a member of the fund and the bank, and East Germany, Albania, and Bulgaria, which had no outstanding debts, were not affected.[38] The application of Johnson Act restrictions on the Soviet Union has been reinforced by its inability to agree with the United States on how to settle the former's substantial World War II lend-lease debt.[39]

As in the case of the strategic embargo, the United States adopted more restrictive policies than its allies. Other NATO countries placed no restrictions on Eastern access to credit, and an effort by the United States in 1958 to impose restrictions through international agreement failed. The Berne Union, a group of governmental and private credit insurance organizations in the developed market economies, agreed to limit commercial credits to the East to five years and to require an initial cash payment of at least 20 percent of the purchase price. The agreement was nonbinding, however, and proved ineffective.[40]

Another form of Western economic warfare sought not to deny the East resources but markets. In 1951 at the height of tensions in Korea, the U.S. Congress passed the Trade Agreements Extension Act, which withdrew all trade concessions negotiated with the Soviet Union and any Communist country (except Yugoslavia). As a result, Eastern countries' products did not benefit from any of the tariff reductions negotiated since the Trade Agreements Act of 1934 and were still subject to the onerous Smoot–Hawley tariffs. Many European states also adopted restrictions on imports from Communist countries, particularly quantitative restrictions.[41]

Thus the East and West, primarily for political reasons, established separate international economic systems with separate institutions, rules, and patterns of interaction. At the height of economic separation during the Korean conflict, East–West trade was actually lower in absolute terms than it had been in 1937.[42] After the end of the Korean conflict and the death of Stalin in 1953 the political–security conflict eased somewhat. As a result, Eastern policies of regional economic isolation were modified, the West's control list was shortened, Western Europe, Canada, and Japan negotiated most favored nation agreements with Eastern Europe and the Soviet Union and reduced quantitative restrictions, and East–West trade increased.[43] From 1953 to 1958 Eastern exports to the West doubled, and from 1958 to 1963 they nearly doubled again.[44]

Nevertheless, as long as the Cold War continued, East–West trade remained unimportant, both as a percentage of world trade and as a percentage of the total trade of East and West.[45] Although both East and West Europe favored greater commerce and took steps in that direction, the United States and the Soviet Union continued, for political reasons, to reject any major change in East–West economic relations. The large self-sufficient economies of the superpowers enabled them to be less influenced by the potential economic advantages of interaction than their smaller and more trade-oriented partners and more influenced by overriding political and security concerns. As late as 1962, for example, while U.S. allies were easing controls the U.S. Congress amended the Export Control Act to prohibit the export of commodities or technical data which would make a significant contribution to the economic as well as military potential of countries threatening U.S. security and in the Trade Expansion Act removed all presidential discretion to restore most favored nation treatment to Eastern countries. Not until the late 1960s and early 1970s when the Cold War ended did the policies of the superpowers change. Political tensions decreased, and forces encouraging East–West economic interaction were able to come into play.

FORCES OF CHANGE IN THE EAST

Both political and economic forces in the Soviet Union and Eastern Europe led to a decrease in political conflict with the West. By the early 1970s the Soviet Union had achieved effective equality with the United States in strategic weapons. Nuclear parity enabled Soviet leaders to view the West with more confidence, to modify the fear of military invasion, and to entertain the idea of limiting expenditures on strategic weapons. The change in nuclear capability thus tended to make the Soviet Union more willing to discuss arms limitation and to seek political accommodation. The Sino–Soviet conflict which flared up in the 1960s reinforced the interest in accommodation. The stationing of Soviet troops on the long Chinese border led to a greater willingness to ease tensions on Western borders and to spend less on nuclear weapons. Increased pluralism in Eastern Europe was also a force for détente. The inability of the Soviet Union to impose political and economic orthodoxy on Eastern Europe encouraged greater accommodation with the West.

With the relaxation of security tension, economic forces for greater East–West economic interaction came into play. Consumers, who had long borne the burden of industrialization, were demanding a rise in the standard of living. Consumerism was a force for reordering budgetary priorities away from military toward civilian expenditures, and a need to decrease military budgets was a force for accommodation with the West.

Another force was the problem of Russian agriculture. Russian agriculture had always been plagued by inadequate production, but the Soviet Union had always adjusted to crop shortfalls by reducing domestic consumption. After 1960 Soviet leaders felt that they could no longer impose such hardships on their people without political risk. Thus, when shortfalls occurred, the Soviet Union turned to the international market to purchase grain.[46] The first major purchase—10.0 million tons—occurred in 1964 following a disastrous crop in 1963. Subsequently, grain was regularly imported in large amounts—about 1.5 million tons per year—primarily from Canada.[47] In 1972 another particularly bad harvest forced the Soviet Union to import over 19 million tons of grain from the United States and to make smaller purchases from other countries.

The problem of industrial growth also increased Russian as well as East European interest in trade with the West. In the 1950s the Soviet Union and Eastern Europe achieved high levels of growth through the quantitative increase in labor, capital, and, to a certain extent, land. High rates of growth were realized by a significant expansion in the labor force—for example, the employment of women, the transfer of labor from agriculture to industry, and long working hours—by the rapid increase in capital formation at the expense of agriculture and of improvement in the standard of living, and, to a lesser extent, by the expansion of cultivated land.[48]

By 1960, however, this expansion, known as extensive growth, had reached its limits. Comecon growth rates declined from an average of 6 percent per year in the 1950s to about 4 percent in the 1970s.[49] The ability to increase quantity was either no longer possible—as in the case of labor—or no longer effective—as in the case of capital. But what was needed to spur growth was not an improvement in quantity factors, rather there had to be an increase in the quality of production. This type of growth, known as intensive growth, is achieved by improving productiv- ity, that is, the efficiency of production. Intensive growth relies primarily on the application of technology: advanced machinery and production processes, sophisticated management techniques, and energy. Since the early 1960s Eastern plans have emphasized the need to achieve growth through the development and application of technology.

The Eastern system, however, has faced severe difficulties in technological development. In the East there was little incentive for plant managers to experiment with new technology. Their rewards were based on fulfillment or overfulfillment of quantitative goals; no incentives were offered for improving the quality of the product or the production process. Indeed, there were disincentives to experiment with new methods because they threatened to interrupt production at least temporarily and thus to jeopardize fulfillment of the quantitative goals. Furthermore, the absence of competition and the existence of guaranteed markets meant that there was no incentive for managers to cut cost or improve quality.

The system was also ineffective in the areas of research and development. Although great emphasis was placed on scientific research, there was little relationship between research and actual production. Unlike the West where most research is carried out by private enterprise, research in the East is generally carried on in research institutes which have few links with factories. Scientists and engineers are thus not positioned to respond directly to the needs of industry or to make industry responsive to scientific development.[50] As a result of these system biases, the East, including the Soviet Union, fell far behind the West in the development of technology.[51]

In the mid-1960s an attempt was made to solve the problem of technology and industrial development through national economic reforms. Planning was decentralized somewhat. Managers were given greater freedom to decide what to produce and how. To encourage efficiency and quality and to stimulate the use of technology, incentives were based on profit as well as on quantitative goals. Prices were made more "rational," and greater reliance was placed on market forces.[52]

However, the reforms did not go far enough. They were strongly opposed by party conservatives and government bureaucracies who saw their power threatened by the potential new power of plant managers. Reforms in Eastern Europe were also opposed by the Soviet Union which viewed the possibility of mixed market and nonmarket economies as a threat to the socialist economic system. With the exception of Hungary and Czechoslovakia, the Eastern regimes were unwilling to risk real reform and introduced only mild changes. By 1970 many of these had been rescinded. In the case of Czechoslovakia military intervention by the Soviet army brought the economic and political reform experiment to an abrupt end in August 1968. And, because of the failure of reform, the Eastern economies continued to stagnate.[53]

The East also attempted to solve the problem of technological development and intensive growth through Comecon. An effort began in the late 1950s to revitalize Comecon and change it from a tool of Soviet dominance to a tool of development. Attempts were made to increase trade within the bloc,[54] as it was hoped that trade would lead to economies of scale, force competitiveness, and thus encourage modernization. Trade was encouraged by agreement on methods for establishing trade prices, a clearing institution (the International Bank for Economic Co-operation),[55] and programs for national specialization in production. In the 1960s technological cooperation was also encouraged through a Permanent Commission for the Co-ordination of Scientific and Technical Research, joint research establishments, and efforts to diffuse scientific knowledge.[56]

Once again, the results were unsatisfactory. Despite all efforts, Comecon trade remained hampered by internal biases against trade, by the lack of complementarity of the Eastern economies, by the poor quality of goods produced in the individual states, and by political unwillingness to delegate power to a supranational body—especially one in which the Soviet Union had a powerful voice. Moreover, intrabloc technological cooperation was not up to the task of overcoming systemic biases against technological innovation.[57]

By the mid-1960s it had become clear that the East could not bridge the technology gap and achieve intensive growth rapidly without foreign technology. To develop its vast natural resources, produce cars and trucks, improve agriculture, and even develop a tourist industry, the East would have to turn to the West.

FORCES OF CHANGE IN THE WEST

While the Soviet Union's primary interest in increased economic interaction with the West was to ease its economic problems of consumerism, agricultural supply, and technological development, the primary interests of the United States in ending isolation were political. There were, however, important economic forces for change. An economic interest in opening relations with the East developed in the United States in the late 1960s and early 1970s at the time of economic crisis in the West. Changing international economic conditions fostered a domestic political consensus favoring increased trade with the East.

As Western Europe and Japan became powerful competitors and threatened the U.S. position in Western markets, American businessmen began to look to the East. The Communist states looked attractive not only as untapped markets but also because of the new interest of the Communist countries in purchasing technology in large quantities from the West. Visions of billion-dollar deals danced like sugarplums in the heads of some American businessmen. Because of the continuing restrictive policies of the American government, however, it seemed that Western Europe and Japan and not the United States would make those deals. As the president of Bendix International described the business viewpoint in testimony before a Senate subcommittee,

> The net effect of our policy has generally not been a weakening of the Communist position but instead has hurt the economy of the United States. By denying ourselves the sales and profits which have accrued to our competitors in Western Europe and Japan, we have damaged only ourselves.[58]

Trade figures bear out the concerns of the American business community (see Figure 10-1). In 1969, for example, U.S. exports of machinery and transport equipment to the Soviet Union totaled $42 million, whereas Japanese exports of the same equipment totaled $70 million, French exports $144 million, West German exports $200 million, and British exports $113 million. Export patterns to other East European countries were similar. In 1969, for example, the United States had exported $5 million of machinery and transport equipment to Poland, whereas France exported $35 million, West Germany $55 million, and the United Kingdom $42 million.[59]

A shift in labor policy paralleled the shift in business horizons. As unemployment rose in the late 1960s and early 1970s, labor's foreign economic policy changed. For most of the postwar era, labor had strongly supported the U.S. policy of embargo and isolation of the East. Reasons for that support ranged from experience with Communists within the labor movement to general anti-Communist attitudes which reflected the American public opinion of the time. Concern of labor over increasing unemployment, however, led to a shift in its traditional opposition to economic interaction with the East. As unemployment soared, labor, like business, became interested in Eastern markets.[60]

Official foreign economic policy was also changing. As the U.S. balance-of-trade position worsened and turned into deficit and as the balance-of-payments deficit increasingly undermined the dollar, American policy makers sought to revitalize U.S. trade. One way they did so was to force a devaluation of the dollar;[61] another way was to initiate new international trade negotiations;[62] yet another way was to open trade with the East.

The interest of business, labor, and government in expanding trade with the East was reflected in the report of Peter G. Peterson, chairman of the Council for International Economic Policy, to President Nixon. The Peterson report, published in December 1971, called for a new aggressive

Figure 10-1   East-West Trade
Trade of the Industrialized West With Communist
Countries (billion U.S. $)

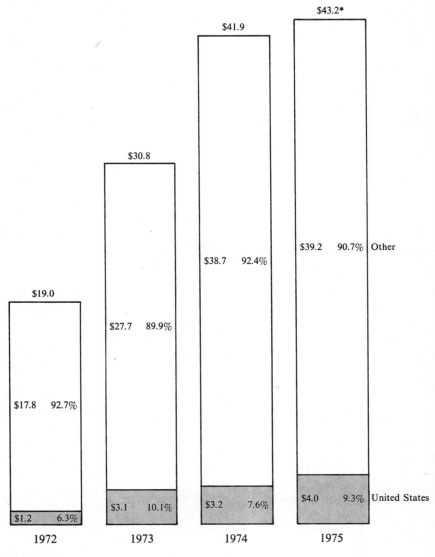

Source: Council on International Economic Policy, *International Economic Report of the President*, (Washington, D.C., March 1976), p. 54.

American trade policy, including increased exports to the East. Significant possibilities for export expansion existed in the East, according to the report, and the development of those possibilities called for a reversal of the old policy of embargo and import control and the development of new arrangements with the East. Peterson mentioned specifically the offering of most favored nation treatment to the East and the expansion of export financing possibilities for American firms doing business with the East.[63]

The interest in Eastern markets was reinforced after the oil crisis by a new interest in Eastern sources of energy and raw materials. There had long been a Western interest in the East, especially in the Soviet Union, as a source of raw materials.[64] However, not until the embargo by OPEC (Organization of Petroleum Exporting Countries) and the drastic rise in the price of oil and not until the Third World's talk of other OPECs did the Soviet Union's vast resource potential become particularly attractive to the West. Western business became interested in helping the Soviet Union develop its raw materials for both export and domestic consumption. Western governments began to see the development of Soviet raw materials both as a source of supply and as a way to keep the Soviet Union from becoming a major purchaser in Western markets.

The economic interest in opening relations with the East was insufficient, in and of itself, to create a change in American policy. While Eastern markets and sources of raw material supply looked increasingly attractive, they were important more for specific industries such as those which hoped to sell technology or grain than for the American economy as a whole. It was the link between economic relations and political concerns that caused a change in policy.

One political concern was a judgment that the embargo had been an ineffective foreign policy. The actual impact of the embargo, the import controls, and the financial restrictions on Eastern economic strength is difficult to determine and is a debated issue. Khrushchev said that it had been very costly because it forced the Soviet Union to manufacture products which it could have obtained more cheaply through trade.[65] Some analysts argue that the West's economic warfare retarded Soviet growth in the long run. Trade, it is argued, may be small, but it plays a very important role in Eastern economies by helping them overcome technological limits.[66] Denial of Western sources of technology thus hinders growth.

Other analysts argue that the economic impact was limited. The large size of the bloc and its members' ability to trade with one another shielded them from many negative economic consequences. Central planning made it easier for the bloc to make the rapid adjustments required by the embargo.[67] Some equipment was available from Western Europe and Japan. Furthermore, although the removal of most favored nation privileges hampered the export of Eastern European manufactured goods, it had little impact on Soviet exports, primarily raw materials not subject to tariffs.[68] In sum, the embargo policy seems to have hampered Eastern growth over the long term but not in a major way. Furthermore, it was not without economic cost to the West—in the form of the loss of exports and the cost of administrative controls.[69]

The embargo seems to have had little effect on the East's military capability. Because of its authoritarian system, the Soviet Union was able to direct massive expenditures into military development and to continue to emphasize heavy industry without political unrest. The embargo probably reinforced the power of those who viewed the West as hostile and who advocated high levels of military expenditures. Embargo did not prevent the Soviet Union from achieving effective strategic parity with the United States.

The political effects of economic isolation were also nil and perhaps even negative for the West. Just as in centuries before, economic isolation in the postwar era has proved to be an ineffective weapon. Isolation provided an excuse for increased bloc autarky and Soviet domination. It contributed, albeit not significantly, to intra-NATO tension due to the conflict over Cocom lists and over U.S. assertion of extraterritorial jurisdiction over U.S. subsidiaries in cases of export control. Finally, it became increasingly ineffective as Western Europe and Japan eased their policies. In many cases the East could obtain goods and technology from European and Japanese companies and even from subsidiaries of U.S. companies abroad.[70]

Gradually American policy makers came to feel that the incentive of greater trade and not the denial of trade would be an effective instrument of foreign policy. The Johnson administration argued that the possibility of increased trade with the West could be used as a bargaining tool in negotiations with Eastern countries. Western trade concessions could be used to negotiate for a variety of Eastern agreements—from the settlement of commercial disputes to protection of U.S. patents and copyrights to greater cultural and information exchange.[71]

Trade, it was argued, could also be used to encourage greater independence within the Eastern bloc. The granting of most favored nation treatment had been used to encourage greater pluralism in the East as early as 1948 when Yugoslavia broke with the Soviet Union and in 1956 when the Gumulka government in Poland sought to decrease dependence on the Soviet Union. In the mid-1960s American policy makers saw a similar restlessness and desire to assert national identity throughout Eastern Europe.[72] Trade, it was argued, could be used to encourage independence from the Soviet Union. Secretary of State Dean Rusk argued in 1966 that

A healthy growth of trade will help to reduce the present dependence of these Eastern European countries on each other and the Soviet Union. They will be encouraged to rebuild the friendly ties they have historically had with the West. Independent action will become more attractive and more feasible.[73]

Interestingly, the West German government in the mid-1960s also sought to use trade policy in a positive way to further its political aims in Eastern Europe. The German *ostpolitik*, or Eastern policy initiated in 1966, was an attempt to use economic interaction to improve its political relations with Eastern Europe and the Soviet Union. Trade liberalization, German participation in joint ventures with East European governments, and German credits and technology transfers were used to set the stage for renewal of political and diplomatic contacts between the Federal Republic and the East.[74]

When the Nixon administration took office in 1969, the American policy of using trade as a negotiating tool and a means of influencing political evolution was extended to relations with the Soviet Union. Improvement in economic relations with the Soviet Union became an integral part of the policy of détente.

The Nixon-Kissinger policy of détente was an attempt to create a stable international system through a greater degree of cooperation between the United States and the Soviet Union. The idea of enhancing the possibility of peace by improving relations with the Soviet Union was not a new theme in American foreign policy. President Eisenhower had tried to improve East–West relations through his "spirit of Geneva" in 1955, President Kennedy through the Non-Proliferation Treaty of 1963, and President Johnson through the "building bridges" policy in the mid-1960s.

Early attempts to ease East–West relations, however, had not been central themes of American foreign policy. Furthermore, they had faltered on the continuing hostility of the Soviet Union. When President Nixon took office and when Henry Kissinger became his chief foreign policy adviser, the easing of U.S.–Soviet relations was elevated to a primary goal of American foreign policy and became the foundation of U.S. world strategy. Furthermore, unlike earlier efforts, the Nixon-Kissinger policy benefited from the Soviet Union's greater interest in improving relations.

Détente was based on the assessment that, even though superpower competition will persist, the possibility of nuclear holocaust makes cooperation imperative. Even though the two superpowers will continue in an adversary relationship, they must seek to establish an environment in which they can regulate and restrain their differences. Détente is both that environment and the means of achieving it. It is conceived of as an ongoing process of mutual relaxation of tensions. This process is a complex one in which numerous dimensions of U.S.–Soviet relations are linked to each other.

As Secretary of State Kissinger put it,

> Our approach proceeds from the conviction that, in moving forward across
> a wide spectrum of negotiations, progress in one area adds momentum to
> progress in other areas. . . . We did not invent the interrelationship between
> issues expressed in the so-called linkage concept; it was a reality because of
> the range of problems and areas in which the interests of the United States
> and the Soviet Union impinge on each other.[75]

The process has several key, interrelated elements: the development
of mutually agreed upon principles of behavior; frequent political consultation, to manage crises and eventually to prevent crises from erupting;
arms control negotiations, to ease political and military instability and to
reduce arms expenditures; and economic interaction.[76]

Economic relations were expected to serve détente in several ways.
Greater economic interaction between East and West could encourage a
downward spiral in political tensions. As Secretary of Commerce Peterson said:

> Closer economic ties bear both cause and effect relationships to relaxation
> of political tension. Improvement in political relationships is a prerequisite
> for improved economic relationships, but, once in place, economic ties
> create a communality of interest which in turn improves the environment
> for progress on the political side.[77]

Thus, trade would create a favorable climate and would reinforce
those internal forces in the Soviet Union which favor greater cooperation
with the West as opposed to those which oppose such cooperation. In
addition, a greater involvement in and dependence on the international
economic system might encourage greater political moderation. According to Secretary Kissinger,

> By acquiring a stake in this network of relationships with the West, the
> Soviet Union may become more conscious of what it would lose by a return
> to confrontation.[78]

Another theme in the trade–détente policy was related to internal
change in the Soviet Union. Some argued that trade would be associated
with the increased presence of Western businessmen and technicians and
with a freer flow of ideas and that such openings in the Soviet system
might encourage social change.

Most importantly, however, trade was to be used as quid pro quo in
negotiating with the Russians. American economic concessions could be
exchanged for Soviet political concessions. The East's desire for Western

grain and technology could be linked, for example, with the West's interest in arms negotiations or Soviet pressure on Hanoi to end the war in Vietnam.

BARRIERS TO CHANGE IN THE EAST

Despite important forces for ending East–West separation, equally important counterforces have impeded change. For the East, the barrier to change was primarily the chronic shortage of foreign exchange. To understand why the East is constrained by chronic foreign exchange problems, it is necessary to examine the problems of *inconvertibility* and *trade aversion under central planning.*

Eastern currencies are not convertible—either into Western currencies or into other Eastern currencies—for many and complex reasons. In part, inconvertibility exists for the same reasons that Western countries sometimes impose limits on convertibility: balance-of-payments problems and lack of sufficient foreign exchange reserves. More importantly, convertibility would disrupt central planning. If foreigners could convert currencies into Russian rubles or Polish zlotys, for example, they could then seek to buy goods in these countries. If Easterners could convert rubles or zlotys into dollars or deutsche marks, they might buy goods abroad. Such free purchasing, however, cannot be permitted because it would disrupt the already precarious central plan under which production and distribution are carefully controlled. "Irrational" pricing in the East also makes inconvertibility necessary. Prices in the East are planned; they are not related to market factors. Certain products are subsidized through artificially low prices. Others are given artificially high prices. Convertibility would enable foreigners to purchase goods which are deliberately kept inexpensive and nationals to purchase abroad goods which are deliberately kept expensive. Such purchases would disrupt planning and create trading disadvantages for the East.[79] As a result, Eastern countries trade with the West and with each other at world market prices.

Even if Eastern currencies were convertible in the sense of being exchangeable for other currencies, they would not be useful for trade because of what is called commodity inconvertibility.[80] Western currencies are convertible not only into other currencies but also into goods. Both foreign and domestic purchasers are able to acquire, for a price, whatever goods they choose, in whatever quantities, and for whatever destination.[81] In the East the distribution of goods is tightly controlled by central planners. Restrictions on the availability of goods are accentuated by overfull employment, that is, the allocation of resources under the plan to their maximum or beyond. There is no surplus, no slack in the system which might become available for foreign or domestic purchasers. Unless their wants have been previously integrated into the plan, foreign purchasers are unable to buy what they want, in the amount they want, and at the time they want in a centrally planned economy. Commodity inconvertibility hampers exports by making Eastern economies less flexible and less able to respond to Western demands for goods.

Because of inconvertibility the only way for Eastern states to make purchases in the West is by using hard, that is, convertible, Western currencies. The major way for the East to acquire these currencies is by selling its products in the West, that is, by exporting. The Eastern economies, however, have faced problems in selling their products abroad. In addition, central planning has created trade aversion.

Because of the characteristics of central planning as practiced in Eastern Europe and the Soviet Union, the East has been unable to produce manufactured goods which are competitive in Western markets.[82] Raw materials, which are produced primarily by the Soviet Union, are relatively homogeneous and thus competitive and exportable. But in general manufactured goods have been unable to meet Western standards, in part because central planners have not been interested in producing goods for export. More importantly, because of the reliance of the plan on quantitative not qualitative production goals, managers have little incentive to concentrate on quality.

The lack of interest in quality is accentuated by the absence of competition in a planned system. Unlike policy in the West, where free competition is part of the theory if not always the reality of the economic system, the East does not encourage competition. The plan directs production on a noncompetitive basis. Furthermore, sellers' markets have inhibited the production of high-quality manufactures. Central planners have sought to use all factors of production to the maximum, committing resources fully and scheduling inputs and outputs tightly. This overfull employment planning often results in shortages and delays. And, because of overfull employment planning and because of a shortage of goods, demand in the East has existed for virtually all goods produced regardless of quality. The existence of a sellers' market also inhibited the development of marketing skills, a barrier to dealing in foreign markets. Finally, centrally planned prices inhibited the production of competitive goods. In socialist countries prices are determined by central planning. For both ideological and policy reasons, prices do not reflect relative scarcities (i.e., supply and demand), as they tend to do in market economies.[83] Such irrational pricing prevents efficient use of resources and inhibits low-cost high-quality production.

The very structure of the foreign trade system is also a barrier to trade created by central planning. In centrally planned economies foreign trade is carried out not by producing enterprises but by a small number of large state organizations which have a monopoly of trade in certain types of products.[84] These organizations make it difficult for enterprises which are not involved in trade to respond and adapt production to the various needs of potential foreign customers.

In sum, because of inconvertibility and trade aversion, both of which stem from central planning, the Soviet Union and Eastern Europe have had difficulty earning sufficient foreign exchange through exports to pay for their growing import appetite. The importance of the foreign exchange constraint was demonstrated in the Soviet Union's first initiatives to the West in the early 1960s and is becoming evident in the recent spurt of East–West trade in the 1970s.

The Soviet Union was the first of the superpowers to initiate change. In March 1959 at the Leipzig trade fair, Premier Nikita Khrushchev announced that the Soviet Union intended to make major purchases of technology—patents, licenses, entire plants—from the West.[85] Premier Khrushchev's initiative was spurred by the Soviet Union's seven-year plan of 1959 to 1965 to solve the structural problems of the Soviet economy and to respond to growing consumerism. The plan established the goal of economic modernization through the development and application of technology and placed greater emphasis than other plans on the improvement of the Soviet standard of living. To achieve these goals, the plan introduced reforms in the economic system and encouraged greater trade. Technological imports from the West were to be used rapidly to eliminate lags in technological development in the Soviet Union.[86] After 1959 the Soviet Union began to import large amounts of machinery from Western Europe and Japan. Because of its more restrictive policy at the time, the United States was not an important source of these imports.[87]

A second initiative was made by Khrushchev in 1963 following that year's disastrous harvest. Instead of reducing consumption as in the past, the Soviet Union turned to imports from Canada and the United States. In 1964 in its first major postwar purchase, the Soviet Union imported 10 million tons of grain from the West. After 1964 the Soviet Union continued to be a significant importer of Western grain.

Although the importation of technology and grain in the early 1960s marked a major departure in Soviet policy, it also revealed important obstacles to change. Premier Khrushchev's ambitious program of technology importation was soon curtailed, principally because the Soviet Union simply could not pay for it.

The agricultural shortages of 1962–1965 strained the demand on the Soviet Union's limited foreign exchange reserves. Western credits were not available in important amounts at that time. To sell gold, as some suggested, did not resolve the foreign exchange shortage. The Soviet Union is able to produce important quantities of gold. Although no figures on gold production are published by the Soviet Union, Western estimates suggest that at best such gold could pay for only 9 percent and at worst only 2 percent of annual Soviet imports.[88] As in the past, then, the solution in 1964 was to curtail imports. The Soviet Union was forced to reduce its imports of Western technology drastically and to use its limited foreign exchange to purchase grain.

The curtailment of Khrushchev's import program suggested yet another limit to East–West trade. In 1964, due to economic problems at home and foreign policy problems abroad, Khrushchev was deposed. His successors reversed his policy of importing Western technology and sought to rely on domestic reform to encourage growth and technological development. These decisions reflected a recurrent theme in Soviet foreign trade behavior. When political factors require, the Soviet Union has been quite willing to forego the economic gains from trade. Trade, at certain times, is seen as important to the Soviet Union, but it has never been seen as an inevitable necessity.

From 1963 to 1966, Soviet imports of technology were greatly curtailed, and Soviet grain purchases, except in 1964, were limited. By 1966, however, as growth rates declined and technological development continued to lag, Khrushchev's successors, Leonid Brezhnev and Alexei Kosygin, concluded that they needed to import Western technology. At the Twenty-Third Congress of the Communist Party in April 1966, Premier Kosygin announced that the Soviet Union would no longer rely solely on domestic research and development but that it would seek to buy technology from the West.[89]

The new Soviet policy was vividly demonstrated shortly thereafter in August 1966 when the Soviet Union concluded a $1.5 billion automobile construction agreement with FIAT, the Italian automaker, to build an automobile plant in the Soviet Union. The FIAT agreement was significant in its size and also in its character, for it involved not only the purchase of licenses and equipment but also the training of Russian technicians in Italy and the use of Western personnel in the Soviet Union.[90]

The ninth five-year plan, announced in 1971, was a return to the Khrushchev seven-year Plan ot 1959–1965 in its emphasis on modernization, consumer orientation, and increased commercial relations with the West.[91]

Important deals in a broad range of industries with other Western European and Japanese companies followed these policy changes. West German exports of machinery to the Soviet Union increased from $96 million in 1960 to $367 million in 1972, Japanese machinery exports increased from $19 million to $160 million, and British exports from $58 million to $108 million. Because of continuing restrictions, American firms did not share in the developing Soviet market. U.S. exports of machinery went from $28 million in 1960 to $1 million in 1962 to $58 million in 1972.[92] Trends in the trade of other Eastern European countries with the West were similar.[93]

In the 1970s as a result of the growing Eastern import appetite and the persistent inability to match that import appetite with export capability, the Soviet Union and the East began to experience trade deficits.[94] According to Soviet statistics, for example, the balance-of-trade deficit with "industrially developed capitalist countries" rose from $129 million in 1971 to a record $5 billion in 1975.[95]

In recent years the Soviet Union and the East have sought to deal with the rising deficit in several ways, one way having been to develop exports to hard currency areas. Export development, however, is a long-term solution which will require greater imports of Western technology in the short term.

Another solution has been to borrow money in public and private Western markets. One indicator of the increased borrowing was the growth in the borrowing of Eastern countries in the Eurocurrency markets. In 1972 publicly announced Eurocurrency bank credits to Eastern countries amounted to $274 million. By 1975 they had climbed to $2.6 billion, and in the first half of 1976 alone they amounted to $1.8 billion.[96] By 1976 the total debt of the Eastern countries to the West was estimated at $32 billion, up $10 billion from 1975. Eastern European countries owed $8 billion to West Germany alone. Western bankers and public officials expressed growing concern about the East's ability to repay additional loans and, thus, the advisability of extending more credit.[97]

Because of these recent concerns about access to Western credit, the East has shown growing interest in industrial cooperation with Western companies. Under such arrangements in Eastern Europe and the Soviet Union, Eastern firms have acquired Western technology and expertise by long-term agreements with Western firms. Industrial cooperation arrangements include licensing agreements and turnkey projects, which involve the supply of complete plants or production lines, for which Western firms are paid overtime in goods produced. They also include more extensive coproduction agreements, joint ventures, and joint construction or other projects in third markets.[98] Under coproduction and joint ventures Western partners typically provide technology, managerial skills, markets, and sometimes capital, and the East provides labor and raw materials. The Western firms are paid for their inputs by receiving a share of the final product, be it a raw material or a manufactured good.

There are several advantages to co-production and joint venture schemes. They provide the East with ongoing access to Western technology and managerial skills, they reduce the problem of foreign exchange shortage by payments in kind, and they help overcome the East's lack of marketing expertise by giving the Western partner marketing responsibilities in Western markets. Thus they help to overcome the foreign exchange shortage by reducing the cost of importing Western technology and by improving export capabilities of the East.[99]

The number of cooperative industrial schemes has been increasing in recent years, but important limits to such schemes remain. Until recently the East has been wary of Western equity participation. Only Yugoslavia, Romania, and Hungary have legal structures for joint ventures involving Western equity participation. Efforts at joint projects in third markets have been hampered by the lack of Eastern firms' flexibility in responding to market needs.

The most important barrier, however, has been financial. American firms are unwilling to invest large sums in the East without U.S. government participation. Whereas Western corporations and private banks are willing to finance a number of small- and medium-sized projects, especially for manufacturing, in Eastern Europe, they are unwilling to undertake the massive projects for raw material production envisioned by the Soviet Union and some Eastern European states without government backing. Furthermore, as business recovers from the recession of the 1970s, Eastern projects will be competing for capital with other projects in more familiar and apparently more secure areas. Industrial cooperation thus will have only a minor impact on the exchange problem.

Another way to overcome the East's foreign exchange problems could be through increasing world demand for Eastern raw materials. The principal recipients of such increased demand would be Poland, which possesses significant coal reserves, and the Soviet Union, which has vast reserves of oil and natural gas. Once again, however, there are insuperable limits. Much of the Soviet Union's raw material production for export is committed to Eastern Europe. For political reasons it seems unlikely that the Soviet Union will deny such exports to its allies. It may, however, shift toward greater exports outside the bloc.

The West, especially the United States, is wary of excessive dependence on the East for crucial raw materials. The political consequences of such dependence are vivid in the minds of policy makers who have just witnessed the action of OPEC. When possible, the West prefers more friendly sources of raw material supply. Most importantly, Soviet and East European materials remain undeveloped. Their exploitation will require vast amounts of capital which will not be forthcoming from the West.

BARRIERS TO TRADE IN THE WEST

While the Eastern barriers to trade are largely economic, the Western barriers are primarily political. American policy makers have been caught between their desire to expand trade for economic and political reasons and their feeling that the East should not get something for nothing, that Western trade concessions should be linked to Eastern political concessions.

Like the Soviet Union, the United States had an early false start on the road to economic détente in the mid-1960s, with the Johnson administration's policy of "building bridges" to the East, which had originated with the Kennedy administration. After the Cuban missile crisis of 1962, both the Soviet Union and the United States sought to step back from the brink of nuclear war. One indication of a change was the August 1963 signing of a treaty to ban nuclear tests in the atmosphere. Another was President Kennedy's October 1963 approval to sell wheat to the Soviet Union and Export-Import Bank's guarantees for medium-term loans to finance that purchase.[100] In connection with this sale, Attorney General Robert Kennedy made a special interpretation of the Johnson act saying that the act did not prevent medium-term credits to finance commercial transactions such as exports. This opinion was a major modification of the Johnson act and broadened the possibility of private commercial credit for the East. The wheat sale, concluded in 1964 after President Kennedy's assassination, was the first American attempt to use trade with the Soviet Union in a positive way to achieve foreign policy goals.

President Johnson sought to expand U.S.-Soviet Union and U.S.-Eastern European trade relations to encourage greater pluralism in the East and greater stability in relations between the United States and the Soviet Union. During his administration a large number of products were removed from the export control list. In 1964 he appointed a Special Committee on U.S. Trade Relations with East European Countries and the Soviet Union, the Miller committee, to

> explore all aspects of expanding peaceful trade in support of the President's policy of widening constructive relations with the countries of Eastern Europe and the Soviet Union.[101]

The committee concluded that

> Trade and government-to-government negotiations which set the framework for trade can be means of reducing animosities between ourselves and individual Communist countries and can provide a basis for working out mutually acceptable solutions to common problems.[102]

The committee found that reduction of trade barriers could be used as a negotiating tool to encourage greater "external independence and internal liberalization of individual Communist nations."[103]

The Miller committee recommended that the president be given discretionary authority to grant most favored nation treatment to individual Communist countries in Eastern Europe. The report also recommended important restrictions on a policy of greater trade. It opposed broad commercial concessions and argued that the United States should demand reciprocal concessions such as patent protection and antidumping regulation from Eastern countries. It opposed any subsidies or artificial encouragement of East–West trade and recommended that credits be limited to no more than five years. It suggested that trade concessions be rescinded if necessary for political reasons. Finally, it opposed the decontrol of strategic goods which would enhance the military capability of the East.

The Miller committee report had support in the business community. The Committee on Economic Development, a private organization of leading American businessmen, issued a report which endorsed the Miller committee recommendations and went further to include a recommendation to ease trade with China and establish a Committee on East–West Trade within the Organization for Economic Cooperation and Development to coordinate Western policies and practices.[104]

In May 1966 a proposed East–West Trade Relations Act was introduced in the House and Senate. The bill, following the Miller committee recommendations, authorized the president to enter into commercial agreements with a Communist country and to grant most favored nation status to individual European countries not receiving such treatment (Yugoslavia and Poland were receiving it).[105]

Despite strong administration support, the East–West trade bill never reached the floor of either the House or Senate in 1966, delayed by the war in Vietnam and by the upcoming congressional elections. In May 1967 the Republican leadership of Congress announced that, as long as the Soviet Union continued to supply North Vietnam, they would oppose any expansion of East–West trade. In June, hearings on the bill were delayed again by the Middle East war and by the Soviet Union's involvement on the Arab side of that conflict. In 1968 the proposed Reciprocal Trade Agreements Act which made provision for increasing East–West trade met a similar fate, largely because of Vietnam.

Meanwhile, Congress moved to increase restrictions on Eastern access to U.S. credits. In 1964 Congress had passed a bill preventing the Export-Import Bank—a public institution which offers credits for U.S. trade—from lending, guaranteeing, or insuring loans to any Communist country unless the president determined that such activities would be in the national interest. In 1967 the president decided to permit the bank to finance the sale of $50 million of precision machine tools for use in the FIAT automobile assembly plant to be built in the Soviet Union. The transaction, which was actually with an Italian firm and not directly with the Soviet Union, had been endorsed by a House subcommittee which had investigated the proposal and by the full House Banking and

Currency Committee which was examining the extension of the Eximbank charter and the extension of its lending capabilities.

When the Senate considered the bill extending the charter, two
amendments were added, passed, and eventually included in the final
legislation. One provision specifically prohibited the bank from financing
in any way machinery to be used for the Soviet automobile plant.
Another prohibited the bank from participating in any financing for any
country at war with the United States or which aided another country in
armed conflict with the United States. The president was given no right to
waive this provision even in case of national interest.[106]

Thus congressional resistance blocked the building of bridges to the
East. After the Soviet invasion of Czechoslovakia in August 1968,
President Johnson abandoned the policy.

In 1969, when the Export Control Act of 1949 expired, Congress
was again seized with the problem of East–West trade. In the few years
since 1966 the political coalition in Congress had shifted. Growing
exports of computers, machine tools, electronics, and other high-
technology products from Western Europe and Japan to the East led
business to press Congress for more liberal legislation. Senator Mondale
introduced a bill to the Senate which would have significantly liberalized
trade restrictions and would have encouraged greater East–West trade.
As Senator Mondale described his reasons for reducing restrictions on
trade with the East,

> The Communist countries of Eastern Europe are not hurt. They can obtain
> what they need from other free world countries. Only the American
> businessman and the U.S. balance of payments are substantially hurt.
> Basically, we deny ourselves the right to compete.[107]

The Senate bill would have limited restrictions to goods having
direct military use which were not available from other sources and would
have put the burden of proof for including products on the control list on
the government. The Nixon administration opposed the Senate bill
arguing, first, that it would remove restrictions without enabling the
president to negotiate a quid pro quo from the East and, second, that it
placed an undue burden on the government by making it responsible for
demonstrating the strategic importance of an item and its nonavailability
elsewhere.[108] The administration, backed by the more conservative House
of Representatives, favored simply an extension of the Export Control
Act of 1949.

The result, the Export Administration Act of 1969, was a compromise between those favoring liberalization and those favoring the status
quo.[109] The act extended the president's power to control exports for
reasons of national security or foreign policy without having to prove

their national security significance. However, it called for a revision of the U.S. control list and made important changes in the criteria for including products on that list. The 1962 amendment's criterion prohibiting the export of goods or technical data which contributed to the economic potential of countries threatening U.S. security was eliminated. Products were to be put on the control list if they contributed to the military strength of the East, not if they contributed to economic strength. Furthermore, it was explicitly stated that the availability of similar products from other Western sources was to be taken into account in drawing up the lists. In 1972 the act was amended to relax further the restrictions on goods available from other sources.[110]

In 1969 there began a series of events which would eventually bring the administration to alter its policy and to support the liberalization of trade with the East. In November 1969 Strategic Arms Limitation Talks (SALT) with the Soviet Union commenced. In that same year the new Brandt government took office in West Germany and moved quickly to conclude agreements with the Soviet Union and the states of Eastern Europe. West German treaties with the Soviet Union and Poland in 1970 settled important territorial conflicts and normalized diplomatic relations. In 1971 an agreement on Berlin was signed by the United States, the Soviet Union, France, and Britain settling the status of that divided city. The settlement of West Germany's relations with the East and the four powers' agreement on Berlin removed a major source of East–West political-security conflict and improved the climate of détente.

In May 1972 President Nixon traveled to the Soviet Union for a summit meeting with Chairman Brezhnev. There, in an atmosphere of great cordiality, they signed the SALT I agreement. There, too, they signed an agreement to establish a high-level Joint Commercial Commission to negotiate a commercial agreement between the United States and the Soviet Union. The commission was charged with the task of coming to an agreement on such trade matters as most favored nation status, credits, establishment of business facilities, and arbitration mechanisms for settling commercial disputes.[111]

In the following six months, the Joint Commercial Commission negotiated a series of agreements designed to normalize U.S.-U.S.S.R. commercial relations and to open the way for increased trade. In July, the United States agreed to provide credit through the U.S. Commodity Credit Corporation for Soviet purchases of U.S. grain. In October there followed a maritime accord which removed certain shipping obstacles to trade. Finally, and most importantly, on October 18, the two countries signed an agreement on commerce and the settlement of the Soviet lend-lease debt.

The agreement of October 18 was to be the key to economic détente and a major building block of détente in general. The Soviet Union agreed to provide facilities for U.S. businessmen and to settle its lend-lease debt by paying $722 million over a thirty-year period. The settle-ment of the lend-lease debt opened the way for Soviet access to private credits by satisfying the Johnson Act requirements. The United States agreed in return to grant most favored nation status to the Soviet Union. MFN had posed a problem for the United States. The granting of MFN status between Western countries assures a natural and mutual increase in trade. As barriers to trade are reduced, private traders react by purchas-ing less expensive foreign foods. The granting of most favored nation status to a state trading country, however, does not assure increased purchases by that country. Because all transactions are controlled by the state, imports can still be limited, not by tariffs but by purchasing policy. Without some assurance that state trading countries will increase imports, most favored nation status works to the advantage of state trading countries. They gain greater access to foreign markets but continue to be able to protect their own markets.[112] Thus the United States sought assurance that the granting of most favored nation status would be mutually beneficial. Under the October agreement the Soviet Union indirectly gave such an assurance by agreeing that trade with the United States would increase rapidly.[113] Finally, at the time of the agreements, President Nixon opened the way for Eximbank loans by declaring that trade with the Soviet Union was in the national interest.

In 1972 the Nixon administration took what it saw as another major step toward economic and political détente by agreeing to a major U.S. grain sale to the Soviet Union.[114] As in 1963, the Soviet Union suffered a bad harvest in 1972. And, as in 1963, the Soviet Union turned to the international market to solve its agricultural crisis. In the summer of 1972, with the consent and support of the American government, the Soviet Union purchased over 19 million tons of U.S. wheat, corn, and soybeans. The Nixon administration felt that the purchase would serve not only its foreign policy goals of improving relations with the Soviet Union but that it would also give a boost to the U.S. balance of payments and serve the administration's agricultural policy of reducing grain stocks and pleasing farmers in an election year.

In the summer and fall of 1972 it seemed that the United States had taken major steps toward ending the economic isolation of the East. The Soviet Union would enjoy most favored nation status, it would now have access to U.S. public and private credit facilities, and it would look to the United States for help in its agricultural problems. These economic changes would, it was hoped, further the process of détente. The year 1972, however, would not prove to be a major turning point; rather, it would be another example of the barriers to change. The Soviet–Ameri-can commercial agreement was officially declared null and void when Congress put restrictions on most favored nation status and Export–Import Bank credits for the Soviet Union. And the grain sale turned into a political embarrassment for the administration.

Most favored nation status for the Soviet Union was the pivotal provision of the October commercial accord. The agreement was to enter into force only after Congress had approved most favored nation status for the Soviet Union. Under the agreement, President Nixon was to submit legislation to Congress which he did by including such a provision in the Trade Reform bill of 1973.

Most favored nation status was of questionable economic importance for the Soviet Union. Most Soviet exports are raw materials which are subject to either no or very low tariffs. The export of Soviet manufactures is probably hampered more by poor quality than by tariff barriers.

One study by the U.S. Tariff Commission argued that most favored nation status would not affect Soviet exports in any substantial way,[115] but the Soviet Union has always given this status great political significance. From the Soviet Union's viewpoint, denial of most favored nation treatment symbolized its exclusion from the international economic system, whereas the restoration of most favored nation status symbolized the end of Western discrimination. The other provisions of the commercial agreement therefore were made contingent on the granting of most favored nation status.

Credits from the West, on the other hand, were of crucial economic importance. As we have seen, the Soviet Union and Eastern Europe face chronic shortages of foreign exchange and thus chronic restrictions on imports from the West. The limited export capabilities of these states and their insufficient gold production have meant that the only solution to problems in the near future is credit from the West. With such credit the East hopes to purchase Western technology to improve its production and eventually its export capability. Improved export capability will, in turn, enable the East to repay Western loans.

Eastern access to Western credit had improved substantially over the years. There are few barriers in Western Europe and Japan to private or public credits. Private credit from the United States had been eased by liberal interpretation of the Johnson Debt Default Act. However, Eximbank credits, blocked until the October agreements, were crucial, as denial of access to Eximbank facilities blocked access to both public and private American credits.

Private banks and companies were unwilling to participate in many loans to the Soviet Union without Eximbank participation or guarantees. And, without a change in the authority of the Eximbank, the Soviet Union was excluded from the large U.S. financial market and from many attractive deals with American firms. While European and Japanese credits and deals were a possible alternative, the Soviet Union in many cases preferred American technology and in many cases needed the resources of the vast American capital market. Thus President Nixon's agreement that the Soviet Union would have access to Eximbank loans was a crucial part of the October package.

Certain leaders in Congress recognized the significance of most favored nation status and Eximbank credits for the Soviet Union and sought to use them as a lever to force the Soviet Union to change its internal policies on emigration. In April 1973, Senator Henry Jackson and Representative Charles Vanik introduced an amendment to the Trade Reform bill which linked most favored nation treatment and Eximbank loans for the Soviet Union and Eastern Europe to freer policies of emigration in these countries. The amendment denied most favored nation treatment and public credits or credit guarantees to any nonmarket economy which "denies its citizens the right or opportunity to emigrate" or imposes more than a nominal tax for that emigration.[116] The executive-congressional debate over the Jackson–Vanik amendment lasted for eighteen months.

The Democratic Congress, testy about Watergate and about not having been consulted in the negotiation of the commercial agreement and pressed by a powerful coalition of interest groups, insisted on a form of linkage which the administration never had in mind. The administration fought back and insisted on its own linkage, that of most favored nation provisions to the overall Trade Reform bill. As a result, as we have seen, relations with Europe and Japan were worsened and trade negotiations with the market economies delayed.

In the end, the administration and, it seemed, the Soviet Union capitulated. In October 1974, just two years after the commercial agreement, Senator Jackson announced a compromise. Soviet and Eastern European trade benefits would be made conditional upon a relaxation of Soviet and East European emigration policies. Secretary of State Kissinger opposed the Jackson amendment in writing but told the senator that the administration had been assured that the Soviet Union would no longer impede emigration. Senator Jackson wrote Mr. Kissinger that he understood that there would be an annual emigration of 60,000 Jews and others from the Soviet Union and that that number would be considered a "benchmark" indicating minimal compliance with the amendment provisions.[117] It seemed that most favored nation and the other commercial agreements which depended upon it were of such significance that the Soviet Union was willing to alter its internal policies in response to external pressure.

Shortly after the agreement on emigration yet another issue arose. An amendment to extend the lending authority of the Eximbank was added to a bill and was being opposed by the administration. The amendment set a $300 million ceiling on new credits to the Soviet Union and provided that the ceiling could be raised only if the president declared it was in the national interest and if Congress concurred with his judgment. Furthermore, the amendment prohibited Eximbank credits for the production, transportation, or distribution of energy from the Soviet Union without Congressional approval and placed a ceiling of $40 million for loans or guarantees for the exploration of energy in the Soviet Union. The amendment, which was passed in December 1974, was unique in singling out one country for special credit restrictions.

The Jackson–Vanik linkage plus the Eximbank restrictions proved to be more than the Soviet Union was willing to accept. The Eximbank provision meant that even a major capitulation such as permitting greater emigration would lead to only small credits. Furthermore, external commercial relations, no matter how important, were not worth the price of internal political change. In December, the Soviet Union denied that it had given any assurances to Secretary Kissinger regarding emigration and charged the United States with interfering in its internal affairs. In January 1975 the United States and the Soviet Union agreed to nullify the 1972 commercial agreement. The Soviet Union would thus not receive most favored nation treatment or be eligible for Eximbank credits. The United States would receive no further lend-lease payments. And, because the lend-lease debt settlement came unstuck, Johnson Act prohibitions on private credits would remain in force.

The 1972 grain sale, like the commercial agreements, also went awry. The sale turned from a step toward détente and a boost to the U.S. economy into a political threat to the policy of détente and an economic debacle. The story of the grain sale is long and complicated. In essence, the Soviet Union succeeded in purchasing a vast amount of American grain at a very low price. In the summer and fall of 1972, Soviet officials purchased 19 million tons of U.S. grain at 1–2 cents per bushel below the market price. Immediately after the sale, and to a great extent because of it, the price of grain doubled. The rise in grain prices led to a rise in food prices and contributed greatly to world inflation. The Soviets had somehow managed to make an incredibly good—some felt too good—purchase.

To make things worse, the sale was subsidized by the U.S. government, which had long paid subsidies to grain exporters. These subsidies were designed to enable U.S. exportation of grain by making up the difference between the domestic price of grain, which was kept higher than the world price, and the world price. A provision in the subsidy laws enabled traders to register subsidies after the actual sale and to receive subsidies based not on the price at the time of the sale but at the time of the registration.

The large grain traders involved in the Soviet deal cleverly waited to register their sales until after the price of grain had risen substantially. As prices soared after the grain sale, subsidy payments also soared. In the end, the government paid several hundred million dollars in subsidies. Not only the Soviet Union but the large grain traders as well had made a great coup. They bought their grain from farmers before the price rise, but they enjoyed large subsidies due to the quick rise in prices following the sale. Understandably, American farmers who had not shared in the profits, American consumers who partly as a result of the sale were faced with rising food costs, and American taxpayers who paid for the subsidies were incensed.

The 1972 fiasco offered several lessons for foreign policy. The grain sale demonstrated the problems for market economies in dealing with state trading countries. By moving in a secret, coordinated, and swift fashion and by using the bargaining strength of a large purchaser, Soviet traders were able to make highly favorable deals with American grain traders. The U.S. government in its various parts, especially the U.S. Department of Agriculture, did not supply information or attempt to manage the Soviet sale to minimize the disadvantages to the private market. Indeed, it seemed that officials in the department cooperated with both Soviet traders who sought to act in secret and American traders who sought subsidies. Thus, by their skill and by the failures of U.S. government management, the Soviet traders were able to use their market power effectively.

The grain sale also demonstrated the problem of fluctuations in Soviet grain purchases. At times of bad harvests, the Soviets became major purchasers in the international grain market. Their erratic interventions could and did upset that market, especially in times of short world grain stocks. Finally, the grain sale suggested the difficulty of using economic means to achieve political détente. The eagerness of the administration to seek Soviet cooperation through the sale probably hindered it from examining the economic consequences of the sale. In the end, by arousing domestic opposition, they may have hurt their cause more than helped it.

After the fiasco, the United States pressed for greater joint management of grain sales. In 1974, the United States and the Soviet Union took a first step toward such management. In the fall of that year, the two countries agreed to negotiate the volume of Soviet purchases of U.S. grain, and the Soviet Union agreed to take less grain than it sought so as not to disrupt world markets. Furthermore, it agreed to receive grain in small, regularly phased shipments, again to minimize market disruption. Finally, the Soviet Union agreed to cooperate with the United States to develop a system to anticipate and manage U.S. supply and Soviet demand. For its part, the United States announced that in the future any sale exceeding 50,000 tons would require approval from the government.

In 1975 the grain issue erupted again. As a result of a bad harvest, the Soviet Union once again made large purchases of American grain. By August, the Soviet Union had purchased over 10 million tons. The reservoir of bad public will left over from 1972 combined with continuing inflation threatened to lead to a major public reaction which would be politically embarrassing for President Ford and which could endanger the very process of détente. In late July, President Ford declared a two-month moratorium on Soviet grain purchases, but this did not stop domestic reaction. The AFL–CIO attacked grain sales sharply saying that they would lead to rising costs for American consumers. In September American longshoremen began a boycott on loading ships with grain bound for the Soviet Union. Faced with such political pressure, President Ford sought to force the Soviet Union to negotiate on the establishment of a system to manage the erratic Soviet purchases. In October, under strong American pressure, the Soviet Union signed a five-year agreement on grain purchases. The Soviet Union agreed to buy 6–8 million tons of U.S. grain each year and to consult with the U.S. government about any purchases above that amount. The United States agreed to supply up to 8 million tons per year unless the total U.S. grain crop fell below 225 million tons, an unlikely event.

CONCLUSION

Unlike the other two systems we have examined, the East–West economic system is not in the midst of crisis. While the 1960s and 1970s have been characterized by significant changes in policies and processes and such problems as the Soviet grain purchases, no major institutional or rule-making problems confront East–West relations. Although East–West economic interaction will continue to increase, economic and political constraints will limit any dramatic growth in interaction. Furthermore, a renewal of intense security conflict could eliminate progress made in the last decade. While some members of the Eastern bloc may join Western institutions—Romania, for example is already a member of the IMF and Poland and Yugoslavia have joined GATT—there will be no reintegration of the world economy and of its management systems. East–West issues will most likely be handled in separate forums such as the bilateral consultation procedures established between the United States and the Soviet Union on the Soviet Union's grain purchases or the albeit abortive Soviet agreement to assure mutual benefit from most favored nation status. Interaction will grow, but separation will likely continue to be the major characteristic of East–West economic relations.

NOTES

1. The chapter concentrates on the East as the Soviet Union and Eastern Europe. Other Communist states—China, North Korea, North Vietnam, and later Cuba—faced a similar separation.

2. Marshall I. Goldman, *Détente and Dollars: Doing Business with the Soviets* (New York: Basic Books, 1975), pp. 4–20.

3. Antony C. Sutton, *Western Technology and Soviet Economic Development 1917 to 1930* (Stanford, Calif.: Hoover Institution on War, Revolution and Peace, 1968); Antony C. Sutton, *Western Technology and Soviet Economic Development 1930 to 1945* (Stanford, Calif. Hoover Institution on War, Revolution and Peace, 1971).

4. See, for example, Jacob Viner, "International Relations Between State-Controlled National Economies," *American Economic Review*, 54 (1944), 315–329.

5. John Lewis Gaddis, *The United States and the Origins of the Cold War, 1941–1947* (New York: Columbia Univ. Press, 1972), pp. 18–23, 174–197.

6. William Diebold, Jr., "East-West Trade and the Marshall Plan," *Foreign Affairs*, 26 (July 1948), 710.

7. On the United Nations Relief and Rehabilitation Administration, see E. F. Penrose, *Economic Planning for the Peace* (Princeton, N.J.: Princeton Univ. Press, 1953), pp. 145–167.

8. Diebold, "East-West Trade and the Marshall Plan," p. 715.

9. Joseph Stalin, *Economic Problems of Socialism in the USSR* (New York: International Publishers, 1952), p. 26.

10. For a discussion of motives and policies, see Zbigniew K. Brzezinski, *The Soviet Bloc: Unity and Conflict*, rev. ed. (Cambridge, Mass.: Harvard Univ. Press, 1967), pp. 3 151.

11. Stalin, *Economic Problems of Socialism in the USSR*, pp. 26–30. Stalin was not alone in his predictions of postwar economic problems in the West. Many Western economists and policy makers were also concerned. See Gaddis, *The United States and the Origins of the Cold War, 1941–1947*.

12. On Marxist justification, see Zygmunt Nagorski, Jr., *The Psychology of East-West Trade* (New York: Mason & Lipscomb, 1974), pp. 58–59.

13. See, for example, Gaddis, *The United States and the Origins of the Cold War, 1941–1947*; Adam B. Ulam, *Expansion and Coexistence: The History of Soviet Foreign Policy, 1917–1967* (New York: Praeger, 1968), pp. 314–455.

14. See Nicholas Spulber, *The Economics of Communist Eastern Europe* (New York: Technology Press of M.I.T. Wiley, 1957).

15. See Charles Prince, "The USSR's Role in International Finance," *Harvard Business Review*, 25 (Autumn 1946), 111–128.

16. See J. Keith Horsefield, ed., *The International Monetary Fund, 1945–1965, Vol. I: Chronicle* (Washington, D.C.: International Monetary Fund, 1969), pp. 263, 359–364.

17. Clair Wilcox, *A Charter for World Trade* (New York: Macmillan, 1949), pp. 164–167.

18. See Ulam, *Expansion and Coexistence*, pp. 432–440. It is debated whether or not the U.S. offer of aid to the Soviet Union was serious. In any case the Soviet rejection was clear. For a critical analysis of U.S. policy, see Joyce and Gabriel Kolko, *The Limits of Power: The World and the United States Foreign Policy, 1945–1954* (New York: Harper & Row, 1972), pp. 359–383.

19. Cited in full in Michael Kaser, *Comecon: Integration Problems of the Planned Economies* (London: Oxford Univ. Press, 1965), pp. 1 12.

20. Nicolas Spulber, "East-West Trade and the Paradoxes of the Strategic Embargo," in Alan A. Brown and Egon Neuberger, eds., *International Trade and Central Planning: An Analysis of Economic Interactions* (Berkeley, Calif.: Univ. of California Press, 1968), p. 114.

21. See Brzezinski, *The Soviet Bloc: Unity and Conflict*, p. 101.

22. Paul Marer, "The Political Economy of Soviet Relations with Eastern Europe,"

in Steven J. Rosen and James R. Kurth, eds., *Testing Theories of Economic Imperialism* (Lexington, Mass.: Lexington Books, 1974), pp. 247-249.

23. Ibid., pp. 244-245.

24. Ibid., p. 234. After the disturbances in Poland in 1956, the Soviet Union agreed to a reimbursement for the inequitable price of coal.

25. Ibid., pp. 233-235.

26. See pp. 263-264 on inconvertibility.

27. Spulber, *The Economics of Communist Eastern Europe.*

28. Ibid., pp. 166-223.

29. For a discussion of earlier actions, see Gunnar Adler-Karlsson, *Western Economic Warfare, 1947-1967: A Case Study in Foreign Economic Policy* (Stockholm: Almquist and Wiksell, 1968), p. 5 and, for text of the Export Control Act, see pp. 217-219.

30. The restrictions did not apply to U.S. territories and most exports to Canada. The controls were designed to deal not only with foreign policy but also with problems of shortages of supply.

31. John P. Hardt and George Holliday, *U.S.-Soviet Commercial Relations: The Interplay of Economics, Technology Transfer, and Diplomacy,* for the subcommittee on National Security Policy and Scientific Developments of the Committee on Foreign Affairs (Washington, D.C.: U.S. Government Printing Office, June 19, 1973), pp. 48-49.

32. Goldman, *Détente and Dollars* p. 49 and, for other export restrictions, pp. 289-290 and Hardt and Holliday, *U.S.-Soviet Commercial Relations,* p. 50.

33. Members were the United States, Canada, Japan, Belgium, Denmark, France, Greece, Italy, Luxemburg, the Netherlands, Norway, Portugal, Turkey, the United Kingdom, and West Germany, (i.e., all the NATO members except Iceland plus Japan).

34. Adler-Karlsson, *Western Economic Warfare, 1947-1967,* pp. 1-3, 31-34.

35. Ibid., pp. 5-6, 36-45.

36. Ibid., p. 220, for text of Mutual Defense Assistance Control Act.

37. See Samuel Pisar, *Coexistence and Commerce: Guidelines for Transactions Between East and West* (New York: McGraw-Hill, 1970), pp. 130-138. See, also, Chapter 4 of this text.

38. In 1972, Romania became eligible when that country joined the International Monetary Fund and the World Bank.

39. Hardt and Holliday, *U.S.-Soviet Commercial Relations,* pp. 55-58; Pisar, *Coexistence and Commerce,* pp. 107-109.

40. See Goldman, *Détente and Dollars,* p. 52; Pisar, *Coexistence and Commerce,* pp. 111-114.

41. Pisar, *Coexistence and Commerce,* pp. 102-107. For other U.S. restrictions on imports, see Goldman, *Détente and Dollars,* pp. 98-102.

42. Spulber, in Brown and Neuberger, *International Trade and Central Planning,* p. 114.

43. Adler-Karlsson, *Western Economic Warfare, 1947-1967,* pp. 83-99.

44. Joseph Wilczynski, *The Economics and Politics of East-West Trade* (New York: Praeger, 1969), p. 56.

45. U.S. Department of State, *The Battle Act Report 1973,* Mutual Defense Assistance Control Act of 1951, Twenty-Sixth Report to Congress, (Washington, D.C., 1974), p. 22; Spulber, in Brown and Neuberger, *International Trade and Central Planning,* p. 114.

46. See Goldman, *Détente and Dollars,* pp. 27-31.

47. Ibid., pp. 194-195.

48. Joseph Wilczynski, *Socialist Economic Development and Reforms: From Extensive to Intensive Growth Under Central Planning in the USSR, Eastern Europe, and Yugoslavia* (New York: Praeger, 1972), pp. 26-33.

49. Franklyn D. Holzman and Robert Legvold, "The Economics and Politics of East-West Relations," *International Organization,* 29 (Winter 1975), 277-278.

50. See Wilczynski, *Socialist Economic Development and Reforms,* pp. 234-237; Goldman, *Détente and Dollars,* pp. 32-33; Holzman and Legvold, "The Economics and Politics of East-West Relations," p. 278. The problems of technology did not apply to the space and military sectors; rather, advances in these fields were made possible by the close

relationship of research with end users, competition among research units and with the West, and preferences on supplies.

51. For indicators of the lag, see Hardt and Holliday, *U.S.-Soviet Commercial Relations*, pp. 15-16.

52. Wilczynski, *Socialist Economic Development and Reforms;* Nagorski, *The Psychology of East-West Trade*, pp. 104-156.

53. Holzman and Legvold, "The Economics and Politics of East-West Relations, p. 288.

54. See Wilczynski, *Socialist Economic Development and Reforms*, pp. 260-299.

55. Wilczynski, *The Economics and Politics of East-West Trade*, pp. 218-220.

56. Wilczynski, *Socialist Economic Development and Reforms*, pp. 252-259.

57. See below on trade aversion. Efforts have not been abandoned. In 1970 Comecon adopted the "Complex Program for the Further Deepening and Streamlining of Cooperation and for the Developing of the Socialist Economic Integration among the Member Countries of the Comecon," a new program for economic integration through joint planning and national specialization.

58. U.S. Senate, *Export Expansion and Regulation*, hearings before the Subcommittee on International Finance of the Committee on Banking and Currency, 91st Congress, 1st Sess., 1969, p. 92.

59. U.S. Senate, *Authority for the Regulation of Exports—1972*, hearings before the Subcommittee on International Finance of the Committee on Banking, Housing, and Urban Affairs, 92nd Congress, 2nd Sess., 1972, pp. 12-13.

60. Goldman, *Détente and Dollars*, pp. 74-75.

61. See Chapter 2.

62. See Chapter 3.

63. Peter G. Peterson, *The United States in the Changing World Economy, Vol. 1, A Foreign Economic Perspective* (Washington, D.C.: U.S. Government Printing Office, December 27, 1971), pp. iii, 28, 43.

64. Peter G. Peterson, *U.S.-Soviet Commercial Relationships in a New Era* (Washington, D.C.: U.S. Government Printing Office, August 1972), pp. 4-6.

65. Wilczynski, *The Economics and Politics of East-West Trade*, p. 284.

66. Goldman, *Détente and Dollars*, p. 46. See Sutton, *Western Technology and Soviet Economic Development 1917 to 1930*, and *Western Technology and Soviet Economic Development, 1945-1965* (Stanford, Calif.: Hoover Institution on War, Revolution and Peace, 1973).

67. Wilczynski, *The Economics and Politics of East-West Trade*, pp. 283-288; Adler-Karlsson, *Western Economic Warfare, 1947-1967*, pp. 7-9.

68. Anton F. Malish, Jr., *United States-East European Trade: Considerations Involved in Granting Most Favored Nation Treatment to the Countries of Eastern Europe*, Staff Research Studies, 4 (Washington, D.C.: U.S. Tariff Commission, 1972).

69. Wilczynski, *The Economics and Politics of East-West Trade*, p. 289; Spulber, in Brown and Neuberger, *International Trade and Central Planning*.

70. In the Freuhof case, France forced the export of trucks to Czechoslovakia despite American government opposition.

71. See testimony of Secretary of State Dean Rusk in U.S. Senate, 88th Congress, 2nd Sess., *East-West Trade*, hearings before the Committee on Foreign Relations, Part 1, 1964, pp. 2-18 and 1966 letter of transmittal of East-West Trade Relations Act of 1966, in Phillip D. Grub and Karel Holbik, eds., *American-East European Trade: Controversy, Progress, Prospects* (Washington, D.C.: National Press, 1969), pp. 1-4.

72. See, for example, President Johnson's Annual Message to the Congress on the State of the Union, "Lyndon B. Johnson," 1965, Book I (January 1, 1965–May 31, 1965), in *Public Papers of the Presidents of the United States* (Washington, D.C.: Office of the Federal Register, 1966), p. 3.

73. Grub and Holbik, *American-East European Trade*, p. 3.

74. See Catherine M. Kelleher and Donald J. Puchala, "Germany, European Security, and Arms Control," in William T. R. Fox and Warner R. Schilling, eds., *European Security and the Atlantic System* (New York: Columbia Univ. Press, 1973), pp. 160-170.

75. U.S. Department of State, *The Bulletin*, 71 (October 14, 1974), 508. This statement by Secretary of State Kissinger is a good statement of the theory of détente.

76. Ibid., pp. 509–516.

77. Peterson, *U.S.-Soviet Commercial Relationships in a New Era*, p. 3.

78. U.S. Department of State, *The Bulletin*, 71 (October 14, 1974), 508.

79. Franklyn D. Holzman, "Foreign Trade Behavior of Centrally Planned Economies," in Henry Rosovsky, ed., *Industrialization in Two Systems* (New York: Wiley, 1966), pp. 242–247.

80. Oscar Altman, "Russian Gold and the Ruble," International Monetary Fund, *Staff Papers*, 8 (April 1960), 415–438.

81. Recent export controls are an exception. The reaction against these controls indicates the importance of the general principle of access to supply. See Chapters 3 and 7.

82. On the problem of trade aversion in the East, see articles in Brown and Neuberger, *International Trade and Central Planning*.

83. Prices are based on the Marxist concept of the labor theory of value, which does not attribute value to capital inputs. Prices are also distorted by the use of the price system to subsidize certain items and to discourage the purchase of others through artificially set prices.

84. Wilczynski, *The Economics and Politics of East-West Trade*, p. 22.

85. Pisar, *Co-existence and Commerce*, p. 35.

86. John P. Hardt, George D. Holliday, and Young C. Kim, *Western Investment in Communist Economies: A Selected Survey on Economic Interdependence*, U.S. Senate, 93rd Congress, 2nd Sess., Subcommittee on Multinational Corporations of the Committee on Foreign Relations, 1974, pp. 1–2.

87. Goldman, *Détente and Dollars*, p. 27.

88. Wilczynski, *The Economics and Politics of East-West Trade*, pp. 198–200.

89. Goldman, *Détente and Dollars*, p. 34.

90. See U.S. House, Committee on Banking and Currency, Subcommittee on International Trade, *The FIAT-Soviet Automobile Plant and Communist Economic Reforms*, 98th Congress, 2nd Sess., 1967.

91. Hardt et al., *Western Investment in Communist Countries*, p. 3.

92. Goldman, *Détente and Dollars*, p. 28.

93. See U.S. Department of State, *The Battle Act Report 1973*, p. 54–55.

94. See, for example, *Quarterly Economic Review, Czechoslovakia, Hungary, Annual Supplement 1976* (London: The Economist Intelligence Unit, 1976), pp. 9, 17; *Quarterly Economic Review, Poland, East Germany, 1976*, 2 (London: The Economist Intelligence Unit, 1976), p. 9.

95. *Quarterly Economic Review, USSR 1976*, 2 (London: The Economist Intelligence Unit, 1976), p. 6.

96. Morgan Guaranty Trust Company of New York, *World Financial Markets*, March 1976, p. 13, and July 1976, p. 8.

97. *Business Eastern Europe*, 5, 30 (July 30, 1976), 236–237. See, also, report of remarks at OECD meeting by Kissinger, U.S. Department of State. *The Bulletin*, 75 (July 19–25, 1976), 78; Nagorski, *The Psychology of East-West Trade*, pp. 157–189.

98. U.S. Department of Commerce, *The United States Role in East-West Trade: Problems and Prospects*. An Assessment by Rogers Morton, Secretary of Commerce (Washington, D.C., 1975), p. 11.

99. See Robert S. Kretschmer, Jr., and Robin Foor, *The Potential for Joint Ventures in Eastern Europe* (New York: Praeger, 1972); Economic Commission for Europe, *Analytical Report on Industrial Co-operation Among ECE Countries* (Geneva: United Nations, 1973); Hardt, *Western Investment in Communist Economies, Business Eastern Europe*, miscellaneous issues.

100. The credits, however, were never used.

101. "Report of the Special Committee on U.S. Trade With East European Countries and the Soviet Union," U.S. Department of State, *The Bulletin*, 54 (May 30, 1966), 845.

102. Ibid., pp. 846–847.

103. Ibid., p. 850.

104. On this and legislative history of the period, see Edwin J. Feulner, Jr., "Recent

Congressional Developments in Trading with Eastern Europe," in Grub and Holbik, *American-Eastern European Trade*, pp. 5-8.

105. U.S. Senate, 89th Congress, 2 Sess., Bill 5-3363.

106. See Feulner, in Grub and Holbik, *American-Eastern European Trade*.

107. Quoted in *The New York Times*, October 23, 1969, p. 1.

108. See testimony of Kenneth N. Davis, Assistant Secretary for Domestic and International Business, U.S. Department of Commerce, in the U.S. Senate, *Export Expansion and Regulation*, Hearings before the Subcommittee on International Finance of the Committee on Banking and Currency, 91st Congress, 1st Sess., 1969, pp. 307-317.

109. Export Administration Act, Public Law 91-184, 91st Congress, 1969.

110. See Hardt et al., *Western Investment in Communist Countries*, pp. 49-50.

111. Ibid., pp. 8-9.

112. Wilczynski, *The Economics and Politics of East-West Trade*, pp. 130-135.

113. Hardt and Holliday, *Western Investment in Communist Countries*, pp. 53-54.

114. On the grain sale, see comptroller general of the United States, *Exporters' Profits on Sales of U.S. Wheat to Russia*, (B-176943), U.S. Department of Agriculture (Washington, D.C. U.S. General Accounting Office, February 12, 1974).

115. Malish, *United States-Eastern European Trade*.

116. U.S. Congress, 93rd Congress, 1st sess., *Congressional Record, Proceedings and Debates*, 119 (April 10, 1973), S6820-S6921.

117. *The New York Times*, December 19, 1974, pp. 18-19.

Conclusion: Toward a New International Economic Order?

This study has focused on two themes: the influence of politics on international economic relations and the political management of international economic relations in the years since World War II.

The examination of international economic relations since World War II has revealed the multiple ways in which political factors have shaped economic outcomes. We have seen that the postwar security system was a significant influence on the postwar economic system. The creation of a bipolar diplomatic–security system led to the separation of Eastern and Western economic systems and provided an important base for the dominant role of the United States in the Western system and of the Soviet Union in the Eastern system. The loosening of the bipolar system through détente, in turn, has tempered East–West economic separation and loosened superpower economic dominance within the respective blocs. We have also seen the influence of domestic policy making on international economic relations. Trade management, for example, has been hampered by the mobilization of multiple interest groups in national policy making. In the domestic policy process, overriding political concerns have often determined economic outcomes. The Marshall Plan and other aid programs, for example, were security policies as well as economic programs. Finally, and most importantly in terms of this study, international economic relations have themselves been a political process of interaction in which state and nonstate actors seek to manage conflict or to cooperate to seek common goals. The management of interdependence, the search for the end of dependence, and the creation of East–West independence, for example, were part of a process of political interaction in which actors sought markets, resources, power, and a multitude of other goals.

The review of the political management of international economic relations in the years since World War II traced the system of political control established after World War II, the reasons for the collapse of the postwar order, and the factors shaping future international economic management. It is to this last subject, the future of the international economic order, that this conclusion is devoted. Each chapter of this book has offered some conclusions about the future of management in particular issue areas—money, trade, investment—and in particular subsystems—West, North–South, East–West. It seems appropriate, in conclusion, to look at the future of the system as a whole and to suggest some answers to the question, Will it be possible to develop new forms of political management which will be able to deal with the problems of our time?[1]

POLITICAL CONDITIONS OF MANAGEMENT

Any new international economic order will be based on political conditions different from the political bases of the Bretton Woods system: the concentration of power in a small number of states, the existence of a cluster of important interests shared by those states, and the presence of a dominant power willing and able to assume a leadership role.

The future order will continue to rely on political management by a core of powerful developed market states. The developed market economies and especially the "big five"—the United States, West Germany, France, the United Kingdom, and Japan—will remain the key actors in the system. The size and vitality of their economies will assure their continuing leadership.

The management group, however, will have to be broadened in some cases and some issue areas. Future management, if it is to be effective, will have to take account of new power centers. The most obvious of these are the petroleum-exporting states. Members of OPEC (Organization of Petroleum Exporting Countries) which have accumulated vast monetary power—especially Saudi Arabia—will have to be integrated into the system of international monetary management. That process has already begun, as we have seen, with the greater role of the oil states in the IMF (International Monetary Fund) and their apparent acceptance of the norms of stabilizing behavior. Further integration—for example, participation in the Group of Ten or Five—will be necessary to assure a stable managed system. In the area of trade and foreign investment, too, new powers will have to be consulted. The developing countries which have reached a take-off stage and whose economies are coming closer to the developed core than to the rest of the Third World will have to play a greater role in international management. States such as Brazil, Mexico, South Korea, and Taiwan whose trade is of great importance to the developed countries and who have vast amounts of foreign investment which they are learning to control will be in a position to demand and receive access to management. Their voices will be heard to a greater extent in trade negotiations and in international discussions regarding the regulation of multinational corporations. The new rich may even join the Organization for Economic Cooperation and Development.

Whereas a few Third World countries will be integrated to a greater extent in international economic decision making, the role of the other states of the Third World in international economic management is unlikely to change. These less developed countries constitute a Fourth World of increasing marginality in the world economy whose only hope is not access to decision making but a greater ability to force the powerful to listen to their demands. The unity of the South, the ability of some states to take disruptive action, and the possible interest of the new rich in championing their cause may enable the Fourth World to place its demands for equity on the international agenda.

Finally, the Eastern countries, too, will continue to play a minor role. Because their future interaction with the market economies will be limited, management changes will not be required. Whereas some Eastern states will participate in the institutions of the Western economic order, their voice will be small. On East–West questions, bilateral agreements or separate multilateral institutions will manage relations.

Among the powerful core there will remain a recognized cluster of common interests. Despite important conflicts raised by economic change and in particular by economic interdependence, the developed market economies continue to support a liberal, capitalist international economy. The postwar experience has reinforced their belief in the need to cooperate to achieve that stable and prosperous economic system. The persistence of the shared goal of cooperation was demonstrated by the behavior of the developed states during the crises of the 1970s. The restraint evidenced during the money, oil, and trade crises and the ability to initiate negotiations for reform testify to the enduring consensus.

There are suggestions that the second tier of states—members of OPEC and Brazil and Mexico among others—share the norm of cooperation. The conservative monetary policies of the oil states, for example, and receptive policies of the others to foreign investment may be signs of consensus. Nevertheless, it seems certain that the new rich will also be likely to press for another goal: international equity. The wealthier Southern states have shown a remarkable solidarity with the other Third World states pressing for their model of a new international economic order.

Although the goal of equity is not rejected by the industrial core, neither is it seen as a primary goal of international economic management nor as a responsibility of the developed market economies. While the South has succeeded in putting equity on the agenda of international economic management and while the developed market economies are willing to carry out some redistributive or development programs, the North is unwilling to significantly alter the operation of the established system. Furthermore, some Northern critics have questioned whether equity as currently demanded by the less developed countries is a legitimate goal. Some charge that redistribution as now conceived will benefit only a few or only a small stratum of the population of less developed countries and not the poorest in the poor countries. Without significant internal political, social, and economic reform within less developed countries international efforts at redistribution and development will be useless, argue many in both the North and the South. Conflict over equity and redistribution therefore is likely to continue to be a political dynamic in the new international economic order.

Finally, the new international economic order will be a system of multilateral management. In the past the management of conflict and cooperation was carried out to a great extent by a single leader. In the nineteenth century Great Britain played the leadership role: in the postwar era the United States acted as the leader of the system. The more even distribution of power among the core states in the future, however, will require the active participation of many states.

Multilateral management is difficult. Agreement among sovereign powers in the absence of government has proved, throughout history, a difficult and often an impossible task. Several factors, however, enhance the possible success of multilateral economic management. The basic consensus among the powerful will be an important factor; so, too, will be the experience in cooperation since World War II. Multilateral management will be facilitated by a variety of formal and informal methods of multilateral decision making developed over the last three decades. A relatively sophisticated and complex structure of cooperative mechanisms has developed in the postwar era, and experience in using these mechanisms has grown.

Even within a multilateral system, however, leadership will be important. Existing institutions are simply insufficiently developed to manage the system alone. Most often, that leadership will have to come from the United States.[2] Unless and until the European Economic Community forms a political unit, the United States by the very size of its economy will be most important international economic actor. Although the United States will be unable to manage the system by itself, management and reform will be impossible without the United States. U.S. initiatives and support for the multilateral order will be crucial for its success.

PROBLEMS OF MANAGEMENT

The new management system will face a multitude of problems, many of which have been touched on in this book: monetary and trade reform, control of multinationals, and economic development. Several, more general, points must be emphasized here. First, there are simply more issues on the agenda for international management than ever before. Interdependence and the demand for the end of dependence have placed heavy strains on the political system of control. Second, because of greater international interdependence and dependence, the solution of many issues on the management agenda will require states to relinquish national control to international management. Yet the need to relinquish national control comes precisely at a time when states are seeking to increase control of the national economy. The conflict between national and international control will be a persistent dilemma.

The speed of change will aggravate all these problems. And the rapidity of change as well as its unpredictability will require flexible management mechanisms—and understanding.

The multiplicity of problems, their complexity, and the rapidity and unpredictability of change give observers and decision makers little time to analyze and understand let alone prescribe appropriate solutions and reach political agreement on those solutions. The simultaneous emergence of inflation and recession, the nature of economic development, the question of resource scarcity, and the impact of national policies on economic activity in other states are all insufficiently understood, but all must be confronted now if the future is to be in any way controlled.

BUILDING A NEW INTERNATIONAL ECONOMIC ORDER

Because of the political setting and the nature of the task, the process of international economic reform will be piecemeal and evolutionary. Reform will result, in part, from international negotiations such as those now taking place in the IMF, the multilateral trade negotiations, and the Conference on International Economic Cooperation. Reform will also grow out of common law, the establishment of rules and procedures through trial and error and through ad hoc responses to problems. International monetary management through consultations among central bankers and finance ministers will most likely evolve through such a process. Reform will come not only from such international agreement and managed change but also through sporadic crises. It was the currency crises of the 1960s and 1970s, not international agreement, which led to the floating exchange rate system. In the absence of agreed rules, structures, and processes, such disturbances may multiply. In some cases crises may be deliberately induced. If conditions are favorable, for example, some Third World commodity producers might attempt to create crisis through cartel action.

The outcome of reform processes will not be a comprehensive international economic order. The political bases are too weak and the problems too complex to lead to anything approaching world economic management. In some areas management will be effective and relatively comprehensive. Issues of interdependence will most likely be managed because they are of greatest concern to the developed market economies. It is quite likely that guidelines for exchange rate management, rules on nontariff barriers, and codes for surveillance of multinationals will be developed. In issues of East–West relations, also, solutions are likely. Because interaction will continue to be limited, progress on regulating East–West interaction is possible. The reduction of U.S. tariff barriers and guidelines for state trading behavior in international markets, for example, are likely developments.

Progress on international equity is much less likely. In most cases, the efforts of the less developed countries to challenge the power and authority of the developed countries failed in the 1960s and 1970s. Evidence suggests that political weakness will continue to plague the South in the future. Some changes—commodity agreements in selected products and greater trade preferences—will be offered by the developed market states. The Third World may also benefit indirectly from management systems developed by the North for money, trade, and multinationals. No major redistribution, however, will occur. As a result, many less developed countries may increasingly turn away from the North to self-reliance and mutual self-help. And as a further result, the confrontation between haves and have nots will remain as a persistent element of international economic relations.

Finally, it is not inevitable that a new international economic order will be established. Although the powerful core has evidenced a high level of cooperation, there is no assurance that cooperation will persist or that it will be successful. The evolutionary process of reform is in many ways precarious, for it relies on mutual restraint and cooperation by the major powers until reform is achieved. In the absence of agreed upon rules, institutions, and procedures, a major economic shock could undermine cooperation and lead to the outbreak of economic warfare as occurred in the 1930s. Nevertheless, the postwar experience suggests that the will and ability to find mutual solutions exists and that cooperation among the powerful will persist.

NOTES

1. For other discussions of this same question, see Miriam Camps, *The Management of Interdependence: A Preliminary View* (New York: Council on Foreign Relations, 1974) and *"First World" Relationships: The Role of the OECD* (Paris: Atlantic Institute for International Affairs and Council on Foreign Relations, 1975); Roger D. Hansen, "The Crisis of Interdependence": Where Do We Go From Here?," in Roger D. Hansen et al., *The U.S. and World Development: Agenda for Action 1976* (New York: Praeger, 1976), pp. 41-66; Fred Hirsch, *Politicization in the World Economy and Necessary Conditions for an International Economic Order* (New York: McGraw-Hill, forthcoming); C. Fred Bergsten, Georges Berthoin, and Kinhide Mushakoji, *The Reform of International Institutions*, A Report of the Trilateral Task Force on International Institutions to the Trilateral Commission (New York: Trilateral Commission, 1976); Egidio Ortona, J. Robert Schaetzel, and Nobuhiko Ushiba, *The Problem of International Consultations*, A Report of the Trilateral Task Force on Consultative Procedures to the Trilateral Commission (New York: Trilateral Commission, 1976).

2. See Marina v. N. Whitman, "Leadership Without Hegemony: Our Role in the World Economy," *Foreign Policy*, 20 (Fall 1975), 138-160.

Selected Bibliography

The bibliography reflects the organization of the book. The first section on general and theoretical works lists general studies and collections which encompass the broad subject of international political economy. The three bibliographical headings that follow denote the three-part division of the study: the Western system, the North–South system, and the East–West system. Each of these has a general subsection that cites works encompassing subtopics for the particular subsystem. Other subtopics correspond to the chapter subdivisions: money, trade, investment, and so on. With a few exceptions individual articles, from general works already cited under general subdivisions, are not cited specifically under the various topical headings.

Publications by governmental and intergovernmental organizations are treated in three ways. Important official studies are included in the appropriate category in the first four sections. Important official serial publications are included in a separate category entitled official publications. Finally, because of space limitations some items are not listed. For example, because the U.S. Congressional hearings bearing on the politics of international economic relations are voluminous they are not repeated here, but are, however, cited in the notes. Those who wish to pursue research in this field should note the significance of hearings such as the Bretton Woods agreements, the Marshall Plan, the North Atlantic Treaty Organization, various trade and foreign aid hearings, and hearings on the problems of the international monetary system, the influence of multinational corporations, and East–West relations. Similar material from international organizations has also been excluded from the bibliography. Researchers should note the importance of proceedings of the various United Nations' bodies such as the General Assembly and UNCTAD and the voluminous material generated by international organizations such as the IMF and IBRD, the GATT, the OECD, and regional organizations.

Major newspapers and journals useful for the study of international political economy are cited in a final section.

GENERAL AND THEORY

Baran, Paul A. *The Political Economy of Growth*. New York: Monthly Review, 1968.

——, and Paul M. Sweezy. *Monopoly Capital: An Essay on the American Economic and Social Order*. New York: Monthly Review, 1966.

Bergsten, C. Fred, ed. *The Future of the International Economic Order: An Agenda for Research*. Boston: Heath, 1973.

——, and Lawrence B. Krause, eds. *World Politics and International Economics*. Washington, D.C.: The Brookings Institution, 1975.

Bhagwati, Jagdish N., ed. *Economics and World Order: From the 1970s to the 1990s*. New York: Macmillan, 1972.

Bundy, William P., ed. *The World Economic Crisis*. New York: Norton, 1975.

Camps, Miriam. *The Management of Interdependence: A Preliminary View*. New York: Council on Foreign Relations, 1974.

Carr, Edward Hallet. *The Twenty Years' Crisis, 1919–1939: An Introduction to the Study of International Relations*, 2nd ed. New York: St. Martin's, 1962.

Cooper, Richard N. "Economic Interdependence and Foreign Policy in the Seventies." *World Politics*, 24 (January 1972), 159–181.

——. *The Economics of Interdependence: Economic Policy in the Atlantic Community*. New York: McGraw-Hill, 1968.

——, ed. *A Reordered World: Emerging International Economic Problems*. Washington, D.C.: Potomac Associates, 1973.

Cox, Robert W., and Harold Jacobson. *The Anatomy of Influence: Decision Making in International Organization*. New Haven, Conn.: Yale Univ. Press, 1973.

Hamilton, Alexander. "Report of the Subject of Manufactures," in Arthur Harrison Cole, ed. *Industrial and Commercial Correspondence of Alexander Hamilton Anticipating his Report on Manufacturing*. New York: Kelley, 1968.

Hansen, Roger D. "The 'Crisis of Interdependence': Where Do We Go From Here?," in Roger D. Hanson et al., eds., *The U.S. and World Development: Agenda* for Action 1976. New York: Praeger, 1976.

Hawtrey, Ralph G. *Economic Aspects of Sovereignty*, 2nd ed. London: Longmans, 1952.

Hecksher, Eli F. *Mercantilism*. 2 vols. Mendel Shapiro, transl. London: Allen & Unwin, 1935.

Hirsch, Fred. *Politicization in the World Economy and Necessary Conditions for an International Economic Order*. New York: McGraw-Hill, forthcoming.

Hirschman, Albert O. *National Power and the Structure of Foreign Trade*. Berkeley, Calif.: Univ. of California Press, 1945.

Hoffmann, Stanley. "Obstinate or Obsolete? The Fate of the Nation-State and the Case of Western Europe." *Daedalus* 45 (Summer 1966), 862–915.

Hudson, Michael. *Super Imperialism: The Economic Strategy of American Empire.* New York: Holt, Rinehart & Winston, 1972.

Kaiser, Karl. "Transnational Politics: Towards a Theory of Multinational Politics." *International Organization,* 25 (Autumn 1971), 790–817.

Keohane, Robert O., and Joseph S. Nye, Jr. "Transgovernmental Relations and International Organizations." *World Politics,* 27 (October 1974), 39–62.

———, eds. *Transnational Relations and World Politics.* Cambridge, Mass.: Harvard Univ. Press, 1972.

Keynes, John Maynard. *The Economic Consequences of the Peace.* New York: Harcourt Brace Jovanovich, 1920.

Kindleberger, Charles P. *Power and Money: The Economics of International Politics and the Politics of International Economics.* New York: Basic, 1970.

———. *The World in Depression, 1929–1939.* Berkeley, Calif.: Univ. of California Press, 1973.

Knorr, Klaus E. *Power and Wealth: The Political Economy of International Power.* New York: Basic, 1973.

Kolko, Joyce and Gabriel. *The Limits of Power: The World and the United States Foreign Policy.* New York: Harper & Row, 1972.

List, Freidrich. *The National System of Political Economy.* New York: Kelley, 1966.

Magdoff, Harry. *The Age of Imperialism: The Economics of U.S. Foreign Policy.* New York: Monthly Review, 1969.

Malmgren, Harald. *International Economic Peacekeeping in Phase II.* New York: Quadrangle, 1972.

Morse, Edward L. *Foreign Policy and Interdependence in Gaullist France.* Princeton, N.J.: Princeton Univ. Press, 1973.

Olson, Mancur, Jr. *The Logic of Collective Action: Public Goods and the Theory of Groups.* Cambridge, Mass.: Harvard Univ. Press, 1965, 1971.

Perroux, François. *L'Economie du XXe Siecle,* 3rd ed. Paris: Presses Universitaires de France, 1961, 1969.

Peterson, Peter G. *The United States in the Changing World Economy.* Washington, D.C.: G.P.O., 1971.

Preeg, Ernest H. *Economic Blocs and U.S. Foreign Policy.* Report 135. Washington, D.C.: National Planning Association, 1974.

Robbins, Lionel. *The Economic Causes of War.* New York: Howard Fetig, 1968.

Schelling, Thomas C. *The Strategy of Conflict.* New York: Oxford Univ. Press, 1963.

Shonfield, Andrew. *Modern Capitalism: The Changing Balance of Public and Private Power.* London: Oxford Univ. Press, 1969.

Smith, Adam. *An Inquiry into the Nature and Causes of the Wealth of Nations.* New York: Modern Library, 1937.

Staley, Eugene. *War and the Private Investor.* Garden City, N.Y.: Doubleday, 1935.

Strange, Susan. "International Economics and International Relations: A Case of Mutual Neglect." *International Affairs,* 46 (April 1970), 304–315.

————. "What Is Economic Power and Who Has It?" *International Journal (Canada)*, 30 (Spring 1975), 207–224.

U.S. Commission on International Trade and Investment Policy. *United States International Economic Policy in an Interdependent World*. Washington, D.C.: The Williams Report. 3 vols. July 1971.

Viner, Jacob. "Power vs. Plenty as Objectives of Foreign Policy in the Seventeenth and Eighteenth Centuries." *World Politics*, 1 (October 1948), 1–29.

Waltz, Kenneth N. *Man, the State, and War: A Theoretical Analysis*. New York: Columbia Univ. Press, 1954, 1959.

————. "The Myth of National Interdependence," in Charles Kindleberger, ed. *The International Corporation*. Cambridge, Mass.: M.I.T. Press, 1970.

Whitman, Marina V. N. "Leadership Without Hegemony: Our Role in the World Economy." *Foreign Policy*, 20 (Fall 1975), 138–160.

Wu, Yuan-Li. *Economic Warfare*. Englewood Cliffs, N.J.: Prentice-Hall, 1952.

Young, Oran. "Interdependencies in World Politics." *International Journal*, 24 (Autumn 1969), 726–750.

THE WESTERN SYSTEM

General

Aubrey, Henry G. *Atlantic Economic Cooperation: The Case of the OECD*. New York: Praeger, 1967.

Calleo, David P., and Benjamin M. Rowland. *America and the World Political Economy: Atlantic Dreams and National Realities*. Bloomington, Ind.: Indiana Univ. Press, 1973.

Camps, Miriam. *"First World" Relationships: The Role of the OECD*. Paris: Atlantic Institute, 1975.

Diebold, William, Jr. "The Economic Issues Between the European Community and the United States in the 1970's," in Steven Warnecke, ed., *The European Community in the 1970's*. pp. 89–110. New York: Praeger, 1972.

———— "Political Economy: Europe and the United States." *Journal of International Affairs*, 30 (Spring/Summer 1976), entire volume.

————. *The United States and the Industrial World: American Foreign Economic Policy in the 1970's*. New York: Praeger, 1972.

Fox, Annette Baker, Alfred O. Hero, Jr., and Joseph S. Nye, Jr. *Canada and the United States: Transnational and Transgovernmental Relations*. New York: Columbia Univ. Press, 1976.

Gardner, Richard N. *Sterling-Dollar Diplomacy: The Origins and Prospects of Our International Economic Order*. exp. ed. New York: McGraw-Hill, 1969.

Hollerman, Leon. *Japan's Dependence on the World Economy: An Approach Toward Economic Liberalization*. Princeton, N.J.: Princeton Univ. Press, 1967.

Taylor, Allen. *Perspectives on U.S.-Japan Economic Relations*. Cambridge, Mass.: Ballinger, 1973.

International Monetary System

Aliber, Robert Z. *National Preferences and the Scope for International Monetary Reform.* Princeton, N.J.: International Finance Section, Department of Economics, Princeton University, 1973.

Aubrey, Henry G. *Behind the Veil of International Money.* Princeton, N.J.: International Finance Section, Department of Economics, Princeton University, 1969.

————. *The Dollar in World Affairs: An Essay in International Financial Policy.* New York: Praeger, 1964.

Bell, Geoffrey. *The Euro-Dollar Market and the International Financial System.* New York: Wiley, 1973.

Bergsten, C. Fred. *The Dilemmas of the Dollar: The Economics and Politics of United States International Monetary Policy.* New York: New York Univ. Press, 1975.

————. *Reforming the Dollar: An International Monetary Policy for the U.S.* New York: Council on Foreign Relations, 1972.

Bernstein, Edward M. et al. *Reflections on Jamaica.* Princeton, N.J.: International Finance Section, Department of Economics, Princeton Univ., 1976.

Calleo, David P., ed. *Money and the Coming World Order.* New York: New York Univ. Press, 1976.

Camu, Louis. "The Dollar Crisis and Europe." *The Atlantic Papers,* no. 3. Paris: Atlantic Institute, 1971, entire volume.

Clarke, Stephen V. O. *Central Bank Co-operation, 1924-1931.* New York: Federal Reserve Bank of New York, 1967.

Cohen, Benjamin J. *Major Issues of World Monetary Reform.* Commission on Critical Choices for Americans, August 1974. Mimeograph.

Cohen, Stephen D. *International Monetary Reform, 1964-69.* New York: Praeger, 1970.

Diebold, William, Jr. *Trade and Payments in Western Europe: A Study in Economic Cooperation, 1947-1951.* New York: Harper, 1952.

Einzig, Paul. *The Euro-Dollar System: Practice and Theory of International Interest Rates,* 4th ed. New York: St. Martin's, 1970.

Farmanfarmaian, Khodadad, Armin Gutowski, Saburo Okita, Robert V. Roosa, and Carrol Wilson. "How Can the World Afford OPEC Oil?" *Foreign Affairs,* 53 (January 1975), 201-222.

Feis, Herbert. *The Diplomacy of the Dollar, 1919-1932.* New York: Norton, 1966.

————. *Europe: The World's Banker, 1870-1914.* New Haven, Conn.: Yale Univ. Press, 1930.

Gardner, Richard N. *Sterling-Dollar Diplomacy: The Origins and Prospects of Our International Economic Order.* exp. ed. New York: McGraw-Hill, 1969.

Harrod, Roy F. *The Life of John Maynard Keynes.* London: Macmillan, 1952.

Hodgman, Donald R. *National Monetary Policies and International Monetary Cooperation.* Boston: Little, Brown, 1974.

Hirsch, Fred. *Money International.* Garden City, N.Y.: Doubleday, 1969.

Horie, Shiego. *The International Monetary Fund: Retrospective and Prospect.* New York: St. Martin's, 1964.

Horsefield, J. Keith, ed. *The International Monetary Fund, 1945–65: Twenty Years of International Monetary Cooperation.* 3 vols. Washington, D.C.: International Monetary Fund, 1969.

International Monetary Fund. *International Monetary Reform: Documents of the Committee of Twenty.* Washington, D.C.: International Monetary Fund, 1974.

——. *Proposed Second Amendment to the Articles of Agreement of the International Monetary Fund: A Report by the Executive Directors of the Board of Governors.* Washington, D.C.: International Monetary Fund, March 1976.

Krause, Lawrence B. and Walter S. Salant, eds. *European Monetary Unification and Its Meaning for the United States.* Washington, D.C.: The Brookings Institution, 1973.

Machlup, Fritz. *Remaking the International Monetary System: The Rio Agreement and Beyond.* Baltimore, Md.: Johns Hopkins Press, 1968.

Meade, James E. "The Case for Variable Exchange Rates." *The Three Banks Review,* 27 (September 1955), 3–27.

Park, Y. S. *The Link Between Special Drawing Rights and Development Finance.* Princeton, N.J.: International Finance Section, Department of Economics, Princeton Univ., 1973.

Rolfe, Sidney E. *Gold and World Power: The Dollar, the Pound and the Plans for Reform.* New York: Harper & Row, 1966.

——, and James Burtle. *The Great Wheel: The World Monetary System.* New York: Quadrangle, 1973.

Russell, Robert W. "Transgovernmental Interaction in the International Monetary System, 1960–1972." *International Organization,* 27 (Autumn 1973), 431–464.

Salant, Walter S. et al. *The United States Balance of Payments in 1968.* Washington, D.C.: The Brookings Institution, 1963.

The Smithsonian Agreement and Its Aftermath: Several Views. New York: Council on Foreign Relations, 1972.

Stabler, Elizabeth. "The Dollar Devaluation of 1971 and 1973." *U.S. Commission of the Organization of the Government for the Conduct of Foreign Policy, Appendix.* Vol. 3. Washington, D.C.: G.P.O., 1976.

Strange, Susan. "The Dollar Crisis 1971." *International Affairs,* 48 (April 1972), 191–215.

International Monetary Relations, in Shonfield, Andrew, ed. *International Economic Relations of the Western World 1959–1971.* Vol. 2. London: Oxford Univ. Press, 1976.

——. *Sterling and British Policy: A Political Study of an International Currency in Decline.* New York: Oxford Univ. Press, 1971.

Triffin, Robert. *Europe and the Money Muddle: From Bilateralism to Near Convertibility, 1947–1956.* New Haven, Conn.: Yale Univ. Press, 1957.

——. *Evolution of the International Monetary System: Historical Reappraisal and Future Perspectives.* Princeton, N.J.: International Finance Section, Department of Economics, Princeton University, 1964.

——. *Gold and the Dollar Crisis: The Future of Convertibility.* New Haven, Conn.: Yale Univ. Press, 1960.

————. *Our International Monetary System: Yesterday, Today and Tomorrow.* New York: Random House, 1968.

Yeager, Leland B. *International Monetary Relations: Theory, History, and Policy.* New York: Harper & Row, 1966.

Trade Among Developed Market Economies

Andrews, Stanley. *Agriculture and the Common Market.* Ames, Iowa: Iowa State Univ. Press, 1973.

Balassa, Bela. *Trade Liberalization Among Industrial Countries: Objectives and Alternatives.* New York: McGraw-Hill, 1967.

Baldwin, Robert E. *Non-Tariff Distortions of International Trade.* Washington, D.C.: The Brookings Institution, 1970.

Bauer, Raymond A., Ithiel de Sola Pool, and Lewis Anthony Dexter. *American Business and Public Policy: The Politics of Foreign Trade.* Chicago: Aldine, Atherton, 1972.

Bergsten, C. Fred. *Completing the GATT: Towards New International Rules to Govern Export Controls.* Washington, D.C.: British North-American Committee, 1974.

————. ed. *Toward a New World Trade Policy: The Maidenhead Papers.* Washington, D.C.: The Brookings Institution, 1974.

Brown, Williams Adams, Jr. *The United States and the Restoration of World Trade: An Analysis and Appraisal of the ITO Charter and the General Agreement on Tariffs and Trade.* Washington, D.C.: The Brookings Institution, 1950.

Cohen, Jerome B., ed. *Pacific Partnerships: United States-Japan Trade: Prospects and Recommendations for the Seventies.* Lexington, Mass.: Lexington Books, 1972.

Curtis, Thomas B. and John R. Vastine Jr. *The Kennedy Round: The Future of American Trade.* New York: Praeger, 1971.

Curzon, Gerard. *Multilateral Commercial Diplomacy: The General Agreements on Tariffs and Trade and its Impact on National Commercial Policies and Techniques.* London: Michael Joseph, 1965.

Dam, Kenneth W. *The GATT: Law and International Economic Organization.* Chicago: Univ. of Chicago Press, 1970.

Dell, Sidney S. *Trade Blocs and Common Markets*, 1st Am. ed. New York: Knopf, 1963.

Diebold, William, Jr. *The End of the I.T.O.* Princeton, N.J.: International Finance Section, Department of Economics and Social Institutions, Princeton University, 1952.

Evans, John W. *The Kennedy Round in American Trade Policy: The Twilight of the GATT?* Cambridge, Mass.: Harvard Univ. Press, 1971.

Hunsberger, Warren S. *Japan and the United States in World Trade.* New York: Harper & Row, 1964.

Johnson, D. Gale. *World Agriculture in Disarray.* London: Macmillan, 1973.

————, and John A. Schnittker. *U.S. Agriculture in a World Context: Policies and Approaches in the Next Decade.* New York: Praeger, 1974.

Kock, Karin. *International Trade Policy in the GATT, 1947–67.* Stockholm: Almquist and Wiksell, 1969.

Marks, Matthew J., and Harald B. Malmgren. "Negotiating Nontariff Distortions to Trade." *Law and Policy in International Business*, 7 (Spring 1975), 327–411.

Metzger, Stanley D. *Lowering Nontariff Barriers: U.S. Law, Practice and Negotiating Objectives.* Washington, D.C.: The Brookings Institution, 1974.

Organization for Economic Cooperation and Development. *Agricultural Policy of the European Economic Community.* Paris: Organization for Economic Cooperation and Development, 1974.

———. *Policy Perspectives for International Trade and Economic Relations.* Paris: Organization for Economic Cooperation and Development, 1972.

Ozaki, Robert S. *The Control of Imports and Foreign Capital in Japan.* New York: Praeger, 1972.

Patterson, Gardner. *Discrimination in International Trade: The Policy Issues, 1945–65.* Princeton, N.J.: Princeton Univ. Press, 1966.

Penrose, E. F. *Economic Planning for the Peace.* Princeton, N.J.: Princeton Univ. Press, 1953.

Preeg, Ernest H. *Traders and Diplomats: An Analysis of the Kennedy Round Negotiations under the General Agreement on Tariffs and Trade.* Washington, D.C.: The Brookings Institution, 1970.

Russell, Robert W. "Political Distortions in Trade Negotiations among Industrialized Countries," in *Prospects for Eliminating Non-Tariff Distortions of International Trade.* Anthony E. Scaperlanda, ed. Leiden, Netherlands: A. W. Sijthoff, 1973.

Schattschneider, E. E. *Politics, Pressures and the Tariff.* Englewood Cliffs, N.J.: Prentice-Hall, 1935.

Shonfield, Andrew. *International Economic Relations of the Western World, 1959–1971.* Vol. 1: *Politics and Trade.* London: Oxford Univ. Press, 1976.

"The Trade Act of 1971: A Fundamental Change in United States Foreign Trade Policy." *Yale Law Journal*, 80 (June 1971), 1418–1455.

Wilcox, Clair. *A Charter for World Trade.* New York: Macmillan, 1949.

The Multinational Corporation in Developed Market Economies

Ball, George W. "Cosmocorp: The Importance of Being Stateless." *Columbia Journal of World Business*, 2 (November–December 1967), pp. 25–30.

Barnet, Richard J. and Ronald E. Müller. *The Global Reach: The Power of the Multinational Corporations.* New York: Simon and Schuster, 1974.

Behrman, Jack N. *National Interests and the Multinational Enterprise: Tensions Among the North Atlantic Countries.* Englewood Cliffs, N.J.: Prentice-Hall, 1970.

———. *U.S. International Business and Governments.* New York: McGraw-Hill, 1971.

Bergsten, C. Fred. "Coming Investment Wars?" *Foreign Affairs*, 53 (October 1974), 135–152.

Boddewyn, Jean J. "Western European Policies Towards U.S. Investors." *The Bulletin*, 93–95 (March 1974), 45–63.

Brash, Donald T. *American Investment in Australian Industry.* Cambridge, Mass.: Harvard Univ. Press, 1966.

Canada. *Foreign Direct Investment in Canada.* Ottawa: Information Canada, 1972.

————. Task Force on the Structure of Canadian Industry. *Foreign Ownership and the Structure of Canadian Industry.* Ottawa: Queen's Printer, 1968.

Conference on the Regulation of Transnational Corporations. February 26, 1976. New York: Columbia Journal of Transnational Law Association, 1976.

Cox, Robert W. "Labor and the Multinationals." *Foreign Affairs,* 54 (January 1976), 344–365.

Dunning, John H. *The Role of American Investment in the British Economy.* London: Political and Economic Planning, 1969.

————, ed. *The Multinational Enterprise.* London: Allen & Unwin, 1971.

Fayerweather, John. "Elite Attitudes Toward Multinational Firms: A Study of Britain, Canada, and France." *International Studies Quarterly,* 16 (December 1972), 472–490.

————. *Foreign Investment in Canada: Prospects for National Policy.* White Plains, N.Y.: International Arts and Sciences Press, 1973.

————. "International Transmission of Resources," in John Fayerweather, ed., *International Business Management: A Conceptual Framework,* New York: McGraw-Hill, 1969.

Feld, Werner. *Nongovernmental Forces and World Politics: A Study of Business, Labor, and Political Groups.* New York: Praeger, 1972.

Gervais, Jacques. *La France face aux investissements etrangers: Analyse par secteurs.* Paris: Éditions de l'Entreprise Moderne, 1963.

Gilpin, Robert. *U.S. Power and the Multinational Corporation: The Political Economy of Foreign Direct Investment.* New York: Basic, 1975.

Goldberg, Paul M., and Charles P. Kindleberger. "Toward a GATT for Investment: A Proposal for Supervision of the International Corporation." *Law and Policy in International Business,* 2 (Summer 1970), 295–323.

Huntington, Samuel P. "Transnational Organizations in World Politics." *World Politics,* 25 (April 1973), 333–368.

Hymer, Stephen. "The Efficiency (Contradictions) of Multinational Corporations." *American Economic Review,* 60 (May 1970), 441–448.

————. "The International Operation of National Firms: A Study of Direct Foreign Investment." Ph.D. dissertation. Cambridge, Mass.: Massachusetts Institute of Technology, 1960.

International Studies Quarterly, 16 (December 1972).

Johnstone, Allan W. *U.S. Direct Investment in France: An Investigation of French Charges.* Cambridge, Mass.: M.I.T. Press, 1965.

Kapoor, Ashok, and Phillip Grub, eds. *The Multinational Enterprise in Transition.* Princeton, N.J.: Darwin Press, 1972.

Kindleberger, Charles P. *American Business Abroad: Six Lectures on Direct Investment.* New Haven, Conn.: Yale Univ. Press, 1969.

————. *The International Corporation: A Symposium.* Cambridge, Mass.: M.I.T. Press, 1970.

Layton, Christopher. *Trans-Atlantic Investments.* Boulogne-sur-Seine, France: Atlantic Institute, 1968.

Levitt, Kari. *Silent Surrender: The Multinational Corporation in Canada.* New York: St. Martin's, 1970.

Litrak, Isaiah A., and Christopher J. Maule, eds. *Foreign Investment: The Experience of Host Countries.* New York: Praeger, 1970.

Mandel, Ernest. *Europe vs. America: Contradictions of Imperialism.* New York: Monthly Review, 1970.

Organization for Economic Cooperation and Development. *International Investment and Multinational Enterprises.* Paris: Organization for Economic Cooperation and Development, 1976.

Ray, Dennis M. "Corporations and American Foreign Relations." The American Academy of Political and Social Sciences, *The Annals,* 403 (September 1972), 80–92.

Robbins, Sidney M., and Robert E. Stobaugh. *Money in the Multinational Enterprise: A Study in Financial Policy.* New York: Basic, 1973.

Robock, Stefan H., and Kenneth Simmonds. *International Business and Multinational Enterprises.* Homewood, Ill.: Irwin, 1973.

Rolfe, Sidney, E., and Walter Damm, eds. *The Multinational Corporation in the World Economy: Direct Investment in Perspective.* New York: Praeger, 1970.

Rubin, Seymour J. "Developments in the Law and Institutions of International Economic Relations: The Multinational Enterprise at Bay." *The American Journal of International Law,* 68 (July 1974), pp. 475–488.

Safarian, A. E. *Foreign Ownership of Canadian Industry.* Toronto: McGraw-Hill of Canada, 1966.

Servan-Schreiber, Jean-Jacques. *The American Challenge,* Ronald Steel, trans. New York: Atheneum, 1968.

Sorenson, Theodore C. "Improper Payments Abroad: Perspectives and Proposals." *Foreign Affairs,* 54 (July 1976), 719–733.

Stopford, John M., and Louis T. Wells, Jr. *Managing the Multinational Enterprise: Organization of the Term and Ownership of the Subsidiaries.* New York: Basic, 1972.

Torem, Charles, and William Lawrence Craig. "Development in the Control of Foreign Investment in France." *Michigan Law Review* 70 (December 1971), 285–336.

Tugendhat, Christopher. *The Multinationals.* London: Eyre & Spottiswoode, 1971.

Turner, Louis. *Invisible Empires: Multinational Companies and the Modern World.* New York: Harcourt Brace Jovanovich, 1970.

United Nations. *Multinational Corporations in World Development.* New York: United Nations, 1973.

———. *Report of the Group of Eminent Persons to Study the Impact of Multinational Corporations on Development and on International Relations.* New York: United Nations, 1974.

U.S. Department of Commerce. *United States Direct Investment Abroad.* 1966, Washington, D.C.: G.P.O., 1970.

U.S. Senate Committee on Foreign Relations. *Multinational Corporations and United States Foreign Policy.* Hearings Before the Subcommittee on Multinational Corporations of the Committee on Foreign Relations, 93rd and 94th Congresses, 1973–1976.

U.S. Tariff Commission. *Implications of Multinational Firms for World Trade and Investment and for U.S. Trade and Labor*. Washington, D.C.: G.P.O., 1973.

Vaupel, James W., and Joan P. Curham. *The Making of a Multinational Enterprise*. Cambridge, Mass.: Graduate School of Business Administration, Harvard Univ., 1969.

Vernon, Raymond, ed. *Big Business and the State: Changing Relations in West Europe*. Cambridge, Mass.: Harvard Univ. Press, 1974.

————. "Multinational Enterprise and National Security." *Adelphi Papers*, no. 74. London: Institute for Strategic Studies, 1971.

————. *Sovereignty at Bay: The Multinational Spread of U.S. Enterprises*. New York: Basic, 1971.

————, ed. *The Economic and Political Consequences of Multinational Enterprise: An Anthology*. Cambridge, Mass.: Graduate School of Business Administration, Harvard Univ., 1972.

Wilkins, Mira. *The Emergence of Multinational Enterprise: American Business Abroad from the Colonial Era to 1914*. Cambridge, Mass.: Harvard Univ. Press, 1970.

————. *The Maturing of the Multinational Enterprise: American Business Abroad from 1914 to 1970*. Cambridge, Mass.: Harvard Univ. Press, 1974

THE NORTH–SOUTH SYSTEM

General and Theory

Alpert, Paul. *Partnership or Confrontation*. New York: Free Press, 1973.

Amin, Samir. *L'Accumulation à l'échelle mondiale*. Paris: IFAN, 1970.

Baran, Paul A. *The Political Economy of Growth*. New York: Monthly Review, 1957.

Barratt-Brown, Michael. *After Imperialism*, rev. ed. New York: Humanities Press, 1970.

Bauer, Peter D. *Dissent on Development: Studies and Debates on Development Economics*. Cambridge, Mass.: Harvard Univ. Press, 1972.

Boulding, Kenneth, and Tapan Mukerjee, eds. *Economic Imperialism: A Book of Readings*. Ann Arbor, Mich.: Univ. of Michigan Press, 1972.

Cockcroft, James D., André Gunder Frank, and Dale L. Johnson. *Dependence and Underdevelopment: Latin America's Political Economy*. Garden City, N.Y.: Anchor, 1972.

Cohen, Benjamin J. *The Question of Imperialism: The Political Economy of Dominance and Dependence*. New York: Basic, 1973.

Dos Santos, Theotonio. "The Structure of Dependence," in K. T. Fann and D. C. Hodges, eds., *Readings in U.S. Imperialism*. Boston: Sargent, 1971.

Emmanuel, Arghiri. *Unequal Exchange: A Study of the Imperialism of Trade*. New York: Monthly Review, 1972.

Erb, Guy F., and Valeriana Kallab, eds. *Beyond Dependence: The Developing World Speaks Out*. New York: Praeger, 1975.

Fann, K. T., and D. C. Hodges. *Readings in U.S. Imperialism*. Boston: Sargent, 1971.

Frank, André Gunder. *Capitalism and Underdevelopment in Latin America: Historical Studies of Chile and Brazil*, rev. ed. New York: Monthly Review, 1969.

———. Latin America: *Underdevelopment or Revolution*. New York: Monthly Review, 1969.

Furtado, Celso. *Diagnosis of the Brazilian Crisis*, Suzette Macedo, trans. Berkeley, Calif.: Univ. of California Press, 1965.

———. *Economic Development of Latin America*. London: Cambridge Univ. Press, 1970.

———. *The Obstacles to Development in Latin America*, Charles Ekker, trans. Garden City, N.Y.: Anchor, 1970.

Galtung, J. "A Structural Theory of Imperialism." *Journal of Peace Research*, 2 (1971), 81–117.

Hansen, Roger D. "The Political Economy of North–South Relations: How Much Change?" *International Organization*, 29 (Autumn 1975), 922–947.

Hirschman, Albert O. *The Strategy of Economic Development*. New Haven: Yale Univ. Press, 1958.

Hughes, Helen, ed. *Prospects for Partnership: Industrialization and Trade Policies in the 1970s*. Baltimore, Md.: Johns Hopkins Press, 1973.

Jalée, Pierre. *Imperialism in the Seventies*, Raymond and Margaret Sokolov, trans. New York: Third World, 1972.

———. *The Pillage of the Third World*, Mary Klopper, trans. New York: Monthly Review, 1968.

———. *The Third World in the World Economy*. Mary Klopper, trans. New York: Monthly Review, 1969.

Johnson, Harry G. *Economic Policies Toward Less-Developed Countries*. New York: Praeger, 1967.

Lichtheim, George. *Imperialism*. New York: Praeger, 1971.

MacEwan, Arthur. "Capitalist Expansion, Ideology and Intervention." *Review of Radical Political Economics*, 4 (Spring 1972), 36–58.

Meier, Gerald M. *Leading Issues in Economic Development: Studies in International Poverty*, 2nd ed. New York: Oxford Univ. Press, 1970.

Miller, S. M., Roy Bennett, and Cyril Alapatt. "Does the U.S. Economy Require Imperialism?" *Social Policy*, 1 (September–October, 1970), 12–19.

Moran, Theodore H. "Foreign Expansion as an 'Institutional Necessity' for U.S. Corporate Capitalism: The Search for a Radical Model." *World Politics*, 25 (April 1973), 369–386.

Myint, Hla. *Economic Theory and the Underdeveloped Countries*. London: Oxford Univ. Press, 1971.

Myrdal, Gunnar. *An International Economy: Problems and Prospects*. New York: Harper & Row, 1956.

———. *Rich Lands and Poor: The Road to World Prosperity*. New York: Harper & Row, 1957.

Nkrumah, K. *Neo-Colonialism: The Last Stage of Imperialism*. New York: International Publishers, 1966.

Nurkse Ragnar. *Equilibrium and Growth in the World Economy: Economic Essays.* Cambridge, Mass.: Harvard Univ. Press, 1961.

———. *Problems of Capital Formation for Underdeveloped Countries.* New York: Oxford Univ. Press, 1953.

O'Connor, James. "The Meaning of Economic Imperialism," in Robert I. Rhodes, ed., *Imperialism and Underdevelopment: A Reader.* New York: Monthly Review, 1970, pp. 101–150.

Overseas Development Council. *The United States and the Developing World: Agenda for Action 1973.* Washington, D.C.: Overseas Development Council, 1973.

———. *The U.S. and the Developing World: Agenda for Action 1974.* New York, Praeger, 1974.

———. *The U.S. and World Development: Agenda for Action 1975.* New York: Praeger, 1975.

———. *The U.S. and World Development: Agenda for Action 1976.* New York: Praeger, 1976.

Pearson, Lester B. *Partners in Development: Report of the Commission on International Development.* New York: Praeger, 1969.

Pincus, John. *Trade, Aid and Development: The Rich and Poor Nations.* New York: McGraw-Hill, 1967.

Ranis, Gustave, ed. *The Gap Between Rich and Poor Nations.* New York: St. Martin's, 1972.

Review of Radical Political Economy, "Dependence and Foreign Domination," 4 (Winter 1972), entire volume.

Rhodes, Robert I. *Imperialism and Underdevelopment: A Reader.* New York: Monthly Review, 1970.

Rodney, Walter S. *How Europe Underdeveloped Africa.* Washington, D.C.: Howard Univ. Press, 1974.

Rosen, Steven J., and James R. Kurth, eds. *Testing Theories of Economic Imperialism.* Lexington, Mass.: Lexington, 1974.

Schumpeter, Joseph A. *Imperialism and Social Classes.* N.Y.: Meridian. 1951.

Seers, Dudley, and Leonard Joy. *Development in a Divided World.* Harmondsworth, Eng.: Penguin, 1971.

Singer, H. W. *International Development: Growth and Change.* New York: McGraw-Hill, 1964.

Singer, Marshall. *Weak States in a World of Power: The Dynamics of International Relationships.* New York: Free Press, 1972.

Spiegel, Steven L. *Dominance and Diversity: The International Hierarchy.* Boston: Little, Brown, 1972.

Sunkel, Osvaldo. "Big Business and Dependence: A Latin American View." *Foreign Affairs,* 50 (April 1972), 517–532.

———. "National Development Policy and External Dependence in Latin America." *Journal of Development Studies,* 6 (October 1969), 23–48.

Sweezy, Paul M. *Modern Capitalism and Other Essays.* New York: Monthly Review, 1972.

Wallerstein, Immanuel. "Dependence in an Interdependent World." *African Studies Review,* 17 (April 1974), 1–26.

Ward, Barbara, Lenore d'Anjou, and J. D. Runnalls, eds. *The Widening Gap: Development in the 1970's.* New York: Columbia Univ. Press, 1971.

Weisskopf, Thomas E. "Theories of American Imperialism: A Critical Evaluation." *Review of Radical Political Economics,* 6 (Fall 1974), 41–60.

Aid

Adelman, Irma, ed. *Practical Approaches to Development Planning: Korea's Second Five-Year Plan.* Baltimore, Md.: Johns Hopkins Press, 1969.

Baldwin, David A. *Economic Development in American Foreign Policy, 1943–1962.* Chicago: Univ. of Chicago Press, 1966.

Bhagwati, Jagdish, and Richard S. Eckans, eds. *Foreign Aid.* Harmondsworth, Eng.: Penguin, 1970.

Bitterman, Henry J. "Negotiation of the Bank for Reconstruction and Development." *The International Lawyer,* 5 (January 1971), 59–88.

Brecher, Irving, and S. A. Abbas. *Foreign Aid and Industrial Development in Pakistan.* Cambridge, Mass.: Harvard Univ. Press, 1972.

Friedman, Milton. "Foreign Economic Aid: Means and Objectives," in Gustave Ranis, ed., *The United States and the Developing Economies.* New York: Norton, 1964.

Gardner, Richard N., and Max F. Millikan, eds. *The Global Partnership: International Agencies and Economic Development.* New York: Praeger, 1968.

Goldman, Marshall I. *Soviet Foreign Aid.* New York: Praeger, 1967.

Goulet, Denis, and Michael Hudson. *The Myth of Aid: The Hidden Agenda of the Development Reports.* New York: International Documentation North America, 1971.

Hadwen, John G., and Johan Kaufman. *How United Nations Decisions Are Made.* Dobbs Ferry, N.Y.: Oceana Publications, 1962.

Hansen, Roger D. *Mexican Economic Development: The Roots of Rapid Growth.* Washington, D.C.: National Planning Association, 1971.

Hayter, Teresa. *Aid as Imperialism.* Middlesex, Eng.: Penguin, 1971.

————. *French Aid.* London: Overseas Development Institute, 1966.

Huntington, Samuel P. "Does Foreign Aid Have a Future?" *Foreign Policy,* 2 (Spring 1971), 114–134.

————. *Political Order in Changing Societies.* New Haven, Conn.: Yale Univ. Press, 1968.

————. "Foreign Aid for What and for Whom." *Foreign Policy,* 1 (Winter 1970–1971), 161–189.

Jacoby, Neil H. *U.S. Aid to Taiwan.* New York: Praeger, 1966.

Levinson, Jerome, and Juan de Onis. *The Alliance that Lost its Way: A Critical Report on the Alliance for Progress.* New York: Quadrangle, 1970.

Little, I. D., and J. M. Clifford. *International Aid: A Discussion of the Flow of Public Resources from Rich to Poor Countries, with Particular Reference to British Policy.* London: Allen & Unwin, 1965.

Mason, Edward S., and Robert E. Asher. *The World Bank Since Bretton Woods.* Washington, D.C.: The Brookings Institution, 1973.

Mende, Tibor. *From Aid to Re-colonization: Lessons of a Failure,* 1st Am. ed. New York: Pantheon, 1973.

Mikesell, Raymond F. *The Economics of Foreign Aid*. Chicago: Aldine, 1968.

Millikan, Max F., and W. W. Rostow. *A Proposal: Key to an Effective Foreign Policy*. New York: Harper & Row, 1957.

Montgomery, John D. *The Politics of Foreign Aid: American Experience in Southeast Asia*. New York: Praeger, 1962.

Nelson, Joan M. *Aid, Influence and Foreign Policy*. New York: Macmillan, 1968.

Ohlin, Goran. *Foreign Aid Policies Reconsidered*. Paris: Organization for Economic Cooperation and Development, 1966.

Packenham, R. A. *Liberal America and the Third World: Political Development Ideas in Foreign Aid and Social Science*. Princeton, N.J.: Princeton Univ. Press, 1973.

Papanek, Gustav F. *Pakistan and Development: Social Goals and Private Incentive*. Cambridge, Mass.: Harvard Univ. Press, 1967.

Park, Y. S. *The Link Between Special Drawing Rights and Development Finance*. Princeton, N.J.: International Finance Section, Department of Economics, Princeton Univ., September 1973.

Pearson, Lester B. *Partners in Development: Report of the Commission on International Development*. New York: Praeger, 1969.

Rubin, Seymour J. *The Conscience of the Rich Nations: The Development Assistance Committee and the Common Aid Effort*. N.Y.: Harper & Row, 1966.

Spero, Joan Edelman. "France and Francophone Africa: The Study of A Dependency Relationship." Ph.D. Dissertation. Columbia University, 1973.

Sunderson, Fred H. *The Great Food Fumble*. Washington, D.C.: The Brookings Institution, 1975.

United Nations Conference on Trade and Development. *Debt Problems of Developing Countries, Report*. New York: United Nations, 1972.

United Nations Special Fund. *The United Nations Special Fund. An Explanatory Paper by the Managing Director*. New York: United Nations, 1959.

U.S. Senate. *Foreign Aid Program, 1957*. 85th Congress, 1st Sess. Washington, D.C.: G.P.O., 1957.

Veit, Lawrence. *India's Second Revolution: The Dimensions of Development*. New York: McGraw-Hill, 1976.

Wall, David. *The Charity of Nations: The Political Economy of Foreign Aid*. New York: Basic, 1973.

Walters, Robert S. *American and Soviet Aid: A Comparative Analysis*. Pittsburgh, Pa.: Univ. of Pittsburgh Press, 1970.

White, John A. *The Politics of Foreign Aid*. New York: St. Martin's, 1974.

Williams, Maurice J. "The Aid Programs of the OPEC Countries." *Foreign Affairs*, 54 (January 1976), 317–318, 322.

Wriggins, Howard. "Political Outcomes of Foreign Assistance: Influence, Involvement, or Intervention?" *Journal of International Affairs*, 22 (1968), 217–230.

Trade

Balassa, Bela. "Trade Policies in Developing Countries." *American Economic Review*, 61 (May 1971), 178–210.

Campos, Roberto de Oliveiro, et al. *Trends in International Trade: A Report by a*

Panel of Experts. Haberler report. Geneva: The Contracting Parties to the General Agreement on Tariffs and Trade, October 1958.

Cordovez, Diego. "The Making of UNCTAD: Institutional Background and Legislative History." *Journal of World Trade Law*, 1 (May–June 1967), 243–328.

———. *UNCTAD and Development Diplomacy: From Confrontation to Strategy.* Twickenham, Eng.: Journal of World Trade Law, 1970.

DeVries, Margaret G. *Export Experience of Developing Countries.* Washington, D.C.: International Bank for Reconstruction and Development, 1967.

Friedeberg, A. S. *The United Nations Conference on Trade and Development of 1964: The Theory of the Peripheral Economy.* Rotterdam: Rotterdam Univ. Press, 1969.

Gosovic, Branislav. *UNCTAD, Conflict and Compromise: The Third World's Quest for an Equitable World Economic Order Through the United Nations.* Leiden, Netherlands: A. W. Sijthoff-Leiden, 1972.

Gruhn, Isebill V. "The Lomé Convention: Inching Towards Interdependence." *International Organization*, 30 (Spring 1976), 240–262.

Haberler, Gottfried. *International Trade and Economic Development.* Cairo: National Bank of Egypt, 1959.

Hansen, Roger D. "The Crisis of Interdependence: Where Do Wc Go From Here?," in Roger D. Hansen, ed., *The U.S. and World Development: Agenda for Action 1976.* Washington, D.C.: Overseas Development Council, 1976.

Knorr, Klaus. "The Limits of Economic and Military Power." *Daedalus*, 4 (Fall 1975), 229–243.

Levin, Jonathan V. *The Export Economies: Their Pattern of Development in Historical Perspective.* Cambridge, Mass.: Harvard Univ. Press, 1964.

Linden, Steffan B. "The Significance of GATT for Underdeveloped Countries." *Proceedings of the United Nations Conference on Trade and Development*, 5 (1964), 502–532.

Little, Ian, Tibor Scitovsky, and Maurice Scott. *Industry and Trade in Some Developing Countries: A Comparative Study.* London: Oxford Univ. Press, 1970.

"Lomé Dossier." *The Courier*, spec. issue 31, (March 1975).

Maizels, Alfred. *Exports and Economic Growth of Developing Countries: A Theoretical and Empirical Study of the Relationship Between Exports and Economic Growth.* London: Cambridge Univ. Press, 1968.

Malmgren, H. B. *Trade and Investment Relations Between Developed and Developing Nations: A Review of the State of Knowledge.* Washington, D.C.: Overseas Development Council, 1971.

———. *Trade for Development.* Washington, D.C.: Overseas Development Council, 1971.

Meadows, Donella H., et al. *The Limits to Growth: A Report for the Club of Rome's Project on the Predicament of Mankind.* New York: Universe, 1972.

Meier, Gerald M. *International Trade and Development.* New York: Harper & Row, 1963.

Meltzer, Ronald I. "The Politics of Policy Reversal: The American Response to the Issue of Granting Trade Preferences to the Developing Countries, 1964–1967." Ph.D. Dissertation. Columbia University, 1975.

Myint, Hla. "The Gains from International Trade and the Backward Country." *Review of Economic Studies*, 22 (1954–1955); 129–142.

Nurkse, Ragnar. *Patterns of Trade and Development*. New York: Oxford Univ. Press, 1961.

Pincus, J. A. *Trade, Aid and Development: The Rich and Poor Nations*. New York: McGraw-Hill, 1967.

Prebisch, Raúl. "The Role of Commercial Policies in Underdeveloped Countries." *American Economic Review, Papers and Proceedings*, 49 (May 1959), 251–273.

Roessler, Frieder. "GATT and Access to Supplies." *Journal of World Trade Law*, 9 (January/February 1975), 25–40.

Streeten, Paul, ed. *Trade Strategies for Development: Papers of the Ninth Cambridge Conference on Development Problems, September 1972*. New York: Wiley, 1973.

United Nations Conference on Trade and Development. *The Kennedy Round Estimated effects on Tariff Barriers: Report by the Secretary General of UNCTAD*. Part I and II. New York: United Nations, 1968.

———. *Toward a New Trade Policy for Development*. New York: United Nations, 1964.

Walters, Robert S. "International Organizations and Political Communication: The Use of UNCTAD by the Less Developed Countries." *International Organization*, 25 (Autumn 1971), 818–835.

Weintraub, Sidney. *Trade Preferences for Less-Developed Countries: An Analysis of United States Policy*. New York: Praeger, 1966.

Wells, Sidney. "The Developing Countries, GATT, and UNCTAD." *International Affairs*, 45 (January 1969), 64–79.

Foreign Investment in Less Developed Countries

Behrman, John N. *The Role of International Companies in Latin American Integration: Automobiles and Petrochemicals*. Lexington, Mass.: Lexington, 1972.

Belli, R. David. "Sources and Uses of Funds of Foreign Affiliates of U.S. Firms, 1967–68." *Survey of Current Business*, (November 1970), pp. 14–19.

Chudson, Walter A. *The International Transfer of Commercial Technology to Developing Countries*. New York: United Nations Institute for Training and Research, 1971.

Furnish, Dale B. "The Andean Common Market's Common Regime for Foreign Investments." *Vanderbilt Journal of Transnational Law*, 5 (Spring 1972), 313–339.

Goodsell, Charles T. *American Corporations and Peruvian Politics*. Cambridge, Mass.: Harvard Univ. Press, 1974.

Hirschman, A. O. "How to Divest in Latin America and Why." Essays in International Finance, 74. Princeton, N.J.: International Finance Section, Department of Economics, Princeton Univ., 1969.

Holland, Susan S., and Esteban A. Ferrer, eds. *Changing Legal Environment in Latin America: Management Implications*. New York: Council of the Americas, 1974.

Hymer, Stephen. "The Multinational Corporation and the Law of Uneven

Development," in Jagdish N. Bhagwati, ed., *Economics and World Order: From the 1970s to the 1990s.* New York: Macmillan, 1972.

International Labor Organization. *Multinational Enterprises and Social Policy.* Geneva: International Labor Organization, 1973.

Johnson, Harry. "A Theoretical Model of Economic Nationalism in New and Developing States." *The Political Science Quarterly,* 80 (June 1965), 169–185.

Lacey, Frank M., and Lic. Maclovio Sierra de la Garza. "Mexico—Are the Rules Really Changing?" *International Lawyer,* 10 (Summer 1976), 560–588.

May, Herbert K. *The Effects of United States and Other Foreign Investment in Latin America.* New York: Council of the Americas, 1970.

Mikesell, Raymond F., William H. Bartsch, et al. *Foreign Investment in the Petroleum and Mineral Industries: Case Studies of Investor-Host Country Relations.* Baltimore, Md.: Johns Hopkins Press, 1971.

Moran, Theodore H. "The Evolution of Concession Agreements in Underdeveloped Countries and the United States National Interest." reprint 289. Washington, D.C.: The Brookings Institution, 1974.

———. *Multinational Corporations and the Politics of Dependence: Copper in Chile.* Princeton, N.J.: Princeton Univ. Press, 1974.

Müller, Ronald. "Poverty Is the Product." *Foreign Policy,* 13 (Winter 1973–1974), 71–102.

O'Connor, James. "International Corporations and Economic Underdevelopment." *Science and Society,* 34 (Spring 1970), 42–60.

Organization for Economic Cooperation and Development. *Stock of Private Investment by Member Countries of the Development Assistance Committee in Developing Countries, End 1967.* Paris: Organization for Economic Cooperation and Development, 1972.

———. *Stock of Private Investment by Member Countries of the Development Assistance Committee in Developing Countries, End 1972.* Paris: Organization for Economic Cooperation and Development, 1974.

Penrose, Edith. "International Economic Relations and the Large International Firm," in Ernest F. Penrose and Peter Lyon, eds., *New Orientations: Essays in International Relations.* London: Cass, 1970.

———. "The State and the Multinational Enterprise in Less-Developed Countries," in John H. Dunning, ed., *The Multinational Enterprise.* London: Allen & Unwin, 1971.

Piñelo, Adalberto J. *The Multinational Corporation as a Force in Latin American Politics: A Case Study of the International Petroleum Company in Peru.* New York: Praeger, 1973.

Reuber, Grant L. *Private Foreign Investment in Development.* Oxford: Clarendon, 1973.

Said, Abdul A., and Luiz R. Simmons, eds. *The New Sovereigns: Multinational Corporations as World Powers.* Englewood Cliffs, N.J.: Prentice-Hall, 1975.

Sampson, Anthony. *The Sovereign State of ITT.* New York: Stein & Day, 1973.

Singer, Hans W. "U.S. Foreign Investment in Underdeveloped Areas: The Distribution of Gains between Investing and Borrowing Countries." *American Economic Review,* 40 (May 1950), 473–485.

Sklar, Richard L. *Corporate Power in an African State: The Political Impact of*

Multinational Mining Companies in Zambia. Berkeley, Calif.: Univ. of California Press, 1975.

Turner, Louis. *Multinational Companies and the Third World.* New York: Hill and Wang, 1973.

United Nations. *Restrictive Business Practices: The Operations of Multinational U.S. Enterprises in Developing Countries, their Role in Trade and Development.* New York: United Nations, 1972.

――――. *The Role of Private Enterprise in Investment and Promotion of Exports in Developing Countries.* New York: United Nations, 1968.

――――. *Multinational Corporations in World Development.* New York: United Nations, 1973.

――――. *Report of the Group of Eminent Persons to Study the Impact of Multinational Corporations on Development and on International Relations.* New York: United Nations, 1974.

U.S. Senate. Committee on Foreign Relations, Subcommittee on Multinational Corporations. *Multinational Corporations in Brazil and Mexico: Structural Sources of Economic and Noneconomic Power.* Washington, D.C.: G.P.O., 1975.

Vaitsos, Constantine V. "Foreign Investment Policies and Economic Development in Latin America." *Journal of World Trade Law,* 7 (November–December 1973), 639.

――――. *Intercountry Income Distribution and Transnational Enterprises.* Oxford: Clarendon, 1974.

Vernon, Raymond. "Conflict and Resolution Between Foreign Direct Investors and Less Developed Countries." *Public Policy,* 17 (1968), 333–351.

――――. "Long-Run Trends in Concession Contracts." *Proceedings of the Sixty-First Annual Meeting of the American Society of International Law.* Washington, D.C., 1967.

Oil and Commodity Cartels

Adelman, M. A. "Is the Oil Shortage Real? Oil Companies and OPEC Tax Collectors." *Foreign Policy,* no. 9 (Winter 1972–1973).

――――. *The World Petroleum Market.* Baltimore, Md.: Johns Hopkins Press, 1972.

Alnasrawi, Abbas. "Collective Bargaining Power in OPEC." *Journal of World Trade Law,* 7 (March-April 1973), 188–207.

Bergsten, C. Fred. "The New Era in World Commodity Markets." *Challenge,* 17 (September–October 1974), 34–42.

――――. "The Threat from the Third World." *Foreign Policy,* 11 (Summer 1973), 102–124.

Clarfield, K. W., et al. *Eight Mineral Cartels.* New York: *Metals Week,* McGraw-Hill, 1975.

Connery, Robert H., and Robert S. Gilmour, eds. "The National Energy Problem." *Proceedings of the Academy of Political Science,* 31 (December 1973), entire volume.

Edwards, Anthony. *The Potential for New Commodity Cartels: Copying OPEC, or Improved International Agreements?* QER spec. issue 27. London: The Economist Intelligence Unit, September 1975.

Engler, Robert. *The Politics of Oil: Private Power and Democratic Directions.* Chicago: Univ. of Chicago Press, 1961.

Fried, Edward R, and Charles L. Schultze, eds. *Higher Oil Prices and the World Economy: The Adjustment Problem.* Washington, D.C.: The Brookings Institution, 1975.

Hartshorn, J. E. *Oil Companies and Governments*, 2nd rev. ed. London: Faber, 1967.

———. *Politics and World Oil Economics: An Account of the International Oil Industry in its Political Environment.* rev. ed. New York: Praeger, 1962, 1967.

Issawi, Charles P. *Oil, the Middle East, and the World.* New York: Library Press, 1972.

Issawi, Charles, and Mohammed Yeganeh. *The Economics of Middle Eastern Oil.* New York: Praeger, 1962.

Kohl, Wilfred L. "The United States, Western Europe and the Energy Problem." *Journal of International Affairs*, 30 (Spring/Summer 1976), pp. 81–96.

Krasner, Stephen D. "Oil Is the Exception." *Foreign Policy*, no. 14 (Spring 1974), 68–90.

Krueger, Robert B. *The United States and International Oil: A Report for the Federal Energy Administration on U.S. Firms and Government Policy.* New York: Praeger, 1975.

Lewis, J. P. "Oil, Other Scarcities, and the Poor Countries." *World Politics*, 27 (October 1974), 63–86.

Mikdashi, Zuhayr. *The Community of Oil Exporting Countries: A Study in Governmental Cooperation.* Ithaca, N.Y.: Cornell Univ. Press, 1972.

———. *A Financial Analysis of Middle Eastern Oil Concessions: 1901–1965.* New York: Praeger, 1966.

Mikesell, Raymond F. "More Third World Cartels Ahead?" *Challenge*, 17 (November–December 1974), 24–27.

Odell, Peter R. *Oil and World Power: A Geographical Interpretation.* Gloucester, Mass.: Peter Smith, 1970.

Penrose, Edith T. *The Large International Firm in Developing Countries: The International Petroleum Industry.* Cambridge, Mass.: M.I.T. Press, 1969.

Sampson, Anthony. *The Seven Sisters: The Great Oil Companies and the World They Made.* New York: Viking, 1975.

Shwadran, Benjamin. *The Middle East, Oil and the Great Powers.* New York: Praeger, 1955.

Spero, Joan Edelman. "Energy Self-Sufficiency and National Security," in Robert H. Connery and Robert S. Gilmour, eds., *The National Energy Problem: Proceedings of the Academy of Political Science*, 31 (December 1973), 123–136.

Szyliowicz, Joseph S., and Bard E. O'Neill, eds. *The Energy Crisis and U.S. Foreign Policy.* New York: Praeger, 1975.

Tanzer, Michael. *The Political Economy of International Oil and the Underdeveloped Countries.* Boston: Beacon, 1969.

Tilton, John E. "Cartels in Metal Industries." *Earth and Mineral Sciences*, 44 (March 1975), 41–44.

Tugwell, Franklin. *The Politics of Oil in Venezuela*. Stanford, Calif.: Stanford Univ. Press, 1975.

U.S. Council on International Economic Policy. *Special Report: Critical Imported Materials*. Washington, D.C.: G.P.O., 1974.

U.S. Federal Trade Commission. *International Petroleum Cartel*. Staff Report to the Federal Trade Commission, 82nd Congress, 2nd Sess. Washington, D.C.: G.P.O., 1952.

Wyman, Joseph C. *Perspective on Copper*. New York: The Research Group of Reynolds Securities, Inc., February 1975.

Yager, Joseph A., and Eleanor B. Steinbert, et al. *Energy and U.S. Foreign Policy: A Report to the Energy Policy Project of the Ford Foundation*. Cambridge, Mass.: Ballinger, 1974.

EAST–WEST ECONOMIC RELATIONS

Adler-Karlsson, Gunnar. *Western Economic Warfare, 1946–1967*. Stockholm: Amquist and Wiksell, 1968.

Altman, Oscar. "Russian Gold and the Ruble." International Monetary Fund *Staff Papers*, 8 (April 1960), 415–438.

Aubrey, Henry G., with the assistance of Joel Darmstadter. *Coexistence: Economic Challenge and Response*. Washington, D.C.: National Planning Association, 1961.

Brown, Alan A., and Egon Neuberger. *International Trade and Central Planning: An Analysis of Economic Interactions*. Berkeley, Calif.: Univ. of Calif. Press, 1968.

Brzezinski, Zbigniew. *Alternative to Partition: For a Broader Conception of America's Role in Europe*. New York: McGraw-Hill, 1965.

———. *The Soviet Bloc: Unity and Conflicts*, rev. ed. Cambridge, Mass.: Harvard Univ. Press, 1967.

Campbell, Robert W. *Soviet Economic Power: Its Organization, Growth, and Challenge*, 2nd ed. Boston: Houghton Mifflin, 1966.

Clabaugh, Samuel F., and Richard V. Allen. *East-West Trade: Its Strategic Implications*. Washington, D.C.: Georgetown Univ., Center for Strategic Studies, 1964.

———. *Trading with the Communists*. Washington, D.C.: Georgetown University Center for Strategic Studies, 1968.

Fallenbuch, Z. M. "Comecon Integration." *Problems of Communism*, 22 (March–April 1973), 25–39.

Gaddis, John Lewis. *The United States and the Origins of the Cold War, 1941–1947*. New York: Columbia Univ. Press, 1972.

Garvy, George. *Money, Banking and Credit in Eastern Europe*. New York: Federal Reserve Bank of New York, 1966.

Giffen, James H. *The Legal and Practical Aspects of Trade with the Soviet Union*. New York: Praeger, 1969.

Goldman, Marshall I. *Détente and Dollars: Doing Business with the Soviets*. New York: Basic, 1975.

Grub, Phillip D., and Karel Holbik, eds. *American-East European Trade: Controversy, Progress, Prospects*. Washington, D.C.: National Press, 1969.

Harvey, M. L. *East-West Trade and United States Policy.* New York: National Association of Manufacturers, 1966.

Holzman, Franklyn D. "Foreign Trade Behavior of Centrally Planned Economies," in Henry Rosovsky, ed., *Industrialization in Two Systems.* New York: Wiley, 1966.

———, and Robert Legvold. "The Economics and Politics of East-West Relations." *International Organization,* 29 (Winter 1975), 275–320.

Kaser, Michael. "Comecon's Commerce." *Problems of Communism,* 22 (July–August 1973), 1–15.

———. *Comecon: Integration Problems of the Planned Economies.* London: Oxford Univ. Press, 1965.

Kelleher, Catherine M., and Donald J. Puchala. "Germany, European Security, and Arms Control," in William T. R. Fox and Warner R. Schilling, eds., *European Security and the Atlantic System.* New York: Columbia Univ. Press, 1973.

Kolko, Joyce, and Gabriel Kolko. *The Limits of Power: The World and the United States Foreign Policy, 1945–1954.* New York: Harper & Row, 1972.

Korbonski, Andrzej. *Comecon.* New York: Carnegie Endowment for International Peace, 1964.

Kovner, Milton. *The Challenge of Coexistence: A Study of Soviet Economic Diplomacy.* Washington, D.C.: Public Affairs Press, 1961.

Kretschmar, R. S., and R. Foor. *The Potential for Joint Ventures in Eastern Europe.* New York: Praeger, 1972.

Malish, Anton F., Jr. "United States-East European Trade." *Staff Research Studies,* no. 4. Washington, D.C.: United States Tariff Commission, 1972.

Marer, Paul. "The Political Economy of Soviet Relations with Eastern Europe," in Steven J. Rosen and James R. Kurth, eds., *Testing Theories of Economic Imperialism.* Lexington, Mass.: Lexington, 1974.

McQuade, Lawrence C. "U.S. Trade with Eastern Europe: Its Prospects and Parameters." *Law and Policy in International Business,* 3 (1971), 42–100.

Mikesell, Raymond F. and Jack N. Behrman. *Financing Free World Trade with the Sino-Soviet Bloc.* Princeton, N.J.: International Finance Section, Department of Economics, Princeton Univ., 1958.

Nagorski, Zygmunt. *The Psychology of East-West Trade: Illusions and Opportunities.* New York: Mason & Lipscomb, 1974.

Peterson, Peter G. *U.S.-Soviet Commercial Relationships in a New Era.* Washington, D.C.: Department of Commerce, August 1972.

Pisar, Samuel. *Coexistence and Commerce: Guidelines for Transactions Between East and West.* New York: McGraw-Hill, 1970.

———, ed. *Conference on East-West Trade, Vienna, May 1969.* Brussels: Management Center Europe, 1970.

Prince, Charles. "The U.S.S.R.'s Role in International Finance." *Harvard Business Review,* 25 (Autumn 1946), 111–128.

Pryor, Frederick. *The Communist Foreign Trade System.* Cambridge, Mass.: M.I.T. Press, 1963.

Schaefer, H. W. *Comecon and the Politics of Integration.* New York: Praeger, 1972.

Schmitthoff, C. M., ed. *The Sources of the Law of International Trade, with Special Reference to East-West Trade.* New York: Praeger, 1964.

Spulber, Nicholas. *The Economics of Communist Eastern Europe.* New York: Wiley, 1957.

Stalin, Joseph. *Economic Problems of Socialism in the U.S.S.R.* New York: International, 1952.

Sutton, Antony C. *Western Technology and Soviet Economic Development, 1917 to 1930.* Stanford, Calif.: Hoover Institution on War, Revolution and Peace, 1968.

————. *Western Technology and Soviet Economic Development, 1930 to 1945.* Stanford, Calif.: Hoover Institution on War, Revolution and Peace, 1971.

————. *Western Technology and Soviet Economic Development, 1945–1965.* Stanford, Calif.: Hoover Institution on War, Revolution and Peace, 1973.

Ulam, Adam B. *Expansion and Coexistence: The History of Soviet Foreign Policy, 1917–1967.* New York· Praeger, 1968.

United Nations Economic Commission for Europe. *Analytic Report on Industrial Co-operation among ECE Countries.* Geneva: United Nations, 1973.

————. *Analytic Report on the State of Intra-European Trade.* New York: United Nations, 1970.

U.S. House Committee on Banking and Currency. *The FIAT-Soviet Automobile Plant and Communist Economic Reforms.* 88th Congress, 2nd Sess. Washington, D.C.: G.P.O., 1967.

U.S. House Committee on Foreign Affairs. *U.S.-Soviet Commercial Relations: The Interplay of Economics, Technology Transfer and Diplomacy.* Washington, D.C.: G.P.O., 1973.

U.S. Senate Committee on Foreign Relations. 93rd Congress, 2nd Sess., *Western Investment in Communist Economics: A Selected Survey on Economic Interdependence.* Washington, D.C.: G.P.O., 1974.

U.S. General Accounting Office. *Exporters' Profits on Sales of U.S. Wheat to Russia.* Washington, D.C.: G.P.O., 1974.

Uren, Philip E., ed. *East-West Trade: A Symposium.* Toronto: Canadian Institute of International Affairs, 1966.

Viner, Jacob. "International Relations Between State-Controlled National Economies." *American Economic Review,* 54 (1944), 315–329.

Wasowski, Stanislaw, ed. *East-West Trade and the Technology Gap: A Political and Economic Appraisal.* New York: Praeger, 1970.

Wilczynski, Joseph. *The Economics and Politics of East-West Trade.* New York: Praeger, 1969.

————. *Socialist Economic Development and Reforms: From Extensive to Intensive Growth Under Central Planning in the U.S.S.R., Eastern Europe and Yugoslavia.* New York: Praeger, 1972.

Wiles, P. J. D. *Communist International Economics.* New York: Praeger, 1968.

PUBLICATIONS BY OFFICIAL SOURCES

Bank for International Settlements. *Annual Reports.*

International Bank for Reconstruction and Development and International Development Agency. *Annual Reports.*

International Monetary Fund. *Annual Reports.*
———. *Direction of Trade.*
———. *International Financial Statistics.*
———. *Selected Decisions of the Executive Directors and Selected Documents.*
———. *Staff Papers.*
Organization for Economic Cooperation and Development. *Flow of Financial Resources to Less-Developed Countries.*
———. Development Assistance Committee, Development Cooperation. *Review of Efforts and Policies of the Members of the Development Assistance Committee.*
———. *Statistics of Foreign Trade.*
———. *Stock of Private Direct Investments by DAC Countries in Developing Countries.*
———. *Trade by Commodities.*
United Nations Conference on Trade and Development. *Handbook of International Trade and Development Statistics.*
———. *Review of Trade and Development.*
United Nations Economic Commission for Europe. *Economic Survey of Europe.*
United Nations Economic Commission for Latin America. *Economic Survey of Latin America.*
U.S. Department of Commerce, Bureau of the Census. *Statistical Abstract of the United States.*
U.S. Department of Commerce. *Survey of Current Business.*
U.S. Department of State. *The Battle Act Report: Mutual Defense Assistance Control Act of 1951.*
———, *Bulletin.*
U.S. Executive. *Public Papers of the Presidents of the United States.*
U.S. President's Council of Economic Advisors. *Economic Report of the President.*
U.S. President's Council on International Economic Policy. *International Economic Report of the President.*

NEWSPAPERS AND JOURNALS

American Economic Review.
American Journal of International Law.
American Political Science Review.
Columbia Journal of World Business.
The Economist.
The Economist Intelligence Unit. *Quarterly Economic Review.*
The Financial Times (London).
Foreign Affairs.
Foreign Policy.
Fortune.
Harvard Business Review.
International Affairs (London).
International Organization.

International Studies Quarterly.
Journal of Common Market Studies.
Journal of Development Studies.
Journal of International Affairs.
Journal of World Trade Law.
Law and Policy in International Business.
The New York Times.
Princeton Studies in International Economics.
Princeton Studies in International Finance.
The Times (London).
The Wall Street Journal.
World Politics.

Index